D0951949

THE NOVEL OF THE SPANISH CIVIL WAR (1936–1975)

THE NOVEL
OF THE SPANISH
CIVIL WAR (1936–1975)

Gareth Thomas

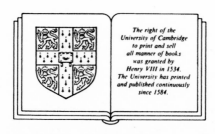

The right of the
University of Cambridge
to print and sell
all manner of books
was granted by
Henry VIII in 1534.
The University has printed
and published continuously
since 1584.

CAMBRIDGE UNIVERSITY PRESS

Cambridge

New York   Port Chester

Melbourne   Sydney

Published by the Press Syndicate of the University of Cambridge
The Pitt Building, Trumpington Street, Cambridge CB2 1RP
40 West 20th Street, New York NY 10011, USA
10 Stamford Road, Oakleigh, Melbourne 3166, Australia

First published 1990

British Library cataloguing in publication data

Thomas, Gareth
The novel of the Spanish Civil War (1936–1975).
1. Fiction in Spanish. 1900 – Critical studies
I. Title
863'.6

Library of Congress cataloguing in publication data

Thomas, Gareth
The novel of the Spanish Civil War (1936–1975)/Gareth Thomas.
p.   cm.
Bibliography.
Includes index.
ISBN 0-521-37158-9
1. Spanish fiction – 20th century – History and criticism.
2. Spain – History – Civil War, 1936–1939 – Literature and the war.
I. Title.
PQ6144.T47   1990
863'.609358 – dc20   89-7352   CIP

ISBN 0 521 37158 9

Transferred to digital printing 2003

SE

For Dorothy

CONTENTS

ILLUSTRATIONS

between pages 116 and 117

Acknowledgements   All photographs are reproduced here by kind permission of the Biblioteca Nacional, Madrid.

viii

PREFACE

In this study I analyse the ways in which Spanish novelists, writing in Spain or in exile during the Franco era (1936–1975), portrayed the Civil War in their works. Some eighty novels have been studied in detail in its preparation. With the exception of the final section, the study concentrates on the novels written in the three decades up to the middle of the 1960s, when the lines between Nationalist and Republican writers were still clearly drawn: no Republican novelist, for example, was allowed to publish in Spain until prior censorship was abolished in 1966. These works are related to earlier examples of universal war literature in order to establish not only similarities but major differences. The distortions occasioned by over-zealous commitment, propaganda or censorship are also examined. A section is devoted to the literary techniques employed by the 'first-wave' novelists of the Civil War, in order to explore the relationship between these works and the *novela popular* of earlier years. The central part of the study analyses the myths that wartime writers created on both sides to sustain themselves and their public during these traumatic days and, later, the gradual disintegration of these hopes and aspirations, whether in victory or defeat. A major aspect of the enquiry is a contrastive analysis of the literary production of Nationalist and Republican writers to discover in what ways their works are differently conditioned by ideology and socio-political phenomena. One Nationalist and one Republican author (J.M. Gironella and F. Ayala, respectively) are chosen for the light they throw on the problem of how to merge the two 'horizons' of the politico-historical novel (the real and the imaginary) – a problem to which critics like Ortega y Gasset saw no satisfactory solution. The final chapter deals with the novels written after the relaxation of censorship, in the final phase of the Franco régime, when the classification 'Nationalist' and 'Republican' begins to lose its meaning, and when some authors seek explanations to these violent events in psychoanalysis rather than in history. There follows a chart showing the number of novels produced in the years 1936 to 1975 and a glossary of terms (often colloquial) which were in common use during the Civil War.

ACKNOWLEDGEMENT

I owe a debt of gratitude to José Alberich — until his retirement, Reader in Spanish at the University of Exeter — whose judgement I value as mentor and friend.

Introduction

SOME DEFINITION is required of the field covered by this study. The 'novel' is a notoriously difficult genre to define, but by common agreement it is written in continuous narrative prose and has a plot and characters who interact with each other. In the Civil War novel, some of these characters may be historical. In addition, there may be large amounts of barely disguised autobiographical information, so that it is often not easy to draw a line between fact and fiction. Memoirs and autobiographies (which exist in profusion) have been excluded.[1] Also excluded are short stories. (F. Ayala's *La cabeza del cordero* has the sustained thematic unity and development that is characteristic of the novel; it is therefore considered here as such.) Occasionally, passing reference may be made to forms other than the novel where these cast light on the particular work being discussed, but they will not in themselves be the object of study. Novels have been chosen which are written in Spanish, by Spaniards.[2] Works in Catalan, Basque or Galician are not included. The 'novel of the Spanish Civil War' is taken to mean novels in which the war itself, or the issues it represents for those taking part in it, whether as combatants or non-combatants, are a major theme. Novels which deal primarily with the pre-war, exile or post-war era are not included unless (like those of Gironella's trilogy) they form part of a series which embraces the war itself. Novels set *in* the war are not included, unless the war is their major theme. Having fixed these parameters, a considerable degree of subjective judgement has to be exercised in deciding what is, and what is not, a Civil War novel.[3] I have often found other critics' choices idiosyncratic, and have attempted to be rigorous in my own choice of titles, but it will be no surprise to find that opinions differ in this respect.

In the course of his illuminating study, *Literature and Propaganda*

(London, 1983), A.P. Foulkes discusses the ideas expressed by J. Ellul in an earlier work, *Propaganda: The Formation of Men's Attitudes* (New York, 1973). What Foulkes has to say about categorising works of literature as 'good' and 'bad' has a direct bearing on the present study, and is worth quoting in full:

> Traditionally, it has been customary to divide literature into 'good' works and 'bad' works. The aesthetic criteria on which such judgements are based are not clearly established, and indeed the history of literature is littered with arguments concerning the relative 'greatness' or otherwise of individual authors or texts. Within Ellul's distinctions, one could differentiate works which question and subvert value systems from works which assimilate and reinforce such systems and one could then proceed into an enquiry into the values which inform the reading and critical reception of the works. Extreme instances of such processes can be observed in the literature surrounding revolution and radical social change.[4]

This study will depart from the convention followed by the large majority of critics who have chosen to treat only novelists of recognised literary merit. While passing reference may be made to the aesthetic quality of the work under discussion, that is not the criterion which will have justified the work's inclusion here. In one way, this has made my task an easier one, since, unlike I. Soldevila, I have not had to identify in advance who are 'les pamphlétaires et les écrivains médiocres', so that these can then be excluded.[5] Nor have I had to decide, as J.I. Ferreras did, which writers are 'ante todo, sinceros',[6] so that they, on the other hand, can be included. By treating here some writers of undoubted mediocrity and even, perhaps occasionally, questionable sincerity, I have greatly extended the range of novelists considered by literary critics such as E. de Nora, who, though he mentions some thirty-five novelists in all, limits himself to detailed consideration of less than a dozen authors in his chapter, 'El impacto de la guerra española en la novela'.[7] Such selectivity has led some to believe, mistakenly, that few novels have been written on the Civil War.[8] In examining in detail a much larger cross-section of novels than has normally been the case, and in focussing more sharply than most previous critics on the novels of the first wave, I hope to be able to elucidate the value systems of these writers and, to some degree, of their envisaged readership, at a time of social and political crisis, when the novel was often used as a weapon of propaganda, recrimination or self-justification.

The year 1966 has been chosen as a threshold in the central sections of the study for a number of reasons. The period 1936–66 comprises two literary generations, both of which were profoundly affected by the trauma of the

Civil War. Most of these writers had lived through the events described; even the youngest of them had experienced their immediate aftermath. By the late 1960s, a generation had emerged which no longer regarded the Civil War as *vivencia*. A major development in 1966 was the removal of prior censorship, in accordance with the new Press Law. Although this by no means implied freedom of expression, it may be regarded as an important step in the right direction. 'Desde 1966 puede observarse una cierta tolerancia respecto a las fuerzas más moderadas de la oposición.'[9] There is no Republican novel published in Spain up to 1966. In 1967, the publication of Angel María de Lera's *Las últimas banderas* ushers in a new era. As P. Iolie observes, in the mid-1960s the attitude of Spaniards living in Spain to the Republican exiles undergoes a marked change.[10] M. Bertrand de Muñoz confirms that the novels of the Republican exiles 'began to be known and to circulate after 1966'.[11] This critic goes further and identifies innovations in form and technique, too, in the later period: 'Following 1966 . . . works clearly different from earlier novels begin to appear. They were books in which the reader senses and observes a profound change in the very first pages, a new technical and formal orientation.'[12] I have used the terms 'Republican novelist', and 'Nationalist novelist' and arranged the bibliography accordingly, because up to the mid-1960s such a division still seems rational. Writers after this date, however, cannot so easily be classified: Benet, for example, defies such categorisation.

Notes

1 R. Sender's *Contraataque*, had it been the author's only contribution to the war literature, would probably not have found a place here. It is a useful counterpoint, however, to his other works.

2 I have been unable to trace the original Spanish version of A. Martínez Pagán's *Génaro*, which has been translated into French by B. Fléxas. The French version has been quoted, therefore, in this case.

D. Aguilera Malta does not strictly speaking justify a place here as he was born in Guayaquil, Ecuador. His work is occasionally quoted, however; he was studying in Spain when the war broke out and experienced life on the Republican side.

3 Novels such as R. Sender's *El rey y la reina* present an interesting dilemma. The symbolism implied, however, in Rómulo's pursuit of the unattainable, and his ultimate failure, surely allow us to consider this a novel *of* the Spanish Civil War.

4 *Literature and Propaganda*, pp. 12–13.

5 'Les romanciers devant la Guerre Civile espagnole', *La Revue de l'Université de Laval*, 14, no. 5 (1960), 428–442 (p. 436).

6 *Tendencias de la novela española, 1931–1969* (Paris, 1970), p. 90. Ferreras takes a deliberate decision to leave out 'escritores de circunstancias'.

7 *La novela española contemporánea*, 3 (Madrid, 1962), pp. 54–105.

8 D. Pérez Minik, for example, in *Novelistas españoles de los siglos XIX y XX* (Madrid, 1957) says of the Civil War as a theme: 'Nuestros novelistas la han eludido siempre. Sus razones tendrán' (p.

336). The reality was that over 100 Civil War novels had been published in Spain and abroad by that time, by Spanish writers. P. Werrie appears to perpetuate the myth when he writes, concerning the publication of Gironella's *Los cipreses creen en Dios* in 1953, that 'tous les récits qui s'étaient jusqu'alors inspirés de cette guerre n'étaient pas des romans' ('Le Roman espagnol d'aujourd'hui', *La Table Ronde*, 193 (1964), 91–101 (p. 94)). Again, the reality was that over 90 Civil War novels had been written in Spanish in this period.

9 S. Vilar, quoted in M.A. Compitello, 'Ordering the Evidence: The Vision of the Spanish Civil War in Post-War Spanish Fiction' (PhD thesis, University of Indiana, 1979), p. 33. This work was published in Barcelona in 1983 with the more accurate sub-title: '*Volverás a Región and Civil War Fiction*'. See also P. Ilie, *Literature and Inner Exile: Authoritarian Spain 1939–1975* (Baltimore, 1980), who confirms that 1966 marks a change of climate: 'Internal unrest and concern with co-existence (*convivencia*) grew stronger after 1966' (p. 16).

10 'What circumstances in the mid-60s permitted the word "exile" first to gain tolerance or sympathy and then respectability?' (*Literature and Inner Exile*), p. 9.

11 In J.B. Romeiser (ed.), *Red Flags, Black Flags: Critical Essays on the Literature of the Spanish Civil War* (Madrid, 1982), p. 212. M. Bertrand de Muñoz's contribution to this collection ('The Civil War in the Recent Spanish Novel, 1966–1976') is a valuable bibliographical reference.

12 *Ibid*, p. 209. The same writer underlines this point later: 'All Spanish Civil War novels written before 1966 were different from those under consideration here' (p. 223).

1
—
Literature,
history and war

THE NOVELS of the Spanish Civil War are far from being 'historical novels' in the normal sense of the term. Their authors are, in the majority of cases, protagonists or eye witnesses of the war. This is not to say, however, that they do not have a sense of recording momentous historical events. Nor could they have been ignorant of the literary antecedents such as Galdós and his *episodio nacional*. Indeed G. Gómez de la Serna, in his study of the *episodio*, directly relates the more ambitious Civil War novels to this literary tradition (while excluding those works which remain at the anecdotal level).[1]

It has been noted that the Spanish Romantic novelists often used distant historical events as the substance of fiction; this may well have been because two of their principal foreign models, Victor Hugo and Walter Scott, were proponents of this type of historical novel and play. The pattern of novel which emerged is described by F. Buendía: 'Desarrolla una acción novelesca en el pasado; sus personajes principales son imaginarios, en tanto que los personajes históricos y los hechos reales constituyen el elemento secundario del relato',[2] and could apply to a number of the novels being studied here; but the time span between the novels' publication and the events they describe is quite different. López Soler's *Los bandos de Castilla* (1830), Cosca Bayo's *La conquista de Valencia por el Cid* (1831), Larra's *El doncel de don Enrique el Doliente* (1834), Espronceda's *Sancho Saldaña* (1834), and others too numerous to mention, are set in the Middle Ages rather than in the recent past, due to the exotic attraction of the period for this particular generation.

The development of the historical novel has been towards a reduction in the space of time between the action described and the date of publication. Baroja's *Memorias de un hombre de acción*, Galdós's *Episodios nacionales* or Valle-Inclán's *La guerra carlista*, *Tirano Banderas*, or *La corte de los milagros* will serve to demonstrate this. Stephen Crane in *The Red Badge of Courage* (1895) is describing a war which took place only 30 years before; Zola in *La Débâcle* (1892) recounts military events which are only 22 years old.[3] In the process, the role allotted to history has increased in importance: 'Ya se acerca tanto la novela a la historia que ésta toma casi más importancia dentro del relato.'[4] Increasing political emancipation and democratic discussion of issues led to more involvement, initially by the middle classes but later by the working classes also, in the intellectual debates of the day, and it is not surprising to see this reflected in literature. In addition, the memoir and the biography have acquired great popularity in a century in which psychoanalysis and interest in people's private lives and thoughts have reached unprecedented levels: the public interest is therefore served by the revelation of an individual conscience. Not surprisingly, 'recent national history exerts a stronger emotional pull on the author than remoter history does, and makes the author reveal his political beliefs and his expectations for the future of his country'.[5] The crisis of conscience occasioned by the 1898 disaster is an illustration of how political events could arouse a Baroja, for example, to fury, and a whole generation to critical self-analysis. The *episodio nacional* seems a convenient means to achieve this, concentrating the mind on specific issues. While in his novels Galdós may broach philosophical and religious themes, in the *episodio*, 'it is the concrete, practical aspect of the national problem which comes to the fore'.[6] Writers following on in this tradition display a 'strong politico-didactic element and a tendency to focus on historically significant public events occurring in the recent past or even in the author's own lifetime'.[7]

Even the greatest novelists, however, have experienced difficulties in wedding the two separate elements: the fictional life of a character (or group) and the social context in which they move. At its most ambitious, it may be compared to fusing the *Iliad*, the story of a group of individuals, and the *Aeneid*, the story of a nation. Writing of Tolstoy's achievement in *War and Peace*, P. Lubbock writes: 'It is a mighty antinomy indeed, on a scale adapted to Tolstoy's giant imagination. With one hand he takes up the largest subject in the world, the story to which all other human stories are subordinate, and not content with this, in the other hand he produces the drama of a great historic collision, for which a scene is set with no less prodigious a gesture.'[8] But even Tolstoy struggles to control his subject matter, picking up his story and dropping it by turns. Nicholas and Natasha often recede into the background while Napoleon or Murat become the chief actors, and 'interminable chapters of comment and explanation, chapters in the manner of a controversial pamphlet', are inserted to make his message clear.[9]

To Ortega y Gasset this would have come as no surprise, sceptical as he was about the capacity of any writer to merge the real and the imagined in this way:

Esta es la razón por la cual nace muerta toda novela lastrada con intenciones trascendentales, sean éstas políticas, ideológicas, simbólicas o satíricas. Porque estas actividades son de naturaleza tal, que no pueden ejercitarse ficticiamente, sino que sólo funcionan referidas al horizonte efectivo de cada individuo. Al excitarlas es como si se nos empujase fuera del intramundo virtual de la novela y se nos obligase a mantener vivaz y alerta nuestra comunicación con el orbe absoluto de que nuestra existencia real depende. ¿Cómo voy a interesarme por los destinos imaginarios de los personajes si el autor me obliga a enfrentarme con el crudo problema de mi propio destino político o metafísico? El novelista ha de intentar, por el contrario, anestesiarnos para la realidad, dejando al lector recluso en la hipnosis de una existencia virtual.

Yo encuentro aquí la causa, nunca bien declarada, de la enorme dificultad – tal vez imposibilidad – aneja a la llamada 'novela histórica.' La pretensión de que el cosmos imaginado posea a la vez autenticidad histórica, mantiene en aquélla una permanente colisión entre dos horizontes. Y como cada horizonte exige una acomodación distinta de nuestro aparato visual, tenemos que cambiar constante mente de actitud: no se deja al lector soñar tranquilo la novela, ni pensar rigurosamente la historia.[10]

The problem may be perceived as twofold. The writer may well have a sense of awe in portraying a Napoleon or a Franco he is very unlikely to know intimately. (It is not surprising, therefore, that Franco is rarely portrayed in the Civil War novel. His portrayal in *Los cinco libros de Ariadna* demonstrates that it is easier to caricature such a character than it is to draw him true to life.) Secondly, the perception of the character on the part of the reader is bound to change with time and with personal circumstances. While this may be true to some degree of imagined characters, it is much more marked in the case of real political figures. This must have been acutely felt by the exiled Republican reader in whom the appearance of a Queipo de Llano or Millán Astray would have provoked quite a different emotional response from that provoked in the reader of today. (Indeed, many readers today would have difficulty in establishing, for example, in Aub's labyrinth of characters, which are historical and which imagined. And of those we consider imagined, how many are historical characters, with different names, recognisable to Aub's intimate circle?)

Having decided to incorporate historical material the novelist is expected by his public to do so truthfully. As H. Klein has indicated, this has made war literature different from most other fiction (at least in the short term):

Fiction has had an immediate factual correlative of which millions were intensely aware. And the overriding criterion applied to war fiction was truth. The tradition of Realism had created the expectation that fiction would be a convincing mirror, would be true to life. With regard to war novels, however, quite a different demand was made which exacted not *verisimilitude*, but *truth to facts* . . . These are proceedings normally used in assessing history, and possibly apposite for the numerous (often apologetic) mémoires and biographies of the great leaders, but they are hardly adequate as the primary considerations for works of fiction.[11]

A concern for truth to facts, even in history itself, is a relatively modern concept. Nineteenth-century positivists attempted to make history a scientific discipline, by analogy with natural science, by accumulating copious data from which general laws could be drawn. More recently, relativist theories of history have emerged which reject the existence of facts, claiming that these do not exist until the historian creates them. Baroja was well aware of this, as C. Longhurst demonstrates in his study of this writer's historical novels.

Al conocimiento completo de un personaje por documentación no se puede llegar más que rara vez. Unicamente en el caso poco frecuente de que haya relaciones de testigos presenciales y se sepa que estos testigos presenciales no tenían ni simpatía ni odio por la figura histórica analizada y estudiada, se podría llegar a este resultado. Pero ¿cuándo pasa esto? Casi nunca. Todas las grandes figuras de la historia, buenas o malas, que se tomen por auténticas están construidas, en parte inventadas, por autores que no las han conocido.[12]

There is no such thing in history as a standard method, as there might be in an exact science. Nor is there an objective basis of fact, such as atomic weight in physics or molecular structure in chemistry. Roquentin, the protagonist of Sartre's *La Nausée*, sets out to write a biography of M. de Rollebon, but despairs of making sense of the multiple sources of information, often conflicting, on which he is basing his work. He comes to believe that the facts arrange themselves according to the order that the historian gives them and not according to any inviolable structure of truth. Roquentin concludes, 'Le passé n'existe pas', and that he would do better to write a work of fiction about his subject.[13] The problem is not new. The bibliographer of the Civil War will appreciate the problems described by R.C. Williams, who in his preface to the bibliography of the seventeenth-century French novel reported difficulties in excluding works of history from the listing because of their 'imaginative quality'.[14] A concern for accuracy in French bibliography dates only from the latter part of the seventeenth century, when a preoccupation with the *vrai* in history was matched by a concern for the *vraisemblable* in narrative fiction, leading to the incorporation of a great deal of historical material.

Prose narrative, taking over as it does the tradition of the epic poem, is 'especially suited to the full re-creation of historical events and state of society'.[15] While the poet can perhaps better capture the immediacy of the event, the novelist often has time to formulate a more comprehensive view. However, such hindsight may not always be beneficial. Human history is inevitably more complex in the realisation than in the recollection. Firstly, political decisions that appear rational at the time may appear less so when weighted with other evidence which is made available to the historian later: the role of the Spanish Communist Party in the events of Barcelona in May 1937 is better understood in the context of Stalin's purge of dissidents within Russia itself, which was not given prominence by the West at the time, as she needed Russia as an ally in the fight against Hitler's Germany. Secondly, the novelist of the Civil War (with few exceptions) knows the outcome of the struggle he is describing, a factor which is bound to influence his entire presentation.[16] In this sense, at least, the narrator is omniscient whether he likes it or not. Fernández-Cañedo points to a conjunction of personal experience and private study in the Civil War novelist, which he considers fruitful:

La existencia de una erudición respecto al tema a tratar facilitará el crecimiento de la obra. Simultáneamente, el preconocimiento de un tema permite al artista aumentar el valor documental de la novela, revelándole qué ángulos exigen mayor detención, qué puntos muertos de las obras anteriores a la suya debe, en su creación, iluminar . . . En la novela de guerra, la experiencia directa del autor es de todo punto necesaria; sin ella, no se logra el matiz de realidad vivida, la emoción, la geografía exacta percibida en el peligro. Me atrevo a afirmar que la conjunción de ambas circunstancias en los escritores de la guerra civil española ha sido beneficiosa para sus obras.[17]

As we shall see later, the sense of 'immediacy' conveyed by many of these novels is achieved at the cost of balance. The tension between the affective world of the protagonist and his historical circumstance is rarely resolved to the reader's satisfaction. Ortega's 'horizons' refused stubbornly to merge. The concept of social realism embodied by Zola, which was to influence European literature so profoundly, seemed incapable of resolving this conflict. It has been expressed by one critic as the attempt to combine the documentary and the visionary:

The novelist, like the scientist, had to be at the same time objective and prophetic, had to do justice to the foreground and background of human existence, the action on the stage and the back projection of social and biological evolution. Transferred to the realm of literature, the achievement of such aims involves the combination of two literary modes – the documentary and the visionary, a combination which involves a potentially awkward mixing of styles.[18]

The events being described sometimes seem so transcendental to the author that he is reluctant to alter them in any way. A remarkable example of this occurs in José Andrés Vázquez's *Armas de Caín y Abel*, in which he suspends the narrative at one point to introduce the factual report of the capture of Seville by General Queipo de Llano. He explains this unusual technique in a footnote:

Para descubrir estos transcendentes episodios históricos, cuyo interés real y verdadero jamás podría ser superado por la ficción novelesca, el Autor ha prescindido en absoluto de su condición de novelista y se ha ajustado rigurosamente al relato hecho por el propio general D. Gonzalo Queipo de Llano.[19]

But he is not alone in this view. Hemingway has written that some events are of such a magnitude that 'if a writer has participated in them his obligation is to write them truly rather than assume the presumption of altering them with invention'.[20] This may well explain the existence in such literature of unlikely situations: fact is often stranger than fiction; the *vrai* may not in fact be *vraisemblable*, as Sender points out in the prologue to *Los cinco libros de Ariadna*: 'Hay muchas cosas autobiográficas (justamente las que parecerán más inverosímiles) y algunas inventadas (las que el lector creerá tal vez auténticas).'[21]

The Civil War novelist, therefore, finds the materials for his construction close to hand, in lived experience. Despite the references critics may make to literary antecedents, we should be aware that in the case of the majority of novelist-protagonists the inspiration springs from the conflict itself. And whilst intellectuals like Aub, Ayala, Sender, Foxá or Gironella were well-read, a host of novelist-protagonists were not. A similar pattern is clearly discernible in the French literature of the First World War:

La guerre ... est fertile en thèmes littéraires, en ce qu'elle confronte l'homme avec la mort, le risque, le situe par rapport aux deux pôles contraires du courage et la peur, l'amène à réfléchir sur ses liens avec la collectivité humaine nationale, et plus immédiatement avec ses compagnons de lutte et misère.

Aussi serait-il vain de chercher des sources littéraires à ces romans de la guerre de la génération des combattants: c'est dans l'événement et dans l'expérience personnelle de l'événement qu'il faut les situer.

Peu d'époques littéraires auront été à ce point tributaires de l'histoire . . .[22]

Although the number of French writers who took part in the First World War has been estimated at around a thousand, in the 16 years between 1915 and 1930 only about 20 titles of novels are recorded. Far more popular as a genre were diaries, memoirs, collections of letters or historical accounts. As in the case of the Spanish Civil War there was great expectancy that the 'definitive' novel of the war would soon appear. The potential market for such a work was enormous, given the millions of ex-combatants who eagerly awaited it. They were to be disappointed: 'On est frappé, à lire d'affilée cette vingtaine de romans nés de la guerre, de la monotonie des traits, de la similitude des situations, des épisodes, souvent même de la technique.'[23]

The war is often packaged in discrete episodes reminiscent of the *roman-feuilleton*, each depicting a typical war-time activity. The most frequent are:

(a) the mobilisation of troops in a garrison town in the rearguard
(b) their joyous departure to the front
(c) the baptism of fire
(d) life in the trenches
(e) the assault
(f) bombardment
(g) resting behind the lines
(h) being wounded and hospitalised
(i) the return to the front

Often, the characters either act as the mouthpiece of the author, or serve as witnesses of the events around them. As such, their stature is diminished by comparison with the hero of the traditional psychological novel.

Authors are faced with the daunting task of portraying a war of huge geo-political and strategic dimensions, far beyond the grasp of a simple character, or else run the risk of portraying only a small segment of the action. Above all, the public insisted on an accurate depiction of events and issues: 'La supercherie eût été grossière et sans doute vite dénoncée, tant le public cherchait dans ce genre de livres des témoignages garantis par une expérience personnelle de l'auteur.'[24]

Intrigue in these novels is restricted to the repercussion on the central character(s) of the chronological events of the war. Most literary critics of the period agree, however, that the public of the 1920s quickly grew tired of the novel of testimony and the diary, often mediocre in quality, and turned to works of historical analysis. There followed a wave of 'demobilisation literature', in which the war was treated in quite a different way, through the medium of humour, poetry and fantasy, with no attempt to chronicle events. Only a small band of right-wing writers look back nostalgically to the heroism of the war. Their typical hero is 'rude et joyeux, avide de gloire et de panache, héro sans le savoir, édifiant exemple des vertus de la race'. Regrettably, a number of patriotic clichés mar these descriptions, which attempt to portray war as something ennobling. Montherlant's *Le Songe* is an example of the genre, in which 'Césarisme et Nietzscheisme s'unissent pour célébrer le culte de la Force et de la Victoire.'[25]

Such triumphalism is unusual in the First World War novel, or indeed the war novel in general to that date, as Louis Aragon has pointed out:

C'est une bien drôle chose que l'influence directe des guerres sur le roman; il n'y a pas d'exemple d'une victoire qui ait inspiré un roman où on voie la guerre, la guerre victorieuse. La victoire russe tient bien peu de place chez Tolstoi. Ce sont les malheurs de la patrie qui l'ont d'abord et surtout inspiré. Soixante-et-onze a donné la *Débâcle* en France, et des contes de Daudet et de Maupassant, mais rien en Allemagne. L'autre guerre, celle qu'on appelait *La Grande*, a produit un tas de romans, pendant et après: mais du *Feu* à *Verdun*, aucun ne décrit la victoire, tous sont centrés sur l'horreur et la vie des tranchées.[26]

This reflected the fact that the mechanised nature of warfare in 1914–18 left little scope for heroism compared with previous wars. For the first time in human history the full potential of Europe's industrial economy was mobilised and harnessed to the war machine. The scale of the carnage defied the imagination, and hence description. Far from being an epic hero, man became an epic victim, taking refuge in the cratered landscape of the battlefield to escape the holocaust. The pacifist novel is the inevitable result of his feeling of hopelessness before events, his anger at the mouthed platitudes of politicians hundreds of miles away. Remarque's *All Quiet on the Western Front* illustrates this reaction.[27]

Around 1929, just over ten years after the First World War, novels begin to appear which attempt to portray the history of the war more objectively. It is no longer considered necessary to have experienced an event personally to describe it: Jules Romains describes the battle of Verdun without having taken part. War novels no longer set out with the primary aim of eliciting pity, horror, indignation or admiration. Rather, they pursue historical truth. This is partly due to the fact of distance, which creates perspective, and partly because in the preceding ten years moralists and political commentators have analysed events: there is by now a considerable baggage of analytical material available. Writers search for a philosophical framework in which to situate the events of the recent past, and many find it in Marxism. In the eyes of these writers the 'post-war' has become the 'inter-war' era: the Wall Street crash and the threat of Hitlerism reveal a perilously unstable Europe. The 'war to end all wars' appears to many to have been a gratuitous waste of human lives.

At this point it may be appropriate to examine the points of comparison between the Spanish Civil War novel and its First World War counterpart. Spain's neutrality in the First World War meant that she was spared these horrors, and with the exception of the Moroccan wars (of which Barea and Sender have left brilliant testimony), would have to wait until 1936 to experience something comparable. The bombing of civilian populations in the large cities (and, memorably, in Guernika), the strafing of fleeing civilians from the air, and tank warfare, have all created a similar sense of hopelessness and anger to that described earlier. But the Spanish war differs in some essential aspects.

Firstly, in much of Republican Spain a social revolution was taking place which gave a real purpose to the war. This is a positive aspect which is lacking in the classical war novel. Man is not here a pawn of the possessing classes sent to fight a colonial war in the interests of capitalist exploitation, but a defender of rights by dint of collective political and syndical action. The protagonist of Aub's 'El Cojo' comes to understand this, although it will cost him his life. The memory of his mother, a washerwoman, sustains Barea throughout similar difficulties. Similarly, in Nationalist Spain, propaganda ensures that the population believes it is defending the civilised Western tradition against Asiatic Bolshevism and Atheism. Those who do not go this far nevertheless see their class interests threatened by the Republic, and have no difficulty in justifying armed rebellion, particularly when it receives the blessing of the Church.

Secondly, the political nature of the conflict created purges which took place with greater or lesser intensity throughout the conflict. Death was just as likely from such a source as it was from a bomb, shell or grenade. The atrocity, as we shall see, occupies a key place in the narrative fiction of the Spanish Civil War and constitutes a much more personalised form of death than trench warfare, artillery attacks or aerial bombardment. The fear of the *timbrazo* is an almost universal preoccupation in the Civil War novel.

Thirdly, although war was mechanised, in some aspects it was extremely traditional. Just as one might have watched the whole of the battle of Waterloo from a hilltop, so there were encounters in Spain which were within one man's compass. There were examples, even at this late date, of cavalry charges.[28]

Fourthly, in the Civil War novel the stress on life in the rearguard among the civilian population is usually much greater. As we have indicated, the fear of the *paseo* or the *checa* is a common theme here, but so are love, domesticity, adolescence and all the more usual subjects of the novelist. This gives the genre considerable flexibility.

A fifth major difference is that whilst Montherlant's *Le Songe* was unusual for its exuberant emphasis on victory, there are in Spain a host of such novels on the Right. As we shall see, the young Falangist hero or *requeté* crusader is commonplace: he takes much pleasure in driving Communists and Masons before him, ridding Spain of anti-Spain. This reflects the fact that he is a counter-revolutionary with a powerful social and political role to play. Gómez de la Serna identifies the 'nuevo tono moral de que le dota el aliento epopéyico' as a feature of the new *episodio nacional* (where for this author '*nacional*' can be equated with the adjective in *Movimiento Nacional*, it would appear).[29] The Republicans, for obvious reasons, do not indulge in victory celebrations.

It is rare to encounter a pacifist novel written on the Spanish conflict; the most brilliant example is Arana's *El cura de Almuniaced*. J.M. Castañón's *Andrés cuenta su historia* and Martín de Lucenay's *El teniente Zacatecas* also fall in this category. It is interesting, but perhaps not surprising, that all three are Republican novels.[30] The collective guilt felt by many novelists on both sides for the violence and destruction caused does not lead them, on the whole, to resort to pacifism.

Finally, there are similarities in the general pattern of production and changing nature of the output in the decade or so following the end of warfare. Lo Ré identified two waves of novelistic production, the first in 1937–39 and the second in 1954–59, with a relative fall in production in between. The crest of the first wave (25 titles in 1939) is considerably higher than that of the second (13 titles in 1954), and publishing activity falls to a single title half-way through this period, in 1947. With regard to content and quality: 'The first wave novels are little more than novelized reminiscences, largely episodic in nature, written from a limited perspective and generally of little artistic significance. The second wave novels are usually better constructed, broader in scope and more profound in conception.'[31]

What is true, therefore, of First World War novels proves also to be true of Civil War novels, with regard to improvement in quality ten years after the event. However, an important difference exists in the socio-political context in which the two sets of novels were produced. If in 1930 a number of French novelists turned to Marxism in an 'inter-war' mood, the reverse may be said of many defeated Republican novelists in exile in 1950, while in Spain itself the dominant ideology of clerical authoritarianism continued in a decidedly post-war, non-conciliatory atmosphere. It will be seen later that the publication of Gironella's *Los cipreses creen en Dios* provoked a storm of protest from the Right,[32] while censorship in Spain ensured that no Republican novel could be published there until 1967.

To summarise the above points concerning war literature, there are many similarities between Spanish Civil War novels and those of the First World War, but some important differences occasioned by the fratricidal nature of the events of 1936–39 and their eventual resolution. As Rieuneau rightly indicates, 'Le propre de la guerre d'Espagne . . . fut de réunir les caractères d'une guerre révolutionnaire et d'une guerre classique, d'une guerre civile et d'une guerre internationale.'[33] In addition, the creation of the two Spains after 1936, and again in different form after 1939, meant that the intellectual climate in which the novels were written was deeply divided. While the Republican novel of exile shares with the First World War novel a general disenchantment with war, the Nationalist novel continues for some considerable time to justify the uprising.

Notes

1 '*Episodios*' are *Madrid de Corte a checa, Una isla en el mar rojo, Checas de Madrid, Madridgrado, El puente, La fiel Infantería* and *Los cipreses creen en Dios*, according to Gómez de la Serna's classification. He excludes *Se ha ocupado el kilómetro 6, Legión 1936, Cada cien ratas un permiso, IV Grupo del 75–27, Fondo de estrellas* and *Pepe Campos*. This list is of course quite inadequate. Furthermore his definition of '*episodio*' virtually excludes exiled writers by definition: '(El episodio) guarda tras de su demoníaca cara destructora otra faz prometedora, creadora, orientada angélicamente [*sic*] hacia un futuro incógnito que se proyecta como ordenado y fecundo' G. Gómez de la Serna, *España en sus episodios nacionales* (Madrid, 1954), p. 113.

2 Introduction to *Antología de la novela histórica española, 1830–1844* (Madrid, 1963), p. 16.

3 A.G. Lo Ré, 'The Novel of the Spanish Civil War, 1936–60' (unpublished PhD thesis, University of North Carolina, 1965), p. 127.

4 *Ibid.*, p. 34.

5 M. de Gogorza Fletcher, *The Spanish Historical Novel (1870–1970)* (London, 1974), p. 127.

6 *Ibid.*

7 *Ibid.*

8 *The Craft of Fiction* (London, 1960), p. 32.

9 *Ibid.*, p. 34.

10 'Ideas sobre la novela', *Obras completas*, 3 (Madrid, 1946), p. 411.

11 *The First World War in Fiction* (London, 1976), p. 5. Klein concludes that war has become a permanent concern of literature, partly due to the Spanish Civil War.

12 P. Baroja, *Obras completas* (Madrid, 1946–52), 5, p. 1140. Quoted in C. Longhurst, *Las novelas históricas de Pío Baroja* (Madrid, 1974), p. 130.

13 Quoted in S.G. Whitmore, 'History Versus the Novel: A Sartrean Concern and its French Antecedents' (unpublished PhD thesis, University of Washington, 1974), p. 77.

14 *Ibid.*

15 H. Klein, *The First World War in Fiction*, p. 4.

16 H.D. Ford, *A Poet's War: British Poets and the Spanish Civil War* (Oxford, 1965), p. 24, maintains that 'the novelist can never really capture the immediacy of war', whereas the poet can.

17 'La joven novela española (1936–47),' *Revista de la Universidad de Oviedo*, 9 (January–April, 1948), 51.

18 H. Klein, *The First World War in Fiction*, p. 45.

19 *Armas de Caín y Abel* (Cadiz, 1938), p. 37.

20 In his preface to Regler's *The Great Crusade* (London, 1940).

21 *Los cinco libros de Ariadna* (New York, 1957), p. xvi.

22 M. Rieuneau, *Guerre et révolution dans le roman français de 1919 à 1939* (Paris, 1974), p. 21. Much of the information in the discussion of First World War literature in this section is drawn from this invaluable source.

23 *Ibid.*, p. 21.

24 *Ibid.*, p. 25.

25 *Ibid.*, p. 144.

26 P. Wattelet (pseud. of Louis Aragon), 'Grandeur et misère des romanciers', *Confluences*, special no: *Problèmes du roman*, 21–24 (1943), 414–415. Quoted Rieuneau, p. 166.

27 *All Quiet on the Western Front* appeared in 1928 and a Spanish translation was published by Editorial Cenit in the following year. By 1936, the work of Remarque, Arnold Zweig, Glaeser, Renn and Johannsen was available in Spanish and was freely read by the younger generation (See G. Gómez de la Serna, *España en sus episodios nacionales*, p. 109).

28 Angel Ruiz-Ayúcar, author of *Las dos barajas*, described to me in a conversation in 1968 how his imagination had been fired by the cavalry charge against the Puerto del Pico, which he had watched from a neighbouring ridge. He claimed that this might have been the last cavalry charge of its kind in history.

29 *España en sus episodios nacionales*, p. 130.

30 M. Bertrand de Muñoz's bibliography (1982) lists a number of other pacifist novels which fall outside the parameters of this study.

31 'The Novel of the Spanish Civil War' (1965). Although it extends to novels of the Russian front, post-war resistance in Spain, exile, etc. the study's conclusion would broadly apply also to the novels contained in my own, more selective bibliography.

32 Even more than 20 years after the war was over the traditional Right was moved to paroxysms of anger by 'objective' novelising on the Civil War. See F. López-Sanz, *Un millón de muertos, pero con ¡héroes y mártires!* (1963) and, even more extraordinary, *Llevaban su sangre* (1966) by the same author, editor of *El Pensamiento Navarro*.

33 M. Rieuneau, *Guerre et révolution*, p. 511.

2

–

Literature,
commitment
and propaganda

THE RISE of mass political movements in the nineteenth and twentieth centuries led to a corresponding evolution in the function of literature. It would be quite wrong to suggest, as some critics have done, that Civil War novels are a return to the nineteenth-century *episodio* and even earlier traditions:

Los *Episodios nacionales* de Galdós, las *Memorias de un hombre de acción* de Baroja, y *El ruedo ibérico* de Valle-Inclán son manifestaciones – siguiendo una preocupación de 'España como problema' que empieza en el mismo Siglo de Oro – de respuesta literaria, de compromiso intelectual con el padecer histórico de todo un pueblo. Puede muy bien decirse . . . que el 'episodio nacional' con su voz comunal, generacional, es la versión española de la novela . . . de la inconformidad, el testimonio y la protesta.[1]

This strangely static view of literature, expressed as it was in the context of the Spanish Civil War novel, ignores the growth of political parties and the increasing pressure on the novel to carry explicit social and political messages. As Benson indicates:

The theme of social protest had existed in literature long before the 1930s, particularly in the Naturalism of European and American writing at the close of the nineteenth century and continuing into the twentieth. But never before had the social protest so involved political considerations. Emile Zola could describe life among the lower strata of Parisian society and Stephen Crane could do likewise about New York's Bowery; but no unified political solution to mitigate social injustices inflicted on the lower classes appeared in the works of these writers. The social protests of the 1930s, however, for the most part, exhibit a strong political influence.[2]

The influence of Marxist criticism on this development cannot be ignored. As early as 1885, Engels revealed in correspondence with Minna Kautsky that he was wrestling with the theoretical problems of committed literature:

I am by no means an opponent of tendentious programmatic poetry (Tendenzpoesie) as such . . . But I believe that the thesis must spring forth from the situations and action itself, without being explicitly displayed. I believe that there is no compulsion for the writer to put into the reader's hands the future historical resolution of the social conflicts which he is depicting.[3]

In a letter in English to Margaret Harkness in 1888, Engels applied these ideas to the novel, showing that his views were substantially the same:

I am far from finding fault with you for not having written a point-blank socialist novel, a *Tendenzroman* as we Germans call it, to glorify the social and political views of the author. This is not at all what I mean. The more the opinions of the author remain hidden, the better for the work of art.[4]

This view of commitment was to prove later to be unacceptably liberal within the Marxist tradition. By 1905 a recrudescence had taken place within the movement's leadership and Lenin was calling for commitment of a quite explicit nature:

Literature must become Party literature . . . Down with un-partisan *littérateurs*! Down with the supermen of literature! Literature must become a part of the general cause of the proletariat, a 'small cog and a small screw' in the social democratic mechanism, one and indivisible – a mechanism set in motion by the entire conscious vanguard of the whole working class. Literature must become an integral part of the organised, methodical and unified labours of the social-democratic party.[5]

This last canonical text was to have a profound influence on the way literature was perceived in Europe, and by the 1930s in Spain a small group of writers (Sender, Arconada, Arderíus, Carranque de Ríos, Díaz Fernández and others) were displaying social commitment in their novels. As Nora points out, they constituted a loosely-knit literary Popular Front some time before the political Popular Front took form.[6]

Clearly it was not possible to impose these views outside the confines of Russia, and the spread of such ideas to another country must have depended on the extent to which the class war had become exacerbated in the individual country concerned. The social stratification of Spain, the recent memories of the Moroccan war and military dictatorship, the failure of agrarian reform and the religious question, all these issues suggested that profound change was needed and that literature could play its part in that country's development. The responses to these issues, as might be expected in a country without a strong totalitarian tradition, were politically diverse:

El simple republicanismo ingenuo, radical o demagógico de unos, se codea con el anarquismo doctrinal, el sindicalismo de acción, el nietzscheanismo y el stirnerismo de otros; el nihilismo o el socialismo humanitario de éstos con el marxismo rudimentario, el trotskismo, o el simple anticlericalismo y antimilitarismo de aquéllos.[7]

However, there can be no doubt that the Soviet experiment was influential in moulding opinion among the Spanish Left. From the moment that Fernando de los Ríos and Daniel Anguiano were dispatched to Moscow in 1921 by the Spanish Socialist Party to investigate its affiliation to the Third International, there were frequent visits to Russia by Spanish politicians and intellectuals. (The two Socialists were accompanied on their visit on that occasion by Julio Alvarez del Vayo (then a foreign correspondent accredited in Germany), and met Angel Pestaña, the CNT moderate, on his way back.) Spanish Communists like La Pasionaria were frequent visitors to Moscow, and Ramón Sender himself spent several months there in late 1933 and early 1934, an experience recounted in *Madrid–Moscú* (1934). Max Aub was also a visitor in 1933. Hugh Thomas reports that 'there was . . . a great increase in Russian literature and propaganda in Spain before the Civil War'.[8]

The political situation in Spain between 1917 and 1923 had been extremely precarious: proletarian revolution seemed a distinct possibility. (The fervour of rural Anarcho-syndicalists during this period is nowhere more graphically described than in J. Díaz del Moral's eye-witness account, *Historia de las agitaciones campesinas andaluzas*.)[9] While it seems inevitable, in retrospect, that literature would respond to these social pressures, in some cases by putting its weight behind them, it is equally inevitable that the counter-revolution should find its own forms of expression. It was Ortega y Gasset, in works like *La rebelión de las masas* and *La deshumanización del arte* who was to articulate the feelings of the élite in the face of the proletarian onslaught. The latter work, published in 1925, claimed that far from involving itself in social realities, art should be the negation of life. This trend, in fact, was already apparent and art was beginning to display tendencies towards:

(a) la deshumanización
(b) evitar las formas vivas
(c) hacer que la obra de arte no sea sino obra de arte
(d) considerar el arte como juego y nada más
(e) una esencial ironía

(f) eludir toda falsedad
(g) (convertirse en) una cosa sin transcendencia alguna

According to Ortegan doctrine, the reality of lived experience and aesthetic expression are incompatible in art: in a deathbed scene witnessed by the wife of the dying man, a doctor, a journalist and a painter, only the latter can produce a work of art from the experience, as only he is detached. Subjectivism in art becomes a taboo. Art survives only in a climate in which it is not intended to mean anything, and the most radical instrument of dehumanisation is the metaphor. In 'Ideas sobre la novela', Ortega prophesies the end of the realist novel and its substitution by a new form, in which contemplation replaces action, as well as external reality: 'Sólo a través de un mínimo de acción es posible la contemplación . . . Sólo es novelista quien posee el don de olvidar él, y de rechazo hacernos olvidar a nosotros, la realidad que deja fuera de su novela.'[10]

Compared with the task of creating a hermetic, imaginary universe into which we can escape, claims Ortega in another essay, 'defender el socialismo o combatir por la libertad son cosas muy fáciles'.[11] In creating a school of dehumanised artists, Ortega can now be seen to have been subverting the trend towards social and Socialist realism, and reasserting the authority of the élite. In this, he is mirroring the politics of his time: 'Dictadura primorriverista en el mundo de la política y orteguiana en las artes y el pensamiento no son sino dos aspectos de la reacción del individuo de *élite*, de la rebelión frente a las *masas*.'[12]

It is not surprising, given the rising tide of proletarian demands in France also, to find similar expression of contempt for 'committed' intellectuals there. In 1927, Julien Benda published *La Trahison des clercs*.[13] 'Devenus "pratiques" et "réalistes," les clercs perdent toute supériorité, se laïcisent. En langage pascalien, on pourrait dire qu'ils ont renoncé à l'ordre de l'esprit pour triompher dans l'ordre de la chair.'[14]

But it was not only on the Left that commitment was to be found. Intellectuals of the Right soon found it impossible to carry out the Ortegan imperative, and indeed upbraided the philosopher of dehumanised art. 'Hay coyunturas de conmoción del mundo o de la Patria en que puede resultar monstruoso permanecer bajo la lámpara de la celda', wrote José Antonio Primo de Rivera in 1935, in a reproach to Ortega.

Una generación que casi despertó la inquietud española bajo el signo de Ortega y Gasset se ha impuesto a sí misma, también trágicamente, la misión de vertebrar a

España. Muchos de los que se alistaron hubiesen preferido seguir, sin prisas ni arrebatos, la vocación de intelectual . . . Nuestro tiempo no da cuartel.[15]

Although the reference is not specifically to the novel, there can be no doubt that all artistic forms are henceforth intended to be weapons in the struggle. The case of the Right is not as closely argued, nor does it rest on such a broad theoretical basis as the dialectic of the Left. An inherent contradiction in it is the contempt in which intellectuals were held by many on the extreme Right, who felt that the treachery of the former lay not so much in the abandonment of metaphysics as in taking sides with the working class. It is frequent to find in Fascist writing of the 1930s attempts to attract eminent literary figures to their ranks. This sometimes reflects the esteem in which they held them in their student days (Ledesma's novel, *El sello de la muerte*, is dedicated to Unamuno, for example); it may also be seen as an attempt to legitimise right-wing ideology and give it greater respectability: 'All the national-syndicalist ideologues had paid homage to Unamuno, Ortega, Angel Ganivet and Pío Baroja, whom they deemed their "precursors" among the Generation of '98 . . . Ledesma had once hoped to attract men of this stripe.'[16] Baroja was interviewed by Juan Aparicio in March, 1931: a transcript appeared in *La Conquista del Estado*, stressing a number of points on which Baroja concurred with the *jonsistas* (contempt for parliament and *leguleyos*, anti-clericalism, rusticity, vitalism, among others). José Antonio wrote to Ortega in 1934, thinking that Falange would appeal to the philosopher. He was mistaken. He later visited Unamuno at the latter's home in Salamanca, in 1935, but found that the ageing professor was critical of the *desmentalización* to which the young were being subjected by right-wing demagogues.

The almost universal disdain of the intellectual class for Fascists in Spain in the pre-war era was inevitable given the movement's stress on irrationalism and on action, rather than reason and contemplation. Unamuno's love of paradox and Baroja's impetuousness were of quite a different order from the ravings of a Giménez Caballero. And Ortega can be forgiven for taking fright on seeing his elitist theories crudely interpreted. All were intelligent enough to realise that the Fascist movement merely wanted figureheads: the correct role for the intellectual, according to this view, was to legitimise the actions of the politicians who realised the 'true destiny' of the country. As one of the Fascists bluntly expressed it:

Los intelectuales hacen alto honor a la política y sirven y completan su eficacia en tanto en cuanto se atienen a su destino y dan sentido histórico, *legalidad* pudiéramos decir, a las acciones – victoriosas o fracasos [sic] – a que el político conduce al pueblo. Otra intervención distinta es inmoral y debe reprimirse ... En la política, el papel del intelectual es un papel de servidumbre.[17]

Clearly this is not a role that is willingly assumed by the writer under normal circumstances. While it may be common to commission certain forms of art it is unusual to do so in the case of literature. The novel emerges from the personal experience and conviction of the author, and it is difficult to see how this could be otherwise.

On the outbreak of war in 1936 the novelist is forced to take sides. The aesthetic theories of Ortega have no place in a context of political and military struggle. The novel, far from disappearing as a spent force, as forecast in 'Ideas sobre la novela', becomes a powerful weapon in the political armoury, and later a critical tool for examining the causes and consequences of the war. Total war mobilises the intellectual class. Whatever theories existed prior to 1936, all forms of literature would at this point have been put at the service of the forces on either side, irrespective of Ortega's essay.[18] The Spanish Civil War must be seen, also, as a major influence in the politicisation of European literature as a whole. Recent history is no longer treated as a gratuitous or exotic fact but as 'une espèce d'auscultation inquiète du passé pour mieux comprendre le présent',[19] a 'being-in-history' rather than a description of it from the outside. As we saw earlier, it is no longer possible to consider the facts of history as objective. The very fact of narration makes them subjective:

Le plus mince incident, dès lors qu'il est narré, se charge peu ou prou de signification. A plus forte raison ce récit développé qu'est un roman: les événements qui le composent tendent spontanément vers un au-delà d'eux-mêmes. Et la proposition se vérifie particulièrement dans les oeuvres qui prennent pour matière la guerre. Il n'est pas possible de traiter une telle réalité comme le prétexte à un exercice de style ... L'attitude du détachement esthétique impliquerait elle-même la négation de l'idée que la guerre est chose importante: il faut que, d'une manière ou d'une autre, la guerre soit jugée.[20]

I. Soldevila has explored the question of objectivity from a number of viewpoints in *La obra narrativa de Max Aub*. From a philosophical point of view, objectivity does not exist. Immediately the subject tries to apprehend the object, the latter becomes, by definition, subjective. It follows, therefore, that 'pedir objetividad al sujeto del acto literario es ... obligarlo al silencio'. Objectivity exists only outside our perceptions and feelings; once we internalise the object we subjectivise it.[21] The psychoanalytical school would claim that perception is no more than knowledge adapted to our intentions and that ideas of the objective and the absolute are illusory. Recall is in any case vague, ambiguous and fallible, since a number of psychological mechanisms such as repression, distortion and projection interfere in the process.[22] It has also been shown that in literature, the claim of the Naturalist to reconstruct reality by means of an accumulation of detail from which the artist is absent is quite alien to the process we undergo in perceiving the real world. We do not see life dispassionately through a lens, nor do we see objects from several angles at once: objects offer us one facet of their reality, and we have to displace ourselves (or they themselves) before we glimpse another. It could be argued, therefore, that art has of necessity to renounce showing us reality and content itself instead with showing us the appearance, or an appearance, of reality.[23]

To speak of 'objectivity' in the war novels makes no sense in the light of the above definitions, since the relation of subject to object, philosophically speaking, is immutable. If the object remained the object, this would mean that the subject had not perceived it: a subject indifferent to the object would have to be blind; the reader would be confronted with a blank page.

This reduction to the absurd is necessary in order to understand the endless heart-searching of war novelists when confronted with the problem of their subjectivity. Not one of them, needless to say, has resolved the problem, since it is incapable of solution. C.A. Longhurst, discussing the issue in the context of Baroja's historical novels, searches for an acceptable compromise and concludes:

Lo único que en toda justicia podemos exigir de la objetividad histórica es un reportaje que posea el máximo grado de fidelidad que permitan las circunstancias, así como cierta neutralidad en lo que se dice y en cómo se dice, de forma que ninguna persona razonable e imparcial quisiera estar en desacuerdo con ello.[24]

But this begs the question of what is neutral, and who might be considered reasonable and impartial. It also puts a premium on moderation, when in fact the literary merit of such works may well lie in their uncompromising attitude. Writing of the output of the Republican novelists in exile, for example, F.R. Benson writes:

The impressive quantity and quality of the literature by these authors in the areas of fiction and non-fiction exceed all foreign treatment of the conflict, including works on the subject published under the Franco régime. If the objectivity desirable in such testimony is lacking, the intensity and vividness imparted by these writers to their work more than justifies critical consideration.[25]

George Orwell too, in reviewing his work, comes to the conclusion that commitment has contributed to the overall quality of his writing rather than the reverse: 'Looking back through my work, I see that it is invariably where I lacked a political purpose that I wrote lifeless books.'[26] Critics from the other extreme of the political spectrum agree that it is the uncompromising nature of the views expressed that give the early works their power of attraction:

La resuelta voluntad histórica, el ánimo de salvación colectiva es el factor que introduce su decisiva voluntad en el alma de los escritores combatientes, cargando sus plumas con una increíble dosis de fe, con un entusiasmo ideológico y vital de primer orden que otorga rango específico y calidad peculiarísima a su obra.[27]

It must be appreciated that in the Civil War a lack of commitment is in itself a political stance: there is no such thing as neutrality. If you are not with the Republic, then you must be against it. Secondly, the magnitude of the events in human terms, and the destruction and suffering they caused, made detachment impossible. 'Anyone who has lived through the hell of Madrid with his eyes, his nerves, his heart, his stomach', wrote Koestler, 'and then pretends to be objective, is a liar.'[28] Such objectivity has more to do with distance, and hence perspective, than with truth. The contemporary (wartime) reader would have subconsciously compared the fictional world created by the author with his own internal vision and found that in many cases they coincided. A different reader, confronted with the same fictional world a generation later, would find that in all likelihood it did not correspond to his vision. Similarly, in the act of creation, the climate in which Sender wrote El rey y la reina is in no way comparable to that prevailing when he composed Contraataque. This is not to say that the one is more 'objective' than the other, but simply that they are conditioned by quite different circumstances. It is not surprising that more recent novels will appear to us as 'objective': it is simply that they correspond more closely to the (subjective) view we have of events.

There are two problems related to commitment, however, which have a crucial bearing on the novel. The first of these is the way in which the author concentrates on the task of 'telling the story'. This is the most ancient of crafts, but one that has to be approached in a workmanlike way. Hemingway, one of the few foreign novelists of the subject to eschew commitment, insisted that his prime task was 'to write straight, honest prose on human beings. First you have to know the subject, then you have to know how to write. Both take a lifetime to learn, and anyone is cheating who takes politics as a way out. It is too easy. All the outs are too easy. And the thing itself is too hard to do.'[29]

For this reason one of the most popular forms of war literature is the diary, memoir or *reportage*, which involves little elaboration once the initial notes have been recorded. Invaluable as they are for the understanding of military, social and ideological issues they are not comparable with the novel as an art form. The war novelist's problem is to find ways of preventing his characters from being submerged by history and ideology. They must occupy the centre of the stage while a 'voice over' tries to draw our attention, or so it seems, to the details of the set. As many 'novelists' of the Civil War are novices in the art of the novel, it is not surprising that they do not succeed in producing Hemingway's 'straight, honest prose'.

The second area of difficulty is that of propaganda, which is commitment extended beyond acceptable limits to include misinformation and falsehood. During the war, as in all wars, it was used as an instrument of indoctrination and in order to create (or destroy) morale. The novel is capable of fulfilling all these functions. The process involves the over-simplification of issues and as such is anti-intellectual. That did not prevent intellectuals, however, from being drawn into it, as H.D. Ford observes in connection with the war poets:

Their black and white view was symptomatic not only of a certain illogicality, but also of an apparent reluctance to cope with a world composed of shades of grey. Whether for political or psychological reasons, or both, they simply refused to differentiate between cause and effect, between the relative merits and weaknesses of both sides.[30]

If this was true of the external observer, it was obviously true of the participants, and early novels are little more than tracts to denigrate or ridicule the enemy, and prove the rightness of their authors' cause. 'If we refer to the nineteenth century as the Age of Ideology', writes A.P. Foulkes, 'then it seems even more appropriate to regard the present century as the Age of Propaganda.'[31] Propaganda may be divided into several categories:

(a) Political and sociological
(b) Agitation and integration
(c) Vertical and horizontal
(d) Rational and irrational[32]

Political propaganda is that issued by Government departments, while sociological propaganda is that 'persuasion from within' which results when an individual has accepted or assimilated the dominant economic and political ideologies of his society and uses them as a basis for making what he regards as spontaneous choice and value judgements. As we shall see, the novelist of the Civil War is heavily exposed to these types of propaganda. During the war years the sources of information were newspapers and radio broadcasts of the zone in which the novelist found himself; these were inevitably biased. In the post-war years Nationalist writers were subjected to strict censorship, and the organs of the State continued to fulfil a propaganda function. In exile, as J.L. López Aranguren has pointed out, the Republican novelist was subject to a form of censorship, 'no por invisible menos operante . . . Examinar con criterio independiente el acontecimiento que ha desembocado en la emigración sería inmediatamente considerado como una ruptura de la solidaridad entre los expatriados y un "pasarse" al otro bando.'[33]

The propaganda of agitation is directed at subverting the established order, while that of integration aims to promote conformity with the status quo. During the war, therefore, Republicans and Nationalists indulge in both forms, justifying their own regime and expressing contempt for the enemy's; in the post-war, Nationalists largely engage in the propaganda of integration, while Republicans have no alternative but to continue agitation or fall silent. The propaganda of agitation loses its *raison d'être* once Franco is accepted into the community of nations.

Vertical propaganda is defined as emanating from a leader, while horizontal propaganda emerges within a group. It will be seen in this study that numerous groups emerged during the conflict on both sides, and that these without exception generated their own propaganda, including novels. In addition, in some cases they absorbed the propaganda emanating from the leader (notably of the Fascist variety).

Finally, rational propaganda takes the form of facts, statistics, economic ideas and technical description, while irrational propaganda is aimed at the feelings and passions. There is a heavy reliance on the irrational element in the case of the Civil War, given the polarisation of issues to extremes. Where statistics are used (Claudel's 'seize mille prêtres', to take a famous foreign example), they are likely to be unreliable.

The aesthetic danger inherent in all propaganda is that it destroys creativity. Instead of exploring ideas and emotions the novelist resorts to ready-made analyses and slogans which are the negation of literature:

Political writing in our time consists almost entirely of prefabricated phrases bolted together like pieces of a child's Meccano set. It is the unavoidable result of self-censorship. To write in plain, vigorous language one has to talk fearlessly, and if one thinks fearlessly one cannot be politically orthodox . . . To be corrupted by totalitarianism one does not have to live in a totalitarian country. The mere prevalence of certain ideas can spread a kind of poison that makes one subject after another impossible for literary purposes. Wherever there is an enforced orthodoxy – or even two orthodoxies, as always happens – good writing stops. This was well illustrated by the Spanish Civil War.[34]

Whatever separation may have existed between literature and politics was largely demolished. As in the case of the First World War, 'what might be termed the spontaneous literary response was . . . embedded and often enmeshed in the official propaganda campaigns'.[35] Louis MacNeice describes this dilemma for the poet when he writes: 'In the Spanish Civil War some poets were torn between writing good propaganda (dishonest poetry) and honest poetry (bad propaganda) . . . In the long run a poet must choose between being politically ineffectual and poetically false.'[36]

References by Hemingway, Orwell and MacNeice, respectively, to 'straight, honest prose', 'plain, vigorous language' and 'honest poetry' reveal a profound malaise about the way in which literature was being exploited for 'dishonest' purposes. As we shall see in detailed analyses of the Spanish novel, such abuse of commitment was to leave many of the works flawed, and unable to transcend the moment at which they were written.

Language, in particular, is the loser. Both George Orwell and, later, George Steiner, have explored the effect of propaganda upon the word, and the way the latter may lose its 'humane meanings' under the pressure of political bestiality and falsehood. 'Actions of the mind that were once spontaneous become mechanical, frozen habits (dead metaphors, stock similes, slogans, etc.). Words grow longer and more ambiguous. Instead of style there is rhetoric.'[37] As Steiner has written, this impoverishment of linguistic resources has a crucial bearing on the possibility of tragic style:

The political inhumanity of our time has demeaned and brutalized language beyond any precedent. Words have been used to justify political falsehood, massive distortions of history, and the bestialities of the totalitarian state. It is conceivable that something of the lies and savagery has crept into their marrow. Because they have been used to such base ends, words no longer give their full yield of meaning. And because they assail us in such vast, strident numbers, we no longer give them careful hearing.[38]

In particular, as we shall see, texts which attempt to shock the reader into a moral condemnation of the outrages of the other side will only be successful if they evoke what Steiner terms that 'mystery of words which lies at the source of tragic poetry'.[39] Novels such as *Checas de Madrid*, by Borrás, ultimately fail because they leave us insensible to the atrocities described. A process of demystification or defamiliarisation is required before the impact intended by the novelist can be achieved:

> When these techniques were first used, notably by Barbusse in his novel *Under Fire* (1917), they undoubtedly functioned in a demystifying way. Wilfred Owen, in the same war, used to carry in his pocket a collection of battle-field photographs which he would silently hand to the armchair warriors he encountered in England between his periods at the front. Barbusse's 'befouled faces and tattered flesh' and Owen's photographs may have been powerful images of defamiliarization 65 years ago but today they would be submerged by the bulletins 'from the front lines of history' which the media dish up with the breakfast.[40]

The novel must therefore continually develop new expressive forms in order to be received as real. We shall see that within ten years of the end of the Civil War authors like Ayala and Sender were exploring new and oblique ways of expressing the tragedy, precisely because there had been many notable failures to do so in the realist novel. Later, in the third wave, defamiliarisation would take totally irrational forms, as in the work of Cela and Benet.

J.P. Sartre, in a canonical essay, 'Présentations des *Temps Modernes*', published in Paris in 1948, called for the writer to be *'en situation dans son époque'*.[41] He condemned Flaubert and Goncourt for standing idly by after the events of the Commune while reprisals were visited on the *communards*, and praised Voltaire, Zola and Gide for putting their pen to the service of *causes célèbres*. It is no accident that Sartre specifically mentions 'l'aide à fournir aux républicains espagnols', while discussing the need for commitment in the writer. He praises Koestler's *Spanish Testament* in this same article as committed *reportage*. It is clear that the Spanish Civil War crystallised the issue of commitment in literature, an issue that until the arrival of the Spanish Republic and the growth of Fascism in Europe had not been perceived with such clarity. In retrospect, it appears to me that writers such as Sender played a major role in creating a European consciousness of *littérature engagée*, the success of which has traditionally been attributed to French writers. (This may well be because the war destroyed the continuity of Spanish literature, and Sender himself devoted himself to less directly committed forms of writing.)

Finally, in advocating committed literature, Sartre shows that he is well aware of the pitfalls to be avoided: 'Je rappelle, en effet, que dans la "littérature engagée," *l'engagement* ne doit, en aucun cas, faire oublier la *littérature*.'[42] A pitfall, unfortunately, into which many Spanish novelists of the Civil War have blundered.

Notes

1 D. Santos, 'Guerra y política en la novela contemporánea', *Estafeta Literaria*, 251 (15 October 1962), 4.

2 *Writers in Arms* (London, 1968), pp. 52–53.

3 Quoted in G. Steiner, 'Marxism and the Literary Critic' in *Language and Silence* (New York, 1976), p. 305.

4 *Ibid.*, pp. 305–306.

5 'Party Organisation and Party Literature', *Novaia Jizn* (November 1905). Quoted in Steiner, 'Marxism and the Literary Critic'.

6 E. de Nora, *La novela española contemporánea*, 2, p. 440.

7 *Ibid.* p. 441. Nora's comment on the technical and stylistic defects of these novels could be applied in equal measure to many of the novels on the theme of the Civil War: 'Cuando el novelista opta por ignorar el destino *personal* de sus tipos, presentándoles *sólo* como "luchadores", corta por así decir la hierba bajo sus pies, falseando incluso el sentido último de la acción revolucionaria, que no tiene como sujetos y objetos las "ideas" defendidas, sino los hombres concretos que, con ayuda de las ideas, aspiran a cambiar *su* condición' (p. 441 footnote).

8 H. Thomas, *The Spanish Civil War* (London, 1971), p. 278.

9 The theme of agrarian reform appears in Arconada's novel, *Reparto de tierras*, among others.

10 J. Ortega y Gasset, 'Ideas sobre la novela', *Obras completas*, 3 (Madrid, 1946), p. 411.

11 J. Ortega y Gasset, 'Notas del vago estío', *Notas* (Madrid, 1928), p. 167. In the light of the subsequent 'struggle for freedom' and 'defense of socialism', this is bitterly ironic: they were anything but easy.

12 I. Soldevila Durante, *La obra narrativa de Max Aub, 1929–1969* (Madrid, 1973), pp. 22–23.

13 Benda defined as 'clercs' 'tous ceux dont l'activité . . . ne poursuit pas des fins pratiques, mais qui (demandent) leur joie à l'exercice de l'art ou de la science ou de la spéculation métaphysique . . .' (*La Trahison des clercs*, Paris, 1927), p. 54. In other words the intellectual classes.

14 M. Rieuneau, *Guerre et révolution dans le roman français de 1919 à 1939* (Paris, 1974), p. 239.

15 'La política y el intelectual: Homenaje y reproche a don José Ortega y Gasset', *Haz*, 12 (5 December 1935).

16 S.G. Payne, *Falange: A History of Spanish Fascism* (London, 1962), p. 50.

17 R. Ledesma Ramos, 'Los intelectuales y la política', *La Conquista del Estado*, 5 (11 April 1931).

18 The fact that Ortega has never been forgiven by some owes more to emotion than to the effects of his influence after 1936. Juan Goytisolo surely exaggerates when he writes, 30 years after the Civil War: 'Las consecuencias de la teoría orteguiana de la deshumanización del Arte han sido incalculables y sus efectos pesan, todavía, sobre la vida cultural del país' (*Insula*, 146 (1959), 6).

19 M. Rieuneau, *Guerre et révolution*, p. 262.

20 R. Pomeau, 'Guerre et roman dans l'entre-deux-guerres', *Revue des Sciences Humaines* (January–March, 1963), p. 84.

21 I. Soldevila Durante, *La obra narrativa de Max Aub*, p. 293.

22 *Ibid.*

23 C.E. Magny, *Histoire du roman français* (Paris, 1950), p. 336. Quoted in Soldevila, *La obra narrativa de Max Aub*, p. 292.

24 *Las novelas históricas de Pío Baroja* (Madrid, 1974), p. 147.

25 F.R. Benson, *Writers in Arms*, p. xxvi.

26 'Why I write', *Collected Essays* (London, 1961), p. 426. It should be noted that Orwell's writings on the Civil War do not extend to the novel: his literary production after the war tended to take the form of essays and *reportage*. However, it is not difficult to imagine *Animal Farm* adapted to the events of May 1937 in Barcelona.

27 G. Gómez de la Serna, *España en sus episodios nacionales*, p. 117.

28 *Spanish Testament* (London, 1937), p. 177.

29 Quoted in C. Baker (ed.), *Ernest Hemingway: The Writer as Artist* (Princeton, 1963), pp. 199–200.

30 *A Poet's War*, p. 134.

31 *Literature and Propaganda* (London, 1983), p. 1.

32 J. Ellul, *Propaganda: The Formation of Men's Attitudes* (New York, 1973). Quoted in A.P. Foulkes, *Literature and Propaganda*, p. 2.

33 'La evolución espiritual de los intelectuales españoles en la emigración', *Cuadernos Hispanoamericanos*, 38 (February 1953), 123–157 (p. 152).

34 G. Orwell, 'The Prevention of Literature', an essay written in 1945. Orwell's pessimistic conclusion at that time was that 'the war produced acres of print but almost nothing worth reading'.

35 H. Klein (ed.), *The First World War in Fiction*, p. 1.

36 L. MacNeice, 'The Poet in England Today', *New Republic*, 102 (1940), 412–413.

37 G. Steiner, *Language and Silence*, p. 96.

38 *The Death of Tragedy* (London, 1961), p. 317.

39 *Ibid.*, p. 317.

40 A.P. Foulkes, *Literature and Propaganda*, p. 79.

41 'Présentations des *Temps Modernes*', *Situations II* (Paris, 1948), p. 13.

42 *Ibid.*, p. 30.

3
—
Literary
genre, narrative
technique and language
in the first-wave Civil War novel

As I HAVE INDICATED in an earlier chapter, the novel of the Spanish Civil War does not always conform to the traditional model of the 'war novel'. While scenes at the front are often included, they may well not form the major part of the work, and numerous novels do not deal with life at the front at all. *Se ha ocupado el kilómetro 6* and *Cuerpo a tierra* may strike us as being paradigms of the war novel, but Aub's *Campos* have an equal claim, as do the numerous works describing life in jails, *checas*, embassies and 'safe houses' of the rearguard. What distinguishes many of these novels from the Remarquian model (though Remarquian echoes are to be detected in a large number of them) is the fact that they are set in a period not only of war but of revolution. The action develops not only on distant battlefields but on the home front in the cities, towns and villages of Spain. Alongside the theme of war, therefore, we find those of revolution and counter-revolution, espionage, crime, adventure, childhood or adolescence, and love. Pre-war and post-war themes may also be treated, in varying degrees. History and invention are combined in different measure, so that works may range from *reportage* to almost pure fiction. The perspective adopted by the author often has a decisive influence on genre; as Sobejano has pointed out, authors may be 'observadores' (W. Fernández Flórez, R. León, F. Camba, T. Borrás), 'militantes' (R. García Serrano, C. Benítez de Castro, R. Fernández de la Reguera) or 'intérpretes' (A. Barea, M. Aub, R. Sender, P. Masip, J.M. Gironella).[1] For Sobejano, 'los novelistas "observadores" se distinguen por imprimir a sus relatos un sesgo cronístico y anecdótico, propio de quienes, durante un tiempo históricamente importante se apresuran a registrar las experiencias personales para informar a la posteridad'.[2] The 'militantes' are in a category which is not dissimilar: 'Trazaron ... el reportaje de las luchas y padecimientos, sin haber llegado a comprender, en clarividente perspectiva, lo que la guerra significaba para todos los españoles.'[3] The third group is characterised by 'una mayor generalidad o ejemplaridad humana'; they go beyond the description of events to their analysis and interpretation.[4]

It is primarily the first two categories that will concern us here, since few of the novels of the first wave achieve the degree of distancing from the event that is necessary for a balanced appraisal. Many of them were produced by men (and occasionally women) who were not, for the most part, professional novelists, but whose diaries, correspondence, newspaper cuttings and memories of things seen and heard (sometimes on the radio) provided the source material for a literary adventure. When two prisoners in *98 horas* discuss the difficulties inherent in recording their experiences in the war, their dialogue includes the following exchange:

— Lo difícil es escribirlo. El tema es fuerte, fuertísimo y por eso la forma se resiste, la expresión se esconde y no se encuentra la que se precisa. Y no sólo es la palabra la que huye, sino algo que flota por encima de todo, la Gracia, que es la más esquiva. Sin esa esencia no hay nada.

— Desde luego que se lucha por encontrarla, pero ya se encontrará, y si no por lo menos los hechos quedan anotados, que ya vendrá el genio, que uniéndolos, hará la obra imperecedera. No se preocupe por ello. Hay que escribir lo que se ve y se siente. Es una obligación que tenemos los que ahora vivimos con los de las generaciones venideras.   (pp. 108–109)

In this same conversation, reference is made to the difficulty of capturing the fleeting moment of inspiration; it allows time for a rapid line drawing, and little more: 'El lápiz triunfa sobre el pincel y la pluma. La impresión es rápida y la forma gráfica tiene que serlo también. Son tan seguidas las impresiones que no da tiempo para dejar terminada la obra' (p. 107). If such depiction of life was difficult in prison, it was doubly so in the trenches, where life was subject to constant interruption; yet many jottings must have accumulated in this way. The protagonist of *Las lomas tienen espinos* is described writing 'versos, una novela, artículos para *El Correo de Andalucía*. '. . . La novela iba muy despacio. No tenía papel bueno y escribía a lápiz sobre dos kilos de papel de envolver que le había traído el cabo de cocina desde Peñarroya. Era papel barato, y por lo demás no merecía la pena gastar otro mejor' (p. 211). He also begins a diary, of which we are given a sample (pp. 258–263). But Manfredi Cano soon abandons the description of the diary, saying: 'Así es el diario de un combatiente. No dice nada. No ve la guerra, no comprende lo que pasa en la línea de batalla, ni por qué entra por un lado o por otro. Luego cuenta las cosas sin detalles. La guerra vista en los "diarios" de los combatientes es una guerra falsa' (p. 264).[5] In one of the earliest surveys of the Spanish Civil War novel, J.A. Fernández-Cañedo drew attention to the haste with which the source materials (in this case, for Nationalist works) have been assembled: 'En permisos, descansos, días de frente inactivo, convalescencia en hospitales, los combatientes se apresuran a pergeñar memorias, escribir biografías de compañeros, petrificar el instante de pánico o de gloria.'[6] M. Rieuneau found that the early French novels of the First World War also had their inspiration in the *carnet de route* or *journal de route*.[7] He noticed too a tendency to divide the war up into neat segments ('the assault', 'hospital', etc.) – a practice he found reminiscent of the *roman-feuilleton*. Other characteristics of the *feuilleton*, such as exaggeration and melodrama, were also to be found among these French writers. It seems that the haste with which first-wave war novels are written, their limited objectives and the relative inexperience of many of their authors, produce works which show similarities with the popular novel. It will be my purpose in this section to examine these resemblances, all the more because critics have tended previously to dismiss many first-wave Spanish Civil War novels as being unworthy of their attention. The growing interest in sub-literary and para-literary genres in recent years reflects a concern that the relationship between literature and society should be properly examined, irrespective of the literary merit of the works under study.[8] Commitment and propaganda played an important role in determining the *content* of the novels. It could be argued that whatever immediately previous literary tradition had existed in Spain, in 1936 it would have been swept away by what came to be known as 'engagement'. It could further be argued that there is no need to search, therefore, for a tradition of commitment in Spanish literature to explain its appearance at this time. The *form* the novel took, however, can only be explained in terms of the novelists' own literary experience – as well as factors such as their envisaged readership and their pursuit of commercial success. The sales figures for the novels, while a most fruitful subject for research, fall outside the limits of this study. The envisaged readership must in this case be expected to have shared the political sympathies of the author, and often, to judge by the youthful protagonists who stride through these novels, not to have exceeded 20 years of age. However, it is the question of how far these novelists were acquainted with Spanish letters, or more specifically, traditions of story-telling, that poses the most intriguing problem for the literary historian.

It seemed to me on reading many of the first-wave novels that in their narrative techniques and language they harked back to the *novela popular* of earlier years. I sought support for this general hypothesis in the studies published by A. Amorós, J.I. Ferreras and L. Romero Tovar in Spain, and in those of a number of critics in France who have written on the same theme. It must be remembered that the nineteenth-century *folletín* continued to be published in Spain until the 1920s.[9] In addition, collections like *La Novela Corta* (1916–25) and *La Novela de Hoy* (1922–32) enjoyed enormous popularity before the Civil War, to judge by their circulation figures.[10] In the post-war era, collections such as *La Novela Actual*, *La Novela Selecta*, *La Novela Corta* and *La Novela del Sábado* continued the tradition. It seems not unreasonable to suppose that the novelists under study here would have been acquainted with this output and perhaps influenced by its conventions.

The popular novelist has a tendency to intrude in his narrative, either in direct intromission, which one critic has termed *excurso narrativo*,[11] or in a heavy-handed manipulation of the plot which lurches this way and that at his bidding.[12] So little distance separates this type of novelist from his readers that he may converse directly with them,[13] and frequently interrupts his narrative to make a moral point.[14] The reader should not be surprised to encounter a sudden conversion in a character;[15] since characters tend to be fixed types, changes will tend to be brusque.[16]

In their depiction of the social scene, authors grossly simplify the events they describe, avoiding any discussion of the complex reality which lies behind them. They are concerned not to engage in a debate with their readership, but rather to reflect what already exists in the collective conscience.[17] Their ideas appear therefore as *discurso*, rather than *problemática*,[18] encapsulating in simplified form what their readers already believe. Political preoccupations are barely in evidence in the *novela popular*;[19] they are totally absent in the *novela rosa*.[20] Clearly, the Civil War novel marks a new departure in this respect (*politización* substituting *erotización* as the major thematic constant), but the tradition of over-simplification, the reduction of societal or class issues to a confrontation between individuals, endures.[21] In addition, as we shall see, the love story often finds a place in the landscape of war, so that facile political idealism merges with sentimentalism to produce a hybrid form of the *novela popular*.[22] The influence of other forms, such as the *novela de aventuras* or the *novela de crímenes*,[23] is also clearly visible. The titles of the works are intended to catch the public attention,[24] and their content is often melodramatic.[25] The characters propound 'filosofía barata',[26] reflecting the low intellectual level of the envisaged readership. There is a strong mystical element in many of the stories: presentiment, prophecy and miracles are common ingredients, and God and the Devil are frequently invoked.[27] The development of the plot may depend on unlikely coincidences.[28] As a general rule, the author is technically incompetent to create the effect he intends, and being unable to describe the complex relationship between man and the universe that surrounds him, he resorts to frenzied descriptions of action.[29] 'No hay distancias, ni tiempo para el protagonista aventurero, ni duerme ni come, ni descansa ni se fatiga.'[30] The novels are characterised by a pronounced manicheism, 'la separación tajante de buenos y malos'.[31] The psychology of the characters is crude; villains, heroes and heroines unmistakably betray their nature in their facial expression.[32] The youthful hero 'posee todos los atributos acostumbrados: valor, sacrificio, liberalidad, amor y . . . belleza'. The heroine is characterised by 'castidad, humildad, espíritu de sacrificio y . . . hermosura'. The villain is physically ugly, perhaps deformed or lame, and displays 'cobardía, avaricia, hipocresía'.[33] The ages of these characters, too, conform to a pattern: the girl still in her teens, the hero in his twenties, and the villain, often an older man.[34] Foreigners are described, both physically and morally, in negative terms.[35] The characteristics of the various social classes are exaggerated.[36] The language used by these authors is often hackneyed, naive or pompous. They go too far in their attempt to avoid the everyday, sometimes resorting to archaic expressions.[37] The result is a strange mixture of styles: 'El estilo oscila entre el popularismo y el deseo de ennoblecer la expresión, sin quedarse en el término medio de la lengua culta.'[38] In reproducing dialogue, attempts are made to imitate popular forms of speech, including dialect.[39] Exclamations and rhetorical questions abound; imagery is generally banal in the extreme; the prose is stilted and it is not uncommon to find errors of language as well as of fact.[40]

For students of the Civil War novel there is much that sounds familiar in these analyses by French and Spanish critics (with the notable exception of the apolitical nature of the popular novel). It may be instructive to examine some of these similarities.

Perhaps the most common feature found in the first-wave novels of the Civil War is authorial intromission,[41] a technique L. Romero found almost universal in the nineteenth-century popular novel in Spain. The *excurso* destroys the illusion that the characters have an autonomous existence within the work. It is as though the author of a play were to walk on to the stage in mid-act and direct asides at the audience to clarify the plot or emphasise his message. Far from being an avant-garde device, challenging the comfortable relationship between audience and characters, it is used to compensate for the author's failure to communicate indirectly through action and dialogue. Either because he does not have confidence in his own technical skills or because he is unwilling to put his faith in his readership's capacity to understand implicit messages, the author uses his own voice to emphasise his point, particularly if that message is propagandist. 'La miseria moral que en el campo rojo es característica común de los combatientes, se ha acentuado con la presencia de milicianas sin pudor, ni concepto de la dignidad femenina', writes Claramunt in *El teniente Arizcun* (p. 34), thus saving himself many hours' work demonstrating this effectively in terms of action and dialogue. Concha Espina's *voluntad de probar* is so powerful that she often abandons her narrative to engage in a lengthy tirade against the enemy or to eulogise her own side. Such examples may be found in *Retaguardia* (pp. 156 and 112). 'Camino cuarto' of *Princesas del martirio* is a lengthy epilogue in the author's own voice.[42] What begins as descriptive narrative at one point in García Serrano's *La fiel Infantería* (p. 556) is soon transformed into a political harangue by the author (p. 558). Earlier, in a section in which he pledges that Falange's violence will be turned against the *caciques* after the war, there is an interesting variation of the technique we are discussing. Realising that he has been speaking for some time with his own voice, the author adds: 'Así lo decía Mario, con el fusil en la mano . . .', belatedly making it sound like an utterance by his character. R. León is ever-present in the pages of *Cristo en los infiernos*, giving full (if tendentious) descriptions of the life of the nation up to the Civil War. To describe parliamentary business, for example, he uses his own voice (pp. 289ff.) even though one of his characters, Margarita Gelves, is a member of the Cortes and could quite easily have been used as a vehicle.[43] M. de Salazar, in *De anarquista a mártir*, seems to forget for pages at a time that he is writing a novel. He gives his account of the reasons for the war (pp. 250–256), abandoning his narrative to do so. The author is never far away, either, in *Camisa azul*. After an objective statement such as 'se hablan de tú y se llaman camaradas' to describe Víctor and his Falangist friends, Ximénez de Sandoval cannot resist making the propaganda point, 'aunque viene cada uno de esos compartimientos estancos que una sociedad estúpida y una Sociología envenenada llaman clases' (p. 24).

Sometimes, as in the popular novel, the author will address a statement even more directly to the reader, appearing to make the latter an accomplice.

Benítez de Castro comments on one of the dialogues in *El espantable caso de los 'tomadores' de ciudades*. ¡Qué conversación tan insípida! ¿Verdad, lector? Fastídiate. No todo ha de ser interesante. Creo que hasta que lleguen a Linaja no hay nada que decirte de especial importancia' (p. 125). This familiar form of address is also to be found in *Un alférez de cursillos*: 'Si fuera lo que leíste, lector, un cuento de guerra o una novela de campaña, fácil la pluma correría en un epílogo de paz de risueños coloridos . . . Pero sería imperdonable, lector, ese falseamiento de hechos . . .' (p. 105). M. Sepúlveda begins chapter 16 of her novel with the words, 'Desearán mis lectores saber que . . .' which is a variant of the same technique. The Nationalist novels in which there is an intrusive narrator are too numerous to mention: Cimorra, Giménez Arnau, Vázquez, Carriedo de Ruiz, Martín-Artajo and many more use this technique.[44]

The Republican novelists are no less intrusive. Martínez Pagán writes after one hyperbolic account in *Génaro*: 'Je dis cela non sans une grande exagération, car faire de la littérature sans exagérer ne serait pas sérieux' (p. 58). The author of *La vida por la opinión* frequently forgets his narrative to give us a personal view of the war. When he wishes to depict a female character, Agus, as intelligent and likeable, he sees no point in beating about the bush: 'Agus era una muchacha inteligente y simpática' (p. 194). This is barely an advance on the descriptive technique of the *folletín* ('el apuesto mancebo,' 'la linda joven'). In *Sueños de grandeza* we find much greater subtlety, but the author is still unwilling to let his message emerge from the action. Instead, he imposes it: 'Sabía ya el pueblo entero lo que significaba la palabra solidaridad . . .' (p. 261). The defensive tone of Sancho Granados is only too apparent in the following comment he makes in *98 horas*: 'Con la muerte de Calvo Sotelo, ejecutada a espaldas y con desconocimiento absoluto del Gobierno . . .' (p. 75).[45] These authors, like their Nationalist counterpart, are an ever-present shadow beside their creations.

Another common form of authorial intromission, sometimes referred to as ventriloquism, takes place when an author uses a character to voice his own opinions. Provided the author is not duplicating views already expressed by himself as author, this need not appear to the reader as excessively manipulative. If there is direct authorial intrusion as well, however, or if the same voice comes from more than one character, the reader will begin to feel that he is the victim of propaganda – unless, that is, the reader's need for propaganda is dominant over the need for aesthetic experience. It is quite clear that these first-wave authors envisaged a readership that needed the reassurance of propaganda, for they provide it not only in their own (i.e. author's) voice, but in the voices of characters sharing their political beliefs, and incredible though it may seem, in the voices of characters with supposedly *opposite* political beliefs.

There are few novelists in this first wave who are capable of portraying a credible enemy. They tend to create either caricatures, or dilute versions of their own side who are clearly misguided and who eventually realise the error of their ways. Benítez de Castro describes *faístas* in Barcelona listening to radio broadcasts by Queipo de Llano, whom they consider to be the only reliable source of information on the war (*El espantable caso de los 'tomadores' de ciudades*, ch. 8). Fadrique de Lorenzana, a self-styled anti-Fascist who helps to run one of the *checas* in *Checas de Madrid*, suddenly speaks with the voice of Borrás: '¿Qué es la revolución? La gran dionisíada del odio. "No sirvo, no agradezco, no amo." Una rebelión contra el cristianismo, una más. Servir, agradecer: eso es cristianismo. La soberbia se revuelve: ¡No! Y se hace la revolución de los que quieren ser dioses' (p. 91). Margarita Gelves, in *Cristo en los infiernos* is supposedly a militant Marxist, but she idolises the hero of the novel, Pablo, who is a follower of Calvo Sotelo, a friend of Onésimo Redondo and the *jonsistas*, and later becomes the organiser of the *requetés*. If Margarita were described as feeling a purely physical attraction towards him, that might pass as an explanation. But on the contrary, she tells him: 'Yo no te quiero como a un hombre. Te quiero como a un santo, como a un ser superior a todos los de este mundo' (p. 277).[46] Her language and attitudes are quite inappropriate to the character she is supposed to represent. Another character, Dr Alegre, who according to Margarita, 'se las da de escéptico, y aún de anarquista a sus horas' (p. 92), speaks enthusiastically of 'ese Bloque Nacional que trae Calvo Sotelo en sus robustos hombros de atleta . . . ¡Este es un hombre y un jefe!' (p. 366). Nor can it be argued that this is the result of a conversion; Dr Alegre later claims: 'Yo soy republicano a rabiar' (p. 430). Such characters are beset by internal contradictions because of the author's inability to portray an ordinary, sincere Republican of the period. Violeta, the beautiful *miliciana* in *Méndez, cronista de guerra*, is supposed to be a Socialist, but tells the dashing Falangist hero Méndez, 'Tú no eres como los otros. Tú eres muy bueno. Tú no eres socialista o comunista. Y por eso te quiero más' (p. 138). She follows him around obediently from this point on. Eduardo, the protagonist of *La mascarada trágica*, is a Marxist who had joined the *Socorro Rojo* in the war, inspired by 'virtudes cristianas' (p. 86). He is described as being an intellectual, yet at no point up to his conversion does he make an intellectual defence of his political ideas, even when provoked into doing so (p. 76). Martingala, described as being an intelligent Anarchist leader in Alicante, in *De una España a otra*, defends Franco's use of German and Italian forces (p. 83), and later kisses the forehead of the executed José Antonio Primo de Rivera 'en nombre de todos sus camaradas'. Unable to sustain the authentic portrayal of an Anarchist, the author decides to convert him into a mirror image of himself. Ximénez de Sandoval, in *Camisa azul*, uses a technique that is only slightly more subtle. After the killing of the Falangist Enrique by left-wingers, his four Falangist comrades take him to the morgue where they meet his working-class father and uncle. While the latter sulks in a corner, the father allows the Falangists to dress his son's body in the blue shirt and black trousers of their Party. Referring to his son's defection to Fascism, he tells the uncle: 'Lo mismo que se borró de la Casa del Pueblo y se fue con los sindicalistas, porque los marxistas les parecíamos blandos y poco revolucionarios, se ha marchado ahora con los fascistas . . . Más socialista que yo no lo eres tú, y creo que tal vez tenía Enrique razón' (p. 40). Such ventriloquism is extremely common in the Nationalist works (which constitute the vast majority of first-wave novels).[47] It is rare for the novelists to recreate the language of the enemy in a convincing way; they make Republican characters refer to 'poblaciones liberadas' when they mean towns which have fallen to the enemy, 'rojos' when they mean their own side, and so on. Reference has already been made to the conversion of a character from one political persuasion to another, usually that of the author. There may also be variations on the theme; for example, a politically indifferent individual may suddenly become committed. Some of the characters already mentioned above (Margarita, in *Cristo en los infiernos*, Violeta in *Méndez, cronista de guerra*, Eduardo in *La mascarada trágica*, Martingala in *De una España a otra*) undergo profound transformations. Juan Pérez in *El espantable caso de los 'tomadores' de ciudades* is converted by the shining example of a Nationalist heroine and abandons the Republican cause, saying: 'Soy muy desengañado. Somos unos tramposos' (p. 134). Ridán, in a *volte-face* which may well have been a concession to the censor, is abruptly converted from indifference to Nationalist fervour in *Provisional* (p. 176). Vicente, in *Retaguardia*, is an unconvincing Socialist for much of the story, and it comes as no surprise when he renounces 'las ideas que sólo producen el asesinato y la cobardía', to become a Falangist (p. 200). The heroine of this novel has already undergone a similar conversion, as has her brother. Conversions brought about for reasons of expediency, when a character finds himself in enemy territory, reflect reality. If such people did not quickly find reasons for supporting the cause of the winning side, they risked imprisonment or worse.[48] Many of the conversions mentioned in this section, however, are of a different order, more akin to divine revelation on the road to Damascus. Sometimes, a character embraces a political cause through weakness or under pressure from someone else. The author will then describe their return to the true cause from which they had been led astray. Such a character is León, in *De anarquista a mártir*, who falls under the evil influence of his wife. Such stories resemble the religious allegories of an earlier age. In this novel, M. de Salazar (like R. León in the case of Margarita Gelves) describes a character whose environment temporarily overcomes his nature, influencing him for the worst. Eventually, however, more benign influences prevail, and the *albedrío* of the character reasserts itself. It is necessary to make clear early in the novel that the hero is contributing to the force of evil in the world reluctantly and against his better judgement: 'La insistencia de Satorre venció la debil resistencia de la voluntad de León' (p. 40). (Despite his redemption, León pays for that early weakness with his life: his plane is mistakenly machine-gunned when he defects to Nationalist Spain.) *En la gloria de aquel amanecer* ends with a dual conversion. Rafaela, a selfish Republican wife and mother, is reunited with her husband as a result of the death of their son, a *requeté*, in the war. 'La gracia divina había hecho en ella efectos rápidos y saludables', writes the author, after describing this process (ch. 21). A similar metamorphosis occurs in Ginesa, the girl who has fallen in love with the novel's hero, Agustín. From a frivolous young thing she is transformed into a Nationalist paradigm, concerned only with the future of the *patria* (ch. 23). Even in the later novels of this first wave, spontaneous conversions are common. An Anarchist is described in *El puente* attending a Fascist meeting and being immediately seduced: 'Había sido anarquista, y un día, con una pistola, se fue a un mitin fascista. En lugar de disparar, apenas le oyó hablar vino con nosotros' (p. 139).[49]

The intrusion of the author, which is such a feature of the traditional popular novel, is clearly a common technique, then, in the works under study. The reader must be left in no doubt about the novel's meaning. The moral dualism present in all these novels impinges directly on characterisation. Characters are portrayed with bold brush-strokes: caricature is the order of the day. The good are saintly, the bad are demonic. E. de Nora's comments on Borrás's novels *Checas de Madrid* and *La sangre de las almas* could be applied to a number of other war novels in this section; significantly, he draws attention in passing to their similarity to the *folletín*:

La visión catastrófica que el autor profesa de la historia contemporánea – la guerra española y la mundial . . . produce un resultado literariamente confuso y casi monstruoso, al moverse el narrador en ambientes creados por su sola fantasía, recargando el lado cruel, tétrico e inhumano de los acontecimientos hasta el puro folletín, que resbala estragando la sensibilidad y la comprensión del lector, sin convencerlo, ni siquiera, como el novelista querría, producirle terror ni indignación alguna.[50]

The nature of Borrás's characters is written in their countenance for all to see: 'Por las dos rendijas oblicuas del mestizo [Fadrique de Lorenzana] asomaba, impasible, la dureza fría y desnuda del rencor' (p. 73). His militiamen and jailers are so evil they cease to be true to life, and consequently do not achieve their intended effect. In *De una España a otra*, too, the militiamen have 'caras patibularias' (p. 56) and Republican prisoners are later described with 'caras aviesas donde el miedo y la rabia ponen tintes verdosos'. In *Navidades sin pan*, the relationship between facial expression and moral character is unambiguous, in a scene in which a militia column plunders a village in Huesca province: 'Aquella mesnada sacrificaba reses y degollaba patos, gallinas y conejos. Algunos milicianos más comprensivos penetraron en las habitaciones llevándose lo que quisieron, mientras otros, de ángulo facial más primitivo, echaban cuadros por la ventana alimentando una hoguera ante la puerta.' A similar scene is described in *Camisa azul* when Nationalists overrun a Republican-held village near Torrijos.

– No se defendían y salían llorando; levantaban los brazos y gritaban ¡Arriba España!
– Pero no nos engañaban. Eran bizcos, barbudos y mellados. Con esas caras de forajidos no se puede gritar nuestros gritos sagrados.
– Con esas caras sólo se puede incendiar y saquear; violar y asesinar. (p. 281)

A militiaman in Miquelarena's *El otro mundo* is described as having 'el azulado descuido barberil que caracteriza a los españoles con ideas democráticas' (p. 89). Much of the description in such caricature centres on the eyes and the mouth (which is invariably curled in contempt). 'Obreros de gorra ladeada y camiseta sucia, con aliento de vinazo y ojos de mala pasión' lust after the heroine in *Camisa azul*. Efrén Laviño (a character based on Enrique Lister) greets the clean-limbed hero of *Tú no eres de los nuestros* with an expression that betrays his contempt: 'En sus labios acababa de esbozarse una sonrisa llena de ironía diabólica' (p. 80).[51]

Numerous examples of exaggerated characterisation will be given in chapters 4 and 5, which deal with the ways in which each side promoted its own cause. The enemy is portrayed as villainous or stupid, or both. In *Méndez, cronista de guerra*, the editor of a Republican newspaper does not understand the word 'STOP' in the telegrams he receives, believing it to be an enemy code word. This form of lampooning is uncommon, however; the enemy is much more likely to display demonic characteristics, like the nurse in *Cartas de un alférez a su madre* (a *novela del sábado*) who, out of revenge for the death of her husband who has been shot as a traitor, insidiously undermines a young soldier's confidence that his sight will be restored after he has been blinded in battle. The description of the popular tribunal which tries Víctor in *Camisa azul* is a splendid example of caricature: the Falangist hero is here tried by three Russian Jews who communicate with each other in Russian, and with the court officials in poor German. 'Los tres judíos cuchicheaban en un bisbiseo felino de suaves eses y de fonética eslava' (pp. 115–116). (At a stroke, the author manages to make a propaganda statement which is anti-Russian, anti-Jewish and anti-Republican.) The three Jews are made to look inferior to the towering Víctor when the latter addresses them in German, which he speaks quite well (having learned it to be able to read Nietzsche in the original version). Such contrast in characterising Republicans and Nationalists is a powerful method of reinforcing caricature. The goodness of a nun may be contrasted with the evil of the enemy. Sor Remedios fulfils such a role in *La mascarada trágica*. The nun who nurses the sick in *Cristo en los infiernos* makes the wayward Margarita Gelves feel envious: 'Por un instante, la esclava de Lucifer sintió una envidia rabiosa, desesperada y frenética, de la dulce esclava del Señor' (p. 245). Pablo ('el apóstol') has the same effect, and constantly lectures Margarita, who is suffering 'la terrible tenacidad de la posesión diabólica' (p. 251). Extremes of character are constantly juxtaposed in this way. Occasionally, the caricature is applied to individuals on the same side. Benítez de Castro lampoons the Nationalist soldier, Pérez, for example, who is supposed to represent the intellectual, but whose 'interminables peroratas' have the effect of clearing the area in his immediate vicinity. (The reader will be expected, here, to identify Pérez with those intellectuals who initially supported the Republic, and are therefore responsible, in the minds of Nationalist writers, for all Spain's ills. This is a disguised attack on the other side.)[52]

Among the Republican novelists of the first wave (much fewer in number), Aguilera-Malta, Cimorra and Samblancat use caricature freely as a technique. Aguilera's aristocrat in *¡Madrid!* hunts on his estate, but instead of shooting hares he dreams of one day shooting serfs (p. 23). His physical description shows him to be sickly and degenerate: 'la piel delicada y granujienta . . . el rostro anguloso, . . . ojos ocultos tras cristales . . . calva inmisericorde . . . cuerpo enano' (pp. 23–24). He has a fat and troublesome wife whom he hates, and an idiot son who is locked away at the top of the palace, until the day he escapes and *chews* the maid to death. The count dreams of the time when the aristocracy will see a return to their former pre-eminence: 'Extirpados los rojos. La propiedad garantizada. Restaurados los privilegios de las altas clases' (p. 43). Not a great deal of subtlety, then, in the portrayal of character; this villainous aristocrat could have come straight from a *folletín*. As in Nationalist novels like *Checas de Madrid*, the enemy carries out its crimes with careless abandon, 'todo ello como una diversión'. But here, those who look on and laugh while atrocities are committed are *señoritos*. In *El bloqueo del hombre*, there is a strong contrast between the landowner's idiot daughter, Blasa, and the progressive schoolteacher, Adelaida. *Caravana nazarena* mercilessly lampoons Republican politicians. It also portrays Alfonso XIII as a sexual athlete from whom village girls had to take refuge for fear of being raped. The monarch ('monoide reinante', 'real monomio') and his nose ('paquidérmica trompa', 'nasal purulencia', 'rinoceróntica protuberancia') are made the butt of Samblancat's mordant satire, which goes beyond the caricature of other writers discussed so far, into a realm of genuine originality.[53]

In order to express their contempt of the enemy, writers of both sides resort to animal imagery. As might be expected, Samblancat has a rich store of such expressions:

El gerifáltico y accipitrino Goded fue destinado a Baleares, para tener a Barcelona y a Cataluña al alcance de su garra. A Franco, buitre de collar desde que nació, se le transformó por mágica arte en canario, sin duda para que hechizase con sus trinos a la bandolera morralla del Tercio y a los mercenarios del Rif, que nunca conocieron madre. A la pezuña porcina de Mola se le entregó otra buena presa: el mando de los cortezudos y los ceporros de las Brigadas Navarras. (p. 22)

Such extended metaphors are unusual, though a similar inventiveness is to be found in R. León's *Cristo en los infiernos*, in his description of the crowds attacking the Montaña barracks:

Aquella hez, masa de carne sin alma, tenía la ferocidad y hasta el semblante del hombre inferior y de la bestia, el sello de la piara y de la horda, la faz del antropoide o del caníbal, la jeta y los morros del paquidermo, el hocico agudo de los cánidos, los belfos de los solípedos, el corvo perfil del ave carnicera, la cabeza aplastada del ofidio.   (p. 484)

More commonly, simple animal similes and metaphors are used.

All the techniques described here are to be found in the traditional *novela popular*. Within that genre, a particularly common sub-genre is the *novela rosa*, and the first-wave war novels display numerous features which are reminiscent of such works. It is noteworthy, however, that the *novela rosa* which deals with the war is uniquely the preserve of the Nationalist novelists, probably due to the state of Nationalist morale during these years and the anti-bourgeois sentiment that existed on the Republican side.[54] Nowhere is this hybrid genre of *novela rosa de guerra* better exemplified, perhaps, than in Concha Espina's series of novels on the war, in which heavy doses of sentimentalism are combined with a highly idealised view of a central hero and heroine. Natural superiority is confused with hereditary aristocracy (perhaps because of Espina's own aristocratic antecedents), so that Alicia, in *Retaguardia*, 'siente el deseo de hallar en sí misma algún antecedente linajudo para adquirir confianza en los buenos adelantos que haga sobre la tierra' (p. 53). This is because she is in love with Rafael, whose parents are 'hidalgos por ascendencia, recoletos y finos por aristocracia natural' (p. 52). The mannered description of Rafael's sister Rosa gives a flavour of Espina's characterisation. 'Muy culta y sensible: de esas mujeres que levantan despacio los ojos a las lejanías como para recoger en ellos toda la luz y esconderla después en el bosque de las pestañas, camino de la conciencia' (p. 52). The choice of a poor crippled girl, Talín, as the heroine of *Las alas invencibles*, gives Espina ample scope to play on the shallow emotions of what was probably a young, impressionable, female readership.[55] The three young female martyrs of *Princesas del martirio* exude 'dulzura' and 'santidad' and share the 'hidalguía natural' of all Nationalists in the novel. Espina's view of herself as the epitome of refinement and sensibility emerges in the short story 'Carpeta gris' (in *Luna roja*) in which a female novelist continues to write in secret in Republican-dominated Spain. One day, her gaze falls on the flowers growing at her window: '¡Qué delicia! murmura, inclinándose a besar los racimos, apasionada y sensible, como todos los artistas' (p. 200).[56] There is an admission in C. Martel's *La guerra a través de las tocas* that this novel is intended mainly for women (it promises therefore to avoid stark realism), but even if the authoress had not told us, we might have guessed by the sentimental tone and the frequent use of diminutives to describe the nurses, one of whom is 'una de nuestras más elegantes y encantadoras duquesitas' (p. 18).[57] The novels are full of stylised descriptions which have been borrowed from the sentimental novels of an earlier period. When Méndez, in *Méndez, cronista de guerra*, returned home wounded, his wife 'deshacía entre los pétalos de sus dedos la perla de una lágrima'. She is later described as 'de ojos marinos y trenzas doradas, de carnes de nácar y rostro de ángel' (p. 57).

   Señorita en la retaguardia is another splendid example of this hybrid genre. The description of a first communion in Seville exemplifies the style:

Ante tanta magnificencia y solemnidad, los pechos de los devotos se hallaban nimbados de dulzura, rebozando de ellos las más puras mieles de lo generoso, y en los de las colegialas palpitaban los tiernos corazones como palomitas alegres y temblorosas.   (p. 20)

The authoress's grasp of the political issues she is describing is tenuous, and the terminology she uses is vague. The heroine inadvertently falls in love with an 'extremista' (p. 146), 'una persona que conspira contra la sociedad' (p. 163); reference is made to 'las cosas políticas y sociales' (p. 213), and no attempt is made at analysis (presumably because her readership would not thank her for it). This is an example of a novel which appears to have been conceived and partly written before the outbreak of war, its action being overtaken by real events. Whereas it begins as a traditional *novela rosa*, it ends as a work of propaganda – an interesting hybrid. Another novel of this kind is *El frente de los suspiros*, by J. de Salas, which, as its title suggests, is directed at the girls who are left behind on the home front: 'La guerra tiene tres frentes: el de los soldados, que lucha, el de los civiles, que trabaja, y el de las mujeres, que suspira' (p. 187). Some sections of *Tú no eres de los nuestros* are pure *folletín*: the description of the heroine in bed, 'maravillosa belleza, pestañas de azabache, labios rojos, sonrisa angelical, dientes de nieve' (p. 100), is a good example. When misled into thinking that her husband has died in a concentration camp, she vows: 'Cuando se haya agotado mi llanto, el claustro será mi fin' (p. 170). The eventual happy ending returns the reader to the warm sentimentality of the *novela rosa*.

   Many more examples can be quoted of this hybrid genre, the *novela rosa de guerra*, to demonstrate its popularity. Claramunt's *El teniente Arizcun* is subtitled 'novela de amor y de guerra'. The love story is woven into the war theme in *Se ha ocupado el kilómetro 6*, *El espantable caso de los 'tomadores' de ciudades*, *En plena epopeya*, *Provisional*, *La mascarada trágica*, *En mi hambre mando yo*, *De una España a otra*, *De anarquista a mártir* and *En la gloria de aquel amanecer*; it is present, but less developed, in *Provisional*. While the *novela rosa* is unknown among Republican writers, they do broach the theme of love in a more realistic vein: Aub's early novels serve as an example, as does Cimorra's *El bloqueo del hombre*. Martínez Pagán is the only Republican author I have encountered who dispatches his bereaved and love-sick heroine to a nunnery at the end of his story (*Génaro*, p. 315). The suppressed eroticism which is such a feature of the *novela popular* is not as commonly found in these war novels. There is a streak of sado-masochism with powerful sexual overtones, however, in *Checas de Madrid*, by Borrás, which would surely have encountered problems with the censor if it had not been a blatantly propagandist work. It is best seen in the description of the debauched aristocrat Angeles, who waits half-naked for the return of her lover 'El Paria' from a *paseo*. Instead, Marrullero appears, having assassinated 'El Paria' in order to possess Angeles. He lashes her body with his leather belt until she submits to his advances (pp. 267–269). On the Republican side, among these early novelists, only Samblancat approaches eroticism. When Carmelina is reunited with Lucas, her words might have come from a Lorca heroine: 'Quiéreme, nada más. Como cuando eras estudiante y las miradas de tus ojos cargados de cariño derrotaban mi pudor y me encendían las caderas; me abrasaban viva toda y hacían estallar las granadas de mis pechos' (p. 146).

Three other genres should be mentioned here for the frequency with which they occur: the crime novel, the detective novel and the adventure story. In the crime novel the emphasis is not on the pursuit of the criminal but on the atrocities he commits. In the detective novel, an attempt is made to pursue a criminal or missing person (though not by a conventional detective, necessarily) and in the adventure story the stress is on action, excitement and changes of scene. *Checas de Madrid*, by Borrás, in the main describes war crimes; but the relentless pursuit of the young Falangist, Federico, by the evil Paco Yeles (who has much in common with the historical figure, García Atadell),[58] introduces the element of detection. Espina's *Retaguardia* is the story of a search by the heroine (Alicia) for the man she loves (Rafael); inexplicably, this remains an unresolved element of the plot at the end of the story, during which numerous grisly crimes are uncovered. The mansion that Margarita Gelves inhabits in R. León's *Cristo en los infiernos* is known in the vicinity as 'el hotel del crimen'. The author himself refers to it darkly as 'misteriosa mansión de folletín o de novela policíaca' (p. 87), taking for granted that his readership will be familiar with these genres and that the analogy will conjure in their minds the image he intends. Soler Moreu's *Navidades sin pan* includes an episode which is in the tradition of the crime story, rather than the war novel. The mysterious Chinaman, Lung, from his den in the *barrio chino* of Barcelona, organises crime in the city. He tricks Camorri (a thinly disguised Durruti) of the wealth he has amassed in the war, then flees the city. Camorri is assassinated for his dealings with the Barcelona underworld, and his body taken to the Madrid front to make it look as though he had died gloriously, in action. The novel stresses the criminal activities of the Left in the black market and in plundering the rich, while the poor queue for bread. The plot of *Méndez, cronista de guerra* is made up of a number of diverse escapades, the inspiration for which might have come from a variety of sources: popular novels of chivalry, cowboy films or more traditional cloak-and-dagger adventure novels.[59] Méndez enters the civil governor's residence by stealth, tip-toeing past sleeping guards, to eavesdrop on the governor's plot to destroy his political opponents. He escapes by tying the curtains together and lowering himself out of the window. Later, he resolves to cross over into the Republican zone in search of the heroine, Isabel, with whom he has fallen in love. 'El espíritu quijotesco de la raza encontraba ocasión de manifestarse: salvar a una mujer cautiva del dragón marxista, era una tentación demasiado fuerte para un español' (p. 62). In Linares, while saving a woman from a burning house, he out-draws a Marxist who tries to shoot him.

There are abundant examples in these novels of melodramatic events, postures and utterances. Ricardo León, in *Cristo en los infiernos*, is perhaps the master of the technique, and the following example, in which the evil Margarita Gelves reveals to the saintly Pablo the love she feels for him, seems to have most of the essential ingredients of melodrama:

Le tendía los brazos, hincadas las rodillas en el suelo, encendido el semblante, alborotados los rizos, siniestras y fulminantes las pupilas verdes.
Pablo no la miraba. Tenía los ojos y el corazón en su Santo Cristo.
Pugnaba entre el deseo de arrojar de su casa aquella furia y la desgarradora compasión de ver un alma tan perdida. ¡Si él la pudiera salvar! . . .
— Dame, Señor — dijo, implorando a su divino Dueño — que yo pueda rescatarla. No soy digno pero Tú eres la infinita Misericordia . . .
La alumbrada se retorcía a sus pies como una lengua de fuego. Parecía la imagen de la eterna condenación.
— ¡Vete, Satanás! — reiteró Pablo, esgrimiendo su crucifijo. De nuevo el Santo marfil tocó — esta vez en la frente — a la posesa.

Margarita retrocedió espantada, con súbitas señales de un escondido terror. Sintióse envuelta en relámpagos cegadores, asordada por silbos estridentes. Percibió en su olfato como un olor sulfuroso, y un sabor urente y metálico en la lengua.

Lanzó después un grito y cayó derrumbada, lívida, convulsa, la mirada quieta, el cuerpo rígido, la cabeza echada hacia atrás. Con indecible angustia y anhelante resuello, sacudida por furiosos espasmos, llena la boca de espuma, quedó luego adormecida en un profundo sopor. (p. 466)

The postures of the respective figures, the muttered imprecation to the Almighty, the stilted utterance, the swoon of the fallen woman – all these elements are redolent of melodrama.

In the battlefront novels, death provides an occasion for melodrama. The final action, dying posture and words of the hero are often stereotyped. In *Se ha ocupado el kilómetro 6*, Julio utters the name of the woman he loves, prays and clutches the Spanish flag (p. 206). In *El teniente Arizcun*, the protagonist is found dead in battle: 'En su mano izquierda, y a la altura de sus ojos, tenía *el Devocionario del Requeté*, abierto en la página en que se lee la oración de la hora de muerte' (p. 51).[60]

We find examples in these works of the *filosofía barata* encountered in the popular novel of earlier times. 'A los muertos no se les resucita', muses the author of the *Se ha ocupado el kilómetro 6* (p. 206). 'A los humildes no les toca más que sufrir y conformarse con la voluntad del Señor y así El no nos dejará de su mano', pontificates Muñoz San Román in *Señorita en la retaguardia* (p. 42). Republican novelists such as Martínez Pagán sprinkle such expressions liberally throughout their narrative. 'Les révolutions durent une minute et passent sur la terre comme un soupir', 'L'amour est court, la vie est longue', or 'Il n'y a pas d'autre justice que celle que dispense Dieu', lack the memorable quality of the successful lapidary phrase; they remain at the level of banality.

Other characteristics of the popular novel, such as coincidences, prophetic utterances and miracles, exist in abundance. Examples of miracles will be given in a later chapter in the context of myth-creation. Prophetic utterance is a tempting device for the Civil War novelist writing after the event. The characters in *Se ha ocupado el kilómetro 6* prophesy several times (pp. 95, 101, 106) that the battle around Gandesa will prove to be a turning point in the war, as it proved to be.[61] During a train journey in 1933, in R. León's *Cristo en los infiernos*, one of the travellers prophesies that the Spanish State will one day be responsible for 'el robo de la riqueza nacional' (p. 323) – a clear allusion to the transfer of the Spanish gold reserves to Moscow during the Civil War. Among the Republicans, Samblancat predicts that the French will turn tail before the enemy when the war extends to Europe (*Caravana nazarena*, p. 107) and Sánchez Barbudo prophesies that the people of Madrid will undergo terrible reprisals at the hands of Franco after the war (*Sueños de grandeza*, p. 253). To be fair to the novelists, many of these events were predictable, so that the prophetic utterance seems quite realistic in the historical context.[62] As for coincidence, this is a justifiable device provided it does not strike the reader as being far-fetched. Morales López stretches our credibility in reuniting his hero and heroine in a burning cellar to which fate has miraculously brought them both by quite separate paths (*Méndez, cronista de guerra*, ch. 28). When the heroine of Carriedo de Ruiz's *En plena epopeya* gets lost on the Madrid front and finds herself in the Republican zone, the hero crosses over in pursuit of her, finds her in a bread queue and takes her back to Nationalist territory disguised as a *miliciana*. It is not supposed to occur to the reader that there would be little likelihood of finding an individual in a city the size of Madrid in the confusion of wartime. Other coincidences of this type are to be found in Pérez y Pérez's *De una España a otra* (the chance meeting of Elena and Juan Ignacio), Vázquez's *Armas de Caín y Abel* (when a miracle brings Fernando and María Isabel together in Seville) and *Cristo en los infiernos* (when Pablo chances upon Federico Gelves, semi-conscious, after the attack on the Montaña barracks).

It will have become apparent from the preceding examples that many of the first-wave novelists are technically deficient. It often appears that they lack the technical resources to create the effect they intend. Sometimes, they may simply be too careless, or in too much haste. Bicho, in *Se ha ocupado el kilómetro 6*, is supposed to be an intellectual, yet never sounds like one. Martingala, in Pérez y Pérez's *De una España a otra*, is supposed to be an illustrious Anarchist leader, but clearly does not think like one, even before his conversion to the Nationalist cause. Authors appear uncertain of the differences between the major ideologies on the Republican side, and are in no position therefore to portray them properly. The traditional popular novel eschewed any discussion of political or religious ideas. The first-wave Civil War novels superficially introduce these taboos into the genre to create an interesting hybrid, but the influence of the original model continues to make itself felt, so that discussion of the issues is neither penetrating nor perceptive. The earlier popular novel had been written by professional hacks for purely commercial ends, while the early Civil War novels were mainly produced by a mixture of non-professional writers and professional journalists (but not novelists) for political as well as commercial reasons. There are many similarities, however, between the popular novel and those under study. This suggests that the exposure of these writers to the popular novels of earlier generations was considerable, and that these influences, together with the exaggerated characterisation to be found in the children's stories they would all have read or heard in their youth, informed their writing of Civil War novels. It is rare to find authors in this first wave like Samblancat, in whom there are clear signs of influence by a major Spanish author (in this case, Valle-Inclán).[63]

With regard to the location of the action of the novels, there is evidence of a desire to describe life on the other side during the war. A surprisingly large number of Nationalist novels are set wholly or partly in Republican Spain. In the case of some authors (Espina, Martín Artajo, Miquelarena, for example) this was a reflection of their own experience. In others, it is pure invention. Benítez de Castro locates the action of *El espantable caso de los 'tomadores' de ciudades* in Barcelona and on the Aragon front seen from the Republican side, of which he had no knowledge. Soler Moreu's *Navidades sin pan* is also set in wartime Barcelona. By far the most popular setting for Nationalist novels which describe the other side is Madrid. The novels of Borrás (*Checas de Madrid*), Carro (*Paco y las duquesas*), Carrere (*La ciudad de los siete puñales*), R. León (*Cristo en los infiernos*), Martín Artajo (*No me cuente Vd. su caso*), Noguera (*La mascarada trágica*), Fernández Flórez (*Una isla en el mar rojo*), Foxá (*Madrid, de Corte a checa*), Camba (*Madridgrado*) and Miquelarena (*El otro mundo*) are based on life in the capital. It is also part of the setting for Ximénez de Sandoval's *Camisa azul*, Pérez y Pérez's *De una España a otra*, Salazar Allende's *Tú no eres de los nuestros* and Carriedo's *En plena epopeya*. *Méndez, cronista de guerra*, by Morales López, is a veritable Cook's tour of Spain, covering several Andalusian cities as well as Madrid, Valencia and Barcelona. Salazar's *De anarquista a mártir* covers a similar range of locations in the enemy zone (Barcelona, Alcoy, Valencia, Albacete, Toledo). Espina relates autobiographical episodes of life in Santander province, an area which also features in Sepúlveda's *En la gloria de aquel amanecer*. By contrast, the Republican novelists of this period show no inclination to describe life in the Nationalist zone, even though this might have offered an opportunity to reinforce their criticism of Nationalist values. This may partly be explained by the fact that, while Nationalist writers in the Republican zone (e.g. Espina) were eventually 'liberated', the reverse was not the case, so that Republican writers in the Nationalist zone simply had to suppress any creative urge they might have had. This does not explain, however, why there existed on one side only a group of writers who were prepared to invent a world on the other side with which they were quite unfamiliar.[64]

Any novelist approaching the Civil War must decide how to manipulate time and space in covering a series of complex events taking place all over the country over a period of several years. Many writers opted for an anecdotal narrative mode, in which a single protagonist or small group is described moving from place to place experiencing the effects of the war. As in the popular novel, action predominates over psychology. *Se ha ocupado el kilómetro 6* is a good example of the anecdotal war novel, in which the action moves from the front to a hospital in the rearguard, from Gandesa to Zaragoza and Valladolid, then back again. The chapters of *Checas de Madrid* are called 'acciones', reflecting their nature. García Serrano's *Eugenio* has no real narrative development: it is a series of vignettes, which the author might have added to or subtracted from without detriment to his story. *La fiel Infantería* follows the fortunes of a group of soldiers engaged in what the author calls 'turismo armado' (p. 434) as they move from Navarre to Castile, as part of the Nationalist advance. Few of the first-wave novelists find ways other than these of manipulating space. Valentín de Pedro uses a roving dog as a focus for the action (but does not try to see the war through the eyes of the dog, which would have been an interesting and innovative technique). Sometimes, we learn what is happening through snatches of a telephone conversation (Samblancat's *Caravana nazarena*, pp. 85–86), letters (Cimorra's *El bloqueo del hombre*, p. 64) or eye-witness accounts by characters the protagonist may meet in hospital or on a train; but it is left to later novelists to refine these techniques.[65]

Since most of these early novels lay emphasis on action rather than the lengthy description of settings or psychology, their tempo (like that of the popular novel) is fast. *Se ha ocupado el kilómetro 6*, described by one critic as 'una obra ágil y rápida',[66] has the breathless quality of the adventure story. The sentences are short and the syntax elementary; the action is divided into neat segments:

Miramos. Es un mosca rojo. Estamos demasiados hombres en la viña. Nos ha visto. Pica. En la carretera hay un camión con una ametralladora anti-aérea. Pasa y nos ametralla. Mala puntería. Nada. Se eleva. Va a picar otra vez. Nos ponemos de pie, porque tirados ofrecemos más blanco. El cacharro del camión se prepara. El mosca baja demasiado confiado en sí mismo. Ello le pierde. La ametralladora le sigue en toda la curva. Le vemos oscilar. No se levanta más. Pierde altura y, de repente, en una pirueta trágica, hunde el morro en la viña. Corren unos soldados. Sacan un bulto informe. Lo veo pasar. Es un muchacho rubillo y pálido.

(p. 102)

An artist would have no difficulty in reducing this description to twenty or so separate frames for an adventure comic. Once this action sequence is removed, little remains of the text. There is no description of the states of mind of the airman or the troops on the ground; our attention is sharply focussed on events. The use of the first person and the present tense reinforces the reader's sense of being an eye-witness to what is being described. But the reader is witnessing only the superficial reality of isolated events; time has been collapsed, so that a sequence which in real life would take perhaps ten minutes occupies only seconds. The profusion of verbs denoting action here quickens the tempo of the narrative. An equally effective technique is to omit main verbs altogether, as Borrás shows in *Checas de Madrid* (e.g. pp. 136–137, where his camera-eye roves around the graffiti of wartime Madrid).

Sometimes, novels seem to have progressed little from the jottings on which they are based. Salinas Quijada's *Un alférez de cursillos* signals the outbreak of the war in a telegraphic style: 'Julio. 31 días. 18. Semana 29. Sábado. Santa Sinforosa y San Federico' (p. 25). Other Nationalist novels in which the action races along are *Méndez, cronista de guerra*, *En plena epopeya*, *Del ruedo a la trinchera*, *De anarquista a mártir* and *Tú no eres de los nuestros*.[67]

R. León belongs to quite a different school of traditional writers whose verbosity and love of moralising slows the pace of the narrative to an exasperating degree. 'Desvirtúa la verdad ... de su testimonio con la pompa retórica de costumbre, ensanchada si cabe: un diluvio de palabras recargadas y amplificatorias apaga, implacablemente . . . la llamada pasional'.[68] Arauz de Robles, in *Mar y tierra*, also develops his plot at a leisurely pace, interrupting the action with lengthy descriptions of rainy landscapes in northern Spain, and *costumbrista* accounts of the life of the fishing and farming communities.[69] But these are exceptions to the general rule. Languorous description is not part of the stock-in-trade of the first-wave war novelist.

On the Republican side, *Caravana nazarena* exemplifies the novel in which restless protagonists ensure a fast tempo: 'Ginés es un azogue. Lleva la barriga llena de gatos, lleva los diablos en el cuerpo y no le dejan parar' (p. 77). Cimorra's *El bloqueo del hombre* includes sections in which the action suddenly lurches forward at a much faster pace than the rest: all the events of 1938 are dispatched in 15 pages, for example, when the author decides to move to scenes of exodus in Catalonia. The subject matter will determine the tempo of the novel in many cases. Sánchez Barbudo, in *Sueños de grandeza*, accelerates the pace of his action when he begins describing the defence of Madrid.

Just as the manipulation of space presents problems to the novelist, so also does the manipulation of time. If we follow the exploits of one character or a group of characters, they cannot be everywhere at once. But momentous events may have taken place simultaneously elsewhere while we have been following the activities of the protagonists. The novelists have to resort to a number of different techniques to cover these different temporal planes. The omniscient narrator is in a position to tell us whatever he wants us to know about the chronological progress of the war. But if he restricts himself to the limited world of a small group, this may involve losing contact with other characters for chapters at a time. Sepúlveda, for example, in *En la gloria de aquel amanecer*, loses sight of Agustín, one of the two Nationalist heroes of the story until, in chapter 16, she takes us back to July 1936 to trace his progress since that time. This use of the 'meanwhile' parenthesis has obvious drawbacks, since the action has to be suspended intermittently in order to bring the story up to date. García Serrano, in *La fiel Infantería*, uses brackets to indicate a flashback (pp. 411–415). Salazar Allende, in *Tú no eres de los nuestros*, begins his story in a French concentration camp in the post-war era, and in Part 2 of the novel returns to the outbreak of the Civil War. Giménez Arnau takes this device a stage further in *El puente* and employs it in each chapter; the chapter begins with the event that, chronologically, should conclude it. This is one of the rare novels of the first wave to employ such a technique. Soler Moreu's *Navidades sin pan* begins and ends at Christmas 1936, after describing in the middle section the events that have led up to it in the preceding months. On the Republican side, novelists struggle with the same technical problems. Cimorra loses sight of the villainous hunchback El Sapo for much of the novel, but tries to disguise the fact by saying: 'No habremos olvidado aquel monstruo que odiaba a sus semejantes...' (p. 177). One of the few novelists to make imaginative use of time planes is Sancho Granados, in *98 horas*, in which the first two chapters are seen in flashback, while the third chapter is even further back in time, with a sudden return to the present (p. 83), to remind us that all these musings are taking place in prison.

The first person narrator might be expected, in such an autobiographical genre, to predominate. To judge by the comments of one critic, the modern Spanish novel suffers from a surfeit of egolatry.[70] In fact, only a minority of novels of the first wave employ a first-person narrator. Benítez de Castro's *Se ha ocupado el kilómetro 6*, Carriedo's *En plena epopeya*, Espina's *Esclavitud y libertad*, García Serrano's *Eugenio* and *La fiel Infantería*, Salazar Allende's *Tú no eres de los nuestros* (from p. 118), Soler Moreu's *Navidades sin pan*, Miquelarena's *El otro mundo*, Camba's *Madridgrado* and Sender's *Contra-ataque* are examples.[71] The third-person narrative is much more frequent.

The reader will search without much success for literary innovation in the first-wave novels. Max Aub is one of the few writers to display virtuosity in the use of devices such as stream of consciousness, for example. Chapter 11 of *Campo de sangre* takes the form of an interior monologue by Paulino Cuartero as he tries unsuccessfully to get to sleep. His thoughts wander in a zig-zag pattern of free association, combining literature, politics, childhood memories and the progress of the war, terminating in the obsessive idea of the fall of Teruel.

La palabra cazada por Paulino Cuartero enlaza ciudades; recuerda cómo, cuando niño, se esforzaba en cazar anillos con un palitroque, montado en el caballo de madera de un tío-vivo. Martorell: Teruel, cogida la ll de la l. ¿Habrán entrado en Teruel?
'Me duele Teruel en el estómago.' (Le dolía de verdad el estómago.) Le dolía Teruel en el estómago.
Don Ignacio Martorell en Teruel, tendero de la plaza del Torico, toma bicarbonato para quitarte [*sic*] el dolor de estómago.
La sola idea de bicarbonato le quita el dolor a Cuartero. Se duerme. (p. 196)

On the Nationalist side, García Serrano uses interior monologue (though less effectively than Aub), either in the first person (*La fiel Infantería*, p. 479) or in the third person (*ibid.*, p. 581). But in the main, these writers appear not to have realised the potential of this technique for expressing the anguish and confusion of the war.

B. Vance has drawn attention to the importance of the multiple protagonist in the novel of the Civil War, a phenomenon which has led to a 'flattening out' of the profile of the traditional hero.[72] While this does not apply to many Falangist novels, in which a single hero is eulogised, it is true that ex-combatants often remember with nostalgia the camaraderie of life at the front and create a collectively heroic group. *Se ha ocupado el kilómetro 6* is the prototype for this category of novels. While it might be expected that the multiple protagonist would have led to multiple view techniques in the novel of the first wave, of the kind found in later works such as M.T. León's *Juego limpio*, this is not the case.

It is in the use of language, in particular, that the reader becomes aware of the shortcomings of most of the first-wave novelists. Their predilection for the ready-made phrase leads to a monotony of language and hackneyed description that takes us back to the conventions of the *novela popular*. Benítez de Castro, whose ranking in the literary histories of the 1940s and 1950s seems difficult, in retrospect, to justify,[73] indulges cliché freely for comic effect in *El espantable caso de los 'tomadores' de ciudades*, in a pastiche of the traditional novel. Sentences such as: 'Sus esculturales espaldas se mostraron olímpicamente al comandante...' (p. 131), followed by a string of rhetorical questions ('¿Dónde iría ella tan decidida? ¿Por qué le volvió las espaldas? ¿Por qué no le hizo caso?'), come straight out of the *folletín*.[74] Referring to the young Falangists who have lost their lives at the hands of the Left, Concha Espina writes in *Retaguardia*: 'Esta siembra de ideales fecundados por el martirio, siempre florece en el pan de una divina salud' (p. 128), seemingly unaware of a most unhappy combination of metaphors.[75] *Princesas del martirio* and *Luna roja* offer numerous examples of this mixture of preciosity and cliché. R. León has been chastised by Chabás for creating a type of novel which is 'blanda como todo pastiche... Sus personajes hablan caricaturescamente como los pobres actores que tienen que representar el teatro de Ardavín o Villaespesa'.[76] The constant repetition of concepts (such as satanism) brings with it a tiresome linguistic repetitiveness; in addition, characters appear in hackneyed descriptions (militiamen 'armados hasta los dientes' for example) over and over again. The official language of the régime's propaganda machine is a powerful influence on the language of these writers, as is perhaps inevitable. Take the following example from Muñoz San Román's *Del ruedo a la trinchera*, describing Franco's rising in July 1936: 'El patriotismo del general Franco, inspirándose en los más altos intereses de la Patria y de la Civilización, hizo que el invicto Caudillo se alzara en armas contra la barbarie marxista, emprendiendo el glorioso camino de la salvación de España' (p. 155). Every element in this text might have been taken from the justifications for the rising appearing in the Nationalist news media. The description of the Republicans as 'hordas marxistas' (p. 161), 'ralea marxista' (p. 179) and the use of other such well-worn epithets only confirm that the author does not wish to create new forms of expression but, on the contrary, to provide his readership with the reassurance of familiar language and concepts. A public aesthetic determines the form and content of these early novels, which explains their lack of originality. Even in an *estampa* less than two pages long, in J. de Pablo Muñoz's *Aquellas banderas de Aragón*, we find clichés such as 'los camaradas que sufrían bajo el yugo marxista' (p. 178). It is not surprising, perhaps, that authors of full-length novels could not escape the influence of official rhetoric. On other occasions (as we have seen in the case of R. León), writers resort to archaic language in the belief that it somehow ennobles their expression. The father of the protagonist in Salinas Quijada's *Un alférez de cursillos* refers to his advancing years with the words: 'Ya la nieve me hiela la sien . . .' (p. 18) – a somewhat anachronistic expression for 1936. Sometimes, archaism and the rhetoric of propaganda are curiously combined. The protagonist of Morales López's *Méndez, cronista de guerra* 'sabía de doncellas sacrificadas en su virginidad por la furia del bandolerismo criminal marxista' (p. 57).

As in the case of the authors of the *novela popular*, many of these writers lack a sense of proportion and good taste, confusing overblown expression with elegance and variety. Vázquez, in *Armas de Caín y Abel*, decries the Second Republic's 'imperio materialista y espantoso, que no deje brotar ni una sola planta del jardín de las espiritualidades del amor fraternal' (p. 34). Borrás uses alliteration in exaggerated fashion in *Checas de Madrid*, when he writes such sentences as: 'El puñado de pedrería centelleó en su puño peludo' (p. 142). On the Republican side, no-one is more guilty of *barroquismo* than Samblancat, who lards his descriptions with innumerable archaisms, puns, epithets and colloquialisms. 'El escritor Samblancat es un expresivista empedernido y exasperado que se hace exasperante. No sabe más que tocar la cuerda de la lengua, las cuerdas vocales. Y así, apenas tiene importancia lo que quiere decir . . . Combina palabras y partes de palabras en el doble juego sincrónico y diacrónico de la lengua y en el doble uso culto y plebeyo de la misma'.[77] His description of Argelès-sur-Mer as 'Argeles-sur-Merd' [*sic*], and the typical concentration camp inmate as 'ser relativamente racional y allí absolutamente racionado' (*Caravana nazarena*, p. 112) has a satirical bite that no other novelist of the Civil War can match. But the profusion of images and circumlocutions with which he bombards the reader eventually prove too much, particularly when the characters speak in the inimitable style of the author. A Nationalist, for example, describing a scene in which a man's hand had been cut off as a punishment for attempting to desert, recounts with black humour: 'Y de un tajo de cimitarra moruna, arrebatada ayer a un mojamé, le han mandado la mano a la copa de un olivo, donde podrá dicho desperdicio cerciorarse a conciencia de si llueve' (p. 80).

Dialogue, if it is to sound realistic, poses a considerable problem for the war novelist, since the soldier's language will be liberally sprinkled with obscenities. The artist must transform this somehow into an expression that is convincing and at the same time socially acceptable; if the Nationalist novelist fails to satisfy the second of these criteria, the censor's department will excise the offending expressions. He must be familiar, too, with the jargon that was freely used during these years: a soldier was unlikely to use the word 'avión' when he had at his disposal 'mosca', 'chato', 'buey', 'pava', 'churrero', 'carro de leche', 'pájaro', and so on. As Pérez Bowie has shown, there is a rich lexicon available to describe death in all its forms during these years,[78] and García Serrano has demonstrated, in his *Diccionario para un macuto*,[79] that the war produced a multitude of creative expressions to enrich the popular culture of the time. Novelists use these resources with varying degrees of success. Benítez de Castro's characters speak in a mixture of written and oral styles. Their conversation is 'infantile and false, frequently distorted by rhetoric,' according to one critic.[80] R. León seems incapable of differentiating characters through dialogue. When Federico and Javier, in *Cristo en los infiernos*, discuss with a group of anonymous soldiers the progress of the war, they all repeat the same ideas in the same exalted language, which bears no relationship to the informal discourse of everyday spoken communication (pp. 528–531). Espina's characters speak with little more authenticity than León's, though they are less declamatory; the dialogue of *Retaguardia* and her other war novels is hollow and lacking in interest. Sepúlveda, in *En la gloria de aquel amanecer*, puts high-sounding moral statements into the mouths of her characters, which militates against realistic dialogue: 'El amor patrio es un estimulante poderosísimo de todos los nobles sentimientos del alma, cuanto más del amor filial' (p. 199), and other such sententious utterances by the main characters have a deadening effect on the narrative. The dialogue of the mythical heroes of the Right is often not intended to be realistic, so on such occasions it would be unfair to judge it by that criterion. When the death-worshipping legionary, Alexis, speaks in Ximénez de Sandoval's *Camisa azul*, it is with the voice of the poet: 'Los brazos fáciles son suaves serpientes venenosas. Los ajenjos delirantes son fuertes llamas envenenadas' (p. 256). Eugenio, in García Serrano's novel of the same name, speaks in a similar poetic style when he renounces the venal pleasures of Hero (alias María Victoria): '¿Me crees capaz de ablandarme ante la brisa?'

In depicting the enemy, Nationalist novelists frequently reproduce the language of the *hampa*, so that Republican characters appear as uneducated and incapable of correct speech. Borrás's *Checas de Madrid* is full of such examples. Civil War slang is freely used; obscenities are thinly disguised

('Me c . . . en sus doce padres', 'hijos de p . . .', etc.). Of the first-wave
novelists, Borrás comes closest to capturing the speech of illiterate
Republican militiamen (of whom there were many, without doubt), but
his characterisation is so extreme that he spoils the effect. The transcription
of vulgar language on the enemy side is to be found in many other novels of
the Right: Pérez y Pérez's *De una España a otra* is a good example. One of the
stock situations in which such language is described in many of these novels
is the *paseo*. Take for example the following extract from Ximénez de
Sandoval's *Camisa azul*:

'Amos anda, chico, Tira 'pa' donde quieras, que en el auto de un marqués se va
'mu' ricamente a cualquier parte. Y la lástima es que el 'chivato' y yo no llevemos
aquí una 'gachí' en vez de este fascista 'litri'.

Almost identical scenes can be found in *Checas de Madrid* and other novels
of the Right. Two novels which attempt to produce the accent of Seville are
Salas's *El frente de los suspiros*, and Muñoz San Román's *Del ruedo a la
trinchera*. This time, the accent is meant to add local colour rather than
denote a lack of culture and civilised values since the speaker is a
Nationalist, like the author. In the latter novel, the transcription is difficult
to follow and becomes tiresome in sentences such as: 'El vá a sé er que se lo
va a poné.'
    An ingredient that is in short supply among these novelists is humour.
When we do encounter it, it is usually at the expense of the other side.
Benítez de Castro's *El espantable caso de los 'tomadores' de ciudades* attempts to
ridicule an *ugetista*, Juan Pérez. García Serrano reports that Remarque's *All
Quiet on the Western Front* was put to lowly use during the Civil War: 'Sus
páginas, luego de leídas, nos servían para los más ínfimos menesteres. Las
usábamos con frecuencia, debido a las aguas de la roca, las conservas y el
calor' (*La fiel Infantería*, p. 463). Chapter 10 of Noguera's *La mascarada
trágica* provides some welcome humorous relief: in a dream, Quinito sees all
Madrid's statues come together to examine Negrín's thirteen articles. When
Philip IV leaves the meeting, he finds that his horse has proved too much of
a temptation for the Republican militiamen: they have eaten it. All such
humorous anecdotes are a way of making fun of the other side. The
Republican response comes, effectively, from a single author, Samblancat,
whose satirical power is formidable. Referring to Alfonso XIII's alleged
cancer, he writes: 'Con razón el pueblo español, cuando se enteró de que Su
Majestad tenía un cáncer, exclamó: ¡Pobre cáncer!' (p. 28). But
Samblancat also lashes out against more moderate Republicans than

himself, as well as the perfidious French, at whose hands he suffered in the post-war era.[81]

As we have already observed, avant-garde techniques are rare in the novels of the first wave. There are elements of surrealism in García Serrano's work, but these are not fully developed (see Ramón's dream, *La fiel Infantería*, pp. 583–588, for an example of the technique). One of the short stories in Puente's *Viudas blancas*, 'El mar', provides an early example of surrealist fantasy on the war theme, though unsuccessful in the execution. It was left to later writers to attempt to develop these techniques further.

There is general agreement among critics about the lack of aesthetic quality in the novels of the first wave. G. Sobejano points to the harmful influence of censorship and cinema, the latter providing cheap thrills for a mass audience:

El [influjo] ejercido por el cinema norteamericano puede decirse que fue negativo. Las intrigas policíacas, los complejos freudianos divulgados en la pantalla, aparte las 'latas' históricas, acarrearon en los medios de la burguesía un gusto absorbente por cuanto fuese tensión, enredo y conflicto, pagados a precio módico y servidos en hora y media de grata escapada.[82]

Torrente Ballester, writing in 1948, laments the lack of technical innovation: 'Cada tema exige su forma, y nosotros no hemos resuelto los problemas formales.'[83] Bertrand de Muñoz draws attention to the influence of journalism, which attempts to satisfy a need for rapid and comprehensive reporting of events.[84] Critics of the literature of the First World War point to the repetitiveness of images and themes in the novels of the war.[85] Conceivably, this may have led to a similarity in the discourse used to describe the war.

The causes of the aesthetic failure of the novels of the first wave are undoubtedly complex. They constitute an extremely interesting collection, despite their poor literary quality: some are traditional battlefront novels, but the majority are hybrids in which there is evidence of cross-fertilisation with other genres and, indeed, other media. The major innovation is to be found, not in any particular narrative technique,[86] but in the injection of a powerful propagandist message into a tradition of popular story-telling which had hitherto been largely apolitical.

Notes
1 G. Sobejano, *Novela española de nuestro tiempo* (Madrid, 1970), pp. 43–73. While passing mention is made of a large number of novelists, Sobejano's attention is directed mainly towards Aub, Ayala, Barea, Sender and Gironella in this chapter, entitled 'La guerra española objeto de novelas'.

2 *Ibid.*, p. 45.

3 *Ibid.*, p. 47.

4 *Ibid.*, p. 50. Sobejano's categories are, as he must know, an oversimplification. Sender is a 'militante observador' in *Contraataque*, an 'intérprete' in *Ariadna*. To classify Benítez de Castro and Fernández de la Reguera together as 'militantes' is perhaps to do the latter an injustice, since his is an altogether more balanced account of the war. The categories need to be further sub-divided if they are to be used for a detailed analysis of the novels.

5 The protagonist has no more faith in the novel he is writing than the author expresses in the diary at this point. 'Lo rompió todo. La novela iba dentro del alma y era imposible echarla fuera. Al intentarlo, como quien salta sobre un barranco sin calcular la distancia, se exponía uno a caer al fondo y hacerse pedazos en las rocas puntiagudas' (p. 342).

6 'La joven novela española (1936–1947)', *Revista de la Universidad de Oviedo*, 9, nos. 49–50 (1948), 45–79 (p. 46).

7 *Guerre et révolution dans le roman français de 1919 à 1939* (Paris, 1974), Part I, chs. 2 and 3, 'Du carnet de route au roman'.

8 According to A. Amorós, in what is a deliberately provocative statement, 'igualmente testigos de España son Pérez Galdós y Corín Tellado' (*Subliteraturas* (Barcelona, 1974), p. 24).

9 See the introduction to V. Carrillo et al., *L'infralittérature en Espagne aux XIXe et XXe siècles* (Grenoble, 1977).

10 L. Urrutia, in 'Les collections populaires de romans et nouvelles (1907–1936)' in V. Carrillo et al., *L'infralittérature en Espagne*, p. 154, mentions a circulation figure of 400,000 for these collections.

11 L. Romero Tovar, *La novela popular española del siglo XIX* (Barcelona, 1976), p. 153.

12 'La autoridad del narrador es absoluta en todos los grados y a ella se pliega la disposición narrativa de la materia novelesca: golpes de efecto, anagnórisis finales, metanoias instantáneas . . . etc.' (*ibid.*, pp. 160–161).

13 See also A. Moufflet, 'Le style du roman-feuilleton', *Mercure de France* (15 January 1931).

14 'Imbriqués dans le même texte, narration et discours moralisant composent une redondance charactéristique de la littérature édifiante' (B. Magnien, '*La Novela del Pueblo*: analyse d'une collection de nouvelles publiées sous la dictature de Primo de Rivera' in V. Carrillo et al., *L'infralittérature en Espagne*, p. 257). This analysis confirms that of A. Moufflet.

15 In a survey of Corín Tellado's stories. A. Amorós comments: 'Al final, para que todo acabe perfectamente, el malvado se convierte bruscamente, como en los folletines' (*Sociología de una novela rosa* (Madrid, 1968), p. 32).

16 'No se trata de un cambio con proceso, sino una sustitución de caracteres' (J.I. Ferreras, *La novela por entregas, 1840–1900* (Madrid, 1972), p. 249).

17 'Una novela popular es ante todo un reflejo de la conciencia colectiva; y reflejo en el peor sentido de la palabra; un reflejo . . . esquematizado, mitificado, falso . . .' (*ibid.*, p. 306).

18 *Ibid.*, p. 308.

19 L. Urrutia, in V. Carrillo et al. *L'infralittérature en Espagne*, p. 159.

20 A. Amorós, *Sociología de una novela rosa*, p. 31.

21 For a most interesting account of the post-1926 *novela popular* and its failure to address the class issue, even in a collection of Anarchist tendency, see B. Magnien, in V. Carrillo et al., *L'infralittérature en Espagne*, p. 254.

22 L. Romero Tovar, in *La novela popular española*, writes that this genre is generally characterised by 'sentimentalismo, truculencia y sensiblería' (p. 29).

23 See *ibid*. pp. 255 ff. for the structural characteristics of such novels.

24 A. Moufflet, 'Le style du roman-feuilleton', and A. Amorós, *Sociología de una novela rosa*. Both give examples of suggestive titles.

25 'La exaltación sentimental de los personajes da lugar a una gesticulación teatral, exagerada' (A. Amorós, *Subliteraturas*, p. 129).

26 *Ibid.*, p. 16.

27 'Aujourd'hui, M. Bernanos est un des rares romanciers qui croient au diable; les feuilletonnistes y croient tous', wrote A. Moufflet in 1931. ('Le style du roman feuilleton', p. 536.) A. Amorós mentions the frequent use of the prophetic utterance in *Subliteraturas*, p. 36.

28 *Ibid.*, p. 128.

29 I. Ferreras describes the successful novel as 'historia escrita de las relaciones problemáticas y en su movimiento constitutivo entre un individuo y un universo' (*Teoría y praxis de la novela* (Paris, 1970), p. 55). The *novela popular* fails to achieve this objective: 'No hay . . . historia constitutiva . . . sino narración de esa historia que no se constituye en la novela, sino que se encuentra ya constituida . . . El autor intenta describir caracteres, pero no logra hacerlos funcionar; intenta sugerirnos un universo, pero no puede recrearlo y la sugerencia se pierde. Al autor sólo le queda el recurso de la acción de los personajes' (*La novela por entregas, 1840–1900*, p. 252).

30 *Ibid.*, p. 262. See also A. Moufflet, 'Le style du roman-feuilleton', section 11, and L. Romero Tovar, *La novela popular española*, p. 124, where similar conclusions are drawn.

31 A. Amorós, *Subliteraturas*, p. 16. B. Magnien, too, refers to the 'dualisme moral' of such novels (V. Carrillo et al. *L'infralittérature en Espagne*, p. 256).

32 A. Amorós, *Subliteraturas*, p. 34, coins the expression: 'el determinismo de la cara', to describe this convention.

33 J.I. Ferreras, *La novela por entregas, 1840–1900*, pp. 257–58.

34 See L. Romero Tovar, *La novela popular española*, and A. Amorós, *Sociología de una novela rosa*, for accounts which are broadly similar despite the different samples chosen.

35 L. Romero Tovar, *La novela popular española*, p. 126.

36 *Ibid.*, p. 129. Also relevant to the present study are this author's comments on the dualism with which the working class is portrayed, 'Se trata de un proletariado con absoluta carencia de conciencia de clase, orgulloso de su situación y de la honestidad con que desempeña su oficio . . . Pero existe otro proletariado marginal y peligroso . . .: criminales a sueldo . . . contrabandistas . . . prostitución de las mujeres . . . perjuros profesionales' (pp. 134–135). This description has a familiar ring to any reader of the first-wave Nationalist novels of the Civil War.

37 'Dans leur style, ces écrivains s'efforcent de se démarquer par rapport au langage quotidien; il faut donner une estampille littéraire de qualité à son récit. C'est ainsi: que j'interprète le caractère recherché, éloquent, du style de la plupart des nouvelles. Mais dans cet effort, les auteurs ne font pas oeuvre de création, ils n'essaient pas de se créer un nouveau style, l'originalité de la langue ne les concerne pas. Ils donnent leur préférence à tout ce qui est la marque, connue et reconnue, d'une litteralité' (B. Magnien, in V. Carrillo et al. *L'infralittérature en Espagne*, p. 258).

38 A. Amorós, *Sociología de una novela rosa*, p. 63.

39 L. Romero Tovar, *La novela popular española*, p. 144.

40 For a full discussion of the language of the *novela popular*, see the works of A. Amorós and L. Romero Tovar already cited.

41 See B. Vance, 'The Civil War (1936–39) as a Theme in the Spanish Contemporary Novel', PhD thesis, Wayne State University (1968), pp. 101ff. and S.G. Eskin, 'Literature of the Spanish Civil War', *Genre*, 4, no. 1 (1971), 76–99 (pp. 94–95).

42 Mention should be made here of the numerous prologues in which authors take the opportunity of addressing their readers directly. This practice, however, is by no means confined to novelists of the first wave. Ayala, Gironella and Sender all provide examples of expansive prologues (though Aub and Barea appear to consider them unnecessary).

43 As R. León was writing *Cristo en los infiernos*, J.-P. Sartre was writing his famous attack on the omniscient narrator, 'M. François Mauriac et la liberté,' published later in *Situations I* (Paris, 1947): 'Eh bien, non! Il est temps de le dire: le romancier n'est pas Dieu' (p. 46).

44 Vázquez and Carriedo de Ruiz also resort to authorial comment in footnotes.

45 The alleged complicity of the Government in Calvo Sotelo's death and the description of the scene in which the arrangements are made are a commonplace in Nationalist literature.

46 This technique is extremely common, in which one character defines another for the reader. It is only one step away from the process whereby the author himself tells us what to think of the character. Neither stratagem requires the novelist to persuade us by indirect means that the character has, or does not have, certain qualities. This is novelising by decree.

47 Even novels published much later use similar techniques. Much of Soler's criticism of the Second Republic in *Los muertos no se cuentan* (1961), is put in the mouth of the disillusioned Republican Rosendo Miralbaix, while no-one effectively puts the pro-Republican point of view.

48 The anti-clerical professor of Greek who taught Matías in *La fiel Infantería* is fearful of retribution when he meets the Falangist hero in the street. He now makes amends for his past mistakes by going to church, and tells Matías: 'Tenían ustedes razón.' (Such public recantation was a wise precaution, whether or not it was genuine.)

49 There is an element of wishful thinking in the descriptions of such conversions. It was always the hope of Falangists that their ranks would be swollen by defectors from the CNT and UGT who accepted at face value Falange's claim that it was a revolutionary movement. In fact, revolutionary Falangists were few and far between. See H. Thomas, *The Spanish Civil War* (London, 1971), p. 444.

50 *La novela española contemporánea*, 2 (Madrid, 1968), p. 378.

51 As manicheism in the Civil War novel becomes less pronounced, with time the caricature of facial description diminishes. There are still traces of it, however, in later writers. In *Las dos barajas* (1956), Rafael Lara is easily distinguished from the Anarchists around him: 'Su aspecto físico era atrayente; carecía de los rasgos brutales de otros milicianos' (p. 31). For a work that appears to have been caught in a time warp, see *Al final del camino* (1966), the cover of which depicts three armed militiamen who are pure caricatures of the kind described here.

52 The literary antecedent of Pérez is the teacher Kantorek, in *All Quiet on the Western Front*. (Both mention Schiller's *William Tell*, for example.) This is one of many parallels between the two novels.

53 Samblancat's novel, while displaying some of the characteristics of the *folletín*, is clearly a highly individual and creative work.

54 With regard to the *novela rosa* of the war years (irrespective of whether it included the war theme or not), I. Soldevila Durante writes: 'La novela rosa prolifera durante la guerra en torno a editoriales sevillanas y burgalesas, y en las páginas de revistas como "Domingo" de San Sebastián. No hemos encontrado una sola editada en zona republicana. Creemos que el dato es altamente significativo como índice del estado de ánimo y las costumbres en las respectivas retaguardias' (*Revista Hispánica Moderna*, 33(1967), 89–108 (p. 100)). My research would corroborate this view.

55 Nora writes of these late novels of Espina: 'La fórmula narrativa de la escritura queda, cada vez más, sobrepasada y lejana: en su prosa redondeada y florida; en su técnica, "novelesca" por exceso, propensa al acarreo de "materiales literarios" que entorpecen la visión fresca y directa de las cosas; en su sentimentalismo y en su problemática' (*La novela española contemporánea*, 1, pp. 340–341). J. Chabás finds these novels comparable in quality to 'la vulgaridad sainetera de Pilar Millán Astray' (*Literatura española contemporánea*, p. 329).

56 A. Moufflet, 'Le style du roman-feuilleton', comments that in the *roman-feuilleton* characters often 'murmur,' which is a convention for revealing what they are thinking at the time.

57 The aristocracy is mentioned with remarkable frequency in the Civil War novels. Nationalist writers like Espina, Foxá and R. León commonly describe aristocratic families. M. Bertrand de Muñoz also includes Castañón (*Bezana roja*), Collantes (*Las vestales*), Contreras Pazo (*Sinaí*), Masoliver (*Barcelona en llamas*) and Siria (*Isabel, la mujer legionaria*) in her list of authors who give a central role to 'aristócratas o burgueses muy acomodados'. (*La Guerra Civil española en la novela* (Madrid, 1982), pp. 657–658.) To these we could add Sender (*El rey y la reina*), Aguilera-Malta (*¡Madrid!*), and a host of novels in which aristocrats play a minor role. Aristocrats abound, too, in the traditional *novela popular*.

58 Yeles hatches a plan to evacuate right-wingers from Madrid and kill them *en route*, after charging

an exorbitant fee for the promise of escape. García Atadell was executed by the Nationalists for just such crimes as these. (See also J. Miquelarena's *El otro mundo* where García Atadell's men wait patiently for the protagonist to emerge from the embassy in which he is sheltering.)

59 Even some of the later novels have cloak-and-dagger elements. Soler's *Los muertos no se cuentan* (1961) includes the description of a wine-cellar which has a flag-stone which can be lifted by an iron ring, to reveal a tunnel a mile long to a nearby wood, where a secret spring moves a stone slab (p. 168).

60 Conchita Carro, in a short story entitled *Paco y las duquesas* (*Novela del Vértice*, 1939) gently pokes fun at the tradition of the stereotyped death. Her working-class hero, Paco, shot by militiamen, dies sitting on the stairs to his grandmother's flat in a posture he has admired many times in the *Tatler*, given to him by his upper-class friends.

61 H. Thomas writes that after the battle of the Ebro, of which the fighting around Gandesa was a central part, 'the Republic had lost all its army in the north of Spain' (*The Spanish Civil War*, p. 704).

62 Less common is the vague but effectively described foreboding to be found in the following passage from Sepúlveda's *En la gloria de aquel amanecer*. The scene takes place outside San Rafael, in the Sierra de Guadarrama, at a time when, unknown to the characters, war is about to break out:

> Matilde y Carmen se sintieron de pronto poseídas de una vaga angustia, de un temor extraño, indefinible, pero lleno de profunda tristeza.
> – No se comunicaron su impresión entonces. Cada una de ellas la encontraba absurda, algo de lo que valía más no hablar.
> – ¿Y las niñas? – preguntó Matilde.
> – Allí, ¿no las ves? Al pie de aquel pino.
> –Venid, hijitas, venid acá.
> Las había llamado casi con angustia, como si las viera expuestas a un peligro.
> Carmen se puso de pie.
> – ¿Si nos fuéramos ya?   (p.64)

63 Remarque's *All Quiet on the Western Front* had influenced (negatively) a number of Nationalist writers, including Benítez de Castro. Foxá, García Serrano, Espina, R. León and others clearly have their roots in the Spanish classics, but they are a minority among this first wave.

64 The autobiographical details of recognised writers are generally accessible, so that we know whether or not their depiction of life in the enemy zone was based on events they experienced in real life. Since many of these first-wave novels are the product of lesser-known writers, however, it is difficult to establish whether such accounts contain a germ of autobiographical truth or not.

65 Gironella, as we shall see, uses a multiplicity of techniques to provide coverage of events in the whole of Spain. Manfredi Cano, in *Las lomas tienen espinos* also introduces devices such as maps, radio broadcasts, newspaper cuttings, speeches, conversations in railway compartments, etc., which offer ample opportunities for a broad geographical coverage.

66 A. Valbuena Prat, *Historia de la literatura española*, 2 (Barcelona, 1950), p. 1136.

67 The very titles of many of these novels lead the reader to expect action and excitement, rather than reflection or analysis.

68 E. de Nora, *La novela española contemporánea*, 1 (Madrid, 1970), pp. 327–328.

69 Arauz de Robles, born in 1898, writes as though he belongs to an earlier generation. His village girls in traditional costume are decorative, but lack a social dimension. They are part of 'la idílica visión de la ría' (p. 9) the author presents from the outset.

70 P. Werrie, 'Le Roman espagnol aujourd'hui', *La Table Ronde*, 193 (1964), 91–101.

71 Some of these so-called 'novels' (*Contraataque, El otro mundo*, for example) are thinly novelised autobiographies. Like Barea's *La forja de un rebelde* they probably contain little fictional material. On the other hand, they use novelistic techniques and select their material to tell a story in an interesting way. They constitute therefore another hybrid genre.

72 'The Civil War (1936–39) as a Theme in the Spanish Contemporary Novel', p. 175.

73 See F.C. Sainz de Robles's *Ensayo de un diccionario de la literatura* (Madrid, 1949) for example (which mentions Benítez de Castro while ignoring Aub, Sender and Barea), or A. Valbuena Prat's *Historia de la literatura española* (Barcelona, 1950), which devotes five pages to this author.

74 In this same section of the novel, after an exaggerated description of nature, Benítez de Castro writes: 'Bonita descripción campestre que suelen hacer todos los buenos escritores para situar a sus personajes en el marco deseado.' The author may appear to be rejecting, here, the traditional crafts of the novelist; in fact he has nothing else to put in their place. There is a similar rejection of literary rhetoric in García Serrano's *La fiel Infantería*, where, after musing on the symbolic nature of the seasons, the narrator chides himself: 'La retórica es un mal de retaguardia; en cuatro meses no se me habían ocurrido tantas cosas' (p. 479). This hardly reflects the author's true position, either, since he frequently indulges in the hollow rhetoric of Falangism to describe his heroes.

75 In the *envío* to the same novel, in the dedication to the two children who lived through the Civil War experiences in the Espina household, we read: 'Si Dios quiere que florezcan los prometedores capullos de su niñez . . .' This metaphor demonstrates greater consistency, if not discernment.

76 *Literatura española contemporánea* (Havana, 1952), p. 328.

77 F. Carrasquer, 'Samblancat, Alaiz y Sender: Tres compromisos en uno', *Papeles de Son Armadans*, 76 (1975), 211–246 (pp. 225–226). Samblancat's style is clearly infectious; this critic continues: 'Acumula sinónimos, variantes, matices, alusiones complementarias y suplementarias sugerencias que desbordan el original sentido de la frase o párrafo, si es que apunta alguno. Y como nada le parece suficiente para ganarse la atención del lector, fuerza el caballo de su estilo a caracolear, escorzar, cabriolar, corvetear y cocear, si a mano viene, hasta hacerle brillar la grupa de sudor, sacar espuma por los belfos y tremolar la crin como un airón, cuando no relinchar como coro de pífanos y cornetas tocando la "floreada"' (*ibid.*, p. 227).

78 *El léxico de la muerte durante la guerra civil española* (Salamanca, 1982).

79 *Diccionario para un macuto* (Madrid, 1964).

80 B. Vance, 'The Civil War 1936–39 as a Theme in the Spanish Contemporary Novel', p. 187.

81 Samblancat even appears capable of punning in English, when he writes, for example: 'Los Estados Unidos – strips and stars for ever!' (*Caravana nazarena*, p. 224). This is either imaginative use of the English language or a misprint. (Given the contempt most of these authors show for English orthography, the latter is a possibility. Cf. the popular song 'Stormy Wehater' [*sic*] to which the characters of Formica's *Monte de Sancha* listen interminably throughout the novel.)

82 *La novela española de nuestro tiempo* (Madrid, 1970), p. 34.

83 'Los problemas de la novela española contemporánea', *Arbor*, 9, no. 27 (1948), 395–400 (p. 400). Although he mentions the Civil War novel specifically, Torrente Ballester seems to have a limited knowledge of those that had been written by that date, as the following comment reveals: 'Es curioso considerar cómo las grandes dolorosas experiencias españolas contemporáneas han quedado sin tratar en la novela presente. Rafael García Serrano ha querido que su propia experiencia militar y política le sirviera de material novelesco, pero *La fiel Infantería* no es una novela' (*ibid.*).

84 'Ciertos escritores utilizan . . . recursos periodísticos y publican libros que llaman novelas' (*La Guerra Civil española en la novela* (Madrid, 1982), p. 20).

85 See H. Klein (ed.), *The First World War in Fiction* (London, 1976), p. 56, and M. Rieuneau, *Guerre et révolution dans le roman français* (Paris, 1974), p. 21.

86 Though G. Sobejano is surely right to single out Aub for having created 'un tipo de relato oral que no puede definirse por Galdós ni por Baroja, ni por Malraux, sus mejores antecedentes, sino con ese neologismo que creo necesario: habladura; o sea un relato de estructura oral y de estilo parlante' ('Observaciones sobre la lengua de dos novelistas', *Diálogos*, 65 (1975), 27–30 (p. 28)).

4

–

Myth creation
and reinforcement
in the Nationalist novel

IN HIS STUDY *Nietzsche en España* (Madrid, 1967), Gonzalo Sobejano discusses the contribution made by the philosopher to Fascism, Nazism and National-syndicalism. There can be no doubt that by the 1930s the influence of Nietzsche was considerable, either by direct contact with his work, or, more frequently, through intermediaries such as Baroja, Maeztu, Azorín, Ortega, d'Ors and others. Giménez Caballero was the first to draw attention to the decisive importance of Nietzsche for the Generation of '98 and subsequent writers in *Los toros, las castañuelas y la Virgen* (1927) and later in *Genio de España* (1932) and *La nueva catolicidad* (1933). Although not always perfectly understood, Nietzsche's ideas had a powerful impact: 'Hemos de admitir que Nietzsche fue utilizado . . . en diversos y quizás erróneos modos, pero en todo caso como fuente de energía, subversión de valores, redención de decadencias y curación mediante la voluntad de poder y jerarquía.'[1] One of the writers who was thus inspired was Ramiro Ledesma Ramos. In a youthful novel, *El sello de la muerte*, Nietzsche appears in a dream with the message, 'El hombre es algo que debe ser superado': the protagonist struggles to suppress sentiment and emotion and instead train reason and will to prevail. This leads him to political radicalism: 'Sentía una gran simpatía por los caudillos revolucionarios, demagógicos, o por aquéllos que figuraban como enemigos del régimen monárquico.'[2] The quotation by Nietzsche which precedes the novel shows the intolerant fanaticism of the young Ledesma, which would eventually lead him to Fascism: 'Llena está la tierra de individuos a quienes hay que predicar que desaparezcan de la vida. La tierra está llena de superfluos . . .' The protagonist describes himself as 'darwinista y nietzscheano' (p. 281), and has no hesitation in committing suicide when he fails to achieve his objectives in his own life.

The group which wrote for *La Conquista del Estado* (Ledesma, Giménez Caballero, Aparicio, Salaverría, Aguado and others) were keen to secure intellectual validation for their elitist theories and they found it in Nietzsche. Salaverría wrote: '¡Hacedme dura a España!'[3] Aguado declaimed: 'La masa troncha las alas de los espíritus que quieren volar. ¿Concebís a Nietzsche o a Unamuno al servicio de una masa fabril?'[4] Certain attitudes follow from these interpretations of Nietzsche; these are, according to Sobejano:

La busca de enemigos cercanos y concretos; el ánimo guerrero: 'Hay que ser soldados'; la postulación de una moral interventora, que desconfíe de lo que no proceda del propio sujeto combatiente; el encauzamiento de la revolución hacia una minoría dirigente por aquélla misma creada; el desprecio de leguleyos, burócratas, renunciadores y resentidos y la entereza para afrontar las luchas del futuro; el aprovechamiento del momento vital en el que se es joven, vigoroso y temible; la elección del camino 'transmutador subversivo', etc.[5]

A careful reading of *La Conquista del Estado* reveals that the 'enemies' are separatists: '(Hay que) fusilar a Maciá por traidor' (p. 173); foreign capitalists: 'el pulpo capitalista yanqui' (p. xix); Liberalism: 'Odiamos el espíritu liberal burgués' (p. 43); intellectuals in politics: 'La política no es actividad propia de intelectuales, sino de hombres de acción' (p. 66); meddling bureaucrats: 'El Ayuntamiento debe desaparecer de la vida rural gallega' (p. 112); the idle rich: 'la vaga y dañina burguesía burocrática y ... rentistas' (p. 114); and the *latifundista* class, whose in-breeding has left it physiologically flawed: 'Sufre de taras hereditarias que la colocan en dificilísima posición para luchar en la vida (p. 147). Communism at this stage (1931) is not considered a threat: 'No hay comunismo, señores' (p. 92), and Anarchists, admired for their revolutionary fervour and violent methods, are considered woefully disorganised: 'La CNT no contaba con un equipo de diez o doce hombres con capacidad de conductores' (p. xix). An unsigned article dated 11 April 1931 contains a key passage on the failure of the Republic, like the Monarchy before it, to produce a 'creative myth' which would appeal to the people: 'Se polarizan las fuerzas políticas sobre esos dos conceptos de Monarquía o República, sin sospechar que ambos perdieron hace muchos años su vigencia como mitos creadores' (p. 61). It is clear that the extreme Right intend to create such a myth; indeed, much of their rhetoric during this period is designed for this purpose. The glories of the past are held out to the Spanish public as a realistic option for the future: 'España ... vive desde hace casi tres siglos en perpetua fuga de sí misma . . . Hemos perdido así el pulso universal. Nos hemos desconexionado de los destinos universales' (p. 1). 'Nosotros, al margen de ellos, frente a ellos, más allá que ellos, sin división lateral de derechas e izquierdas, sino de lejanías y de fondos, iniciamos una acción revolucio-naria en pro de un Estado de novedad radical' (p. 2). Following Unamuno's imperative, they aim to imbue the people with 'locura colectiva' in order to 'rescatar el sepulcro de don Quijote' (p. 23); the Fascists are protecting 'los valores supremos del hombre' (p. 107); Spain is 'la reserva de Occidente' (p. 106) and 'sangre de imperio' (p. 134).[6] Such terms later became the stock rhetorical devices of the extreme Right. A curious omission from the rhetorical armoury of *La Conquista del Estado* is religion, which as we shall see was to play an important role in the novel of the Right. In their political manifesto of February 1931, mention is made of the Spanish people as 'ecuménico, católico' but only in the sense of having a universal mission, 'El mundo necesita de nosotros, y nosotros debemos estar en nuestro puesto' (p. 3). Significantly, Baroja's anti-clerical remarks are freely reported in an interview with Aparicio on 14 March 1931: 'El cura, cual el eunuco de un harén, se lo prohibe todo (a los obreros): cinematógrafo, teatros, civilización' (p. 11). It became expedient later to make Catholicism an essential ingredient of the creative myth and adjust the rhetoric accordingly. This was facilitated by the fact that Onésimo Redondo and José Antonio were Catholics, and succeeded in reconciling their Fascism with their religion.[7] Redondo's *El Estado nacional* (a collection of his speeches made in 1931–33, published in 1943) glorified heroism: 'Tenemos que restaurar . . . el afán de crear la aptitud para el heroísmo' (p. 47), and war: '¡Amemos la guerra, y adelante!' (p. 54). José Antonio's speeches and articles (collectively published in *Obras completas* (Madrid, 1942) reveal a similar liking for danger: 'Aspiramos . . . a ser los primeros en el peligro' (p. 29), power: 'las flechas del poderío' (p. 29), violence: 'la dialéctica de los puños y de las pistolas' (p. 19), and militarism: 'la vida como milicia' (p. 443). This led him to issue on behalf of Falange the following call to arms as early as December 1933: '(Falange) llama a una cruzada a cuantos españoles quieran el resurgimiento de una España grande, libre, justa y genuina' (p. 443). By this early date, the creative myth was substantially complete. The myth required a hero, which history would supply in due course in the person of the martyred José Antonio, and of the *Caudillo* who survived the Civil War, Francisco Franco. These were the paradigms in history for numerous literary heroes. Giménez Caballero had anticipated the event in *La nueva catolicidad*, in which a bizarre combination of Nietzschean and Sorelian hero was predicated as the future model:

Friedrich Nietzsche – instruye, sueña, melodiza un nuevo ideal heroico –. Un nuevo semi-dios. El *Superhombre* que deberá ser al hombre como el hombre al mono, tipo de una especie futura, de una autocracia ideal que habría de conducir una vida fuerte y alegre . . .

Por otra parte, Sorel en Francia, contemplando la moral mezquina y cobarde a que se había reducido el proletariado en su lucha con la burguesía industrial, proclama el derecho a la violencia, como norma de heroicidad en los humildes. La acción directa, sindical.

De esa conjunción fundamental del *máximo individuo* – del superhombre, del *Nuevo Titán* nietzscheano – y de la masa soreliana rebelada en violencia, en acción sindical – iba a surgir el nuevo concepto del Héroe.

Iba a surgir – su encauzador en la historia actual del mundo –: Benito Mussolini.

Más tarde: con otras características delimitadas en la raza germánica: Adolfo Hitler. Y han de surgir todavía nuevas modalidades de ese tipo actual del *Héroe* . . .[8]

The Spanish Civil War provided ample opportunity for these ideas to be tested against experience, and the novels under study are in many cases a glorification of the armed struggle in which the Nationalist hero is the protagonist. There is little room for pacifism here; as we have seen, this contrasts strongly with the European novel of the First World War. In his preface to *Se ha ocupado el kilómetro 6* (sub-titled 'Contestación a Remarque'), Benítez de Castro inveighs against 'esos papanatas que se bautizan con el nombre pomposo de pacifistas' (p. 12) and considers war a natural and inevitable occurrence. Like the process of giving birth, it involves suffering, but 'no habrá madre que, por inmenso dolor que le cueste, se niegue a dar luz al fruto de sus entrañas' (p. 9). Domínguez, the sergeant in D. Manfredi's *Las lomas tienen espinos*, finds Remarque's philosophy equally distasteful: 'Las novelas de la guerra en el estilo de Remarque no le gustaban. "La guerra es algo más que piojos, fango, palabrotas y tripas fuera . . ."' (p. 215). Those who shelter in the rearguard as *emboscados* rather than exposing themselves to danger at the front are to be despised: 'Gozaba con ponerles en ridículo y en el fondo de su conciencia hervía la esperanza de que alguno le hiciera cara un día y le planteara una pelea. Sería estupendo volver al frente diciendo que le había partido la boca a un emboscado . . .' (p. 247). Later Domínguez affirms proudly 'Yo soy un hombre, un macho, un soldado' (p. 247). In the prologue to *Cristo en los infiernos*, Ricardo León exalts the traditional heroic virtues of Spain and the 'sentimiento religioso y militar de la vida, las disciplinas militares de la obediencia y del servicio, frente al satánico *non serviam*, origen de todas las rebeldías; el sentimiento heroico del deber contra el concepto falso, muelle, pacifista y glotón de la felicidad' (p. 8).

It is perhaps in the Falangist authors that this cult of violence reaches its apogee: 'Donde no hay soldado, no hay hombre', affirms García Serrano in *La fiel Infantería* (p. 580). 'Los fuertes tienen derecho a todo' (p. 581). Rafael, in *Eugenio, o proclamación de la Primavera*, despises the urban peace of a prosperous Basque town on a visit to see his friend: 'La civilización pacifista – la del progreso indefinido – lo subordina todo a la higiene y a los ensanches' (p. 55), and goes on to advocate 'la pedagogía de la pistola' (ch. 5). Ximénez de Sandoval's hero in *Camisa azul*, Víctor, embraces violence openly: 'A nosotros no nos asusta la violencia, que nos parece sagrada' (p. 45). For such characters as these the war is an exhilarating and adventurous experience, in which courting death becomes a game to be played out each day. 'La guerra es un juego "de farol" como el pocker' (*ibid.*, p. 143). War is described as fun: 'Las marchas en camión son divertidas . . . Somos unos cuantos amigos en plan de *camping* . . .' (Benítez de Castro, *Se ha ocupado el kilómetro 6*, p. 35). Boyish games are played and rituals established, as for example in putting out the camp fire (*ibid.*, p. 175). Nothing, however, detracts from the ultimate sacrifice of death in battle, in which the soldier is the 'novio de la muerte'. Ramiro Ledesma had expressed his admiration for such self-sacrifice in *El sello de la muerte*, attributing the following words to Nietzsche: 'Ama al que quiere crear algo superior a él y sucumbe' (p. 260). The man who risked his life in such a mission was god-like: 'La posición natural del hombre es la vertical: sobre sus densas piernas, un mozo es casi un semidiós. Con un arma en los brazos, más que un semidiós. Con un enemigo delante, ya está completo el poema . . .' (*La fiel Infantería*, p. 511). At the moment of the attack, perhaps the ultimate in 'limit situations', men feel intoxicated: 'Cuando la metralla cae a un lado y a otro, y se avanza, las manos se crispan en el fusil y uno se emborracha de gloria' (*Se ha ocupado el kilómetro 6*, p. 46).

The desire for self-immolation in defence of the fatherland is found not infrequently in these novels: 'Yo llevo meses deseando que me alcance una bala . . . todos tenemos envidia a los que vierten su sangre por España, y no digamos a los que pierden por ella un brazo, una pierna: esos son los privilegiados' (M. Sepúlveda, *En la gloria de aquel amanecer*, p. 183). García Serrano approaches the problem with greater scientific rigour. For him there are four categories of dying:

    (a) 'Muerte de circunstancias' e.g. in an accident
    (b) 'Muerte burguesa' e.g. of an illness
    (c) 'Muerte de deber' e.g. in the course of duty, perhaps as a soldier
    (d) 'Muerte de voluntad' e.g. by choice, as a martyr

Eugenio, the protagonist of his first story, freely chooses the last of these. His violent death at the hands of the Communists befits the hero: 'Entregó veinte años sin estrenar por la Patria, la Falange y el César' (*Eugenio*, p. 92). Ramón, in *La fiel Infantería*, is furious because he has been removed to hospital and deprived of a glorious death: '¿Por qué ahora venía la muerte, desde otro siglo, muy literaria, muy blanca, muy civilizada, con violetas en la cintura, cuando él se había alistado para la muerte frenética sobre la tierra conquistada?' (p. 581). Víctor, in Ximénez de Sandoval's *Camisa azul*, has no greater ambition than to die gloriously: 'Era . . . intenso en su acento y en sus ojos el deseo de Víctor de morir heroicamente, de redondear de gloria la armonía de las veintitrés esferas de cristal de sus años mozos' (p. 399). Pepín, in Salinas Quijada's *Un alférez de cursillos*, exclaims, '¡Qué bonita la guerra! ¿Veinte bajas? . . . ¡Qué lástima!' War is glorified partly as a cult of violence, and partly as a cathartic process in which pain and suffering purge the Spanish soul after centuries of neglect. This owes more to the Catholic ascetic tradition of self-abnegation and flagellation, perhaps, than to Nietzsche: 'Aprendían los españoles en la prueba esa gran lección de propio desprendimiento y de conformidad con el dolor, que hacía mejores a los malos y admirables a los ya buenos antes' (M. Sepúlveda, *En la gloria de aquel amanecer*, p. 184). 'Nos purificamos por el dolor' (p. 207). Death in war assures the hero of immortality. Clearly it is in the interests of all propagandist literature to offer such a guarantee in order to ensure the enthusiastic participation of the soldiers, but Falangist mythology was extremely effective in this area. As Pérez Bowie points out, many of the phrases used by the Nationalists subvert the normal Catholic mythology:

Tales fórmulas, privativas sin excepción del discurso de la derecha, designan esa otra vida a la que la víctima se encamina al morir, echando mano de la fraseología acuñada por la mitología falangista en torno a la figura del combatiente muerto. A éste se le encomienda la tarea de velar desde el cielo, desde 'el puesto en los luceros,' por la suerte de los compañeros vivos y por el triunfo de las ideas en cuya defensa sucumbió. El cielo no es entonces ya el lugar de eterno reposo sino el de la eterna vigilancia.[9]

The death of José Antonio before a firing squad in Alicante jail undoubtedly fuelled the myth of the Absent One and strengthened the cult of leadership from which Franco was to profit indirectly. As Payne has pointed out, 'ideal identification with José Antonio proved a necessary and welcome dodge for the Salamanca *camarilla* . . . José Antonio was the hero, the martyr, the troubadour, the transcendent reference, the perfect symbol – in short, everything that the leaders of the "New Spain" were not.'[10] Clear indications are to be found in the Nationalist novel of the power exercised by this myth. In *Camisa azul*, the report of the trial originally published in the Alicante daily *El Día* (18 November 1936) is reproduced, interspersed with comments by the characters of the novel who repeatedly compare José Antonio's plight with Christ's trial by the people before his crucifixion. José Antonio is 'elegido por Dios para acusar ante la Historia . . . las traiciones de toda una España indigna' (p. 387) – a role later assumed by Franco. Even the worst enemies of the Falangists, the Communists, concede, 'Vuestro Jefe es una maravilla. Al contrario de los nuestros, es el primero en el peligro y el deber' (p. 93). Noguera eulogises: 'Franco es el cruzado que salva al mundo occidental de la destrucción cierta de su cultura' (*La mascarada trágica*, p. 46). 'Franco, a quien Dios nos envía . . .' (p. 66). Eduardo, one of the central characters of the novel, undergoes a political conversion when he realises that Franco is in fact defending the underprivileged: 'Eduardo iba a Franco porque veía encarnada en él la verdadera revolución contra un mundo de injusticias y de inhumanidades hundidas con sus bayonetas y sus leyes para alzar a los humildes' (p. 117). Both Franco and José Antonio are depicted as Quixotes, tilting at 'molinos de pan espiritual' in *Checas de Madrid* (p. 258). Ricardo León uses equally traditional imagery to lament the lack of a *caudillo* in Spain until the arrival of Franco: 'Lo que (Pablo) quería era exaltar el eterno espíritu español de Caballería y de Cruzada. Y para ello urgían, sobre todo, la unidad de mando y de acción . . . En España nunca faltaron los héroes. Formidables vasallos hubo en todo siglo, pero no siempre hubieron [*sic*] buen señor' (*Cristo en los infiernos*, p. 266). The characters of Benítez de Castro's *Se ha ocupado el kilómetro 6* express 'fe ciega' in Franco's leadership (p. 106), and consider him virtually infallible (p. 127). He is 'el Caudillo que sólo Dios puede habernos enviado' (p. 127). The cult reaches its height in Manfredi's *Las lomas tienen espinos*, in which an *alférez* recounts that 'había tenido a

Franco un día tan cerca que no había podido resistir la tentación de tocarle el capote . . . Y que luego había estado varios días sin lavarse la mano' (p. 164).

Such hero worship as this, stemming as it did from a long intellectual tradition of authoritarianism, supported more recently by theories of a super-race or 'select minority', was bound to produce a generation of heroes in literature. The Spanish Civil War novel is rich in such stereotypes, which are an essential part of the 'creative myth' disseminated by the Franco régime. García Serrano's novels are perhaps the best-known examples: *Eugenio* is dedicated to José Antonio and its hero symbolises the new era into which Spain has entered, the Fascist millennium. This hero is 'fuerte, sano, valiente' (p. 37), of sound racial stock ('bien engendrado'), quick to anger, impetuous and violent. We first encounter him smashing the windows of the French Embassy, a suitable symbol of liberalism and decadence. 'El sol le unge héroe. Las mujeres parece que lo miran como a un predestinado. Va sereno, gozoso' (p. 39). Ramón, in *La fiel Infantería*, is guided by the Caesarean myth: 'Sólo nos guía y alienta la voz del César, sólo del César' (p. 531), and the three student heroes of this novel are never happier than when marching and singing 'Cara al sol', in a mythical union with the fatherland: 'Sabían que estaban celebrando unas míticas bodas con su patria y que toda aquella sangre – inmensa sangre – era nupcial' (p. 509). This union of the youth of Spain with the destinies of their country was precisely that advocated by Ledesma in his essay *Discurso a las juventudes de España*, in which he had seen the potential of harnessing youthful impetuosity to political goals. For the first time Spanish youth was made to appear a moral force in its own right:

Que las juventudes tienen que adoptar una táctica de acción directa, es decir una moral de desconfianza hacia todo lo que no proceda de ellas y una decisión de imponer por sí mismas las nuevas normas, es algo incuestionable.
Eso va implícito en la actitud que antes hemos dicho corresponde a nuestros jóvenes: la actitud del soldado.[11]

Young, sporting, handsome Nationalist heroes strut around this literary world with supreme confidence. 'Ramón . . . un tiempo, campeón de los cien metros' (*La fiel Infantería*, p. 581), 'Ramón predestinado. Ramón superior' (*ibid.*, p. 591). Of the hero of *Manolo*, by Francisco de Cossío, we are told, 'En el fútbol . . . nadie metía más goles que él' (p. 16).

The climax of *Las alas invencibles* by Concha Espina transfers this idolatry into the air and introduces a female admirer whose passion for the

Nationalist hero, despite the discomfort of their surroundings, suddenly erupts:

[Talín] se pone en pie, apoyándose con temerario impulso en el borde de la nave. Sin saber lo que dice, grita, con los ojos ciegos de llantos y de resplandores:
– ¡Te quiero, Fidel, te quiero!
Su voz transida de inquietudes, se deslíe en el aire, que la sorbe y la empapa con inmensa dulzura.
El piloto, a la vanguardia del aeroplano, va sumido en las múltiples atenciones de su ciencia, llena de arte y de riesgo, emuladora de la divina . . . va pensando con orgullo en la brillantez de su destino.   (p. 183)

Although a more complex example, it shows that the authoress considers by the end of her novel that she has created a demi-god, a mythical creation whose heroism and flirtation with danger make him irresistibly attractive. This is the stereotype of the Nationalist hero.

Agustín, a brilliant law student, is the protagonist of M. Sepúlveda's *En la gloria de aquel amanecer*. He displays 'arranques de varonil entereza, rebeldías, iniciativas, ambiciones las más de las veces desmedidas . . . Tenía algo peculiar suyo, un dinamismo innato que le atraía voluntades, simpatías, una afabilidad con los humildes y una dignidad con los altos y poderosos, privativas de la sangre linajuda que en sus venas llevaba, todo ello realzado por un físico apuesto, de una gallardía netamente varonil' (pp. 25–26). The suggestion here is of physiological or genealogical superiority due to his aristocratic antecedents. (The description is not unlike that of José Antonio given by his friends.)

Pepín, in *Un alférez de cursillos*, by Salinas Quijada, walking through a hail of bullets in the attack on Bilbao, 'reía gozoso de la epopeya triunfal' (p. 84).

There is an interesting example in *Méndez, cronista de guerra*, by Morales López, of heroism being made the prerogative of one political group, in this case Falange. The woman Méndez saves from certain death in Linares while pretending to be a Republican, tells him that she recognises from his act of bravery that he must be a Falangist: 'Tiene que ser así, porque sí no, no hubiera hecho lo que ha hecho por mí . . .' (p. 95). The author has moved from the already dubious premise that all Falangists are brave to the syllogism that all brave people are Falangists. There could be no better example of Fascist mythology and the state of development it had reached by 1939, the date of this novel's publication. Like many other Nationalist heroes, Méndez causes women to fall slavishly in love with him – 'Estoy dispuesta a . . . servirte de esclava si ése es tu deseo' (p. 149) – because he stands head and shoulders above other men.

One of the few authors to have seen the heroic potential of casting a bullfighter as Falangist hero is Muñoz San Román, in *Del ruedo a la trinchera*. 'Veneno', a bullfighter from Seville, joins the Falangist *fuerzas de choque*, and the union of politics and violence is consummated:

Había que ver a 'Veneno' con aquel su cuerpo erguido marchando con suma marcialidad, con el mismo gusto y entusiasmo como cuando hacía el paseo delante de su cuadrilla, en las plazas de toros, entre sus compañeros los patriotas falangistas de su compañía, alegre el rostro, decidido el ademán, con su camisa azul y su escudo del yugo y las flechas al pecho, con un orgullo de poder servir a la Patria que le rebosaba por todos los poros de su cuerpo y le iluminaba el alma con incendios que le rebrillaron los ojos.   (p. 190)

The comparison which is made here between the thrill of the bullfight and that of battle is another example of life being portrayed as sport, a concept found in Ortega and common in authors of the Right.

The crusader is another powerful mythical creation of the war novel. H.R. Southworth's *El mito de la cruzada de Franco* was perhaps the most publicised attempt to dispel this myth,[12] which stemmed from the publication on 1 July 1937 of the Spanish bishops' joint letter to 'Bishops of the Whole World'. This gave the Civil War the status of a Crusade, claiming, falsely, that a Communist plot to take over Spain had been hatched by the Comintern in February 1936.[13] The Nationalists could claim they were fighting, therefore, in a 'just cause', though this was hotly contended by liberal Catholics in the rest of Europe.[14]

The Carlist *requeté*, unlike the Falangist prototype, owes little to Nietzsche and everything to the native Spanish tradition. This timeless crusader is to be found in novels such as *El teniente Arizcun*, by Jorge Claramunt. 'Javier Arizcun tiene veintidós años, es fuerte como el roble, apasionado, impetuoso . . . y buenísimo. Un navarro de cuerpo entero, que siente a España en sus venas con energía indomable' (p. 7). He dies in an assignment for which he competes fiercely with his comrades, although they all know it means almost certain death. When his body is found, 'en su mano izquierda, y a la altura de sus ojos, tenía el *Devocionario del Requeté*, abierto en la página en que se lee la oración de la hora de muerte' (p. 51). Ricardo León's characters too are surrounded by an aura of saintliness. Pablo, the protagonist of *Cristo en los infiernos*, inspires quasi-religious adoration on the part of Margarita: 'Apenas le veo entrar me dan ganas de hincarme de rodillas como si viera a un santo' (p. 228). Onésimo Redondo, 'clarísimo espejo de la raza', is termed 'apóstol de Castilla' (p. 265) despite his Nazi sympathies.

The novelist is faced with a separate set of problems in depicting the Nationalist heroine. The sinewy masculinity and iron will of the male stereotype gives way to an altogether softer and virginal character. In *El espantable caso de los 'tomadores' de ciudades*, by Benítez de Castro, the description of Mariluz among the Republican troops leaves no doubt in the reader's mind that she must secretly be a Nationalist: she is too beautiful to be anything else. 'Las guedejas sueltas de sus rubios cabellos, los ojos entornados por la fatiga, la boca pequeña y bien formada, la frente espaciosa y clara, el cuerpo virgen . . .' (ch. 7). Benítez de Castro attempts to stress the asexual nature of comradeship in war, but without much conviction. 'Si esa mujer no fuera de uniforme, si ese uniforme no fuera la camisa azul, yo la habría mirado de otro modo. Pero la he visto como una combatiente y como una compañera de lucha' (p. 80). The novelist's ambivalent attitude to the value of women in the struggle is best summed up perhaps in his double-edged compliment to the workers of the Auxilio Social: '¡Olé por las niñas de Auxilio Social! Valen más que algunos hombres' (p. 28).[15] The ideal woman is middle or upper class, beautiful, elegant and well-spoken. Pilar, in *El teniente Arizcun*, is described as a miller's daughter but has bourgeois tastes. As Mainer has pointed out, 'junto a la exaltación de la revolución nacionalsindicalista, un larvado anhelo de aristocraticismo – bellos uniformes, mantillas de blonda – invadió el país, hasta caer en la cursilería de las madrinas de guerra y las chicas-topolino'.[16] Concha Espina's heroines are good examples of this literary stereotype. In *Retaguardia*, Rosa is forced to scrub the floors in the *comité rojo* and Felipe is appalled to see her engaged in such lowly activities: 'Se fija en las manos . . . agrietadas por la aspereza de un trabajo tan impropio de los dedos gentiles que saben hacer un bello encaje, un bordado finísimo, una primorosa costura, una excelente labor de taquimeca, unas inmejorables traducciones literarias, al castellano, de cualquiera idioma vivo' (p. 102).[17] The three virgins of *Princesas del martirio* are 'del más puro abolengo racial,'[18] and Pilar in particular is the embodiment of virtue: 'Pilar reúne en sus facciones el privilegio angelical y toda ella se mueve dentro del soplo seráfico, con una beatitud indecible' (p. 211). While getting ready to meet her death at the hands of the Republicans, another of the three young women, Olga, 'baja los ojos, cuidando de no pisar una humilde flor que ha visto a sus pies' (p. 82). The extraordinary degree to which these traits of delicacy and saintliness are stressed is evidence of the authoress's intention to create a myth. To criticise the novels for lack of realism would be to miss the point. Espina, despite her affiliation to Falange, displays what Nora terms 'una concepción maternalmente tradicionalista de la vida social y privada'.[19] A more modern heroine is to be found in Pérez y Pérez's *De una España a otra*, in which Elena Calvo, a Falangist, exerts a powerful influence on her political enemies in Alicante. So strong is her personality and so glowing her example that the Anarchist Martingala is inspired to kiss the forehead of the dead José Antonio after his execution: 'Le he besado en la frente en tu nombre y en el de todos sus camaradas' (p. 91). It is only when an even more heroic figure appears in the form of the Falangist José Ignacio (later to become her husband), that Elena is relegated to a secondary position. In this novel, as in all other Nationalist novels of the 'first wave,' the love affair is treated with extreme decorum. While immorality reigns supreme among the *milicianas*, the sexual *mores* of Nationalist heroines are above reproach. (It is not unknown for Nationalist soldiers to be described visiting the brothel, but the exemplary hero is not usually described engaging in such activity.)

It will be apparent from the description so far of Nationalist paradigms that while unswerving in their pursuit of their ideal, they will be incapable of base or criminal acts. It became an important part of Nationalist mythology to claim that justice was administered strictly in accordance with established law and that only those Republicans guilty of crime were tried and punished. In the early months of the war, thousands of summary executions took place, the dubious legal pretext being that a state of war had been proclaimed to exist on the day of the rising. 'It was assumed that the Government of the Republic were the rebels and the Nationalists the legitimate power.'[20] However much the Nationalists (including the novelists under study) tried to disguise the fact, systematic killing was an essential element in their holy war:

The largest simple category of deaths were the reprisals carried out by the Carlists, the Falangists and the military themselves. Physical liquidation of the enemy behind the lines was a constant process throughout the war ... The repression took place in three stages. At the outbreak of war, the arrests and wholesale shootings of such persons corresponded to the revolutionary terror in the Popular Front zone; but there were a great many more victims, because such arrests and shootings were officially sanctioned and because so large a percentage of the population were considered hostile. In the second stage, the Nationalist Army, conquering areas which had been held by the Popular Front, carried out heavy reprisals in revenge for those of the revolutionaries and in order to control a hostile population with few troops. In both Andalusian and Castilian villages there are many testimonies concerning reprisals in the order of 60 for 6, 90 for 9, and so forth. In the third stage, which lasted at least into the year 1943, the military authorities carried out mass court-martials followed by large-scale executions.[21]

There are powerful indications in the war novels that the authors wish to portray their warriors as being magnanimous. Benítez de Castro (who must have known otherwise) makes one of his characters say: 'Aquí no se fusila a nadie. Mientras están con el enemigo se les combate, porque es necesario. Pero en cuanto se pasan o los cogemos, no hay por qué. Se les da de comer y se les conduce a la retaguardia . . . ¡Si viera usted la alegría con que nos abrazan!' (Se ha ocupado el kilómetro 6, p. 166); indeed, such a scene is later played out (p. 188). The description of Arévalo in Ruiz Ayúcar's Las dos barajas is that of a town where no-one feels threatened by reprisals; the workers are well-paid, well-fed and relaxed: 'No tenían aire de temer que afuera les esperara un cura para pegarles un tiro' (p. 103). In La fiel Infantería, when a Republican position is overrun, the captured Republicans are treated with humanity:

Amarillos de miedo, creían en su seguro fusilamiento . . .
– Toma, hombre, toma.
Le daban coñac a uno que no se sostenía en pie.   (p. 578)

A legionary who has just taken part in the battle for Badajoz, in Carmen Martel's La guerra a través de las tocas, reports: 'Pudimos entrar en la Plaza de Toros, en donde llegamos a tiempo de salvar la vida a cien prisioneros' (p. 69), but makes no mention of the massacre of between a thousand and two thousand unarmed militiamen which is reported to have taken place there.[22] The Communist Bonilla, in Noguera's La mascarada trágica, remains in Madrid at the end of the war and prepares to take his punishment: he is astonished to find that the liberating army treats the population with great kindness. Similar treatment is afforded to the population of Cartagena in Los canes andan sueltos: 'Los soldados de Franco eran españoles . . . a pesar de su saludable aspecto, y no entraban en las ciudades asesinando a la gente, violando mujeres, etc.' (p. 290). Pérez y Pérez dismisses 'todos aquellos cuentos del aceite de ricino y demás tonterías' (De una España a otra, p. 79) and ridicules the idea that a fallen enemy pilot could come to any harm: 'Si cayese en las líneas de Franco no me pasaría nada' (p. 149). This is borne out in a scene in Se ha ocupado el kilómetro 6 where a fallen Russian pilot is dutifully looked after (p. 102). Concha Espina is at pains to point out at the end of Las alas invencibles that there are no reprisals in Nationalist Spain (p. 184) and in Retaguardia dismisses claims of atrocities against women, children and old people as 'absurdas invenciones' (p. 118) dreamt up by the Communists.[23] Domingo Manfredi, in discussing the capture of Seville (*Las lomas tienen espinos*, p. 20), grossly understates the violence that took place there, involving the deaths of 9,000 people in a few short weeks.[24] While Moors and legionaries are mentioned, their numbers and role in the events are deliberately underplayed. There is no doubt that the presence of such troops on the Nationalist side made it difficult for the latter to sustain claims of magnanimity. These troops were notoriously ruthless.[25] Carmen Carriedo de Ruiz attempts to create a new image for the Moorish troops in *En plena epopeya*, where instead of being rapists and castrators, they are 'hijos de Magreb, fieles y leales, creyentes y bravos, almas de niños . . .' (p. 62). In one scene, a Moorish soldier knocks on the door of the house in a captured village. When a mother answers the door, carrying a baby in her arms, the soldier pats the child on the head, gives it a sweet and moves on (p. 130). Such scenes can only be intended to counter the rising tide of international outrage at the atrocities being committed, allegedly in defence of Christian civilisation.

There is some embarrassment evident in these novelists also, over the extent to which the creation of a consistent Nationalist mythology was negated by the presence on Spanish soil of not only Moroccan troops but also German and Italian divisions. In the case of the first group, as we have seen, the attempt was made to revamp the image. In C. Martel's *La guerra a través de las tocas* the Moors are 'leales y caballeros' (p. 45), believe in God (p. 50) and join Franco's troops in a 'santa hermandad' (p. 158). It was left to Gironella to pose the essential contradiction ('¡Cruzada! ¿luchando los moros y los nazis al lado de Franco?') which led to bitter recriminations from right-wing critics as late as 1961. What is noticeable in the Nationalist novels in general is their reticence in dealing with the issue. On the battlefront somewhere near Guadalajara in 1937, María Sepúlveda speaks of the Nationalist forces as being 'Requetés, Falangistas, caballeros Legionarios, todos los que integran las fuerzas del Ejército vencedor' (*En la gloria de aquel amanecer*, p. 213). It seems extraordinary that no mention is made of the 30,000 Italian troops who made up more than half the attacking force in this battle.[26] Ricardo León had substantially completed *Cristo en los infiernos* before the outbreak of war, but extended it to take in the first six months of the conflict. He is well aware of the international involvement on the Republican side and mentions several battalions of the International Brigades by name as well as describing them in action. It is curious therefore that he makes no such mention of German or Italian involvement: the

Army of Africa is transported across the Straits not with Fascist air and sea transport but by the intervention of Nuestra Señora de África: 'En amorosa merced a la oración ferviente del Caudillo, Nuestra Señora de África, la *Morenita* ceutí, guiaba otra vez . . . las naves y los tercios españoles' (p. 513). Domingo Manfredi gives the International Brigades a significant role in the defence of Málaga, which in fact they took no part in at all.[27] He curiously fails to mention, on the other hand, the role played by Italian tanks or the 5,000 Italian troops involved in this battle. Ruiz-Ayúcar makes no attempt to disguise Italian involvement but makes the propaganda point that this was of no real help to the Nationalists anyway. Thus the ignominious defeat of the Nationalists at Guadalajara is expressed in terms of a battle fought entirely between Italians and the International Brigades: 'Los españoles, de espectadores de este gran arreglo de cuentas internacionales, en el que sólo intervenimos prestando unos kilómetros cuadrados del territorio como palestra' (*Las dos barajas*, p. 191). At a stroke, the Republicans are thus deprived of any glory and the Nationalists of any blame. This author is contemptuous of Italian involvement in general: 'Los italianos parecía que habían venido a España más para hacer el amor en retaguardia que para luchar en el frente' (p. 253). Nor is the intervention of German troops highly valued either: 'Los oficiales con que trató Lara daban poca importancia a la ayuda prestada en hombres por los italianos o alemanes' (p. 253).[28] In Pérez y Pérez's *De una España a otra*, the Anarchist Martingala, speaking in November 1936, denies that Italy or Germany are providing aid to Franco at that stage, though he admits Republicans *are* being supplied from abroad: 'Mientras el pleito se ventilaba entre españoles, era una cosa, nadie tenía derecho a meterse, y la prueba es que, digan lo que quieran los rojos, ni Alemania ni Italia se han metido. Pero ahora . . . ¿Qué quieres que haga Franco más que aceptar las ayudas que le ofrezcan los países totalitarios?' (p. 83). It is inconceivable that a Republican at this stage of the war would not have been aware of the extent of foreign aid to Franco since July 1936.[29] Patriotic pride, however, was extremely sensitive on this point and Nationalist mythology did not easily accommodate these facts. Concha Espina, writing in Luzmela (Santander), would surely have been better informed about the campaign in the North than to believe that Communists were responsible for the destruction of Guernika (*Esclavitud y libertad*, p. 206). With two sons fighting in this campaign – they 'liberated' Luzmela on 26 August 1937 – it is hard to believe that she was unaware of the reality of the situation. Myth, however, is more important than reality in the war of words.

Perhaps the most powerful myth elaborated by the participants in war is that they are the representatives of Good, in a struggle to the death with Evil: 'el mito maniqueo del ángel y la hidra'.[30] The very titles of some of the Civil War novels (*Armas de Caín y Abel, Cristo en los infiernos, Princesas del martirio*) illustrate their intention: to create a struggle between the forces of light and darkness which attains epic proportions. The fact that numerous historical realities have to be distorted is subordinate to the principal aim of myth creation. In Vázquez's *Armas de Caín y Abel* the two brothers Ricardo and Fernando are reincarnations of the biblical characters. The Communist Ricardo is an unprincipled, evil, drunken Atheist: 'Se han levantado y puesto frente a frente los espíritus dispares de Caín y Abel. El Mal contra el Bien' (p. 16). Borrás creates characters of satanic dimensions in *Checas de Madrid*: 'Esta es la lucha de los buenos contra los malos; lucha elemental, eterna. El Arcángel batiéndose con el Rebelde' (p. 164). The Republicans practise the most barbaric forms of torture, not for any political purpose but for sheer sadistic pleasure: 'Aman y practican el mal por el mal' (p. 237). In *Princesas del martirio*, Asturias is described as being infected by 'el satanismo ruso' (p. 57), while the Nationalists are 'los amigos del bien' (*Retaguardia*, p. 104). R. Léon's *Cristo en los infiernos* contains numerous such references: '[el] satánico *non serviam*' (p. 8), 'satanismo francés . . . nihilismo ruso' (p. 83), 'las batallas del demonio contra Dios' (p. 113), and the wholesale condemnation of Spain's enemies as 'las potencias secretas del satanismo internacional' (p. 382). When the Nationalists win the battle on the Aragon front, in *La guerra a través de las tocas*, the authoress exclaims: '¡El Angel venció otra vez a Lucifer!' (p. 163). Earlier the reader had been left in no doubt as to the identity of this holy messenger: 'Franco es el hombre del BIEN, el que lucha contra el MAL' (p. 52). When Juan Ignacio and Elena escape to Nationalist Spain, in *De una España a otra*, they go 'del infierno al paraíso' (p. 171). The parable recounted by don Emilio Flores in *La mascarada trágica*, which gives the novel its name, tells of an inventor who has created live puppets. He controls them, but allows them a certain freedom of action. When they organise a masquerade, the Devil steals in and tangles up the strings that control them, causing total confusion. The message is that during the Republic, individuals incapable of exercising power responsibly took control, and that this ultimately led to mob rule and social chaos. The Nationalists represent a return to order and hierarchy. (There are echoes in this allegory of the biblical account of the Creation, in which an orderly universe is conjured out of chaos.) In Salinas Quijada's *Un alférez de cursillos*, good and evil are recognisable even in death: the faces of the dead after the battle for Bilbao reveal clearly which side they belonged to. As for the living, their appearance and behaviour also sharply differentiates each side from the other. The Republican prisoners display 'unas caras hostiles, lombrosianas, de hampones y errabundos . . . Seguían con aire de desafío, con denuedo fanfarrón, con chulería enfermiza, mientras unos azules cedían trozos de pan blanco, quitándoselo de la boca, a los mismos que antes buscaban en su corazón el blanco de la bala. Con nobleza, sin ruindad' (pp. 92–93). Perhaps the best example of all of the manichean distinction between the two sides is to be found in Benítez de Castro's *Se ha ocupado el kilómetro 6*, in which he sums up the Civil War as follows:

Aquí se hallaron los vestigios de la Revolución francesa en forma de liberales, masones, ateos, amorales, librepensadores, unidos a los asiáticos bolcheviques, para los que resultaba idéntico plantear la batalla en España o en las alturas del Tibet. Contra ellos se presentaron los definidos como amantes de la frontera, del hogar patrio, de la religión, de la grandeza, del orden, de la familia, que resultaron, por ser España el campo elegido, españoles. Y rugieron durante tres años los hijos de los Reyes Católicos, al lado de los voluntarios en legión, contra la plebe asiática de todas las procedencias, que esperaba, ansiosa, desde hacía más de veinte años, el momento de lanzarse al degüello. Vencimos.   (p. 11)

Catholic mythology, in particular, was to prove a fundamental component of the Nationalist novel. The idea of the war as a Crusade is commonplace in the early novels: embarrassments such as the fact that some of the most devout Catholics in Spain, the Basques, were fighting on the Republican side, were not allowed to get in the way of this central myth. For Pablo Guzmán, in *Cristo en los infiernos*, the war is a second *Reconquista*: 'Una vez más en la Historia va a decidirse en España el destino de la civilización' (p. 156). In this novel, Ricardo León conjured up an Arcadian vision of a rural Spain living in peace and harmony, free from the curse of materialism. The hero, Pablo Guzmán, strives towards an ideal based on 'la Economía, cristiana y (el) Estado corporativo' (p. 177), best represented by the political programme of Acción Católica. When he travels through Andalusia, now safely in Nationalist hands, he finds the workers happily engaged in bringing in the harvest of grapes: 'Aquí la vendimia no era un motivo de explotación ni de odio sino una fiesta de amor' (p. 178). This highly romanticised vision, which contrasts strongly with the reality of life in that area described by Díaz del Moral or Brenan, is intended to represent a 'breve anticipo de una España rural pacífica, opulenta, laboriosa, fiel a sus tradiciones, reorganizada en lo futuro bajo un nuevo régimen aristocrático y democrático a la vez' (p. 179).[31] For Rafael Araluce, in Salazar Allende's

Tú no eres de los nuestros, religion offers an alternative to politics, which have simply served to divide Spain: 'Buscad la paz y el bienestar en vosotros mismos, no en los demás. Volved la espalda a la política. Amparaos en la religión que os enseñaron vuestros mayores' (ch. 1).

The devotion of Nationalist soldiers to their religion occupies a major part of these novels, and the propagandist intention is often apparent. A soldier in *La guerra a través de las tocas* describes daily prayers: 'Rezábamos el Rosario todas las tardes, asistiendo a él los soldados libres de servicio, los cabos, los sargentos y los oficiales . . . y era tan grande la devoción que teníamos al Santo Rosario que, a veces, llegaba la hora de la cena mientras estábamos rezando y nadie se movía a cogerla, ni los rancheros lo repartían' (ch. 4). As might be expected, such soldiers are frequently rewarded with miracles: 'Milagro fue lo de Sevilla, y otro milagro lo de Córdoba, y otro el paso y batalla del Estrecho, y otro . . .' (*Cristo en los infiernos*, p. 529). Three militiamen trying to destroy the statue of the 'Sagrado Corazón de Jesús', in the same novel by Ricardo León, suddenly find their weapons mysteriously turning against themselves. One kills himself by stabbing himself in the chest, another turns his pistol on himself and a third dies when a bullet ricochets off a marble plinth. Similar stories are reported at two other churches in Madrid (p. 551). In an explosion, described in Vázquez's *Armas de Caín y Abel*, the only thing to remain standing is an iron cross; this event is described as 'un nuevo milagro de los que reitera cada día a los cruzados de España la infinita misericordia de Dios' (ch. 9). God intervenes in Muñoz San Román's *Señorita en la retaguardia* to save Antonio from death and enable him to repulse a Republican attack single-handed (p. 229). Many other such examples exist.[32]

An effective method of reinforcing the Nationalist mentality was to stress the existence of an external enemy. If Catholicism became the guiding light of Nationalist propaganda, the forces of darkness were Atheism, Freemasonry and Jewry. Southworth has demonstrated that anti-Semitism was purely circumstantial: prior to the war, Fascists such as Giménez Caballero were in fact pursuing a pro-Jewish policy in an attempt to integrate Sephardic Jews into a Spanish-speaking commonwealth.[33] Anti-Semitism first appeared in the Spanish Fascist movement in the writings of Onésimo Redondo, due in part to German influences: 'Tanto los italianos como los alemanes ofrecían abundante material anticomunista a la Falange . . . Buena parte de los libros, folletos, revistas y películas brindados comportaban una propaganda política, que en el caso alemán, se centraba en lo racista y antijudío.'[34] There is no doubt that anti-Semitism was fomented in clerical circles too during the war. E. Fernández Almuzara, writing in *Razón y Fe* in May–August 1939, noted that Henry Ford's *El judío internacional*, 'corre, ahora, por España y se ha puesto muy de moda'.[35] It should also be remembered that Cardinal Gomá, in his first pronouncement of the war in a radio address from Pamplona on 26 September 1936, explained that the Nationalists were fighting against the anti-Spain, the Jews and Masons who had poisoned the Spanish people with Tartar and Mongol ideas, and who were erecting a system manipulated by the Semitic International.[36]

The Nationalist war novelists echo these sentiments in general terms, while never producing any evidence to support their claims. The Catholic reactionary Ricardo León refers to the pernicious influence of the 'judería internacional' on several occasions in *Cristo en los infiernos*, and Dr Alegre in the same novel speaks contemptuously of 'Margarita Nelken y esas otras judías alemanas' (p. 89) as being responsible for ushering in a new age of barbarism.[37] The aristocratic Gelves family sees its lineage tainted by Jewish blood, 'sangre, más que azul, negra como las moras', and becomes materialistic and conspiratorial thereafter: 'Los Rubíes infunden a los Gelves un espíritu más solapado y mercantil, de hipocresía y de cautela, propio de gentes misteriosas criadas, como las lechuzas, al olor del aceite y del incienso' (p. 70). In Carrere's *La ciudad de los siete puñales*, Russia is termed 'la diplomacia judía más peligrosa y tenebrosa del mundo' (p. 11). In *Camisa azul*, as we have seen, José Antonio's death is compared to that of Christ at the hands of the 'chusma judía'; the war has been caused by 'dirigentes políticos vendidos a una revolución judaica' (p. 112). Republicans fall in battle 'vomitando blasfemias judío-marxistas' (p. 226) – though interestingly the author does not reveal what these might be. Similar condemnation of the Jews is to be found in *Méndez, cronista de guerra* (ch. 7), *Señorita en la retaguardia* (ch. 32) and *De una España a otra*, among others.

Denigration of the Jews often goes hand in hand with that of the Freemasons. Five members of the 1931 Republican cabinet had been Freemasons, and Azaña apparently became one in 1932.[38] The anticlericalism of the Republic is a matter of historical fact: what the novelists of the war do, however, following the propaganda of the time, is to make the Freemasons the instruments of foreign governments plotting the downfall of Spain. Borrás best exemplifies this line of argument when he describes those governing the Republic as 'anglófilos o afrancesados, papanatas instrumentos de lo extranjero por medio de la Masonería, instrumentos conscientes o inconscientes, por acción, o por brutalidad, o por cobardía de nuestra servil obediencia a los amos: Inglaterra y Francia' (*Checas de Madrid,* p. 244). This view is shared by don Emilio, a character in Noguera's *La mascarada trágica* who embarks on a long diatribe against France and England. The main culprit behind the subversion of Spain's fortunes is 'la democracia capitalista francesa, judía y masónica' (p. 133) – a many-headed monster. Criminal elements in Madrid amass fortunes by looting their victims, with 'la protección del Gran Oriente' (Borrás, *Checas de Madrid,* p. 200) which is 'la Orden que lo dirige todo' (p. 63). A similar view is expressed in Espina's *Retaguardia*: 'Esos de la masonería siempre salen ganando ... El conjuro de la secta aborrecible envuelve a la familia en una especie de protección oculta' (p. 228). The Freemason don Julián, in *Cristo en los infiernos,* is at the heart of every intrigue; described as 'la caricatura del Anticristo' (p. 27), he makes a fortune in smuggling arms, for which purpose he foments revolution wherever he can. 'La hidra masónica-marxista' is the enemy in *La guerra a través de las tocas* (ch. 4). In *Méndez, cronista de guerra* (ch. 7) the Nationalists battle to save Spain from 'un internacionalismo judío y masónico'. Similar clichés abound in *La mascarada trágica, En plena epopeya* and *Las alas invencibles.*

The rapid growth of the Communist Party in the course of the war, due to the fact that the Soviet Union quickly became the major supplier of arms to the Republic, presented the novelists of the Right with an irresistible propaganda weapon. Republicans are invariably termed 'rojos', irrespective of their political shade. A number of authors perpetuate the myth that Spain was about to become a victim of a Communist plot to take over the country – a point of view widely reported in the right-wing press at the time. Benítez de Castro does not hesitate in categorising the war as 'una lucha de independencia . . . contra el próximo, inmediato peligro de la invasión exterior' (*Se ha ocupado el kilómetro 6,* p. 11). Salazar's *De anarquista a mártir* (pp. 250–256) contains a lengthy disquisition on the justification for the war and a description of the Communist coup allegedly planned for August 1936. *Cristo en los infiernos* includes numerous references to the same plot: Margarita Gelves returns from a visit to Russia, bearing 'el plan completo de la revolución del 36' (p. 422), which was to be the prelude to 'la invasión de Europa, la gigantesca ofensiva de la Revolución universal' (p. 536).

The depiction of Communism in the early Nationalist novel is extremely stereotyped. While it advocated throughout the war a 'moderate, non-revolutionary social policy'[39], it is invariably portrayed as collectivist, egalitarian and extremist, its members owing total allegiance to a revolutionary Russia. Attacking troops in *Se ha ocupado el kilómetro 6* scream '¡Viva Rusia!' (p. 108); the people of Madrid in *Checas de Madrid* do the same, adding for emphasis '¡Muera España!' (p. 27). In *Retaguardia*, egalitarianism appears to mean that anyone can do anyone else's job: '— Todos somos iguales — han dicho aquí los comunistas —. Y han puesto a un sujeto ya poco estimable como hortera, al frente de un ilustre organismo literario' (p. 87). In *La mascarada trágica*, Quinito concludes that Communism 'es para los fracasados, para los envidiosos, para los perversos sexuales, para los degenerados del tipo de Azaña, Galarza, Casares Quiroga y demás casos clínicos de la patología española' (p. 76), though none of the politicians mentioned was a Communist — indeed, Galarza was 'an old enemy of the Communists'.[40] This illustrates the distortion that the novelists of the 'first wave' perpetrate in simplifying the issues of the war for propaganda purposes. Many of the writers have little idea of Marxist ideology and often do not distinguish between libertarian Communism and the Stalinism being practised in Spain during the war. Communists are blamed in particular for creating the class hatred that had developed in Spain in the twentieth century, and little attempt is made to explain this in terms of the extremes of social injustice that were evident within the country. Alicia, in *Retaguardia*, is a good example of prevailing attitudes. When she discusses with Vicente, who has been to the United States, the differences between that country and Spain, he comments on the similarity of the clothes people wear, whatever their social class. Alicia argues that Spain is the same: 'Cualquiera menestrala viste, por lo menos, como yo. Y muchas campesinas también' (p. 37). She adds that Vicente can earn more in a day taking rich passengers on excursions than a doctor earns in the same time: '¿Entonces? . . . ¿Quién tiene los privilegios que tanto se persiguen?' (p. 38). Ricardo León finds it incomprehensible that the miners of Asturias should feel any dissatisfaction with their lot: 'No había minas en Europa donde fueran las jornadas tan breves ni los jornales tan altos. Pero los sacrilegios y los crímenes, el odio mortal a Jesucristo y sus Apóstoles, nada tienen que ver con los problemas económicos' (*Cristo en los infiernos* p. 387). Protests about social injustice in *El espantable caso de los 'tomadores' de ciudades* are put in the mouth of the comic Republican figure Juan Pérez, whose obvious physical and social well-being contrasts strongly with his allegations of social exploitation:

— 'Esto no puede ser. Esto no puede seguir así. Queremos pan y lo tendremos.'
Y comía que se las pelaba. (p. 10)

In one of the stories in Concha Espina's *Luna roja*, the local doctor tells a member of the UGT, after a debate on social questions, 'Tú . . . no has hecho más que dolerte de supuestas injurias sociales' (p. 136) and claims that a lot of so-called 'workers' are idlers anyway.

It is unusual for these novelists to describe life in Russia: it is more commonly condemned from afar as 'un país de esclavos' (Pérez y Pérez, *De una España a otra*). In Salazar's *De anarquista a mártir*, however, a whole section of the novel is devoted to a visit to Leningrad. León and Lucía find life there wretched and tyrannical. Deviants are suppressed and in the collectives peasants are whipped. The couple are forced to share a tiny, evil-smelling room with a total stranger, who proceeds to seduce Lucía 'con la despreocupación característica del problema reinante en Rusia'. Although he has to pretend to be poor, this Russian is in fact extremely rich, as he is a member of the secret police (ch. 10). The idea that women are objects of common ownership in a Communist society is echoed in Salazar Allende's *Tú no eres de los nuestros*: 'Entre comunistas, la mujer, como nada que tenga algún valor, puede ser para nadie objeto de propiedad' (p. 78).

The treatment accorded to Anarchists is characterised by similar distortion. The two 'Anarchists' described in *De anarquista a mártir* are intended to represent different aspects of the same fundamental creed; instead they are grotesque caricatures. One of them, Antonio, 'despreciaba el trabajo manual, considerándolo como algo penoso a lo que no debía descender' (p. 10). Inexplicably he believes in a small, ruthless élite which will terrorise the rest of society into submission: 'Extenderemos por el mundo cadenas de hierro y haremos de los hombres ruedas de nuestra máquina de progreso que permitan a una minoría selecta gozar de su triunfo' (p. 39). We are informed by the author that 'millones de pesetas se invertían en propaganda anarquista y centenares de vividores sin escrúpulos cobraban sumas de importancia' (p. 26). Since the CNT had not even been in the habit of collecting for a strike fund, and boasted only one paid official until 1936, this fictional account is very wide of the mark.[41] The collectivisation which was the policy of some – but by no means all – Anarcho-syndicalists is described in *Se ha ocupado el kilómetro 6* (p. 99) as though it is the policy of the Republican Government, when in fact the Government was invariably an ally of the *individualista* and small farmer.[42] Free love is another concept, perhaps because of the inappropriateness of the term, which is misinterpreted by Nationalist novelists; in their lexicon it invariably comes to mean debauchery. In *Checas de Madrid* a pregnant *miliciana*, when asked who the father of her child is, answers: '¿Y yo qué sé quien es? ¿Tú no ibas los domingos al Pardo, cuando los chíbiris? Yo fui con los de mi taller . . . Entre unos y otros me afiliaron a lo del amor libre y cada domingo . . . una chica con un chico diferente. Decían que para acabar con los celos, las ideas burguesas, el hogar: las pamplinas' (p. 79). State education under the Republican Government allegedly includes the showing of pornographic films to children to rid them of sexual inhibition:

– Ahora los niños marxistas, enterados de las funciones sexuales, proceden con alegre improvisación, como quieren.

– Y hay niñas de trece años con hijos. Y todas las niñas . . .

(*Checas de Madrid*, p. 232)

Modesty prevents Borrás from continuing, but the sense is clear enough. Not only the very young but the very old too are encouraged to indulge in illicit sexual practices. The geriatric inmates of the old people's home in Madrid, in *La mascarada trágica*, segregated before the revolution, are brought together when militiamen take over and urged to commit acts of debauchery with each other (p. 42).

The theme of Republican immorality, corruption and perversion is perhaps one of the strongest elements in Nationalist propaganda, arising out of the manichean interpretation of the Civil War, already discussed. That such instances existed, that atrocities on a massive scale did take place is undeniable, and a voluminous literature testifies to it. Marx's view of history was that to a large extent it is the propaganda of the victors; for all the Nationalist novelists writing in Spain during and immediately after the war, the exposure to such propaganda was intense. The scale of the executions taking place in Spain up to 1943 testifies to the atmosphere of recrimination and revenge that must have existed. The decision, on 26 April 1940, to prepare a general indictment of the Second Republic for crimes committed against Spain, is indicative of the prevailing attitude.[43] The resulting catalogue of atrocities committed by one side during the war is to a large extent factually accurate. It reveals the difficulty confronted by the novelist attempting to describe the scale of the horror: nothing, it seems, could be more horrific than the facts themselves. *Checas de Madrid*, though published in 1940, seems inspired by the same sources as those of the *Causa General*. (That such pornography of violence could be published while the literature of contrary ideas was being suppressed, is eloquent testimony to the function of the censor.) Carriedo de Ruiz's *En plena epopeya* contains footnotes indicating that the descriptions are 'rigurosamente exacta(s)': this is because scenes like the one describing 'pobres niños abiertos en canal y colgados de los balcones' (p. 61) are the stuff of nightmares. The torture of the *checas* (*Las dos barajas*, *Los muertos no se cuentan*, *Madrid de Corte a checa*, *Checas de Madrid*), mass killings in the jails (*Los canes andan sueltos*, *Cristo en los infiernos*), the rape of a woman by a whole company of soldiers (*Méndez, cronista de guerra*), and innumerable individual atrocities are to be found in the Nationalist novels. They are included here under the general heading of 'myth creation and reinforcement', not because they did not take place – most of them *did* – but because such violence is attributed solely to the enemy. Like the *Causa General*, most Nationalist novels make no mention of their own side's guilt in the affair.

The perpetrators of the Republican horrors described above are stereotypes. The dominant characteristics of the typical Republican are licentiousness, greed, duplicity, cruelty and vulgarity. A powerful image which symbolises for these Nationalist authors the whole revolutionary movement of the 1930s, is that of those below simply wishing to substitute those above. This appears clearly in *Cristo en los infiernos*, in which a militiaman says of the wealthy middle classes: 'Ahora se ha vuelto la tortilla . . . Nosotros a disfrutar de lo suyo, a hincharnos de comer y de beber en sus palacios, y revolcarnos en sus tumbonas . . . ¿eh? Y ellos a la cochina calle, a trabajar para nosotros . . .' (p. 489). In *Las dos barajas*, Lara reduces the question to one of sex, with which he suggests the revolutionaries could have been bought off: 'El jornalero andaluz sin trabajo, envidiaba al señorito, tanto como el cortijo, las mujeres hermosas que le acompañaban. Y le odió igual por la risa cristalina y la boca fresca de la señorita que iba un día con él a caballo, que por la cosecha de aceitunas. Si a los obreros les hubieran entregado, hasta que se saciaran, las mujeres que deseasen, es dudoso que nunca hubiera habido revolución ni guerra' (p. 173).[44] When the revolution does come, the Republicans are described as living in the lap of luxury, enjoying their ill-gotten gains. *El espantable caso de los 'tomadores' de ciudades*, *Checas de Madrid*, *Las alas invencibles*, *Cristo en los infiernos*, *De anarquista a mártir*, *Navidades sin pan* include such references in abundance.

The image of the illiterate militiaman, first popularised in *El miliciano Remigio pa la guerra es un prodigio* (1937), was to become a stock-in-trade of the Nationalist novelists. As Pérez Bowie has pointed out, the propaganda of the time actively fomented such stereotyping: '(Los) rasgos diferenciales fueron monstruosamente exagerados por la propaganda oficial de cada zona, lográndose así su reducción a unos estereotipos de gran efectividad'.[45] On the Nationalist side, this involved making the Republicans sound uneducated, 'para poner de manifiesto su baja extracción social'.[46] There are powerful examples of such vulgar language in *Checas de Madrid*, *Cuerpo a tierra*, *El espantable caso de los 'tomadores' de ciudades* and other novels. When Republicans requisition her typewriter, in the autobiographical *Esclavitud y libertad*, Concha Espina asks: 'Pero, en el Frente Popular, ¿hay quien sepa escribir?' (p. 87). Two captured Socialists in *La fiel Infantería* display 'cultura de carro de mano' (p. 451); this is not untypical of the contempt shown for the enemy's intellectual level.

Finally, mention ought to be made in this discussion of Nationalist myth creation of the air of superiority which generally characterises Nationalist figures, and the marked xenophobia which frequently accompanies it. Occasionally this finds expression in racism: '[el] puro abolengo racial' of Concha Espina's heroines, mentioned earlier, or '[la] raza sin par en la historia del mundo' of Sepúlveda's *En la gloria de aquel amanecer* (p. 87). More often it is expressed as exalted nationalism, as in José Vicente Puente's *Viudas blancas*:

> Locura, paroxismo, furia y fiebre: Todo y nada
> ¡Español, español, español!
> Un orgullo hasta levantarse la frente
> ¡Nacer en España! Privilegio de Dios.

Since Republicans too are Spanish, this presents the novelist with a difficult paradox to resolve. Manfredi Cano opts for the explanation: '[Los rojos] son españoles de segunda . . . Y nosotros de primerísima' (*Las lomas tienen espinos*, p. 34). Concha Espina too considers Republicans 'seres inferiores' (*Princesas del martirio*, p. 43). With regard to outsiders, few foreigners escape without criticism. As we have seen, German and Italian intervention is almost universally understated. There is praise for Portugal in *Del ruedo a la trinchera*, as 'humanitaria y riente' (p. 177), but Soler believes Spain to be struggling to 'ganar esta guerra contra el mundo entero' (*Los muertos no se cuentan*, p. 197). The French are singled out for particularly harsh treatment in *Se ha ocupado el kilómetro 6*, *Tú no eres de los nuestros*, *Cristo en los infiernos* and *Las lomas tienen espinos*; France and Great Britain receive brickbats in *Checas de Madrid*, *La mascarada trágica* and *Viudas blancas*. The International Brigades are frequently referred to as 'mercenarios', 'la hez de Europa' or 'la escoria internacional'.

The spiritual superiority of the Nationalists overcomes the superiority in arms and men that is often described as a characteristic of the Republican side. Three to four hundred Nationalists hold off 13,000 Republicans in *El espantable caso de los 'tomadores' de ciudades* (p. 56), and 200 face 10,000 in *Las lomas tienen espinos* (p. 169). Twenty thousand 'foreign' troops are described attacking 3,500 Nationalists at Gandesa, in *Se ha ocupado el kilómetro 6* (p. 115), when the reality was that, at this time, 'between the Pyrenees and Teruel, Franco possessed over half a million men under arms'.[47]

As Southworth has demonstrated, 'toda la trama de la sociedad intelectual franquista está tejida con . . . hilos endebles de mentiras y verdades a medias sobre la guerra civil'.[48] I have attempted to demonstrate that the novelist is party to this collective agreement, whether conscious or otherwise, to create a mythology which will both explain the war and sustain the régime of the victors. The 'sociological' and 'irrational' propaganda referred to in an earlier chapter are freely indulged, and probably reflect the fact that the novelists themselves are subjected to intense 'vertical' and 'horizontal' propaganda in the media and the organisations to which they are affiliated. Literature is placed, therefore, at the service of a political cause. The national disaster of 1898 generated much discussion and analysis of 'the problem of Spain'; the events of 1936–39 give rise, not to debate, but to a shrill propaganda war. The rhetoric of Falange, which some found difficult to take seriously in times of peace, seemed highly appropriate to the 'limit situation' Nationalists later found themselves in. The Nietzschean hero, while initially attractive to a genuinely revolutionary minority, had to be clad in the Christian armour of the crusader before he could be projected as a popular hero: the anti-Christ becomes Christ militant. It is interesting to see that, while Spanish Fascism has many points of comparison with its French counterpart, no such virulently anti-Catholic writers as Céline or Rebatat emerge in the Spanish movement.[49] If a truly autonomous Fascist mass movement had developed, Franco's Decree of Unification, merging Carlists and Falangists in 1937, would have been unworkable. Also, in literature we would have seen many more novels like *Eugenio, o proclamación de la Primavera*. The ex-Falangist Dionisio Ridruejo is perhaps the harshest critic of all in denouncing the mythology that the régime created, and artists then propagated, when he lists the various characteristics ('directivas') of the Spanish Fascist movement, the last of which is:

una más bien estética, que hundía sus raíces en el vitalismo nietzscheano, tardíamente como tónico para combatir la depresión de la primera postguerra europea y que desencadenaba entre los jóvenes una especie de neorromanticismo, con la preferencia del vivir apasionado y peligroso sobre el vivir habitual y racionalizado, del acto heroico sobre la ley inteligente y de la compañía de soldados o la parada de masas sobre la asamblea de jurisperitos o el comicio electoral. El cultivo retórico de esta embriaguez de estilo permitiría luego llamar revolución a una operación de policía y, lo que es más grave, vivirla espiritualmente como si lo fuera.[50]

Notes

1 *Nietzsche en España*, p. 650.

2 R. Ledesma Ramos, *El sello de la muerte* (Madrid, 1924), p. 214. The novel was written in 1923, when Ledesma was only 18 years old. It is dedicated to Miguel de Unamuno.

3 *La Conquista del Estado* (Barcelona, 1939), p. 84.

4 *Ibid.*, p. 329.

5 *Nietzsche en España*, p. 658. Sobejano's points are here based on a reading of Ledesma's *Discurso a las juventudes de España*.

6 The word 'imperio' is sometimes used in the normal sense of the term, sometimes in a more general sense: 'Hay muchos espíritus débiles y enclenques que creen que esto del imperio equivale a lanzar ejércitos por las fronteras. No merece la pena desmentir una tontería así. Por de pronto, el imperio sería la idea común que adscribiese a los pueblos hispánicos un compromiso de unidad' (*La Conquista del Estado*, p. 135 (30 May 1931)). This illustrates the obfuscation, presumably deliberate, which characterises much Falangist rhetoric.

7 Giménez Caballero had to resolve a similar conflict. 'Como todos los fascistas españoles, Giménez Caballero, al salvaguardar la fe en Dios, en Cristo, se opone a Nietzsche' (Sobejano, *Nietzsche en España*, p. 652).

8 *La nueva catolicidad*, pp. 127–129. Quoted by Sobejano, *Nietzsche en España*, p. 653.

9 J.A. Pérez Bowie, *El léxico de la muerte durante la Guerra Civil española* (Salamanca, 1983), p. 66.

10 Stanley Payne, *Falange* (Stanford, 1970), pp. 190–191.

11 R. Ledesma Ramos, *Discurso a las juventudes de España* (Madrid, 1935), p. 74.

12 H.R. Southworth, *El mito de la cruzada de Franco* (Paris, 1963). This study does not deal with the Spanish war novelists, however, except for Gironella and (fleetingly) Barea and Aub.

13 H. Thomas, *The Spanish Civil War* (London, 1971), referring to the documents alleging a Communist plot, states 'it seems certain that these were forgeries' (p. 150 footnote 2).

14 See H.R. Southworth, *El mito*, ch. 8, 'Católicos antitotalitarios'. The French Catholics Maritain, Mauriac, Duhamel and Bernanos were vociferous in their condemnation of Nationalist atrocities in the name of religion. There can be little doubt that Nationalists were sensitive to these criticisms and that they redoubled their efforts to give the Civil War the status of a Crusade. This may explain the 'aura of moral purity' cultivated by Falange; as Payne testifies, 'their propaganda differed radically from that of most European fascist groups in its emphasis on Catholicism and Christianity. This religious theme continued to swell as the war progressed.' (*Falange*, p. 127.)

15 Sección Femenina had been set up by Falange in 1934 and numbered 580,000 members by the end of the war. Auxilio Social was set up in the first year of the war to incorporate women formally in the war effort. In the latter part of the war, unmarried women were compulsorily required to serve in these organisations (Payne, *Falange*, p. 203).

16 J.C. Mainer, *Falange y literatura* (Barcelona, 1971), p. 37.

17 Cf. the hands of the aristocratic Francisco de Borja, in *Camisa azul*: 'Isidro ríe con risa ingenua y sana, mientras el hijo de duques y hermano de marquesitas rubias le pone sobre el hombro su mano fina con un sello de oro en el que hay grabados escudos y cimeras' (p. 160).

18 Concha Espina's admiration for the breeding of her heroines is perhaps explained by her own noble lineage. A friend of Alfonso XIII, she was born of the Casa de los Tagle, of Santillana del Mar. See Josefina de la Maza, *Vida de mi madre, Concha Espina* (Alcoy, 1957).

19 E. de Nora, *La novela española contemporánea*, 1, p. 341.

20 H. Thomas, *The Spanish Civil War*, p. 226.

21 G. Jackson, *The Spanish Republic and the Civil War* (Princeton, 1965), pp. 533–534.

22 *Ibid.*, p. 269.

23 The estimate of 'Red' prisoner deaths through execution or disease between 1939 and 1943 is 200,000. See *ibid.*, p. 539. In fairness to the Nationalists, it must be said that Jackson's figures are challenged by R. Salas Larrazábal, in his well-documented *Pérdidas de la guerra* (Barcelona, 1977).

24 H. Thomas, *The Spanish Civil War*, p. 223.

25 In Badajoz, Franco had to issue an order restraining Moors from castrating the bodies of their victims – 'an established Moorish battle-rite' (H. Thomas, *ibid.*, p. 319 footnote).

26 'The Guadalajara attack was undertaken on the right by . . . 20,000 legionaries, Moroccans and some Carlists. On the left 30,000 Italians . . .' (H. Thomas, *ibid.*, p. 495).

27 F. Borkenau, *The Spanish Cockpit* (Michigan, 1963), p. 224. Borkenau was an eye-witness of the Málaga campaign.

28 Ruiz-Ayúcar fought in the *Flechas Negras* side by side with Italian troops. In personal conversations he has spoken with considerable sarcasm of the lack of commitment of the Italians.

29 According to J. Coverdale, as early as 31 July 1936 'newspapers around the world published on the front page the news that the Italian government was providing aid to the Spanish rebels' (*Italian Intervention in the Spanish Civil War* (Princeton, 1975), p. 4).

30 J.L.S. Ponce de León, *La novela española de la guerra civil* (Madrid, 1971), p. 49.

31 León's Spain is one in which property relationships would remain essentially unchanged (*Cristo en los infiernos*, 176), so his Arcadian dream, in practice, means little more than a return to the pre-war situation.

32 When militiamen searched Concha Espina's house at Luzmela they failed to find the family's shot-gun. Espina's daughter, in a biography of her mother, attributes this to divine intervention: 'De seguro un ángel la escondió entre sus grandes alas . . . Sí, sin duda ángeles andaban por la casa . . .' (Josefina de la Maza, *Vida de mi madre, Concha Espina*, p. 197).

33 H.R. Southworth, *Antifalange* (Paris, 1967), p. 33.

34 M. García Venero, *Falange en la guerra de España* (Paris, 1967), p. 323.

35 Quoted in H.R. Southworth, *Antifalange*, p. 35. Advertisements in the same journal announced the publication, by the Jesuit publishers Ediciones Rayfe, of *Los protocolos de los sabios de Sión*.

36 Quoted in G. Jackson, *The Spanish Republic*, p. 386.

37 Margarita Nelken, initially a left-wing Socialist deputy for Badajoz, joined the Communist Party in 1937. She was a champion of agrarian reform.

38 H. Thomas, *The Spanish Civil War*, p. 47 footnote.

39 *Ibid.*, p. 245.

40 *Ibid.*, p. 551.

41 *Ibid.*, p. 65. During the war itself ruthless individuals and criminal elements undoubtedly used requisitions and expropriations for their own advantage, but this did not reflect the ethos or morality of the Anarcho-syndicalist movement in general.

42 See H. Thomas, *The Spanish Civil War*, ch. 44, for a full discussion of collectivisation, which was a result of social revolution, rather than Government policy, in 1936.

43 Ministerio de Justicia, *Causa General: La dominación roja en España* (Madrid, 1943).

44 Gironella repeats this idea in *Un millón de muertos*, in which a character 'se vengaba, al igual de José Alvear, de las muchas mujeres burguesas que desde su fealtad física y su escasa educación había amado en vano' (p. 341).

The relationship between revolution and sexuality had also been explored by one of Koestler's acquaintances in Berlin, a certain Dr Reich. 'He was a Freudian Marxist; inspired by Malinovsky, he had just published a book called *The Function of the Orgasm* in which he expounded the theory that the sexual frustration of the proletariat caused a thwarting of its political consciousness; only through a full uninhibited release of the sexual urge could the working class realise its revolutionary potentialities and historic mission' (*The God that Failed* (London, 1950), p. 43).

45 J.A. Pérez Bowie, *El léxico de la muerte*, p. 36.
46 *Ibid.*, p. 49.
47 H. Thomas, *The Spanish Civil War*, p. 690.
48 H.R. Southworth, *El mito*, p. 6.
49 Paul Sérant, *Le Romantisme fasciste* (Paris, 1959), ch. 5.
50 Dionisio Ridruejo, *Escrito en España* (Buenos Aires, 1962), p. 79.

5
–

Commitment
and propaganda
in the Republican novel

THE NOVEL of the Left differs from the novel of the Right in that its social commitment stems from a body of theory, namely Marxist dialectic. The doctrine of Socialist realism promulgated at the Soviet Writers' Congress of 1934 inevitably made its influence felt in left-wing circles in Spain, as in the rest of Europe. As Edmund Wilson has indicated, however, such an attempt to legislate masterpieces into existence was doomed to failure.[1] The relationship of the 'superstructure' of higher activities which Marx identified: politics, law, religion, philosophy, literature and art, to the economic base and its methods of production in a given time and place, is a complex one. It is an oversimplification to believe that the economic base is the sole active cause and everything else a mere passive effect. Indeed Engels argued that there is a reciprocal interaction between these elements, so that literature may influence the life of a period down to its very economic foundations. As is well known, Marx loved Shakespeare, and both Marx and Engels admired Goethe and Balzac. Neither saw art simply as a weapon. Trotsky rejected the idea of proletarian literature and culture and considered them dangerous because 'they erroneously compress the culture of the future into the narrow limits of the present day'. The proletarian dictatorship was not after all a lasting phenomenon, but a transitional phase leading to a culture which would be above classes, a truly human culture. This is not to deny, of course, that works of art can be weapons. In a sense the *Divine Comedy* was a weapon for Henry of Luxembourg, whom Dante was eager to impose on his countrymen. Shakespeare's *Henry IV* and *Henry V* may be seen as instruments of Elizabethan imperialism, but they are also weapons in the deeper sense in the struggle of modern European man emerging from the Middle Ages and striving to understand the world and himself. Wilson writes:

The truth is that there is short-range and long-range literature. Short-range literature preaches and pamphleteers with the view to an immediate effect. A great deal of the recent confusion of our writers in the Leftist camp has been due to their not understanding or being unable to make up their minds whether they are aiming at long-range or short-range writing.[2]

He concludes that because of this confusion, revolutionary periods are not the most favourable for producing works of art. The French Revolution gave us only the orations of Danton, the journalism of Camille Desmoulins and a few political poems by André Chénier. The Russian Revolution produced the political writing of Lenin and Trotsky and the poetry of Alexander Blok.

It is impossible therefore to identify the highest creative work in art with the most active moments of creative social change. The writer who is intent on producing long-range works of literature should . . . thank his stars if there is no violent revolution going on in his country in his time. He may disapprove of the society he is writing about, but if it were disrupted by an actual upheaval he would probably not be able to write.[3]

But write these Spanish novelists did, many of them putting their art at the service of the Republican cause. Just three months before the war broke out, Ramón Sender published a canonical text in the Marxist-Leninist politico-literary review *Leviatán*, in which he defined the role of the committed artist. In doing so he made a ferocious attack on previous generations of writers who devoted themselves to 'describir lo importante que era el amor metafísico con ropa interior de seda, a desmenuzar el mito de la muerte, a divulgar las complejidades morales del adulterio y a exaltar entre la pequeña burguesía un tono de vida preocupado por futilezas de forma'.[4] Sender calls for the application of what he terms the 'principio vital', the dynamic force which emanates from the working class:

Los mismos burgueses, al llamar arte social a nuestras obras, confirman, sin quererlo, varias cosas: primero, que nuestra literatura tiene una actitud positiva en la vida. Segundo, que esa actitud es beneficiosa para los hombres; que si se identifica con la ideología de los trabajadores, es porque solamente en ella está vivo el sentimiento desinteresado de la humanidad.[5]

He goes on to elaborate on an idea he says was put to him by Valle-Inclán. The replacement of the feudal system by the bourgeoisie produced great literature: Cervantes, Molière, Shakespeare; the replacement of the bourgeoisie by the proletariat will similarly produce writers of genius. (It is interesting to note that Sender does not quote examples closer to hand, say, in recent Russian history, where precisely such a social revolution took place. Failure to find such examples would bear out Edmund Wilson's analysis, mentioned above.) At all events it is impossible, Sender maintains, for the novelist to ignore the working class any longer:

La posición del novelista ante las masas es el gran problema de la novela de hoy. Ya sabemos que no es posible una labor de creación de espaldas a ellas. En ellas está el principio activo, como está el 'radium' en las canteras de mineral. La labor del genio, del novelista genial de nuestro campo, que saldrá un día, será aislar ese principio y acondicionarlo establemente en sus obras.[6]

Few Spanish writers reflect more clearly than Sender during this his most pro-Communist period the influence of the decisions taken at the Soviet Writers' Congress two years earlier. Fundamental to this concept of literature is that it must not be neutral, and that it must serve the cause of progress as defined in the Marxist dialectic. This makes it quite unlike earlier literary forms, even though there may be superficial similarities:

Lo que diferencia el realismo burgués del nuestro es que nosotros vemos la realidad dialécticamente y no idealmente. Nuestro realismo no es sólo analítico y crítico, como el de los naturalistas, sino que parte de una concepción dinámica y no estática de la realidad. Nuestra realidad, con la que no estamos satisfechos sino en cuanto forma parte dinámica de un proceso en cambio y avance constante, no es estática ni produce en nosotros la ilusión de la contemplación neutra.[7]

As we shall see, Sender was to move away from this position in his post-war writing: what is significant is that this was the stance of a left-wing intellectual on the eve of the Civil War, anticipating in literature the abandonment of neutrality that was soon to affect all Spaniards in their daily lives.[8] Sender had, of course, already spent many years involved in left-wing activities. An ardent admirer of Kropotkin at the age of 14, he was encouraged to read libertarian tracts by the Anarchist Angel Checa, who prepared the rising in the Zaragoza barracks in 1920 and later met a violent death. Sender was imprisoned for several months in 1927 for his political activities; he was a member of the CNT and of a small Anarchist circle of seven members known as 'Espartaco'. He describes the demands he put to Alcalá Zamora (at that time the chairman of a Republican committee) in 1930 on behalf of the workers' movement: 'Yo representaba algunos grupos de acción. Solíamos ponerle condiciones en nombre de los sindicatos y teníamos con él autoridad porque éramos los que hacíamos las cosas.'[9] He collaborated with a number of Anarchist newspapers, including *Solidaridad Obrera* and *La Libertad*, and later edited the Communist newspaper, *La*

Lucha. As Marra-López points out, referring to this pre-war phase, 'casi toda su obra en este tiempo es un magnífico reportaje, animado por una doble intención: testimonio de su tiempo y conciencia revolucionaria'.[10] Of his Civil War works, *Contraataque* is the most overtly political, attempting as it does to convince the outside world that the war is being waged in the defence of liberal, bourgeois democracy.[11] The Communist Party is not interested in establishing a dictatorship of the proletariat:

Aplastar el feudalismo y a la Iglesia como órgano de la casta feudal, no representaba llevar el esfuerzo tan lejos como para implantar la dictadura del proletariado, ni aun en el caso de que ese aplastamiento fuera obra de los obreros y los campesinos, como tenía que ser, según había predicho el Partido Comunista Español, que acertó de lleno.   (*Contraataque*, p. 11)

This point, together with a justification of the execution of Fascists behind the lines, is the basic propaganda message of the work and is repeated a number of times. As a writer and combatant, he is aware of the ambivalence of his role in the war; during a visit to a writers' organisation in Madrid, he expresses contempt for the armchair participants in the war who appear neither to write nor fight:

Los había visto tantas veces en tantos lugares que habían entrado en la categoría de esos *desconocidos familiares* que llegan a pesar en la vida de uno. Solían estar en los escenarios de los teatros, sin ser actores ni autores; en los centros de escritores, sin escribir; en los cenáculos de pintores, sin pintar. Como diletantes en todas partes, yo esperaba haberlos visto también en las trincheras, aunque no disparaban; pero ahí fallaba su *snobismo*.   (p. 73)[12]

The atmosphere in this unnamed organisation of writers contrasts strongly with that described in the offices of Cultura Popular, described later. This latter group had requisitioned a *palacio* in the Calle de Sacramento which was a hive of activity, organising dispatches of newspapers, films, theatre groups and travelling libraries to the front and the rearguard. Sender comments: 'Yo me sentía muy a gusto en aquel ambiente, que representaba bastante bien mi manera de ver la cultura' (p. 103). Considered a writer by the soldiers at the front, he is seen as a soldier by those working in Cultura Popular. The difficulty of producing 'long-range' literature under these conditions is hinted at in his definition of *Contraataque* as 'recuerdos, escritos velozmente, sin propósitos de composición literaria' (p. 301).[13] Ten years are to pass before Sender returns to the theme of the war in *El rey y la reina*, a theme which is skilfully interwoven with that of personal idealism in the form of Rómulo's pursuit of the absolute.

In the larger social scene represented by the war, Rómulo imagines that the soldiers, too, are fighting 'to get back to their past, their lost lives.' Rómulo [Sender] means the deformation of their true humanity by an unjust and twisted social organisation as well as by their ignoble choice to serve the interests of the temporal 'person' at the expense of the human species and of their own dimension towards the eternal, their 'essential selves,' *hombría*. Indirectly then – through an implied parallel between Rómulo and the Spanish masses, – the novel is a commentary on the Civil War.[14]

In *Mosén Millán* (later to be retitled *Réquiem por un campesino español*), published in 1953, Sender is more involved in the social and political issues but avoids the direct statement of his position we find in *Contraataque*. Commitment here takes the form of presenting the facts in such a way that the reader comes to the conclusion that in the Civil War the proletariat fell victim to an alliance between the greedy possessing classes and a subservient Church. Peñuelas is at pains to point out that this conclusion is no longer the result of a political conviction on the part of the author but arises naturally from the events he describes:

El símbolo y la tesis aparecen indirectamente, de forma implícita, como una consecuencia que se desprende sola, y algo al margen, de los hechos narrados . . . En ningún caso el símbolo y la tesis aparecen como encarnación dialéctica de teorías abstractas.[15]

This raises the issue of the extent to which commitment involves supplying the answers as well as the questions. There is no doubt that Sender has moved away from his avowed Communism, in *Contraataque*,[16] and as we shall see later there is profound disillusionment in *Los cinco libros de Ariadna* at the unscrupulous conduct of the Communists in the war; nevertheless, his definition of the problems remains as rigorous as ever in *Réquiem por un campesino español*, as does his condemnation of the enemies of the people. To that extent, it is a committed work.

The importance of relating literature to class consciousness at a time of social upheaval is illustrated in an episode in M.T. León's *Juego limpio*. Camilo, the priest, while recuperating in a Republican hospital after being wounded in a Nationalist attack, is given the job of reading aloud to soldiers who have lost their sight. By chance he chooses a story by Gorky, and discovers that this strikes a chord with these men, who henceforth will not accept readings from any other author. He realises it is because Gorky describes a world of injustice which has been swept away by the revolution: '¡Esa miseria está barrida y nace en esa Rusia que parecía de estiércol un mundo distinto!' (p. 27). No Spanish writer can capture their imagination in the same way, because none has emerged to plead the cause of the proletariat so eloquently: 'Máximo Gorki estaba más cerca de mis muchachos hablándoles de sus mujiks apaleados, que cualquier autor de buena lengua castellana' (p. 28).

Max Aub, too, speaks of injustice, but his commitment is not that of a Communist. He peoples his magic labyrinth of novels and short stories with intelligent characters who, though they support the Republican cause (in most cases), seek a variety of solutions to the problems posed. Much of the thought-provoking political material of the novels is to be found in the intellectual discussions between the main characters: Templado, the Socialist who disagrees with the Communists but admires their discipline and decency; Rivadavia, the Atheist and Liberal-Democrat; Herrera, the Communist army captain; Cuartero, the Catholic, and so on. Although Templado is seen by some to be nearest to Aub himself in his political beliefs, many other points of view receive a fair hearing. Aub's commitment is not based on narrow party loyalty: 'Su compromiso es con la realidad más amplia y no sólo con una causa determinada.'[17] He shows in the conversation between Laparra and Lugones in *Campo abierto* that he is aware of the Leninist definition of literature as 'una parte ínfima, una ruedecilla, un pequeño tornillo del gran mecanismo del partido'; but he makes Laparra say:

Eso no puede satisfacer a un escritor, a un pintor, a un músico, a menos que deje de serlo y venga a convertirse en comunista, es decir: que se decida a sacrificar lo suyo en pro de la construcción de un mundo nuevo. (p. 376)

A similar discussion occurs later in the same novel between Gorov (a combination of Ehrenburg and Koltzov, in reality) and Templado, when the latter expresses concern about maintaining the quality of literature when it is put to social use:

La calidad ¿para quién? – cortó Gorov – ¿Para las minorías selectas? No, compañero. La calidad ya vendrá después, si viene. Se puede sacrificar en pro de un mundo nuevo, de un hombre medio nuevo, de un hombre general. Las exquisiteces tuvieron su tiempo. (p. 453)

Aub himself is caught on the horns of this dilemma. Like Francisco Ayala, he was nurtured in the school of dehumanised art in an age heavily influenced by Ortega. Like Ayala, he was transformed by the experience of 1936–39 and its aftermath. As Ricardo Doménech has shown, the work which marks the turning point in his consciousness is the short play *Pedro López García* (1936), the story of a shepherd's gradual awakening to the significance of social revolution – a theme similar to the one he later explored in the short story 'El Cojo'. Aub sees the need to place his art at the service of the Republic, but unlike younger writers is already conditioned to write in a certain way:

Consciente de la necesidad de un determinado teatro, exigido por las circunstancias, el autor ha de echar mano del único cauce expresivo que tiene a su alcance: un cauce expresivo de factura simbolista, producto de los sutiles años gongorinos. Vemos librada así, en el seno mismo de esta obra, una de las batallas de pensamiento más importantes de nuestra época: la entablada entre un arte irracionalista y un arte racionalista, entre las 'bocanadas de ensueño' y el 'retorno a la objetividad,' por un lado, y a la fraternidad, por el otro.[18]

Aub inveighs against Ortega for having persuaded a whole generation to turn their backs on popular culture, and to behave irresponsibly: 'Considerada la creación como juego, pierde el escritor todo sentido de responsabilidad.'[19] It follows that if the intellectual class is irresponsible and does not communicate with the people (*pueblo*), the latter will have scant regard for art in any of its forms; an anonymous character in *Campo abierto* says:

¿Cómo quieres que respeten lo que nadie les ha enseñado a respetar? ¿Qué es un Greco, para un hurdano, más que la muestra de lo más inútil que ha producido un mundo que lo ha tenido hundido en la basura? Y quema, y roba, y mata. Y tiene razón. Su razón. (p. 369)

Aub must be aware of the fact that his own work is, for the most part, just as inaccesible to the Spanish working class as the art of El Greco. His aim will be not to influence this class directly but to raise the consciousness of the reading public of its social predicament.[20] To Aub's credit, he does so without resorting to propaganda, except in a few cases (e.g. some of the stories in *No son cuentos*). Soldevila gives an example of his attention to historical fact: he was concerned to correct a detail in the second edition of *Campo del Moro* when he read that 'Ercoli' (Togliatti) was *not* present when the Negrín Government met for the last time.[21] There are also whole sections (e.g. p. 124) in this same novel which are slabs of history unrelated to the main narrative, in which the author takes the opportunity of commenting upon historical characters and events which have come to mind. Don Leandro's digression in *Campo de sangre*, occupying almost 50 pages, is a dramatic example of the technique, which takes us on this occasion to Spain's more distant past. *El laberinto mágico* is a blend of private and national tragedy, a labyrinth in which chaos often reigns, but where the author himself is guided by 'un idéal socialiste de foi en un monde où s'épanouiraient justice et liberté et qui serait enfin, et pour cela même, à la mesure de l'homme'.[22] For some critics there is too much discussion of politics.[23] For others, 'a lack of historical intent'.[24] Soldevila strikes the correct balance, I think, in finding dramatic quality in the conflict between personal and political worlds, 'le déchirement des êtres partagés entre leurs liens affectifs et leur engagement politique'.[25]

It would be fair to say that many novelists who write on the war are characterised by their concern for historical truth. The truth of the novelist will rarely satisfy objective criteria, however. What matters is that there is not deliberate or wilful distortion, even where there may well be political commitment. One of Aub's characters says: 'Si cualquiera se atreve a levantarse y exclamar: "Voy a decir la verdad," consiste en decir horrores de sus enemigos' (*Campo abierto*, p. 500). Aub's Socialism does not deprive him of that 'sinceridad de artista que sabe desligarse de sus convicciones políticas para atender exclusivamente a la verdad'.[26]

Arturo Barea, at first sight, seems an unlikely candidate to be an honest exponent of the Civil War: he was employed for some time in the Press and Propaganda Section of the Ministry of State in Madrid, with responsibility for censoring telegrams and other communications by foreign journalists. Having been persuaded by his early upbringing, his job in a bank and military service in Morocco that Spanish society was essentially unjust, he became a militant Socialist. There is no doubt that his political beliefs coloured his writing; what is admirable in *La forja de un rebelde*, however, is his 'tierna y áspera sinceridad apasionada'.[27] (The passion and sincerity of Barea's commitment is, perhaps inevitably, not always admired by critics of the Right.)[28] 'Escribir era para mí', writes Barea, 'parte de la lucha, parte de nuestra guerra contra la vida y la muerte, y no sólo una expresión de mí mismo' (p. 797). His commitment is disguised in the early section of the trilogy, in the description of his upbringing in Avapiés, by the technique of reporting events through the eyes of a child, without comment; as he grows older, his description of the 'explotación sistemática' of his class becomes explicit; he comes to recognise the value of trade unionism and political action. Just as Aub, of foreign parentage, was in some senses an outsider trying to identify with the Spanish working class, so Barea, son of a laundress but educated with the children of the well-to-do middle class, seems to be seeking a class identity. The Civil War offers him the opportunity of putting his talents at the service of the class with which he identifies emotionally and to which he considers he owes allegiance. He is not blind, however, to the mistakes committed during the Civil War, nor to the irresponsibility of the lumpenproletariat in the first days of the revolution (*La llama*, ch. 8); he attempts to give a truthful account: 'En su versión de la guerra española, no hay arenga política; la prédica partidaria . . . se sustituye por la directa exposición de los hechos. El narrador parece aguardar que de esos hechos se desprenda la prédica y luego, de esa prédica, la convicción.'[29] 'Rehuye todo partidismo unilateral, una vez sentada su actitud democrática de militante obrerista.'[30] The version given of the war by Hemingway, although sympathetic to the Republic, comes in for heavy criticism from Barea because of its lack of truth: 'He falsifies most plausibly the causes and the actual form of the tragic violence of my people.'[31] What Barea seems to miss most is the class identity of Hemingway's characters, the description of their roots: 'Even the genuine characters are curiously detached from their background. One never quite knows why they fight for the Republic . . .'[32] It is significant that Barea, like Ayala, stresses authenticity more than commitment to the Republican cause. It may be that he takes the latter for granted in Hemingway, but clearly commitment alone is not enough if it falsifies reality. Benedetti contrasts the attitude of Barea with that of Koestler in this respect:

Scum of the Earth, por ejemplo, es el libro de un marxista que, además, es un hombre corriente; *La forja de un rebelde*, en cambio, es la obra de un hombre corriente que por añadidura es un marxista. En Barea la actitud política no es lo principal; lo principal es la actitud del hombre. Naturalmente, éste como marxista no es un arquetipo, porque llegado el instante crucial no actúa de acuerdo a la línea partidaria sino a lo que a sí mismo se aconseja.[33]

After the war was ended, Barea (like Aub and Sender) remained a fervent critic of injustice and a believer in the correctness of the Republican cause. He is also (like them) prepared to concede that political commitment alone is not enough. The political cause itself has been defeated for the time being but the social situation which engendered it remains. These novelists are reluctant to propose specific political remedies but continue in their diagnosis of a chronic disorder. Of Barea, one critic writes:

Desde su alienación social y personal buscó el novelista lo ético en principios socio-políticos que según él podían restaurar la dignidad del hombre. La catástrofe de la guerra civil y la derrota que ésta supuso para Barea desde el punto de vista moral determinaron una nueva valoración más general y absoluta de la condición humana.[34]

The dignity of man referred to here was vitiated by the social injustice to which large numbers of Spaniards were subjected. A major theme of the Republican novelists is the division that exists between the social classes. According to Borkenau this was a symptom of the sickness of a declining social order:

Spain is the country where the spontaneity of the 'people' as against the aristocracy, the bourgeoisie, the intelligentsia, and, in the last decades, the clergy, is most conspicuous. Such a deep severance of the people from ruling groups, such a passing of the initiative to the lowest stratum of society, is always a symptom of deep decay and disintegration of an old civilization.[35]

Class antagonism was particularly sharply felt in the rural areas of Spain where agrarian conflict has been described by one historian as 'the most crucial of those several component confrontations within the civil war'.[36] The intransigence of the landlords in southern Spain drove the peasants to a state of desperation, which often ended in violence. The moderate reformism of the PSOE under the Republic infuriated many of them. Membership of the Federación Nacional de Trabajadores de la Tierra, founded in 1930, had reached almost 400,000 only two years later, and at the same time the proportion of rural labourers in the UGT had reached 38 per cent. In retrospect, this degree of political activity may be seen as the last attempt to achieve redistribution of wealth in these areas by political means. The Republican Government had tried to meet the demands of the labourers by introducing a number of moderate reforms. By preventing the hiring of outside labour while local labour in a given municipality remained unemployed, the law of municipal boundaries (términos municipales) effectively deprived landowners of one of their most effective weapons: the importing of cheap labour to break a strike. By setting up arbitration committees (jurados mixtos), the Government gave the braceros a machinery for negotiation. An eight-hour working day was introduced, which meant that labourers working the traditional day of sunrise to sunset became entitled to a good deal of overtime. Another law of compulsory cultivation (laboreo forzoso) prevented the landowners from starving out the labourers by refusing to work the land. The tactics of the Right, however (particularly through the Asociación Católica Nacional de Propagandistas and its electoral organisation, Acción Nacional), soon showed 'the futility of moderate reformism in the face of latifundista intransigence'.[37] Civil governors often connived with local landowners and the Civil Guard to prevent social legislation being applied. Lock-outs in rural estates became commonplace. During the bienio negro of 1934–35, when the Right gained control, agrarian reform fell into abeyance and the little that had been achieved was largely undone. For all the good intentions of the Republic, 'conditions . . . were in 1936 much the same as they had been since the *Reconquista*, or even the Romans'.[38]

There is no better literary expression of the problem to be found in the authors under study than in Aub's short story 'El Cojo'.[39] The main character, 'El Cojo', is offered a tenancy by a local landowner he meets by chance in a brothel in Motril. 'Aquella mañana había rechazado con mal humor el arriendo de aquella casucha, sus viñedos y sus cañaverales a varios campesinos a quienes debía algunos favores electorales, pero ahora con el calor del alcohol . . .' (p. 19). The landowner is not accountable in society for his actions; his capricious behaviour may mean starvation for several families, but no matter. El Cojo agrees to cultivate the land, 'para el amo, como era natural' (p. 16). When the Civil War breaks out, Socialists and Communists share out the land to the workers; the word 'natural' acquires a quite different meaning, associated this time with natural justice rather than with convention: 'Tú eres un obrero, has trabajado bien esa tierra, es natural que te corresponda, ¿comprendes?' (p. 27). The growing awareness of the peasant that this land is no longer a parched, cruel landscape, but something with the potential to feed himself and his family and allow them to live in dignity, forms the basis of the story. The approaching Nationalist army, described significantly as 'algo antinatural' (p. 38), is not enough to frighten El Cojo, who has gained in moral stature since becoming his own master – in a spirit of fraternity, nonetheless, with the other peasants in the area. When his daughter Rafaela is machine-gunned from the air by Nationalist planes on the Málaga road, she gives birth before she dies to the child who will surely carry on the struggle which is lost for the time being. El Cojo, facing almost certain death as he waits to do unequal battle with the Nationalist forces, is at one with the world and inseparably bonded, now, to the earth he has tilled all his life: 'El Cojo se enriscaba en la tierra, sentía su cintura y su vientre y sus muslos descansar en el suelo, y su codo izquierdo hundido en la tierra roja' (p. 46).

Life in an Aragonese village during these same months is the subject of Arana's *El cura de Almuniaced*, and here the unconventional priest, Mosén Jacinto, attempts to bridge the gap between the oligarchy (*fuerzas vivas*) and the working class. Stripping away conservative convention, he reveals the hypocrisy of the so-called 'gente decente' and their 'buenas costumbres.' The village money-lender, don Froilán, is a case in point: 'Para don Froilán, las buenas costumbres eran prestar al treinta por ciento; tener jornaleros por dos pesetas cuando la siembra y la recolección, disponer de los votos y hacer mangas y capirotes en el Ayuntamiento' (p. 18). The Republic awakens hope, however, in the land-labourers: 'Ya no tenían aquel gesto resignado y mustio, aquella opacidad y lejanía que le hacían verlos como sombras. Hablaban ahora de reparto de tierras, de crédito . . . Al caer la tarde los veía pasar hacia "el sindicato" charlando animadamente . . .' (pp. 21–22). Mosén Jacinto is a hard-working priest, not afraid to roll up his cassock and work in the fields if need be, and he even lends money interest-free to the peasants if they cannot afford to buy seed to sow. Such priests, as we will see in a later section, are uncommon in the Republican novel. Not surprisingly, he is left unharmed by the revolution, and he dies, symbolically, at the hands of a Moorish soldier, a victim of the counter-revolution.

Martínez Pagán, in *Génaro*, describes the fleeing refugees making their way through Catalonia as peasants exploited by the landowners. With heavy irony, he writes: 'Oui, ils étaient méchants. Ils voulaient la parcelle de terre que pendant tant d'années ils avaient arrosée de leur sueur . . . Ils voulaient vivre: ils avaient la nausée de leur misère' (p. 235). Referring to the custom of the absentee landlord, he commiserates with 'des paysans qui devaient payer la dîme à un maître inconnu qui vivait là-bas à Barcelone' (p. 237). One of the scourges of rural Spain, the absentee landlord was indirectly responsible for the system of *caciquismo* on which so much political corruption was based.[40]

Typical of the landowning classes as seen by the Republican novelist is doña Mañolita, in Cimorra's *El bloqueo del hombre*. The action takes place in the Castilian village of Cabezuela de la Jara, in which doña Mañolita is the local landowner. During the *bienio negro* she reigns supreme, getting the free-thinking village teacher dismissed by suggesting she had taught her girls the doctrine of free love. Because one of her labourers is seen in the teacher's company, she dismisses him too, along with his two brothers. When the Popular Front wins the elections of February 1936, however, the brothers are given a small plot of land by the landowner, out of fear of reprisals. What is more, the schoolmistress is reinstated. As in other cases, this *fuerza viva* is revealed to be nasty, vengeful, capricious and hypocritical, smashing the effigies of her saints when they do not heed her prayers.

As we have seen, Sender, during his Communist phase, interprets the social question as a struggle between progress and the forces of feudalism which survive in Spain despite their evident anachronism. The claim of the extreme Right that they represent revolutionary change elicits an angry response: *Réquiem por un campesino español* is described as 'el esquema de toda la guerra civil nuestra, donde unas gentes que se consideraban revolucionarias lo único que hicieron fue defender los derechos feudales de una tradición ya periclitada en el resto del mundo'.[41] Doubtless for the same reason, in *Los cinco libros de Ariadna*, he is able to differentiate between the two forms of class violence exercised by the Republicans and the Nationalists (here termed 'moruecos'), respectively:

Los moruecos mataban por salvar sus privilegios. Los nuestros mataban por principios . . . Mataban para tener escuelas, lugares de trabajo más cómodos y para evitar que los ricos haciéndose más ricos empujaran todavía los pobres hacia abajo. Mataban por principios morales y pensando en el futuro más que en el presente. En el campo contrario había gente de principios también, pero de momento querían salvar sus cuentas corrientes, sus dividendos, la mano de obra barata, los criados con salarios bajos y los privilegios, añadiendo a ellos los que confiere la sangre del enemigo, vertida.   (p. 278)

One of the representatives of this caste in the same novel is Lucero del Alba, a magnificent creation as the twisted caricature of a Spanish nobleman. On the famous train journey, he brings Ariadna to his carriage to accompany him as she is a 'persona decente'. His language is characterised by frequent references to honour and justice, authority and hierarchy, 'mando' and 'imperio'. (He is in favour of annexing Portugal (p. 208).) When the Carlists stop the train and demand to be allowed to shoot the prisoners, Lucero del Alba offers them his wife instead. The arrogance of this class, as perceived by Sender, is summed up when Lucero del Alba complains: 'Hoy no me encuentro bien. No es que esté enfermo, pero no me siento a gusto dentro de mi piel. No me siento bastante petulante' (p. 193). When he realises he is safe from any reaction on the part of his victim, he confides later: 'Voy recuperando poco a poco mi fachenda y mi arrogancia de clase' (p. 196). Despite his pretensions to seriousness, Lucero del Alba is a ridiculous character. It is he who constantly draws attention to the 'gran epígono, cabeza de linaje, honra de la raza' (Franco) whose emaciated body lives on stubbornly beneath his statue in the Campo de Marte: for his constant interruptions, he is expelled from the OMECC assembly in which much of the novel's action unfolds. A pompous figure, he is later caught unawares by a burst of steam from the train at the very moment of offering himself to Ariadna so that she can become pregnant in order to avoid execution. Once on the train, his secret orders blow out of the window. Even his physical gestures are revealing: 'Maniobraba en diferentes bolsillos en busca de cerillas con gestos atléticos como si fuera más grande de lo que era' (p. 207). Lucero del Alba represents that feudal caste which has not yet realised that it has outlived its usefulness, and while striving to appear dignified and honourable, in reality is neither. 'Imaginando el mundo gobernado por hombres como (él),' says Ariadna, 'yo no podía menos que sentir ganas de reír' (p. 209).

Sender often intimates that the days of this class are numbered. In *Contraataque* an old militiaman explains that progress is inevitable: all social upheavals lead to gains by the working class; he suggests that by this 'ratchet effect' humanity progresses inexorably:

> – ¿Qué pasó en la guerra europea? Yo, cuando vi lo que hacían los alemanes, dije: 'No puede ser; perderán.' ¿Qué pasó luego? Que perdieron y que los barones y los grandes capitalistas se arruinaron, y los trabajadores ganaron jornales mejores y subieron en la escala social. Nadie pudo evitarlo. En Francia, en Inglaterra, en todas partes, después de una racha de sangre y de codicia, quiéranlo o no, la vida se afirma más en lo justo. Los que no comían, comen.   (p. 253)

Sender traces his preoccupation with social questions to the day when, at the age of seven, in the company of a priest, he visited a dying man in a cave near his home. The episode is included in *Réquiem por un campesino español*. Referring to this event many years later, in one of his conversations with Peñuelas, Sender comments: 'Creo que condicionó toda mi vida.'[42] The description of the imaginary village of *Réquiem* and of the alliance of social forces which brings about the death of Paco el del Molino, is carried out with great skill: Don Valeriano, the administrator of the Duke – the local absentee landlord – and two other local dignitaries are the only members of the congregation at the requiem mass held for Paco after his assassination by the Nationalists. The tragedy revolves around the question of agrarian reform: the Duke rents out pasture land to six villages in the area; when the Republic arrives, these rights are transferred to the village council, to which Paco is elected. 'Se decía que con el arriendo de pastos, cuyo dinero iba al municipio, se hacían planes para mejorar la vida de la aldea' (p. 61). When the Civil War breaks out the *pistoleros* of the oligarchy wreak terrible revenge on the village, killing men savagely and later machine-gunning the women. Don Valeriano, the ex-*cacique*, is installed as mayor and the reforms are halted. The people living in caves nearby, it is suggested, will have to wait a lot longer for an improvement in their conditions of life.

El rey y la reina, while it takes place in a far more luxurious setting than this village on the borders of Lérida, poses the same dilemma of the gulf that separates the classes. The pivot around which the story revolves is the fateful interview between the gardener Rómulo and the naked duchess in her indoor swimming pool, where in a whimsical moment she has the maid usher him in to deliver a message. She explains her lack of embarrassment to the maid by saying: '¡Un jardinero no es un hombre!' (p. 14). When she looks at him later, he reflects: 'No se mira así a un ser humano . . . sino a un animal o a un mueble' (p. 28). The life of these two characters in a limit situation, when the palace is requisitioned by the Republican militia, makes them see each other eventually in human, not class terms. So at the end of the novel the duchess can say, as she dies in Rómulo's arms: 'Tú eres el primer hombre que he conocido en mi vida' (p. 177). This is not to say that *El rey y la reina* is primarily a novel of social commitment: there are numerous other strands running through the work that make it a general comment on the human condition. However, the gardener Rómulo displays the quiet dignity and common sense that we find in other working-class characters in Sender's novels; 'Tenía una cabeza romana de campesino cordobés. Hablaba poco y sus ideas sobre las cosas y las personas eran muy sólidas. Como todos los campesinos, había hecho su filosofía y le gustaba generalizar' (p. 13). The duchess's early view of him as being below the category of a real man reminds us of the numerous examples already quoted in a previous chapter of proletarian characters portrayed in Nationalist propaganda; these are illiterate, evil-smelling, debauched and brutish. Rómulo is not the prototype of the Republican proletarian hero we shall meet later in this chapter, but he does at one stage go off to the war and distinguish himself by his courage (p. 151).

The commitment of Max Aub is tempered by his ultimate concern for human relationships above political theory. As Soldevila has pointed out, Aub's ideal (as expressed in his essay 'El falso dilema') appears to be a Socialist economy in a Liberal State, a marriage of liberty and equality; but in his novels he never quite manages to achieve such a synthesis: his characters argue, usually inconclusively, about the two problems of social justice and individual freedom.[43] There seems little doubt, however, that Aub is on the side of the exploited. La señá Romualda, in *Campo abierto*, a splendidly drawn character who supports the policies of Largo Caballero, is outraged at the mere thought of the social inequalities around her:

¿Qué razón hay para que los hijos de los pobres sean pobres y los hijos de los ricos, por el hecho de serlo, nazcan entre sedas? Eso no hay Dios que lo justifique y hasta que no se remedie, el mundo no será mundo . . . Y los militares no vienen más que a quitarle al pueblo lo que éste ganó a fuerza de sangre y de trabajo. ¡Que trabajen todos, rediez, que para eso tenemos dos manos y salimos desnudos al mundo! Cuando piensa en la desigualdad social la Romualda siente que le hierven las entrañas.   (pp. 277–278)

At the other end of the social scale from Romualda are the two characters, Juan Manuel Porredón and Jesús de Buendía y O'Connor, in *Campo cerrado*. The former is 'ex-ministro de la monarquía, tonto', the latter 'banquero . . . nació presidente de consejos de administración' (p. 179). When they discuss the rising, the role of international capital is ever present: 'Nuestros amigos podrían ser un poco más prudentes; en Amsterdam ha subido hoy Almadén como les ha dado la gana' (p. 180).[44] What Aub criticises in both these cases is the lack of social mobility that characterises Spanish society, as well as its lack of humanity. It is a growing awareness of these issues that leads to Fajardo's conversion, in *Campo de sangre*, from an aimless and dissipated intellectual to a devoted Communist. It is as if a light is suddenly turned on in the darkness: 'Los hombres le parecieron nuevos . . . Cuando le sugirieron que se ocupara, con otros "intelectuales," de poner a salvo las obras de arte, se negó en redondo: quería ser militar, militante, no ocuparse para nada de la salvación del espíritu como no fuese directamente a través de los campesinos y obreros' (p. 247). This view is more extreme than Aub's own, but he shows by the description he gives that he prefers the new Fajardo to the old.[45] Another character who receives generous treatment in Aub's description is the roguish Manuel, el de la Font, in the story of the same name (in *No son cuentos*). Son of a poor laundress, Manuel explains to someone who asks why he became a Republican: 'Desde siempre . . . he visto trabajar a mi madre' (p. 86).

As we have seen, Barea's conviction stems from a similar source: *La forja de un rebelde* is dedicated to his mother, 'la señora Leonor' (a laundress), as well as his wife. Of all the writers on the war, Barea is perhaps the most acutely aware of social class, due to his upbringing in Avapiés. The naturalistic descriptions of the wretchedly poor of this quarter in the pre-war period constitute by far the most brilliant pages of the novel; they haunt the reader long after he has encountered them: 'La señora Segunda es una pobre de pedir limosna y además le falta la nariz por un cáncer que se la ha comido y se le ven los huesos de dentro de la cabeza' (p. 99). But this old woman is kindly and helpful: she looks after Barea's sister and cooks for the family; she likes the children to kiss her on the cheek to show they are not disgusted by her physical appearance. What people have to do to escape this wretchedness may not always accord with bourgeois morality, either. The thumbnail sketch of Manzanares, a character in *La ruta*, reveals someone destined to live a life of crime if he is not to starve: '¿Cómo quieren que sea una persona decente con noventa pesetas y un pulmón seco?' (p. 436). When he steals a wallet at the station, on his return from soldiering in Morocco where he was badly wounded, there is no criticism of his action. On the contrary, Barea raises his glass to him in the station bar (p. 427). In the villages near Madrid where he spends his holidays, Barea finds a rigidly stratified rural society: '(Navalcarnero) está dividido en dos gentes: unos que visten como en Madrid y otros que van con blusa y pantalón de pana' (p. 67). In both Navalcarnero and Novés, the rich and poor classes frequent the *casino* appropriate to their caste. When Barea arranges for four Popular Front speakers to come and address meetings at Novés prior to the elections of February 1936, he is expelled from the *casino de los ricos* and made an honorary member of the *casino de los pobres* (p. 524). This is a clear example of the writer having to take sides, even before a shot was fired in the Civil War. The power of the *cacique* and the network of *fuerzas vivas* existing in such villages is well described by Barea. The zig-zag path of their fortunes during the Republic is outlined in the first chapter of *La llama*. Don Heliodoro, the *cacique*, feels threatened during the first two years, but returns to the offensive after the Asturian revolution. He has gained power over the village by money-lending and exploitation of the farm-workers, depriving these of the opportunity of work if they rebel, and blocking the farmers' attempts to sell their produce direct to Madrid. He exercises this power in tacit collaboration with the civil guards and the priest. Wherever Barea looks he finds the labouring classes discriminated against: only the sons of the wealthy can afford to buy themselves out of military service in Morocco (p. 336), and only the children of the middle classes have access to higher education; even the progressive Residencia de Estudiantes is beyond the economic means of the working class (p. 143). Barea's work transcends propaganda because of his search for his own identity in the events he describes. As José Ortega states, here is a good example of Goldmann's concept of the novel as the synthesis of biography and social chronicle: 'La penetración de la realidad corre paralela al autoanálisis existencial que realiza el novelista y ambos procesos forman parte del proceso dialéctico, unificante y totalizador.'[46]

Sánchez Barbudo, in *Sueños de grandeza*, gives us a glimpse of what a genuinely integrated society might look like. Wartime Madrid is described in terms not unlike those used by Orwell to describe Barcelona in the early months of the war in *Homage to Catalonia*. The privileged classes have had to accept a new status:

Los cafés estaban llenos de soldados, de hombres del pueblo que parecían más seguros de sí, más alegres, más *individuales* que nunca . . . Junto a Arturo comía una señorita aristocrática, amoldada a la nueva vida, así como su padre, el viejo caballero de barba blanca y cuello duro que sorbía el caldo sin protesta ni rencor. Comían sin alegría, es cierto, pero sin odio.   (pp. 272–273)

Mosén Jacinto, in *El cura de Almuniaced*, is torn between the warring classes. He cannot accept the ruling classes as 'his' ('los suyos'): indeed, he dies dissociating himself from their cause. Earlier in the novel, he had reflected: 'Eran los *suyos* gentes petrificadas, hundidas hasta las cejas en polvos de milenios. Acercarse a ellos era verlos desnudos de gestos y chisteras, falsos, vacíos, chatos de fanatismo y crueldad' (p. 21). His dilemma is that he realises that the new order being proposed has little place for people of his own persuasion. Like Barea, in his contempt for the *fuerzas vivas* he condemns himself to being a *déclassé*.

The presence of a powerful class consciousness in the Republican novelists leads in many cases to the creation of an archetype who will serve as the bearer of their message: the proletarian hero. In Sender, this character is often a peasant: Paco el del Molino (*Réquiem*), Rómulo (*El rey y la reina*) or the numerous heroes to be found in *Contraataque*. It is as though in rejecting the so-called bourgeois virtues, the author has to replace them with other, more fundamental values. The message is summed up in an early novel, *Mr Witt en el cantón*:

La diferencia entre su manera de ver y la mía es bien simple: yo creo en el hombre, usted cree en la fuerza que el mito religioso, el mito aristocrático, el mito imperial se han organizado alrededor. Pero al final, el barro de la Biblia, el hombre salido del barro, dará su forma permanente a las sociedades, Mr Witt.   (p. 100)

As M. Joly has indicated, Sender has to jump a generation in his own family history to reach his peasant roots.[47] From a sense of loyalty to peasant ancestry he develops a conviction to 'opposer sa propre croyance en un homme "fondamental" à une conception de l'homme produit d'une soi-disant société, société qui n'est au fond que la conjugaison intéressée de forces répressives'.[48] Sender evolves a theory of the *hombre ganglionar*, whose essential humanity places him above so-called 'civilised' man: 'Me ha ayudado hasta hoy el repertorio de los valores más simples y primarios de gentes de mi tierra. No del español de la urbe . . . sino tal vez del campesino de las tribus del norte del Ebro' (*Los cinco libros de Ariadna*, prologue, p. ix). Rómulo is just such a man: 'El jardinero es el español elemental, heroico, fuerte, que deja una roca con su nombre allí en el frente.'[49] Paco el del

Molino, too, is the embodiment of traditional peasant loyalty, as emerges in *Réquiem* in his answers to the visiting bishop:

– ¿Qué quieres ser tú en la vida? ¿Cura?
– No, señor.
– ¿General?
– No, señor, tampoco. Quiero ser labrador, como mi padre.   (p. 22)

The heroism of the soldiers in *Contraataque* is of a different order, since the work has limited propagandist aims. In some ways the descriptions mirror those of the early Nationalist novels. When 40 men are requested for a suicide mission, nearly 100 volunteer (p. 248); men go into battle 'con el pecho descubierto y a veces una canción en los labios' (p. 234); a *miliciana* dies revealing a 'pecho virginal' (p. 123); the enemy are 'hordas rebeldes' (p. 100) and 'hienas' (p. 115). The defence of the Alto del León and the formation of the Compañías de Acero give Sender the opportunity to adopt an epic tone. But in the description of a dead soldier clutching the earth, the author shows indirectly his concern for the Spanish peasantry and their aspirations:

El muerto tenía un gesto de frenesí, un gesto crispado, como si en lugar de la tierra tuviera entre sus manos el pecho joven de su novia . . . ¡Llévate la tierra de España entre las uñas, camarada, y apriétala bien! ¡Es tuya, tuya, tuya para siempre!
                    (p. 144)

As we have already seen in 'El Cojo', Max Aub, too, is capable of creating the epic hero. J. Chabás considers his novels have 'mucho de crónica y no poco de cantar épico'.[50] I. Soldevila Durante identifies the same elevated tone, which he associates with the people's brave defence of their colletive interest:

La epopeya parece imposible en el mundo científico de 'la realidad conocida experimentalmente,' donde la organización prescinde de mitos y de milagros. Pero leyendas, milagros y mitos siguen siendo la base de la antropogonía popular. Y quizá por ello, cuando el pueblo se erige de nuevo en protagonista de la historia, a la manera heroica, la epopeya vuelve a ser posible.[51]

What makes Aub different from any other novelist of the war is the sheer number of his characters. In the chapter entitled '6 de noviembre, por la noche' in *Campo abierto*, he introduces over 200 barbers by name: there are over 500 characters in all in this one novel. The proletarian hero is here seen as if in fairground mirrors which multiply his (or her) image dizzily as the work unfolds. The heroic figures are usually not those who reappear in other novels in the *Laberinto mágico*: their existence is often brief and their end violent. Aub's admiration for his collective protagonist, particularly in the defence of Madrid, is deeply felt: he discovers, perhaps for the first time, 'une société dont il est profondément, presque viscéralement, solidaire'.[52] In choosing a unanimist technique Aub is giving literary form to that solidarity. As Don Leandro says in *Campo de sangre* before he dies: 'Aquí la Historia es cuestión del pueblo.' Aub adopts a position diametrically opposed to the Falangist authors and their Nietzschean hero: his creation is often 'l'homme fruste et primitif, totalement inconscient de son propre héroïsme, dont le sacrifice . . . consiste à mourir pour ce qui représente, sans qu'il le sache, sa raison d'être'.[53] This heroism is a centripetal force which draws in other characters despite themselves. The final pages of *Campo de sangre* bear testimony to this. As Sancho walks beside an old woman in Barcelona in March 1938, after a bombing raid, she looks up at the skies defiantly and promises: '¡Pasarán por arriba, pero no por abajo!' This ambiguous remark, so reminiscent of Unamuno's 'Venceréis, pero no convenceréis', gives added courage to Sancho as he is caught up in the crowd on its way to urge the Government not to surrender: 'Sancho pierde la noción de quién es. De pronto tiene cien brazos, mil bocas, diez mil voces. Se siente masa. Hay que luchar' (p. 510). The description of the taking of Barcelona barracks at the beginning of the war, described in *Campo cerrado*, offers similar examples of popular heroism and is comparable with the best pages of Malraux in his novels of revolution. Durruti's men capture the Hotel Falcón on the same day:

> Disparan por el gusto de disparar, como si el plomo que envían llevara flameando el rabioso derecho de vivir de la humanidad esclava de Barcelona . . . Tienen su vida en la mano, la pasan, la notan, saben por qué viven. Son, están; no son ni fulano, ni mengano; están todos a una; ligados, enraizados, enlazados . . .
>
> (p. 213)

The solidarity of the people, their 'afán de solidaridad inasequible'[54] and their tenacity in the face of overwhelming odds gives them epic grandeur despite their often humble social status. The farm labourer in *Campo abierto* who goes to collect a rifle to protect (like El Cojo) his newly acquired plot of land, is a man of few words; those he utters reveal his origins. But he has acquired dignity and pride in the revolution:

– ¿A qué Organización perteneces?
– A denguno.
– ¿A qué partido?

– A denguno.

– ¿Qué eres?

– Labrador. – Rectificó: – Campesino.   (p. 440)

Templado comments that even if such people were told that defeat was inevitable, they would carry on the fight. Aub describes them with such a sure touch that one senses he must have encountered many such individuals. Like la señá Romualda, in charge of 500 women defending the Calle de Embajadores, they were shrouded in anonymity before the war began. Suddenly their reserves of humanity and courage are called upon and they show the stuff they are made of. Again and again in these pages we find the same heroism that inspired Goya to paint his '2 de mayo'.

The people of Madrid are the collective hero of many other Republican war novels. Samblancat (*Caravana nazarena*, p. 68) makes the barbers' syndicate the backbone of Madrid's defence in early November 1936, and offers scant praise to the professional soldiers. Sánchez Barbudo (in *Sueños de grandeza*) describes a scene almost identical to one in *Campo abierto* (p. 469): 'Los viejos, silenciosamente, en una casa de Embajadores, afilaban los cuchillos grandes de la cocina' (p. 248), and like Aub, describes the women rallying their menfolk (p. 253). The characters of *Sueños de grandeza* forge the same bonds of solidarity with their fellow men that Aub describes in all his novels of the war: 'Aquél que sólo un día rompe las paredes de su estrecha posición y se encuentra con otros hombres, con la verdadera vida, no puede ya nunca volver exactamente a ser quien era' (p. 258). They are compared on several occasions to don Quixote, 'ese ser esquelético, ansioso de justicia y de aventura, de pan y de Dios' (p. 283). Like him, they fail in their search for the ideal, but are magnificent in defeat.

Sancho Granados, in *98 horas*, adopts a propagandist stance reminiscent of contemporary newsreels, and uses la Pasionaria's slogan, 'más vale morir de pie que vivir de rodillas', to set the tone of his description of the defence of Madrid (pp. 36ff.). The people of the city (described as 'Pueblo' or 'PUEBLO') become a symbol of heroism. In the Sierra de Guadarrama, a man with a wooden leg unstraps it and throws it from him when the fighting begins, so that he cannot run away (p. 129).

Herrera Petere's *Acero de Madrid* is a hymn of praise to the Communist Fifth Regiment, which is the embodiment of the people: 'Era el pueblo inteligente . . . organizador, el pueblo de Madrid en pie de guerra' (p. 129). Acts of individual heroism such as those of Coll, Cornejo, Carrasco and Gran, who assault tanks single-handed, are not unlike those found in the novel of the Right; their iron discipline is reminiscent of that of the Nietzschean hero: 'Gran estaba acostumbrado a zambullirse en enero en el agua helada, a disciplinarse y a vencerse, a practicar bien el deporte y a ganar concursos' (p. 197). But these are two-dimensional heroes, intended as illustrations of Communist propaganda and little more.[55]

The title of Valentín de Pedro's *La vida por la opinión* is taken from Lope's *El alcalde de Zalamea*, in which the farm labourer Juan tries to protect his honour from being stained by an army captain. The military uprising of 1936 and the defence put up by the working class obviously suggested a parallel. The description of the crowds in the underground, sheltering from bombs, expresses the solidarity of the people and their 'ternura colectiva' (p. 43). Their 'heroísmo casi sobrehumano' is contrasted with the cowardice of 'algunos intelectuales' who pack their bags and flee to Nationalist Spain when they see the strength of popular feeling (pp. 55–56).

María Teresa León reserves some of her most lyrical writing in *Juego limpio* for the description of the defence of Madrid. In his flashback to the war, the priest Camilo recalls 'un heroísmo de aleluya callejera pequeño y audaz' (p. 116), and he prays, '¡Señor, escuchadme! ¡Que no muera Madrid! ¡Déjalo en la irisada memoria universal!' (p. 117). Once again, the hero is the proletariat, collectively, rather than any individual.

The Anarchist novelist Angel Samblancat offers quite a different kind of hero from that typically found in the Republican novel. Ginés Azlor, the central character of *Caravana nazarena*, displays an intolerant and violent disposition that bears comparison with that of Eugenio, García Serrano's young Falangist hero. When the offices of a Republican newspaper on the floor below their own are attacked, Ginés and his two friends throw down sofas, books and a piano on the heads of the assailants – an action Samblancat himself was quite capable of, it appears.[56] It is clear from Samblancat's description of the three students as 'los tres mosqueteros' that we are intended to admire their swashbuckling methods; this will depend, however, on the sensitivities of the reader. One of the three, Lucas is made responsible for killing Melquiades Alvarez and Martínez de Velasco in the carnage at the Model Prison in Madrid on 23 August 1936. No excuse is given except that the prison was a 'fonda de lujo y gran hotel de fascistas'. Lucas and Ginés then proceed to carry out 'carnicerías espantosas' elsewhere (p. 69). The heroism of the protagonists is akin to that of the slayers of dragons or brigands in folklore and legend rather than the kind discussed elsewhere in this chapter: '[Lucas] se cansó de degollar infieles y de mandarles bienaventurados a Alá en la Cuesta de San Vicente, en la Plaza de España y en la montaña del Príncipe Pío' (p. 70). Like some of the Falangist heroes described earlier, Ginés is prepared to commit suicide when his cause fails. Lucas restrains him with what appears to be a Nietzschean appeal to hard-heartedness:

Lo que ahora procede y lo que define el heroísmo de la era que comienza es no protestar, ni afligirse, ni enfadarse, ni estragarse en inútiles voces y gestos . . . Y, sobre todo, blindarse el corazón con triple plancha de acero imperforable.

(p. 106)

Samblancat's trio are untypical of the Republican hero but by their very contrast they help us to define the qualities of the archetype: an ordinary character, often a peasant or man of modest means, who has glimpsed the future, either in the reforms of the Republic or in the social revolution of the Civil War itself, and strives to make this vision a reality. His participation in the war is usually expressed as a defence against aggression and the tyranny of centuries. He does not glory in war, but considers it a duty to his class, a gesture of solidarity and fraternity. The war is often a catalyst, enabling the character to perceive his own humanity in a way he has never done before, to become part of the mass.

Another major area in which Republican war novelists demonstrate commitment is in the religious question: their works are imbued with anti-clericalism. The history of Republican legislation in this area, in the constitution of 1931, is well documented and for that reason will not be discussed here.[57] Less well appreciated perhaps is the extent to which newspapers, magazines and books had become imbued with anti-clericalism by the time the war began. According to one writer, there were 146 anti-religious newspapers in Spain in 1936, though not all of them displayed equal virulence.[58] In Madrid alone, the following were classified by this same author as 'Atheist' newspapers: *La Libertad*, *El Liberal*, *Heraldo*, *El Socialista*, *El Sol*, *Mundo Obrero*, *Orto*, *Octubre*, *El Comunismo*, *CNT*, *La Tierra*, *La Lucha*, *Juventud Roja*. Numerous publishing houses which followed the same tendency – in particular, La Biblioteca de los Sin Dios, in Madrid – 'inundaron las librerías y los quioscos de España de los títulos más blasfemos y procaces'.[59] The war novelists, then, are carrying on a tradition already well established in journalism and popular literature at the time.

As a prominent left-wing journalist, Sender was at the centre of this anti-clerical culture; the priest in *Réquiem*, Mosén Millán, is the embodiment of

Plate 1   A Republican soldier takes delivery of a consignment of books on the Madrid front. Reading novels led in some cases to writing them. Notice the antique firearm over his shoulder.

Plate 2   At the Feria del Libro in Barcelona, on 15 June 1938, visitors were urged to buy books to send to soldiers at the front. This campaign, organised by the Alianza de Intelectuales, was intended to keep up the morale of an army confronted by defeat.

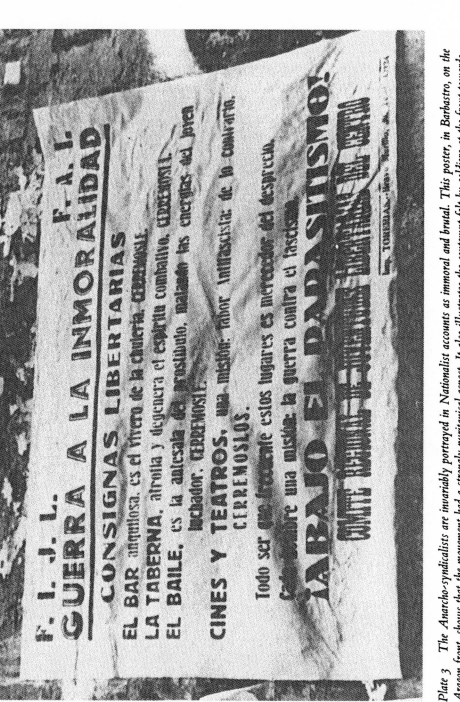

Plate 3 The Anarcho-syndicalists are invariably portrayed in Nationalist accounts as immoral and brutal. This poster, in Barbastro, on the Aragon front, shows that the movement had a strongly puritanical aspect. It also illustrates the contempt felt by soldiers at the front towards *emboscados* living in the comfort of the rearguard.

Plate 4   The Guerrillas del Teatro were organised in Madrid by María Teresa León from the headquarters of the Alianza de Intelectuales, a requisitioned palacio at no. 7, calle Marqués del Duero. Their travels around Republican Spain are described in Juego limpio.

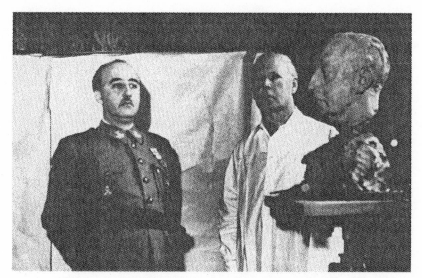

Plate 5   'S.E. el Caudillo posando ante Georg Kolb que le está modelando un busto'.
Burgos, November 1938. The Nationalist propaganda machine was by now promoting
the cult of personality: Franco was to be responsible only 'to God and history'.

Plate 6   The design section of the Nationalists' propaganda department in Burgos, November 1938. The concern for political unity is apparent from the poster in the background; the huge emblem of the yoke and the arrows testifies to the central function of FET y de las JONS in

Plate 7   On 17 March 1938, the Department of Anthropology of the University of Barcelona was damaged in a bombing raid. The human skeleton amid the debris of war has been adorned with a Moorish head-dress and photographed, perhaps as an ironic reminder of the part Africa was playing in Franco's defence of European civilisation.

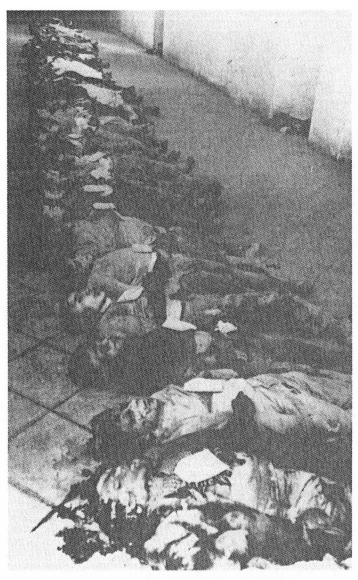

Plate 8   Barcelona, 30 January 1938. A Nationalist bombing raid cost the lives of 308 people, of whom 47 were children. The photograph illustrates the way in which atrocities such as this were exploited for purposes of propaganda, to the extent (Steiner has argued) that they lost their meaning.

Plate 9 The punishment cell of the checa in the calle Zaragoza in Barcelona. The lack of flat surfaces was intended to ensure that prisoners suffered permanent discomfort. There are numerous accounts by Nationalist novelists (e.g. Borrás) of the tortures inflicted by chequistas on their victims.

Plate 10   The front at Teruel, 31 December 1937. Soldiers of the 11th Division brave the intense cold of mid-winter. Fighting froze to a standstill at one stage, in temperatures of 18 below zero.

Plate 11 *A Republican soldier, exhausted after the battle for Teruel, contrives to get some sleep. Danger and discomfort in the form of cold, hunger and lice were the constant companions of these men, many of whom had received only rudimentary military training.*

Plate 12 Burgos, 15 November 1938. The Cuadro Artístico de Frentes y Hospitales organised an entertainment for the wounded soldiers of the Hospital Musulmán, to which members of the public were invited. The wounded Moorish soldier, recruited to serve in Franco's 'crusade', is bewildered by events, but still inspires respect.

Plate 13 From a hilltop above Toledo, members of a Republican battalion, 'El Socialista', look down on the beleaguered Alcázar, which survived all attempts by the Republicans to take it, until eventually it was relieved by Franco's army on 27 September 1936.

Plate 14   Toledo. A view of the Alcázar before its destruction.

Plate 15   Toledo. A view of the Alcázar, showing the results of months of Republican bombing and mining of its foundations. Ayala's 'El tajo' describes Nationalist reprisals for these events.

Plate 16 The moment of the capture of Gerona by the Nationalists, during which part of the city was set on fire. The Nationalist caption attributes this destruction to 'fuerzas marxistas' prior to their abandoning the city, but Hugh Thomas blames Nationalist incendiary bombs. The cathedral around which much of the action of Gironella's trilogy takes places towers above the rest of the city.

Plate 17   The Refugio Luis Sirial, in Valencia, provided a brief resting place for this mother and daughter, evacuated from Málaga after the fall of the city in February 1937. The civilian population's flight from Málaga is a recurrent image in the literature of the Civil War.

DDD   DDD   DDD APPEL SPECIAL MULTIHAVAS   10 H 30 MADRID Mar 28

REUTER ANNONCE MADRID MADRID CAPITULA + FULLSTOP +

Plate 18   The Reuter announcement of the fall of Madrid on 28 March 1939, against a background of Nationalist sympathisers who have taken to the streets in celebration. Such scenes are described in Lera's Las últimas banderas.

EXCELENTISIMO SEÑOR COMISARIO GENERAL DE INVESTIGACION Y VIGILANCIA.

El que suscribe , Camilo José Cela y Trulock , de 21 años de edad ,
natural de Padrón (La Coruña) y con domicilio en esta Capital , Ave-
nida de la Habana 23 y 24 , Bachiller Universitario (Sección de Cien
cias) y estudiante del Cuerpo Pericial de Aduanas , declarado Inútil
Total para el Servicio Militar por el Tribunal Médico Militar de Logro
ño en cuya Plaza estuvo prestando servicio como soldado del Regimiento
de Infantería de Bailén (nº24) , a V.E. respetuosamente expone:
Que queriendo prestar un servicio a la Patria adecuado a su estado físico , a sus conocimientos y a su buen deseo y voluntad , solicita el
ingreso en el Cuerpo de Investigación y Vigilancia .
Que habiendo vivido en Madrid y sin interrupción durante los últimos
13 años , cree poder prestar datos sobre personas y conductas , que pu
dieran ser de utilidad .
Que el Glorioso Movimiento Nacional se produjo estando el solicitante
en Madrid , de donde se pasó con fecha 5 de Octubre de 1937 , y que por
lo mismo cree conocer la actuación de determinados individuos .
Que no tiene carácter de definitiva esta petición, y que se entiende so
lamente por el tiempo que dure la campaña e incluso para los primeros me
ses de la paz si en opinión de mis superiores son de utilidad mis servici
Que por todo loexpuesto solicita ser destinado a Madrid que es donde cree
poder prestar servicios de mayor eficacia , bien entendido que si a juicio
de V.E. soy mas necesario en cualquier otro lugar , acato con todo entusiasmo y con toda disciplina su decisión.
Dios guarde a V.E. muchos años.
La Coruña a 3o de Marzo de 1938 . II Año Triunfal .

Plate 19   Cela's application to the Nationalist authorities to work for the Cuerpo de
Investigación y Vigilancia, dated 30 March 1938 (see note 20 to chapter 9).

the historical failure of the Church. In the very first paragraph of the novel, the priest is described avoiding contact with the olive branches left in the church after Palm Sunday; this is symbolic of his lack of human contact with the villagers, his lack of love for humanity. His prayers have become automatic responses without meaning: 'Cincuenta años repitiendo aquellas oraciones habían creado un automatismo que le permitía poner el pensamiento en otra parte sin dejar de rezar' (p. 8). Above all, he is a static force: he begins and ends the novel waiting passively for an event that is destined never to occur, like a character in a Pinter or a Beckett play. As Peñuelas says, the story revolves around two poles, 'una espera (la del cura) y una ausencia (la del pueblo)'.[60] Mosén Millán always takes the side of the *cacique* against the people, and when, through weakness, he allows Paco to be shot, his attitude betrays his alienation from humanity: 'Callaba, con los ojos cerrados y rezando' (p. 80). Paradoxically, *Réquiem* is a religious work, for it demonstrates at so many points how the priest has abandoned his ministry without realising it: in uncovering his hollow religiosity, it unconsciously calls for a return to Christian compassion.[61]

Sender is less charitable in his depiction of the Church in his other war novels. He makes clear in *Contraataque* that he regards it as an agent of feudalism; moreover, without the financial support of the State it could not survive, since those whose interests it furthered were too selfish to reciprocate with donations of money (p. 15). The cruelty of Rome in giving support to Nationalists who bombed children and civilians (p. 215) is echoed in individual acts of violence by priests. In one episode a priest tricks a militiaman into pouring a glass of water and then stabs him in the stomach (p. 111). The Dominican monastery in Atocha is described as a 'foco insurrecto' at the outbreak of war and its occupants, unprovoked, fire on the workers (p. 95).[62] There is the usual example of the priest (in this case 'gordo, bajito con caderas ampulosas y piernas muy cortas') being looked after by a *sobrina*, 'clásica ama de cura' (p. 51). On one of the few occasions when he meets a good priest, Sender cannot resist the comment: 'Un cura que cree verdaderamente en Dios y en el bien es muy difícil que llegue a obispo' (p. 298). Both the Papal Nuncio and the Bishop of Madrid-Alcalá have mistresses who cuckold their husbands in *Los cinco libros de Ariadna* (p. 98). Don Absalón's niece is known as 'la arcipresta' because of her sexual relations with the archpriest (p. 203), who has earlier been denounced for 'vender bajo mano obras de arte que sacaba de la iglesia' (p. 186), More ominously, priests are often associated with killing (pp. 148, 245–247, 251). Sometimes they are ridiculed: when the Archbishop of Santiago speaks at the imaginary OMECC Assembly which is the focal point of the novel, he is incoherent and the Chairman ignores his remarks (pp. 251–252).

Max Aub has been accused by one critic of not addressing himself in *Campo abierto* to the religious question and so leaving out an essential part of Civil War history.[63] Aub makes it abundantly clear elsewhere in his work, however, what his views on this question are. The title of *Campo de sangre*, taken from Matthew 27: 8, refers to the field bought with Judas's thirty pieces of silver and the innocent blood of Christ. ('That is why it has been called the Field of Blood to this day.') The theme of treachery runs through the whole of the *Laberinto mágico*; the people have been betrayed by their Church, as well as other agencies.[64] Priests have become 'los hacer-dotes' and little more (*Campo cerrado*, p. 102). The church burnings in Barcelona in July 1936 are described with enthusiasm; an old man exclaims to Serrador:

– ¡Si no las queman, volverán!
– ¿Quiénes?
– Curas y diablos.   (p. 243)

Don Leandro (*Campo de sangre*) comments: 'No me divierte que quemen los conventos . . . Pero si los queman por algo será' (p. 307). In the same novel, Rivadavia claims that by supporting the cause of Fascism the Church has in fact abandoned its Christianity: 'Los fachas de verdad no creen en Dios. Creen que ellos son Dios. Si los curas que les sirven creyeran en Dios, no les servirían. Les sirven como si ellos fuesen Dios. Ya no distinguen entre Dios y César, porque el César es Dios' (p. 120). Cuartero later analyses the same problem from a different angle: 'Franco ha respetado los curas por fascistas, no por cristianos. Si no, los monda' (p. 185).[65] The Church's role in identifying individuals for the Nationalist death-lists is also referred to with some bitterness: '(Teruel) siempre ha sido una capital de muchos frailes, y para la cuenta es fácil: acabaron con todos los que no iban a misa' (p. 253). One finds similar comments in the short stories. 'Alrededor de una mesa' (in *No son cuentos*) features a fanatical Falangist priest who rewards the Catholic family that has sheltered him in wartime Barcelona by denouncing them to the authorities. Those availing themselves of the services of a brothel in 'El Cojo' include *canónigos*. 'Manuel, el de la Font' includes a lascivious priest who is at the same time the local *cacique*: 'Todas las criadas de la casa salían preñadas. Las mandaba al campo, luego se colocaban de amas de cría en Barcelona' (*No son cuentos*,

p. 77). But perhaps the bitterest comment of all from Aub is reserved not for the priesthood but for the figure of Christ himself. In 'Santander y Gijón', when the population have Franco's forces before them and the sea at their backs, we are reminded of the biblical description of Christ walking on the water: 'Jesús no hubo más que uno; en Santander perdió la ocasión de convencer a muchos' (p. 99).

The anti-clericalism of Arturo Barea is just as profound as any we have studied so far. Alborg terms it 'un anticlericalismo *ab ovo*, temperamental, sorbido en el aire . . . sin razones de hondura intelectual'.[66] José Ortega sees Barea as a fundamentally religious person disenchanted with a reactionary Church which falls far short of his ideals: 'Pertenece . . . al catolicismo heterodoxo, conflictivo, agónico, unamuniano.'[67] An earlier influence than Unamuno was Barea's grandmother, who tells him when he is still a small boy: 'No olvides nunca que los curas son unos sinvergüenzas' (*La forja de un rebelde*, p. 71). He remembers a fat priest who lived nearby with 'una muchacha muy guapa que las lavanderas dicen riendo que es su hija, pero que él dice es su sobrina' (p. 13). When he begins school one of the priests caresses and kisses the boys; another has the reputation of being a womaniser; others display other forms of eccentric behaviour. Barea concludes: 'La verdad es que la mayoría de los curas parece que están algo locos' (p. 98). But the sexual frustration of the priests who teach him is not his main concern. More serious is the fact that the Jesuits attempt to direct a family inheritance into their coffers, a manoeuvre which is blocked by the grandmother in an angry scene (p. 136). When Barea reaches adulthood, his anti-clericalism is reinforced. The village priest in Novés, don Lucas, 'es de los de la cáscara amarga'; incapable of charity towards the villagers, he believes only in repression, 'palo, mucho palo' (p. 514). The physical description of Barea's priests tells us a great deal: they often have repulsive features, as though the author is still seeing them through the eyes of a small frightened boy: '(Don Lucas era) llenito de carnes . . . un poco cerduno por sus ojillos diminutos y la abundancia del pelo, barba y vello, con labios gruesos y rojos y manos anchas, casi manazas' (p. 512). 'El padre Ayala era sucio y grasiento, el hábito pringoso, sus zapatones enormes, con gruesas suelas, sucios de siempre, las uñas de sus dedos planos ribeteadas de negro' (p. 547). When, in July 1936, he hears that the school he attended as a small boy is in flames, Barea goes there only to be told that the Jesuits provoked the incident by firing on the people with a machine-gun. He confirms that he believes this story to be true: 'Había visto demasiado de sus preparaciones para no creer que habían usado las iglesias y los conventos como almacenes de guerra' (p. 568). While it is extremely difficult to establish the truth of any particular incident, H. Thomas is in no doubt that 'practically nowhere had the Church taken part in the rising. Nearly all the stories of firing by rebels from church towers were also untrue.'[68] Barea may well have been given this explanation for the burning of the school; whether it was true is questionable.

Aguilera Malta, in *¡Madrid!*, also relays similar stories of the Church militant. One of the characters, Dr Montilla, claims: 'La Iglesia se prepara a beber sangre, a repartir el botín . . . Bajo los santos y bajo los altares, hay verdaderos nidos de ametralladoras y de bombas' (p. 45).

One of Arana's characters in *El cura de Almuniaced* – the Anarcho-syndicalist Fermín – explains the anti-clericalism of his militiamen by telling Mosén Jacinto: 'Comprenda usted que muchos de estos hombres han sido tiroteados desde las iglesias, que en muchos conventos de Barcelona se han encontrado depósitos de armas y que algunos frailes se han dedicado a disparar desde tejados y azoteas' (p. 59). When the priest expresses disbelief, Fermín claims to have seen it with his own eyes. (This is unusual in incidents of this kind; they tend to be related second-hand.) Subconsciously, the priest knows that the Church has lost the support of the people. In his dream (pp. 60–61), he has visions of preaching to an empty church: 'De pronto advertía que la iglesia estaba vacía. Sólo quedaba Fermín, otra vez niño, jugando al toro con el perrillo de San Roque.'[69] In the dream, there also appear 'calaveras de pájaros' and 'un polvo negro, roído de gusanos', both symbols of the death and decay of the institution. Mosén Jacinto is that rare character in the Republican novel: the good priest. His liberalism is contrasted strongly with the narrow parochialism of the verger on the one hand, and the lofty conservatism of the bishop, on the other. He is intelligent enough not to be concerned by the destruction of the wooden statues of the saints ('troncos carcomidos') as long as the figure of Christ and the central Christian message are safeguarded. The dénouement of the novel, however, demonstrates Arana's thesis that there was no place in Nationalist Spain for a socially progressive priesthood.

Camilo, M.T. León's priest in *Juego limpio*, undergoes a political conversion through his contact with the Republican theatre group, 'Guerrillas del Teatro'; he dissociates himself at the end of the story from the victory of the Nationalists and therefore, indirectly, from Catholic immobilism.

It will be seen from the above examples that Republican anti-clericalism is almost inseparable from ideas of progress and social renewal. The anger of these writers is explained by the fact that they feel betrayed by their priests. They have, almost without exception, been brought up in the Catholic faith; but all voice their condemnation of a Church that has neglected the social problems of its day. The process of polarisation that took place in 1936 makes its influence felt on novelists in that they tend towards caricature, the expression of uncompromising views and the creation of stock situations. This is nowhere more apparent than in the religious question.

Limitations of space prevent any extensive analysis of examples of Republican commitment and propaganda on other themes, but these should at least be mentioned. The portrayal of the Civil Guard as 'tricornios obrericidas' (*Caravana nazarena*, p. 126) allying themselves with the ruling oligarchy is a commonplace in these novels.[70] The role and scale of foreign intervention on the Nationalist side is, as one would expect, mercilessly exploited: the military contribution of 'aquel conglomerado italogermanomarrocohispano' (*¡Madrid!*), the price the Nationalists will eventually have to pay for this and, in particular, the description of these 'foreigners' killing, looting and raping on Spanish soil, feature in many of the stories. Nationalist atrocities, especially the bombing of the civilian population, are recounted at length, often with exaggerated statistics. Attempts are frequently made to show that Republicans are magnanimous towards enemies captured in battle or in the rearguard, even though history shows this was patently not the case; authors attempt to explain in moderate terms (with the exception of Samblancat) the need to purge fifth-columnists who have themselves committed violent acts. Finally the shortage of Republican arms due to what is considered perfidious non-intervention by the majority of the international community, and the accompanying shortage of food, occupy an important place in this literature.

Writing of the historians of the Spanish Civil War, Paul Preston maintains that 'not having a regime to defend and chastened by defeat, the writings of the exiled Republicans were less blatantly propagandistic. [Although they were] partisan and self-justificatory, the urgent need to explain defeat prevented a total disregard for truth.'[71] There is a marked difference in tone between those novels that were written in the war years (*Contraataque*, *¡Madrid!*, *Acero de Madrid*) and later works. While the former were short-range *obras de circunstancias* with propagandist intent, Republican novels published after the war do indeed eschew, for the most part, 'a total disregard for truth'. Even Aub's *Campo cerrado*, written between May and August 1939, which shows no lack of commitment, is much more than propaganda. The description of the crescendo of revolution and the enthusiasm of the Anarcho-syndicalists in the last section of the novel, apart from the fact that it constitutes some of Aub's best writing, also rings true. Barea's sincerity also seems beyond doubt – he lays himself open to criticism for the way in which he treated his wife precisely because of his honesty. Sender refuses to make party political points after *Contraataque*, and like Francisco Ayala, seeks more deeply for solutions to human problems. Arana, Lamana, and Masip avoid the distortion that accompanies propaganda and write 'straight, honest prose'. By comparison with the Nationalist novelists, these writers are (a) fewer (particularly in the early years: my bibliography shows that up to 1941, Nationalist writers had produced eight times as many Civil War novels as Republicans), and (b) of better quality (since, with few exceptions, writers and artists tended to be Republican rather than Nationalist). The cult of violence to be found in the Falangist novel is rarely encountered here. War is usually portrayed as a painful necessity, a stubborn defence of the human right to a dignified existence. While the proletarian hero is a protagonist-symbol of many such novels, and is often surrounded by that same aura of moral purity which characterises the Right, the manicheism of the Republican novel is less pronounced. It did not claim, nor could it, that God was on its side. Finally, it is noticeable in this so-called 'novel of the Spanish Civil War' that the political, economic and social background is rarely neglected. The committed novelist is drawn not so much by the sound of the explosion as by the clash of elements which caused the spark.

Notes

1 'Marxism and Literature' in D. Lodge (ed.), *Twentieth Century Literary Criticism* (London, 1972), pp. 241–252.
2 *Ibid.*, p. 250.
3 *Ibid.*
4 'El novelista y las masas', *Leviatán*, 24 (May 1936), 31–41 (p. 31).
5 *Ibid.*, p. 34.
6 *Ibid.*, p. 35.
7 *Ibid.*, p. 37.
8 Those who have interviewed Sender in recent years have, not surprisingly, come away with quite a different impression of the writer and his attitude to commitment from that described here. They tend, in my view, to underplay this aspect of his earlier work. Cf. the comment of Peñuelas: 'El "compromiso" de Sender – en el sentido corriente de la palabra – [es] sólo relativo y circunstancial' (*La obra narrativa de Ramón J. Sender* (Madrid, 1971), p. 66). It would be more accurate to divide Sender's work into different phases, some of which involve more political commitment than others.
9 M.C. Peñuelas, *Conversaciones con Ramón J. Sender* (Madrid, 1970), p. 84.
10 *Narrativa española fuera de España (1939–1961)* (Madrid, 1963), p. 345.

11 The English version of *Contraataque*, *The War in Spain*, was published by Faber in 1937. The original Spanish version was published in the following year. There was obviously propagandist value in publishing such a work in English at the earliest opportunity. The English version was described in a contemporary book review as 'by turns rhetorical, propagandist, deeply emotional and photographic' (David Garnett in *The New Statesman and Nation* (31 July 1937), 187).

12 Perhaps surprisingly for an ex-major in the Fifth Regiment, Sender claims never to have fired his pistol once in the whole course of the war (Peñuelas, *Conversaciones*, p. 277). This indicates the primacy of his literary commitment over his role as a combatant.

13 Aub terms it 'una novela de la guerra . . . sin alma, ni aliento', despite its obvious commitment (*Discurso de la novela española contemporánea* (Mexico, 1945), p. 104).

14 Charles L. King, *Ramón J. Sender* (New York, 1974), p. 112.

15 *La obra narrativa de Ramón J. Sender*, p. 153.

16 He writes (p. 22) that Queipo de Llano, 'creyéndome a mí comunista – lo que me ha sucedido muchas veces en la vida y no tiene nada de particular, puesto que lo soy . . .', had expressed support for this cause.

17 E. Rodríguez Monegal, *Tres testigos de la guerra civil* (Caracas, 1971), p. 86.

18 R. Doménech, in the introductory essay to *Morir por cerrar los ojos* (Barcelona, 1967), p. 39. For the debate on art and propaganda which took place among contributors to the review *Hora de España*, of whom Aub was one, see Monique Roumette, '*Hora de España*' in Marc Hanrez (ed.), *Les Ecrivains de la Guerre d'Espagne* (Paris, n.d.), pp. 201–213. The group submitted a collective manifesto to the Second International Congress of Writers, held in Valencia in 1937, in which they claimed to be pursuing an art which was the 'ideological equivalent of the human content of the revolution', but rejected the 'pale decorative symbols to which Socialist realism reduces the working class'.

19 *Discurso de la novela española contemporánea*, p. 95.

20 As an exile, Aub is distanced from the Spanish working class geographically as well as intellectually, a double frustration.

21 I. Soldevila Durante, *La obra narrativa de Max Aub (1929–1969)* (Madrid, 1973), p. 257.

22 In M. Joly et al., *Panorama du roman espagnol contemporain, 1939–1975* (Montpellier, 1979), p. 123.

23 'Es posible poner en duda la oportunidad de conceder tanto lugar a las cuestiones políticas en la obra literaria [de Aub]' (I. Soldevila Durante, *La obra narrativa de Max Aub*, p. 255).

24 M. de Gogorza Fletcher, *The Spanish Historical Novel (1870–1970)* (London, 1974), p. 130.

25 M. Joly et al. *Panorama*, p. 127.

26 E. González López, '*Campo cerrado*', *Revista Hispánica Moderna*, 11 (1945), 251–252 (p. 252).

27 E. de Nora, *La novela española contemporánea*, 3 (Madrid, 1962), p. 62.

28 'La obra tiene un marcado sentido crítico anti-reaccionario que, por lo unilateral, pierde en calidades artísticas, forzando la narración para llevarla por un cauce predeterminado' (F. Yndurain, 'Novelas y novelistas españoles, 1936–1952', *Rivista di Letterature Moderne*, 3, no. 4 (1952), 277–284 (p. 282)).

29 M. Benedetti, 'El testimonio de Arturo Barea', *Número*, 3 (1951), 374–381 (p. 380).

30 G. de Torre, 'Arturo Barea: *La forja de un rebelde*', *Sur*, 205 (1951), 60–65 (p. 64).

31 'Not Spain but Hemingway', *Horizon* (May 1941), 350–361 (p. 356).

32 *Ibid.*, p. 357.

33 M. Benedetti, 'El testimonio de Arturo Barea', p. 375. Barea was a Socialist who defined himself as 'almost a Communist'.

34 J. Ortega, 'Arturo Barea, novelista español en busca de su identidad', *Symposium*, 25 (1971), 377–91 (p. 389).

35 *The Spanish Cockpit* (Michigan, 1963), p. 5.

36 P. Preston, 'The Agrarian War in the South' in P. Preston (ed.), *Revolution and War in Spain, 1931–1939* (London, 1984), p. 159, from which much of the background information for this section is taken.

37 *Ibid.*, p. 169.

38 H. Thomas, *The Spanish Civil War* (London, 1971), p. 77.

39 The first of the stories in *No son cuentos* (Mexico, 1944) – 'El Cojo' – is dedicated to another novelist of the Civil War, Paulino Masip. It was considered by Nora to be the best short novel the war had produced.

40 'Many regarded their estates as they would distant colonies and visited them rarely. They left the administration of their property in the hands of a local agent, the *cacique*, who also ensured its political docility' (H. Thomas, *The Spanish Civil War*, p. 78).

41 M.C. Peñuelas, *Conversaciones*, p. 131.

42 *Ibid.*, p. 200.

43 *La obra narrativa de Max Aub*, p. 237.

44 For an interesting historical account of the value of Spanish raw materials to the international community (particularly Germany and Italy), see Angel Viñas, 'The Financing of the Spanish Civil War' in P. Preston (ed.), *Revolution and War in Spain*, pp. 266–283.

45 The aimless intellectual or uncommitted writer is not uncommon in Aub. Templado inveighs against the dehumanised attitude of Roberto Breña, just such a character, in *Campo abierto* (pp. 296–300). There are similarities between Lledó (*Campo cerrado*) and Ferrís (*Campo de los almendros*) in this respect.

46 'Arturo Barea, novelista español en busca de su identidad', p. 379.

47 M. Joly et al. *Panorama*, p. 142.

48 *Ibid.*, pp. 142–143.

49 Peñuelas, *Conversaciones*, p. 166. In *The God that Failed* (p. 57) Koestler derides the cult of the proletarian hero which the Communists had promoted in the 1930s: 'In all books which we read or wrote the ideal proletarian was always broad-shouldered, with an open face and simple features; he was fully class conscious, his sexual urge was kept well under control; he was strong and silent, warm-hearted but ruthless where necessary, had big feet, horny hands and a deep baritone voice to sing revolutionary songs with.'

50 *Literatura española contemporánea* (Havana, 1952), p. 661.

51 *La obra narrativa de Max Aub*, p. 320.

52 I. Soldevila Durante, in M. Joly et al. *Panorama*, p. 124.

53 *Ibid.*, p. 125.

54 D. Pérez Minik, *Novelistas españoles de los siglos XIX y XX* (Madrid, 1957), p. 301.

55 *Acero de Madrid* is an early work, being already completed by February 1938, which explains its haranguing tone. Herrera Petere collaborated in various literary reviews promoting the war effort, including *El Mono Azul*.

56 'In the sphere of justice, the Anarchist lawyer Angel Samblancat, at the head of a C.N.T.–F.A.I. militia, had in the first days of the Revolution invaded the Palace of Justice, thrown out of the window legal documents, contracts, leases, crucifixes, and killed a large number of lawyers and judges' (H. Thomas, *The Spanish Civil War*, p. 252). In the prologue to his novel *Caravana nazarena*, Samblancat admits personal responsibility for the deaths of a hundred Nationalists, and regrets it could not have been double this number (p. 13).

57 See Antonio Montero Moreno, *Historia de la persecución religiosa en España, 1936–1939* (Madrid, 1961) for a well-documented Catholic account of events.

58 Constantino Bayle, *Sin Dios y contra Dios*. Quoted in Montero, *Historia*, p. 36.

59 Montero *ibid.* p. 37.

60 *La obra narrativa de Ramón J. Sender*, p. 146.

61 In the context of this novel, Julia Uceda writes: 'Sender es a mi juicio el único novelista español actual cuya obra tenga dimensión y sentido religiosos' ('Realismo y esencias en Ramón Sender', *Revista de Occidente*, 82 (Jan 1970), 39–53 (p. 47)).

62 The pretexts the Republicans found for excusing popular assaults on churches and *conventos* are somewhat far-fetched. In the 1931 attacks, *Heraldo* (11 May) reported, like Sender in this episode,

that friars had fired on the workers. On the following day, *El Socialista* wrote that caches of arms and explosives were being stored in these buildings. Montero finds these explanations 'pintorescas' (*Historia*, p. 25).

63 Fernández Figueroa, '*Campo abierto*', *Indice de Artes y Letras*, 53 (15 July 1952).

64 It was originally Aub's intention that *Campo del Moro* should be entitled *Los traidores* (Soldevila Durante, *La obra narrativa de Max Aub*, p. 97).

65 Southworth claims that the execution of eleven Basque priests by the Nationalists demonstrates that Franco was more concerned with politics than with religion (*El mito de la cruzada de Franco*, pp. 100ff.).

66 *Hora actual de la novela española*, 2 (Madrid, 1962–63), p. 231.

67 'Arturo Barea, novelista español en busca de su identidad', p. 386.

68 *The Spanish Civil War*, pp. 227–228.

69 The parallel with *Réquiem por un campesino español*, published just three years later, is striking.

70 H. Thomas, concluding that the Civil Guard 'had a deserved reputation for ruthlessness', interestingly quotes from Sender's *Seven Red Sundays*: 'When one joins the Civil Guard . . . one declares civil war' (*The Spanish Civil War*, p. 75).

71 *Revolution and War in Spain*, p. 4.

6
–

The gods
that failed:
disillusionment in the
novel of the Civil War

IN PREVIOUS CHAPTERS we have seen the important role that mythology and ideology played in the creative process of these novelists. Given the price the Nationalists paid for victory and the nature of the regime they saw installed, it might be expected that post-war novelists writing in Spain would exhibit signs of disenchantment that the heady rhetoric of the war years had not produced more encouraging results. Republican writers, forced into an exile which for many would prove permanent, had time to lick their wounds and reflect on whether their political cause, and the means adopted to pursue it, had been just. Many of the Civil War novels published after 1939 reveal the dismay of the authors that the noble causes for which the war was allegedly fought had been swept away, either in the passion of the historical moment or in the intrigue and manipulation of internal and external factions. For reasons which will become apparent, this dismay is much more in evidence in the Republican novel than in the Nationalist novel, though it may in reality have permeated the two sides in equal measure.

The Nationalist novel

In 1962, Dionisio Ridruejo published in Buenos Aires his indictment of the Franco régime, provocatively entitled *Escrito en España*.[1] (There was at that time no possibility of publishing such a work in Spain, given the censorship that prevailed.) Ridruejo had been Director General of Propaganda during the Civil War. A devoted Falangist, he had also fought on the Russian front, not, as he makes clear, simply to combat Communism, but actively to promote the cause of Fascism. He was later to

renounce his membership of Falange and resign as editor of the review
Escorial.[2] His stormy relationship with the régime (during which he had
several personal interviews with Franco) led to his banishment (*residencia
forzosa*) to Ronda and later to the environs of Barcelona, a punishment
which lasted until 1947. The harsh measures taken against Ridruejo
indicate that the expression of political disillusionment in Spain in the
1940s was an extremely sensitive issue; they also suggest that such
disillusionment may have been widespread: there seems little point in
banning someone to far-off places unless he represents a genuine threat and
is in some senses representative of a body of opinion (the very reasons for
which Franco had been banished to the Canaries by the Government under
the Second Republic). It may be instructive, therefore, to remind ourselves
what it was Ridruejo objected to in the 'New Spain' he had fought to
create.

Firstly, he reminds us that in the Civil War the Nationalists committed
acts which were repulsive to him and many of his fellows:

Si declaro que participé con plenitud en la esperanza y el entusiasmo, no ocultaré
tampoco que el recelo y a veces el disgusto me acompañaban también como les
sucedería a muchos falangistas. Tanto por la orientación represiva como por el tipo
de intenciones que manifestaban muchos de los dirigentes oficiales, la guerra de las
derechas, la guerra policial, se nos revelaba con descaro y solamente la fe en el
número y una especie de conciencia de la mayor oportunidad histórica, nos hacía
pensar que, al final, podríamos darle otro carácter.[3]

The internal power struggle, though not publicised, was nevertheless
continuing behind closed doors: 'La lucha interna por el control del
régimen siguió siempre, aunque rara vez alcanzase expresiones externas.'[4]
When the Catalan campaign was won and Barcelona 'occupied' (he
avoids the usual Nationalist term, 'liberated'), Ridruejo claims to have been
appalled by the violence and hypocrisy of the victors: 'Las primeras
medidas de ocupación – mezcla de hosquedad represiva y beatería
empalagosa – me pusieron al borde de la náusea.'[5] Echoing the 'No es eso'
of earlier intellectuals at the advent of the Republic, he comments:

Todo era insatisfactorio: el Partido era una comparsería; la Jefatura del Estado y el
Partido – una en la persona – nada tenían que ver entre sí; los sindicatos deberían
ser una ficción; el Ejército imponía su poder; la Iglesia tiranizaba la política
cultural con criterios calomardianos y proyectaba una autoridad ejecutiva
inaceptable sobre la sociedad laica; las reformas sociales en la Banca, en la tierra, en
la industria, ni se barruntaban de lejos; la represión misma – regulada ya – era

antipopular y abría entre los falangistas y su sonada clientela obrera un abismo sin fondo.[6]

His analysis of the regime leads him to a total renunciation of the political credo for which he had fought on the Russian front; instead, he advocates either a return to democratic values or genuine revolution:

La pretendida síntesis falangista entre los valores nacionales y tradicionales y los valores sociales y revolucionarios me parecía vaga y retórica. Harto más clara me parecía, en cambio, la conveniencia de intentar una integración de los bienes concretos, las adquisiciones históricas de las anteriores fases del proceso histórico – estado de Derecho, libertades efectivas, derecho al pensamiento y a la creencia, vida privada, pluralidad de formas de vida y asociación . . . Volver a la Democracia, cantando humildemente el *mea culpa* o decidirse por la revolución genuina, sin miramientos.[7]

Ridruejo's disenchantment stems mainly from a feeling of having been duped by the ruling classes. Although he and others fought in good faith believing they were changing Spanish society, he believes they were unconsciously being manipulated for the protection of oligarchic interests:

Hay que distinguir con gran cuidado lo que la guerra fue como vivencia subjetiva general de lo que fue como conspiración oligárquica destinada a consumar el secuestro del Estado y a eliminar del juego histórico toda fuerza popular – tomando esta palabra en su más amplio sentido – sin excluir las propias fuerzas que habrían de servir de peonaje para la maniobra . . . Todo lo que la guerra significó como vivencia colectiva se ha disipado, mientras en la situación actual aparece con toda desnudez y únicamente el logro acabado de la maquinación conspiratoria.[8]

With the benefit of hindsight, Ridruejo realises that the creation of the Nationalist myth eventually stood in the way of any real progress. The oligarchy, fearing that Falange's revolutionary zeal would be translated into real social and economic change, had promoted the illusion, conveniently shrouded in rhetoric, of a nostalgic past which would somehow be reconstituted in a rosy future. No rigorous analysis of the facts had taken place; nor indeed was it ever to take place:

Que este modo particular de conciencia militante no podía favorecer el desarrollo de una conciencia pública valedera y constructiva, es cosa clara: todo aquel futurismo – en ocasiones apoyado en la visión del pasado – era mesiánico, milagrero y hazañoso y en cierto modo preparaba la futura dispensa personal a que se entregarían colectivamente los españoles. De ahí que, en definitiva, la verdadera oligarquía del país, que no andaba metida en libros de caballerías ni apetecía otras novedades que las del refuerzo de su propio poder, no necesitase un gran esfuerzo para mantener toda aquella turbamulta de ilusiones fuera de campo.[9]

The general demoralisation that Ridruejo exhibits is deepened still further by his experience of 'la frecuente facilidad con que hombres que parecían haber luchado por ideales se avenían a venderlos por un plato de lentejas'.[10]

If this author has been quoted so extensively, it is because he may be seen as representing the conscience of his generation. Like many Republican novelists, and like the contributors to The God that Failed (which is discussed later), he is courageous enough to renounce previously held beliefs and admit that mistakes have been made for which he shares responsibility, by omission if not directly.[11] The fact that Civil War novelists publishing in Spain in the period Ridruejo describes cannot be quoted as evidence of generalised spiritual despair is related to the question of censorship. We know in the case of Ridruejo that he became progressively alienated from the regime from the moment of Falange's unification with the Carlists.[12] Disenchantment was probably not, therefore, a phenomenon which was late to develop amongst the politically aware: its roots are in the Civil War and its immediate aftermath. Even if censorship had not existed, it is likely that in the war years the prevailing intellectual climate would have prevented dissident intellectuals 'breaking ranks'. As the political formations regrouped in post-war Spain, however, it was surely only censorship that prevented some of these writers from giving full expression to their frustrated ideals in the novel of the Civil War. Ridruejo himself is explicit about censorship: 'La sistemática interferencia de la censura – que en ocasiones llegó a dictar alteraciones graves de mis textos – me descorazonó por completo' (p. 27). Writing about the period 1939–1957, Ferreras maintains that 'un novelista puede ser católico en lo religioso o falangista en lo político, pero fuera de estas dos posiciones, el novelista no puede ser nada'.[13] In fact, as Ridruejo has shown, these parameters were even further restricted, and 'progressive' Falangists (and indeed Catholics) found themselves alienated. García Serrano's La fiel Infantería met strong ecclesiastic disapproval because of its Falangist lack of piety, and was withdrawn from bookshops immediately after publication in 1943: it was not to reappear until 1958. As early as December 1936, a decree had been passed which banned the publication or circulation of 'libros o impresos pornográficos, marxistas o disolventes'.[14] From May 1937 onwards, two censorship departments operated in La Coruña and Seville. An ordinance of April 1938 placed under the control of the Department of Press and

Propaganda the publication, distribution and sale of books of all kinds. In July 1945, the Cortes approved the 'Fuero de los Españoles' which defined the duties and the rights of Spaniards. Article 12 of this charter granted the Spanish people freedom of expression and of the press, provided they did not advocate the overthrow of the fundamental principles of government. It is clear from the 1962 report of the International Commission of Jurists, however, that this article was honoured more in the breach than in the observance.[15] In the case of the control of newspapers and reviews, the report concluded, 'the authorities responsible for the control of the press do not confine themselves to preventing the publication of opinions and news which seems undesirable to the regime; they also issue directives to editors to pass over certain internal or external events in silence or to treat them in a special way'.[16] Topics forbidden by the directives of the Ministry of Information included 'the regime, the succession of the Caudillo, certain activities of members of the Government . . . and in general anything likely to be disapproved of by the censorship of the Roman Catholic Church. It is also forbidden to spread scandal . . . or to publish information of the kind which would place the national situation in an unfavourable light.'[17] In December 1960, a large number of artists and writers (said to be around 350 in all) addressed a letter of protest to the Minister of Information complaining about the 'system of intolerance, confusion and uncertainty' under which they laboured, and as a result of which 'Spanish writers and scholars live in a sort of exile'.[18] The pressure to abolish pre-censorship grew progressively in the 1960s until in March 1966, Fraga Iribarne's Press Law brought it to an end.[19] In the case of the Nationalist novel of the Civil War, therefore, every example under study here (with the exception of those dealt with later in chapter 9) was subject to prior censorship – a fact that is essential to their understanding. No Republican novel of the Civil War was published in Spain until 1967.[20] It seems likely that a great deal of novelistic talent in post-war Spain was diverted from the war novel because of the threat of censorship, which may explain in part the relative inferiority of this literature when compared with works on other subjects and, indeed, when compared with the Republican novel of the Civil War written in exile. This hypothesis is supported by at least two pieces of evidence. Firstly, the *angst* displayed by Ridruejo in *Escrito en España* is much more apparent in novels published in post-war Spain which are *not* war novels than it is in the Nationalist war novels themselves. Laforet's *Nada* and Cela's *La familia de Pascual Duarte* were the first in a series of pessimistic descriptions of human society in which violence was never far below the surface, and often erupted.[21] Secondly, innovations in novelistic technique are rarely found in the Nationalist war novels: they are more often to be found in Spanish novels on other themes.[22] It is not the purpose of this study to analyse the phenomenon of censorship in its totality; its effect on the Nationalist novel must be taken into account, however, if we are to explain the paucity of critical self-analysis in the works under study. It is striking that in the years when the regime was at its most defensive, hardly any first editions of war novels appeared in Spain: between 1943 and 1949, only four new war novels were published (*La fiel Infantería* (later withdrawn), 1943; *¡Hombre!*, 1944; *Legión 1936*, 1945; *Isabel, la mujer legionaria*, 1946), compared with over 60 first editions between 1936 and 1942. Not a single new Nationalist war novel was published in 1947, 1948 or 1949. It is not until Gironella publishes the first novel of his trilogy in 1953 that the Nationalist writers on the war give serious attention to the questions of conscience voiced by Ridruejo. During these bleak years the novelists live in that 'inner exile' mentioned earlier, a motif on which Paul Ilie has elaborated in *Literature and Inner Exile*. In that study he stresses that exile affected those left behind as much as those who departed: 'Each segment is incomplete and absent from the other . . . Francoism . . . seeks to compensate for the missing segment through self-sufficiency, which it accomplishes by negating the value of what has been lost.'[23] The triumphalism of the regime and its operation of the mechanisms of social control were a disincentive to any writer wishing to engage in critical self-examination in the war novel.[24]

It was always open to the novelist to express the horrors of war, since that was in itself a politically neutral statement. Remarque had shown, however, that by stressing the horrors of war and making the soldiers appear as cannon fodder, rather than epic heroes, the novel could become a political statement. Only Fernández de la Reguera's *Cuerpo a tierra* (1955) comes close to such a depiction of the war. The stress throughout is on the pure discomfort of trench life (a point made strongly by Orwell in his recollections of the same Aragon front): the cold, hunger and lack of sleep; the stench and the lice that are man's constant companions. The feeling of revulsion is all the stronger because the author thrusts us into the midst of the carnage after only a few introductory pages: 'Un proyectil mató a cuatro hombres. A uno le arrancó de cuajo la cabeza. La hizo reventar como una granada. Los hombres del pelotón huyeron despavoridos' (p. 24). It is not surprising that the uninitiated run away, or indeed attempt to desert; but this is one of the rare authors on the Right to admit that desertion and defection took place. The protagonist Augusto takes a detached view of such events.

When he hears that six soldiers have crossed over to the Republicans, his concern is purely pragmatic. The enemy will now know their weaknesses: '– ¡Sólo faltaba eso! Ahora sabrán esos tíos que somos bisoños, que nuestros morteros son una eme pinchada en un palo, que no tenemos bombas de mano . . .' (p. 51). Later, when his comrade-in-arms Campos is condemned to death by firing squad for deserting, Augusto is one of the soldiers entrusted with the execution. This time, far from denouncing Campos, Augusto is preoccupied with understanding his motives, which are unclear. He also feels compassion for the man: 'Augusto piensa que el sentimiento de la compasión es un atributo de los verdaderos valientes' (p. 95). Augusto himself, while enjoying the camaraderie of life at the front, is anti-heroic; after more than a year in the front line he is near breaking point and arranges, through a friend, to get a transfer: 'Que me destinaran a un cuerpo en el que el peligro y las incomodidades fuesen menos' (p. 206). In some ways, Cuerpo a tierra owes more to the novel of the First World War than to the conflict on which it is based. War is here converted into an infernal machine, to which Augusto will inevitably succumb: 'La máquina de la guerra no se podía detener y avanzaba engrasada por la muerte, abandonando sus despojos' (p. 259). The battlefield after the Aragon offensive of autumn 1937 is strewn with so many bodies, they cannot be buried. Instead they must be burned: 'Negros, horripilantes. Una visión dantesca. Luego enterrarían los despojos. Fue lo último que contemplaron al dejar el pueblo: los montones humeando en el atardecer. La brisa trajo un hedor repulsivo . . . Los camaradas muertos. Los enemigos muertos' (p. 142). Later, in the battle of the Ebro, a dam of corpses is described, in details which are intended to disgust the reader:

Las emanaciones eran tan insufribles que se abrió una presa para arrastrarlos. Subió el nivel del río, recogió los cadáveres que aún quedaban en su lecho y en las orillas. Al llegar a Torrelameu, depositó su dramático arrastre, aumentando el grosor del macabro dique y su pestilente exudación. El agua lamía las carnes putrefactas, blancuzcas, arrastraba humores y piltrafas humanas. Y cuando el caudal del río bajó a las veinticuatro horas, verdes moscas y gordos gusanos hervían en la charca de vísceras y carne en putrefacción.   (p. 290)

Many of the novelists deal with the horrors of war, but Fernández de la Reguera is the first Nationalist war novelist to attain these Remarquian proportions. The purpose behind these images of death contrasts strongly with that which motivates writers such as Borrás in their depiction of atrocities. Cuerpo a tierra is a lament for those who fell in battle, written by a sensitive soldier who took part; it is imbued with sadness rather than partisanship.[25] It is interesting to compare this work with another published in the same year, *Las lomas tienen espinos*, by D. Manfredi, in which the physical discomfort of warfare is described, but in such a way as to reflect the valour and stoicism of the soldiers. In addition, the novelist has lost none of his Falangist zeal, so that the work is a latter-day first-wave novel in tone, with additional documentation added from the standard history books available at that time.

If it is difficult to find examples of disillusionment with the bestiality and carnage of war among this group, a characteristic many of them share is their contempt for those who lead a comfortable life in the rearguard. Fernández de la Reguera is again more outspoken than most. On his return to Zaragoza on leave, Augusto is jostled by a fat bourgeois in a crowd which is watching a parade. 'Ni se disculpa. Ni se da cuenta seguramente. Está acostumbrado a pisar, aquí y donde sea – en la retaguardia –, firme . . . Para él, todo el quid está en gritar recio y en estirar mucho el brazo. Paga los subsidios y se enriquece con la guerra. ¿Los soldados? Para eso están: para sacarle las castañas del fuego a él' (*Cuerpo a tierra*, pp. 197–198). Significantly, Augusto does not give the Fascist salute. In the following veiled reference, Augusto seems to be referring to Nationalist repression in the rearguard: 'El soldado no alimenta odios. Eso queda para los homúnculos' (p. 138). Peasants in the village through which the troops pass do not line the streets cheering, as in the propagandist novel. 'Las puertas estaban cerradas hoscamente' (p. 218). They provide firewood only under threat: 'No les daría "ni esto". Con "el negro" de la uña se entiende. Uñas rapadas, rapaces, de arañar para adentro y escarbar terrones' (p. 219). They symbolise Augusto's alienation from the society he is fighting to defend.

García Serrano, too, is contemptuous of the armchair warriors on the home front. In *La fiel Infantería* he gives vent to his feelings about those men who have stayed behind 'en los casinos, en las terrazas de los cafés, en los balcones, junto a las mujeres . . .' He continues:

El 19 de julio calibró a las gentes: unos salimos y otros no. Aquel día se jugaba España definitivamente, y mientras nosotros marchábamos al choque cubiertos de rosas, ellos nos lanzaban las rosas desde el cielo de su indiferencia o de su cobardía. Bien limpia la chaqueta, entonada la corbata y lustrosos los zapatos, veían pasar la Patria en mangas de camisa, ronca y brava, un poco callejera para su británica elegancia. (p. 450)

Aun gustando la miel que nos brindaban al pasar los caciques y los cobardes, estábamos todos seguros – todos – de que un día habríamos de volver los fusiles contra sus aplausos, que tenían voluntad de asqueroso dinero con que hacernos mercenarios.   (p. 451)

Given the violence of this last statement, it is not surprising perhaps that the conservatives in the Franco camp saw this novel as a threat in 1943. (The sentiments expressed here accord with those of Ridruejo quoted earlier.) García Serrano had already singled out one political group, CEDA, for criticism in an earlier enumeration of Falange's enemies: 'Nos aplaudían las beatas, los explotadores, los usureros, los terratenientes, los de la Ceda' (p. 429).[26] In *Plaza del Castillo*, published in 1951, the rich and privileged are still in his sights: 'Se ganará. Pero ¿y después? Mire, la tribu de los privilegiados es mucho más difícil de combatir que la de los revolucionarios de barricada y quema de conventos. Me produce mucho más miedo un banquero español que ese pobre Lenin español con su tartera de caviar y dinamita' (p. 217). But this time, despite the combative language, there is no threat, simply the hint of frustration. The author occasionally recalls the promise of bread and justice that his party made to the people and suggests that those with privileges have no intention of allowing such pledges to be honoured. When Joaquín visits a rich aristocrat to try and persuade him to cede some land to the workers, the landowner derides the idea: 'Es imposible este pueblo nuestro. Se muere de hambre y se harta de fornicar. Luego vienen los hijos y tengo que pagar yo. Mire usted, joven: no le pago el gusto a nadie, al menos mientras pueda elegir.' But despite this aristocrat's contempt for such ideas, he cynically supports those that put them forward, knowing they will help bring a victory which will secure his future: 'Joaquín . . . estaba seguro de que aquel hombre gélido, siempre a salvo, apostaba fuerte por ellos' (p. 365). This is more than contempt for those that live in comfort in the rearguard: it is the realisation that this privileged group is in fact manipulating the combatants for its own ends, and that the much vaunted right-wing revolution is a dead letter.

A similar antagonism is described in E. Romero's *La paz empieza nunca*, in which Perico Mencía complains that he went to war against 'terratenientes y . . . comunistas'. The former now maintain that their motives were principally to put an end to anarchy. 'Si yo digo que sí, que bueno, pero que además hay que hacer la revolución social, entonces dicen que soy un *failangista* [*sic*], un totalitario, un amigo de Hitler y un partidario de los hornos crematorios en los campos de concentración' (p. 286). When a comment is made that the important thing now (the novel was published in 1957) is to produce more so that more can be shared out, someone else retorts: 'Pues ahí está la madre del cordero, que aquí muchas personas que tú y yo conocemos, ni producen ni reparten' (p. 287). Later, in an impassioned discussion with Perico, López expresses his disillusionment that Falange has become fossilised and has not achieved its objectives:

Ha sido una carga enorme de ilusión la que llevamos un día para que la hayamos gastado . . . Siempre estaré aguardando la llegada de una Falange que pueda justificar plenamente por qué fui combatiente en la guerra civil y en la guerra mundial . . . Esperaré siempre la llegada de una Falange que anule del todo mis sufrimientos, mis daños, mis dolores, mis decepciones, mis pérdidas, el vendaval espiritual de mi vida.   (p. 404)

In *Las dos barajas*, by Ruiz-Ayúcar (published in 1957), Paloma voices what is perhaps the author's view when she complains that the ideals for which she risked her life have been lost:

Desde los días exaltados del Alto del León a los días frívolos de San Sebastián, el movimiento ha recorrido mucho terreno hacia atrás. Volvemos a los errores que motivaron la guerra antes de haberla ganado. Da miedo pensar que tanto sacrificio, tanta sangre y tanto heroísmo puedan resultar inútiles. Muchos combatientes dicen que al terminar la contienda tendrán que dar una segunda vuelta, pero que entonces no será contra los mismos enemigos.   (p. 308)

However, this is an isolated example of such protest. Such moments constitute an island of disillusionment in a sea of complacency and triumphalism.

Giménez Arnau's *El puente* (1941) provides an early example of the disillusioned hero, but the sense of *angst* here (particularly in the third section of the novel) stems from his feeling that he is part of a lost generation which, in sacrificing itself to the Civil War, has become a bridge between a younger and an older generation but lacks any *raison d'être* of its own: 'Nosotros somos un simple puente, al que ninguna de las dos orillas acepta como tierra propia. Cumplimos nuestra misión, que era simplemente hacer posible el contacto entre el ayer y el mañana' (p. 333). The protagonist's alienation from post-war society is symbolised in the final pages by his departure to Equatorial Guinea. Walking down the street on his way to the station, he has to stand aside for the new generation, 'una formación universitaria que desfilaba militarmente en sentido contrario' (p. 365). There is no better example of the soldier's feeling of being undervalued and rejected when he returns to civilian society. There is little evidence here, however, of a more general questioning of whether the Nationalists' stated objectives were achieved: the protagonist's malaise is generational and existential rather than political or moral.

Juan Cepas, in *Provisional* (1959), takes liberties that earlier writers could not. This may rightly be considered a novel of reconciliation which urges Spaniards not to hark back to traditional values and dreams of *grandeza*: 'Hay que olvidarla. Lo primero que hay que hacer es arrancarle a cada español el testamento de Isabel la Católica que lleva en la cartera' (p. 100). When the speaker, Antonio, is coming close to being accused of being a Republican, he retorts: '¡Tú lo has dicho!: por un pelo. Como muchos de nosotros. Eso es lo monstruoso de esta guerra, que siendo necesaria, la suerte designó el campo para muchos de sus combatientes' (p. 101). In a so-called war of ideas, the protagonist Ridán complains, 'han tenido que morir inmolados tantos hombres sin ideas' (p. 141). When the Nationalists drive through a newly conquered village, they are cheered by 'una población que recibió con alegría, más que a los vencedores, a los que representaban el fin de la guerra' (ch. 32). Towards the end of a novel full of such sentiments, Cepas makes his protagonist do a sudden *volte-face*. He describes his entry into Valencia at the end of the war in the following terms: 'En aquel momento comprendí que hasta ahora mi entusiasmo de juventud no me había dejado ver claro: que lo que habíamos hecho era algo muy grande; algo que pasará a la historia con letras de honor' (p. 76). The most likely explanation for this abrupt change of heart is the influence, tacit or otherwise, of the censor's department when the novel came to be published. Anti-heroic sentiment is to be found in another second-wave novel, L. de Diego's *La presa del diablo*. The propaganda clichés of the Right are here used for humorous effect. The release of Republican prisoners at the request of the village priest provokes complaints among extremist elements. 'Cuando una docena de mozalbetes de Medina de Pomar – que de creer a mi tío eran unas mierdas – fueron a preguntarle por qué había intervenido en la fuga de tan calificados y peligrosos agentes de Moscú, don Pío les contestó con palabras imprevisibles en un sacerdote: "porque me ha salido de las narices"' (p. 117). Later, when Carlos asks him whether it would be right to go off to the war, the priest answers: 'Vete en buena hora. Nadie tiene derecho a privarte de una oportunidad así de hacerte un verdadero hombre' (p. 119). Notably absent are the exhortations found in first-wave novels to wage a crusade for Christian civilisation. Nor is there any heroism in Carlos's gesture: 'Fui a la guerra convencido de que quedaba muy poco que hacer' (p. 121). Army life is boring for much of the time: 'Era aquella una vida de cuartel monótona, desesperante' (p. 134). What is more, the soldier's need for sexual gratification combined with the wretched living conditions and privations of some of the women left behind on the home front, lead to prostitution. In a scene reminiscent of many encountered in the war novels (Ayala's story, 'El Regreso', for example), Carlos visits a girlfriend of his brother, who had been killed at Teruel. On hearing of the death, Carmen confesses: 'No me acuerdo de tu hermano, no me acuerdo del mío que no sabemos dónde está hace dos años, ni de mi padre que lo asesinaron como al tuyo; no me acuerdo de nadie. Soy hace tiempo eso que la gente llama, que se llama una prostituta' (p. 148).

La presa del diablo, a Nationalist novel, reflects the same tension between bonds of friendship and political beliefs that is the success of many Republican novels (particularly the cycle by Aub). The scene has already been described in which the priest releases enemy prisoners. Felimo, who was saved from drowning by Luis and his brother Carlos, when they played together as children, later becomes Luis's jailer during the Civil War; he releases him knowing he will defect to the Nationalists. At the end of the novel, Carlos captures Felimo in a mopping-up operation in the mountains, but gives Felimo a sporting chance of escaping, which ends in the latter's death. Such crises of conscience are potentially fertile areas for the novelist to explore but are dealt with relatively superficially in most Nationalist novels, particularly in those of the first wave. In a later novel, *Plaza del Castillo*, García Serrano expresses similar conflict in the scene in which the young Felisín, in the days leading up to the Civil War, is entrusted with the secret that the right-wing militant Vallejo, who is pretending to be drunk, has in fact been wounded. He has to swear not to reveal this secret even to the girl he loves, Paloma, who is one of the group taking Vallejo to safety, in ignorance of the real facts: 'Felisín sentía que no iba a tener más remedio que decirle la verdad a Paloma, porque entre Paloma y él no es que no debiera haber secretos, sino todo lo contrario: tenía que haber un secreto que les uniese más y más hasta que Dios quisiera unirles por el tremendo secreto de los hijos' (pp. 182–183). The torment is short-lived, however, and like all García Serrano's heroes, he places duty first: 'El deber estaba por encima de todas las cosas, por encima de Paloma misma, y eso que Paloma era lo más alto que él podía imaginar, querer y servir' (p. 183). This illustrates the difficulties inherent in the Nationalist novel which carries a political message: psychological depth is often sacrificed for ideological persuasion; the potential for describing the spiritual tribulations of the characters is often squandered in this way.

If the Nationalist novelists feel guilt, it is rarely expressed directly. R. León pays lip service to remorse in *Cristo en los infiernos*, when he writes: 'Todos somos culpables, más o menos, por acción o por omisión, de estas conmociones históricas. No vale hurtar el hombro a la responsabilidad y al castigo, ni establecer una barrera farisaica entre los "buenos" y los "malos," entre los "puros" y los "impuros." El problema no es tan sencillo' (p. 543). Having devoted over 500 pages to proving the opposite, however, León cannot sincerely hope to persuade the reader at this point.[27] It was left to a Republican novelist, Francisco Ayala, to create characters who were truly 'inocentes-culpables' and to express genuine moral despair in the war novel.

There seems little doubt, that *Los cipreses creen en Dios* (1953), which is dealt with in a later chapter, had a profound influence on the later novelists quoted here (Fernández de la Reguera, E. Romero, L. de Diego, J. Cepas, in particular). Gironella's ambivalence about the rights and wrongs of the Nationalist cause and his creation of the weak and anti-Fascist protagonist Ignacio broke the traditional mould and invited others to follow. Censorship did not allow a resounding *mea culpa* but, by the emphasis placed on the horrors of war, by expressing dismay at some of the activities and attitudes on the home front, and by deliberately omitting rhetoric, a small group of Nationalist novelists showed that the quarrel with others was ending, and the quarrel with themselves was about to begin. It must be stressed, however, that numerous so-called 'second-wave' novels (*Los canes andan sueltos* (1952), *Las lomas tienen espinos* (1955), *Los muertos no se cuentan* (1961)) still exhibited much of the revanchism of the early propagandist novels.

The Republican novel

In his study of six foreign writers on the Civil War, F.R. Benson sets out to examine the 'disillusion effected by the pernicious betrayals among the Republican factions and the eventual defeat of the Loyalist cause'.[28] Some writers of the Second World War seemed to him 'to have extended beyond disillusion to a desperate and consuming nihilism'.[29] It seems appropriate, therefore, to investigate whether the native Republican novelists reacted in the same way. It is interesting too, to discover in what respects, if any, their disillusion differs from that of the Nationalist writers we have just discussed.

The effects of exile on the novelist have received extensive critical treatment and it is not my intention to go over that ground here. Suffice it to say that the conditions under which these novels were produced differed radically from those which prevailed in Spain in the period under discussion, as did the public which was destined to read them. Those authors who were committed to reflecting the views of the Spanish proletariat were now doubly removed from the object of their commitment; but even liberal writers like Ayala asked. '¿Para quién escribimos nosotros?'[30] Despite the difficulties inherent in being refugees, Republican authors produced a steady flow of novels throughout the 1940s and beyond. Although the overall production of Nationalist novels far exceeds that of Republican novels, the bulk of the former was produced in the years 1936 to 1942. From 1943 onward the difference in number produced by each is less marked. Indeed, at intervals (e.g. 1948–53), there is a flurry of new Republican war novels which far exceeds the numbers appearing in Spain during the same period.[31]

The Republican novel's stress on the horrors of war demonstrates that this is a universal in war literature. Whether the object of the novel is to glorify heroic exploits, as in the epic, or to condemn carnage, as in the pacifist novel, the physical description of bloodshed and suffering can serve the author's purpose. Cimorra's description of the dead at Guadalajara as 'cadáveres hinchados como ranas muertas, enormes y bamboleantes' (*El bloqueo del hombre*, p. 121), or the description of a pregnant woman blown apart in a bombing raid, 'las tripas con el crío que iba a nacer, unos metros más allá, revueltos con las cagarrutas y con el polvo' (p. 130), demand a reader with a strong stomach. The intention is to defamiliarise scenes which have become commonplace. M.T. León's description of a horse mortally wounded in a bombing raid shows the preoccupation of the novelist to maximise the effect of such descriptions by introducing unexpected detail. To the horse's owner the animal was like a friend. As he cradles the head of the animal in its death throes, 'acudieron perros ... Se habían puesto a beber la sangre del amigo antes de que muriese definitivamente' (p. 99). Close on the heels of the dogs come the starving people of Madrid; a butcher buys the carcass for 500 pesetas and cuts it up there and then for sale to the passers-by. Such scenes have a disquieting effect, subverting as they do our conventional mental constructs. A familiar world suddenly becomes terrifyingly unpredictable. The opening pages of Aub's *Campo abierto* are another good example. In Valencia, Gabriel Rojas attends the birth of his daughter and is then sent to fetch the doctor. In the street he is shot from behind by an anonymous sniper. 'Le dieron por detrás, en medio de la cabeza, donde empezaba a calvearle el pelo' (p. 16). The fortuitous nature of the killing, and the juxtaposition of birth and death, give this episode its force. Numerous descriptions of the bombing and shelling of civilians are interspersed in the narrative (not always necessarily with a propagandist intent). A typical example occurs at the end of *Campo del Moro* where Lola, after hanging herself, is taken to be buried. When a shell bursts in the middle of the funeral cortège, Aub's description combines physical revulsion with psychological perception. As in so many scenes in war literature the horse symbolises the suffering of the people: 'El caballo sobrevivió un cuarto de hora, suelto, corriendo por el campo desierto, pateando sus tripas' (p. 254).[32] The final image with which the author leaves us is that of the demented Soledad 'chupando *una* mano destrozada, sucia de barro y sangre' (p. 256), watching uncomprehendingly as people die around her. The sufferings of the battlefields in the First World War, geographically restricted as they were, remained largely unseen by the civilian population. In some of the large cities of Spain the Civil War scenes of carnage, albeit on a smaller scale, could be witnessed relatively frequently. It is clear that these left a lasting impression on the war novelists. In *La llama*, Barea describes with mixed feelings of fascination and revulsion part of a human brain stuck to a shop window after a shell blast:

Contra la luna estaba aplastado y aún contrayéndose convulsivo un trozo de materia gris, del tamaño del puño de un niño. A su alrededor, pequeñas gotas temblonas de la misma sustancia, habían salpicado el cristal. Un hilillo de sangre acuosa se deslizaba por el cristal abajo, surgiendo de la pella de sesos, con sus venillas rojas y azules, en la que los nervios rotos seguían agitándose como finos látigos.   (p. 704)

The description is as objective as that of a hospital camera recording a surgical operation. Barea admits, however, to being sickened by such scenes to the point where his mental balance was seriously threatened, and it seems likely that his premature departure from Spain was as much due to his mental state as to Communist persecution.[33] He describes himself as 'encadenado a mí mismo y dividido dentro de mí mismo' (p. 710) – clearly a state of extreme despair.

In Sánchez Barbudo's *Sueños de grandeza*, the siege of Madrid proves too much for one of Arturo's relatives, Carmiña, who goes mad. This prompts Arturo to ponder on the fragility of our mental state and of the human values on which our relationships depend:

Arturo pensó entonces que aquella locura era como una puñalada, como una rasgadura en el velo que nos hace fácil la existencia. Estaban rotos para ella los hilos del tejido, no había continuidad en el espacio ni en el tiempo. No había moral tampoco, no había Dios; y su alma sufría hundida en el tormento del fuego.   (p. 269)

Carmiña's madness also symbolises for him the failure of the Spanish revolution, the frustration of the Republicans' hopes for a better future: 'En ella vio, macabramente, la encarnación de España entera, el fin trágico de todas las ilusiones y sueños de grandeza' (p. 272).

V. de Pedro's *La vida por la opinión* finishes on a similar note of disillusionment. As Madrid prepares to surrender, the crowds in the underground station no longer display the same human qualities as when the war began:

La fe que encendió en el pueblo de Madrid aquel maravilloso heroísmo de noviembre de 1936. Y esta fe los hacía solidarios en su desgracia, serenos en la aceptación de su destino, conformes con su miseria transitoria. Pero ahora se había perdido la serenidad. Todo vínculo de solidaridad se rompía. Se había perdido la fe, ya no había esperanza. (p. 237)

The dog Argos, whose life we have followed in the course of the narrative, is captured on leaving the underground by a group of children pretending to be Nationalist soldiers. In a scene reminiscent of *Duelo en el Paraíso* he is beaten and tied to a tree, where they pretend to execute him by firing squad. War has brutalised not only many militiamen in the novel, but also a new generation of Spaniards who lived through the experience. This view is echoed in Sancho Granado's *98 horas* in which he describes the war as 'guerra cruel que había de llenar de sangre y de odio – esto último tal vez lo peor – a muchas generaciones' (p. 23). This is a burden of responsibility that both sides have to bear.

Arana's priest in *El cura de Almuniaced* has the presentiment, rightly, that his peaceful rural existence and his spiritual harmony will be destroyed for ever by the war. What most preoccupies him, like Sender in *Contraataque*, is that he will end up by hating his enemy: 'Mañana, quizás luego, sería tarde para aquel goce tan puro: la guerra estaría allí, tapándole los ojos con puñados de odio; porque él odiaría también a los que odiaban, arrebatadamente, con aquella calentura en la sangre que parecía subir de la tierra y envolverlo todo. Otra vez la cólera de Pedro sería en él . . .' (p. 30). The theme of the destructive effect of passion on Christian forbearance runs throughout the story, and the death of the priest is the consequence of the prophecy he makes here.

Although, as we have seen in an earlier chapter, Republican novelists are mostly critical of the oppressing classes, some see the danger of creating such extreme class antagonism that groups will never again be able to live together. The intensity of feeling in a village is so described in Cimorra's *El bloqueo del hombre*: 'El odio del vecino A es sobre los vecinos B y C que viven allí y a quienes ve a tales horas todos los días y que tienen el objeto del odio, la finca, los bueyes, la herencia en el lugar precisamente. Todo en unos metros cuadrados' (p. 39). Such hatred is often embodied in a (Republican) villain – in this case the sadistic hunchback, El Sapo – not dissimilar to portrayals of Republican characters found in Nationalist novels. Republican novelists do occasionally concede, therefore, that such *incontrolados* existed on their side and were responsible for civilian deaths. Sender describes in *Ariadna* the killing of four wounded militiamen in cold blood by one of their comrades who is instructed by a superior officer 'Sácame de enmedio a estos tíos porque me desmoralizan la gente' (p. 261). This brutality is just as perverse as any described on the enemy side by the same author, and has no propaganda purpose.

The title of M.T. León's *Juego limpio* is a reference to the depths to which both sides sank during the war. At one point in the novel Claudio laments: 'Somos el preludio de algo espantoso, porque la guerra ya no tiene nada de caballeresco ni es cortesía, ni siquiera juego limpio y bárbaro: la guerra es únicamente la pelea de dos perros rabiosos' (p. 79). Such references reflect the disillusionment of a considerable number of these novelists that their ideals had been lost from sight and that all that remained was the phenomenon of the war itself.[34] As P. Collard points out, such disillusionment is common to most social novelists of the 1930s. Their literature 'refleja generalmente, por una parte, la esperanza de que la República traiga consigo una *Vida nueva* y, por otra, las desilusiones producidas precisamente al no cumplirse dichas esperanzas.'[35]

In London, in 1950, Arthur Koestler and others published a set of essays entitled *The God that Failed*, in which they renounced their beliefs in Communism as an answer to the problems of the West. Explaining the pessimistic tone of the writing, Koestler comments: 'As a rule, our memory romanticises the past. But when one has renounced a creed or been betrayed by a friend, the opposite mechanism sets to work. In the light of that later knowledge, the original experience loses its innocence, becomes tainted and rancid in recollection.'[36] Ignacio Silone's essay exposes the Communists' tactic of lying quite blatantly if it will serve their purpose to do so: the end justifies the means. He also finds quite unacceptable their dependence on theory and their contempt for values: 'On a group of theories one can found a school; but on a group of values one can found a culture, a civilization, a new way of living together among men.'[37] André Gide personalises the argument and talks of the Communists' contempt for loyalty in human relationships: 'An excellent way of earning promotion is to become an informer; that puts you on good terms with the dangerous police which protects you while using you. Once you have started on that easy slippery slope, no question of friendship or loyalty can intervene to hold you back.'[38] Communist duplicity is condemned in Stephen Spender's essay, in which he decries their scant regard for their so-called allies in the Popular Front: 'The fatality of the Communists was to think only of forming united fronts in order to seize control of them from within.'[39]

Echoes of these criticisms are to be found in a number of Republican novels, but none is as ferocious in its attack as Sender's *Ariadna*, since the author clearly feels that he was duped by the Russians in the 1930s and his life was threatened by them. Like the former leader of the PCE, Jesús Hernández,[40] he accuses the Russians of deliberately depriving the Spaniards of the arms necessary to win the war and even shipping back to Russia Spanish-made weapons, industrial tools and equipment of all kinds (*Ariadna*, p. 280).[41] The American Michael tells the chilling story of Earl, an American soldier in the International Brigades who happens to have no living relatives; he also bears a close resemblance to an English-speaking Russian official of the NKVD, called Vasiliev. A complicated conspiracy is hatched in which the young idealist Earl is liquidated and his passport delivered to Vasiliev, enabling him to take Earl's place and become a Russian spy in the United States.[42] The Russians who participate in this conspiracy do so with diabolical enjoyment. Other major sections of the novel are taken up with similar episodes which have an autonomous existence: they are not required by the internal development of the narrative, but demonstrate the author's 'voluntad de probar'. Pages 112–142, 152–156 and 286–293 are devoted to Michael's experiences in Moscow. In one scene, his Communist girlfriend Aniska takes him back to the few square metres of living space she shares with four other people. When he tries to caress her, she shows him statistics for the industrialisation of the Ural. Like all Communists in this novel, she puts her loyalty to the Party above love or friendship. Fedor, the Party official, speaks in the clichés described by Koestler in *The God that Failed*: 'Nosotros somos materialistas dialécticos y ustedes materialistas empíricos . . . Nuestro pacifismo . . . es dinámico y de naturaleza defensiva' (p. 124). His thoughts are determined largely by what *Pravda* has dictated.[43] Michael's denunciation in these pages of the theory of Socialist realism in literature is in fact Sender's formal renunciation of the beliefs he had expressed in 'El novelista y las masas'.[44] His attack on the totalitarianism, brutality and methods of social control exercised by the

Communists is trenchant. A naked man Michael meets in the park is an ex-schoolteacher who lost his job because, not having read his newspaper on the day the German Communists voted with the Nazis in the Reichstag, he told his class of children that Thaelmann would never do such a thing. He now has to expiate his sins by working in inhuman conditions, waist-deep in water, constructing the Moscow underground. In another episode, the dog Brooklyn, who has mysteriously landed in an American plane which carries no crew or passengers, represents Western individualism: he refuses to do the circus tricks that the Russian dogs have been trained to do (p. 150). He displays the Anarchist spirit that Sender admits in the prologue to the novel is closest to his own, saying: 'No soy capaz de formar en la fila de los perros de circo ladrando a compás y llevando en la boca el bastón del amo' (p. xiii). As Michiko Nonoyama points out, this episode is a fundamental attack on Stalinism:

Detrás de este episodio hay una crítica aguda de la fórmula estalinista de la transformación de la naturaleza humana. Buscando la contrapartida de la teoría de Michurin-Lysenko en el campo de la sicología, Stalin redescubrió a Pavlov. Trasladando las teorías de los reflejos condicionados de Pavlov al hombre, éste se convierte en un mecanismo reactivo cuya conducta, inclusive los procesos mentales de orden superior, puede comprenderse mediante el conocimiento de la ley de condicionamiento y puede controlarse a través de la aplicación de este conocimiento. De modo que Stalin encontró en el modelo que Pavlov da de la personalidad, la fórmula que coloca la naturaleza humana bajo el poder arbitrario del ambiente educativo controlado por el Estado.[45]

Clearly influenced by his experience in the Civil War, Sender portrays the Communists as wishing to empty man of any spiritual content he may have and fill his head with Party clichés – clichés which do not represent their true policies but which are designed to achieve certain predetermined goals. Language plays a powerful role in this, as we see in the description of the cult of personality which has grown up around the Vodz (Stalin).[46] The subordination of personal values to political expediency is clearly seen in the Vodz's murder of his own wife and in numerous acts of personal disloyalty by Communists. The arrival in Spain of the Russian ambassador (Rosenberg), 'contrahecho, con hocico de gárgola', brings with it a sinister atmosphere. 'Todo se va poniendo triste, melancólico, siniestro y agrio . . . seco y color de cementerio' (pp. 285–286). Spanish Communists are described behaving obsequiously to their Russian masters: 'Los periódicos que llegaron a la ciudad traían un nuevo lema: "Vale más morir de pie, que vivir de rodillas." Firmaba una mujer que se llamaba Dolores a quien yo conocía. No era probable que Dolores ni Verín murieran de pie. En cuanto a vivir de rodillas, estaban viviendo en esa posición incómoda a los pies del Vodz desde hacía muchos años y seguirían así el resto de su vida' (p. 407).[47]

The Spanish Communists, therefore, are no different from those who surround the Vodz in Moscow, all watching each other to ensure that they are making the correct responses to his statements, concerned only to ensure that they retain their place in the hierarchy. One of the greatest admirers of the Vodz (also called the 'Uro') is Sonia, a Russian who has been sent on a mission to Spain. In a section of the novel which is full of paradox, Sonia explains why she idolises the man responsible for the death of both her parents: 'El Uro es un monstruo pero la vida es monstruosa. El hombre es un criminal nato y lo humano es odiar, asesinar, destruir, traicionar, mentir . . . y dominar. Por eso el Uro es el más humano de los seres hasta hoy conocidos y por eso yo lo adoro' (p. 360). Such characters as this are morally perverted, and in emphasising their dehumanised qualities to the point of caricature, Sender creates monsters far more sinister than the Republican villains portrayed in Nationalist novels. Also, by creating a series of stories within stories, like a Russian doll which reveals ever more surprises as it is taken to pieces, the author adds to the sense of mystery reflecting the deviousness and labyrinthine complexity of the Communist conspiracy which Bolloten has described so well.[48] The story of the murdered American Earl, for example, was first told by Vera to Michael, who then recounted it to Javier. Malakov's tale about Stalin is within Michael's story of his inteview in the Kremlin, which in turn is part of Javier's testimony to the mysterious organisation OMECC. Ariadna, from behind a veil, reports Michael's account of Aniska's words to him.[49] This oblique approach to events, so radically different from the structure, as well as the message, of Contraataque, distances the author from them, but in no way reduces the disillusionment and bleak pessimism he feels. The distance may serve, however, to reduce the author's sense of guilt, to which he refers in the prologue: 'Todos somos culpables de lo que pasó en España. Unos por tontería y otros por maldad. El hecho de que la tontería esté de nuestra parte (de parte de los mejores) no nos salva ni ante la historia ni ante nosotros mismos' (pp. xii–xiii). Ariadna is the only one of Sender's war novels to show disillusionment. There is a brief reference in El rey y la reina to the Communists' love of slogans,[50] but it is good-humoured and the theme is not developed.

Max Aub's view of Communism, which is explored above all in Campo de sangre, is detached by comparison with Sender's; he does not express the same disillusionment, but does show he is aware of the dangers. When asked by the American Hope whether he is a Communist, Templado bridles; he claims that the Communists are aiming at world domination, that they put undue stress on discipline and undervalue freedom and ethical values. While there is much he admires in the Communists, Aub shows by his portrayal of Gorov in *Campo abierto* that he considers the Russians untrustworthy. In a conversation with a Republican minister about truth, Gorov remarks: 'En política decir la verdad es entregarse en manos del adversario' (p. 325). In a later conversation with Templado, he comments: 'Los sistemas políticos prueban su excelencia por la fuerza, y exclusivamente por ella . . . La única manera de tener razón es acabar con los enemigos' (p. 459). Such dubious principles are never advanced, however, by Spanish Communists like Herrera, in *Campo de sangre*.

Arturo Barea, in *La forja de un rebelde*, describes the manoeuvres of the Communists in Madrid (among them María Teresa León) to remove his future wife Ilsa from her post and put in their own people (p. 732). He describes the feeling of impotence he has on discovering that plots are being hatched against them: '¿Qué podíamos probar en contra? ¿Cómo podíamos luchar contra esta acumulación de antipatías y odios personales, intrigas políticas, y las leyes inflexibles de la maquinaria del Estado . . .?' (p. 733). His major criticism is directed at the young, ambitious neophytes of the Party who increasingly occupy positions of influence in the ministries:

Lo que más me chocaba en la mayoría de ellos, era que pertenecían a un mismo patrón: jóvenes ambiciosos (o miedosos, tal vez) pertenecientes a la clase media alta que se habían declarado comunistas, no como lo habíamos hecho en Madrid, porque nos parecía el partido de los trabajadores, sino porque unirse a ellos era unirse al grupo más fuerte y tener parte en su poder disciplinado. Habían saltado por encima del socialismo humanista y habían adquirido una máscara de eficiencia y rudeza. Admiraban a Rusia por su poder, no como una promesa de una nueva sociedad, y su actitud me daba escalofríos.   (p. 767)

His description of Ilsa's husband, Poldi, in action as an SIM interrogator leaves no doubt that he deplores the fanaticism with which the Communists pursued their goals: 'Ahora estaba ejerciendo lo que concebía su deber y lo terrible era que su poder sobre los otros le proporcionaba un placer. En la luz amarillenta sus ojos estaban hundidos como las órbitas de una calavera' (p. 767).[51]

Examples of virulently anti-Communist sentiment are to be found in V.

Alba's *La vida provisional*. In the very first pages the other Spanish left-wing groups are described as pawns being manipulated by the Communists who, in an attack on the Huesca front, take advantage of the opportunity to shoot their Republican comrades in the back. Later, they are described selling bread as pig-food so as deliberately to keep it in short supply (p. 56). Paula, the character who voices many of the criticisms of the Communists, nevertheless rejoins the Party after a period in the political wilderness, arguing that ultimately it is power that has corrupted them, not their political beliefs themselves: 'No hay ricos decentes. Es imposible. Y cuando se tiene el poder, es como si se fuera rico . . . todos nos volvemos iguales. No hay manera de estar en el poder y ser decente' (p. 76). Disillusionment with the Communists' methods turns to general disillusionment in political action, but grudging acknowledgement that there is no other solution.

J.R. Arana, in *El cura de Almuniaced*, appears to respect the motives of the Communists but cannot accept their materialism: 'Quienes niegan a Dios y ponen en su lugar al hombre que ha de venir, están jugando con palabras. Ellos también tienen sed de pureza y hambre de esperanza, pero no saben de dónde les viene esa inquietud, que es ansia de vida eterna y verdadera. Se dicen dialécticos e ignoran la gran síntesis de Cristo, Dios, Hijo del Hombre' (p. 28). This interpretation of the problem is unusual for its stress on Christian belief.

Republican despair at the factionalism on their own side is not motivated solely by Communist infiltration during the Civil War. Max Aub's characters are frequently infuriated by the lack of collaboration between the various individuals and groups; indeed, much of the conceptual substance of *El laberinto mágico* comes from the discussion between such characters, who are eloquent in putting their case but seldom compromise. '[Los] puntos de vista . . . quedan . . . sin solución, es decir sin que ninguno de los dos contrincantes acepte la opinión del otro, o intente ponerse en su lugar siquiera.'[52] This is not, therefore, a Hegelian dialectic which takes the thesis and the antithesis and achieves some form of synthesis. 'Los amigos del *Laberinto* . . . comparten sensaciones y sentimientos, pero prácticamente nunca coinciden en sus puntos de vista.'[53] Rivadavia complains, in *Campo de sangre*, about the Spaniards' political intemperance: 'Aquí el cogollo es la intemperancia, la falta de moderación. No hay más justicia que la propia: raíz del fracaso de la República' (p. 92). As might be expected, the Communist Herrera is highly critical of the Anarchists' emphasis on revolution rather than on military victory and their refusal to adopt a constructive political role: 'Mucho hablar de construir el mañana' (p. 97).

Rivadavia admires the Anarchists and is exasperated by them at the same time:

Entre nosotros no hay nada más poético, de posible materia poética, que los hombres de la FAI. Lo malo es que no están hechos para este mundo: lo deshacen. Hay pueblos enteros incapaces de concebir un mundo ordenado por la razón: los africanos y muchos pueblos orientales. El místico es individualista y el anarquismo español tiene ese gato en la barriga.   (p. 159)

As Soldevila Durante has indicated, it is possible to construct a picture of *homo hispanicus* from the pages of Aub's war novels. He appears to be 'simplista, irracionalista, cruel, impaciente, expeditivo, antilegalista, antifeminista, envidioso'. In politics, he is 'enemigo de partidos, de la autodisciplina individual y de grupo, caudillista'.[54] This has led to the creation of 'un pueblo dramático que puede aliar sin escrúpulos el máximo furor ético con la praxis más inmoral'.[55] Don Leandro's analysis (in the chapter 'Don Leandro y los anarquistas', *Campo de sangre*) leads him to the conclusion that the problem is insoluble: 'El remedio de España está en que no lo tiene' (p. 301). This paradox is later clarified: Anarchists are more interested in problems than solutions. A solution implies a form of steady state, whereas the *search* for a solution involves a dynamic. 'Contrarios a todas las soluciones, no por nada, sino porque significan estancamiento, sedentarismo, necesaria organización, futura estructura . . . la paz carece de sentido. Lo primero que abandonarían en ella sería su propio ser' (p. 311). In the same novel Sancho embarks on a long tirade against the divisions on the Republican side, concluding obscenely: 'Cada can lame su picha y Dios la de todos' (p. 96). Rivadavia returns to his attack on factionalism in *Campo abierto*, where, after berating the Anarchists for their lack of realism, he continues: 'Para eso de las ilusiones tanto montan los comunistas como los anarquistas y hasta, si me apuras mucho, los republicanos' (p. 293). In this novel, the conversations in the café La Granja on 6 November 1936, punctuated by reminders that the enemy is at the gates of Madrid, give the impression of Nero fiddling while Rome burns. Republican divisions come to a head in the description of the Casado coup in *Campo del Moro*, in which Aub sides firmly with the Communists in not wanting to capitulate to Franco's demands for an unconditional surrender. Templado curses the Anarcho-syndicalists roundly for conspiring with Casado: 'FAI: Fulleros Auténticos Ijos de puta . . . CNT: Cobardes Nacionalistas Traidores' (p. 128). Riquelme expresses similar emotions: 'Si pudiera se abriría el pecho para que saliera todo el rencor que le amarga la boca. Pestilencia. ¿Por qué tanto imbécil? ¿Por qué tanto ciego? ¿Por qué tan distintos los hombres unos de otros?' (p. 161). Vicente Dalmases is so infuriated by the Casado conspiracy, which he attributes to personal grudges rather than political judgement, that he is physically ill: 'Le regurgitan todos los insultos, las palabras más soeces. Sin poder remediarlo . . . Vicente siente arcadas, arroja lo poco que tiene en el estómago' (p. 244).

One of the few Anarchist writers on the war, A. Samblancat, uses the war novel to attack his political enemies on the Republican side. Azaña (thinly disguised as Cucaña) and Marcelino Domingo (as Aprilino del Martes) are mercilessly pilloried; they are accused of financial and sexual malpractice, respectively. The whole Republican cabinet of 1931 is dismissed as an 'equipo de juerguistas' (*Caravana nazarena*, p. 21). Lerroux's alleged sterility is made fun of. The Socialists are dismissed as 'otros cuatro gatos mayantes y en busca de cordilla, como las restantes murgas de izquierda' (*idem.*). Miaja is not credited with any responsibility for the defence of Madrid: 'Miaja se enteró de que había defendido a Madrid leyendo *Los Lunes de El Imparcial*' (p. 68). When the Republican administration abandons Madrid for Valencia, the departing functionaries are called 'bandadas de ratas burocráticas' (p. 65). His references to the Spanish gold reserves sent to Moscow imply that much of it was misappropriated on the way ('los que arramblaron con carretadas de oro del Banco de España' (p. 124)). In addition, Samblancat indicts the Republicans for handing over Eduardo Barriobero, ex-President of the Revolutionary Tribunal in Barcelona, to the Nationalists at the end of the war.

All the novelists mentioned here illustrate S.G. Eskin's assertion that divisions are much more apparent on the Left than on the Right:

> The left is far more self-critical, partly because it is more wracked by intramural conflicts than the right. Minor conflicts of ideology occur in right-wing literature – as between a heavily religious orientation and a more secular Falangist activism or between pure militarism and political partisanship – but the definitive tone is of unquestioned and unified dedication . . . The literature of the left, however, reflecting deeper, more public and unresolved divisions, is a veritable anthology of factionalism.[56]

Disillusionment with the home front is expressed with a good deal more frankness by Republicans, free of the constraints of the censorship that was imposed on their Nationalist counterparts. C. Cimorra, in *El bloqueo del hombre*, describes a woman trying to take away the contents of a requisitioned mansion, an action which outrages 'el erudito del Café Colonial' (p. 100). In the same novel, 'El Sapo' is a sadistic murderer who symbolises the *antihombre*. In Martínez Pagán's *Génaro*, extremism and irrational conduct abound: 'Ceux qui avançaient des idées de vérité et un bel idéal de rédemption humaine se virent tournés en dérision et humiliés... Il n'y eut pas un coin d'Espagne où ne pénétrat le virus: c'était la pourriture nationale' (p. 27). He describes first licence, then tyranny, on the Republican side: women lapsed into immorality (p. 99) and corruption invaded the rearguard: 'Il n'y avait d'héroïsme qu'au front' (p. 246). In V. de Pedro's *La vida por la opinión*, Isabel is murdered and robbed by a militiaman, an event which prompts her father to question his Anarchist belief in man's natural goodness: 'La realidad lo ponía frente al cadáver de su hija, asesinada por quienes, roto todo freno social, se entregaban a los más espantosos crímenes, descubriendo una naturaleza de fieras' (p. 98). For an early novel, this work is unusual for the degree to which it criticises the side on which its sympathies lie.[57] The villainous chauffeur 'El Patas', in Samblancat's *Caravana nazarena*, rapes and robs the heroine Maruja. The author's description of the vengeance wreaked on him by Maruja's lover, Lucas, gives a flavour of the violence of the period: 'Liquidó de un modo concienzudo lo del Patas, rompiéndole la cabeza a tiros en tantos pedazos que hubo que recogerle del suelo con cuchara el caletre' (p. 142).

Sueños de grandeza, in spite of being an early novel (it was written between 1938 and 1942), contains clear denunciations of the Republican violence and immorality which followed the heady optimism of the early days of the war: '¿Qué quedaba ahora del viento de julio? ¿Qué quedaba de aquel fuego? Quedaban las sombras y el crimen' (p. 15). The author's view is that the people abused the freedom with which they suddenly found themselves, 'una libertad que habíase convertido en estupidez, borrachera y sordos golpes' (p. 16). Within a short time, their sensitivities to the sufferings of others had been dulled, so that crime no longer provoked indignation or protest (p. 34). While war brought out the good qualities in some, it brought out the bad in many more. 'Muchas mujeres se prostituían o se dedicaban simplemente a poner en práctica sueños eróticos largamente acariciados' (p. 261). Amid the scenes of emotion in the defence of Madrid, the protagonist Arturo is suddenly overcome by gloom: 'Pese a su propia exaltación de horas antes, estaba seguro de que todo sería inútil y la venganza mayor' (p. 253). These seem to be honest sentiments, despite the fact that they are expressed with the benefit of hindsight.

If Sender had much to say on the iniquities of Stalinism, he has little to say about the disillusionment he felt concerning other activities on the home front. Aub, by contrast, is restrained in his criticism of the Communists;[58]

but he is highly critical of corruption, intrigue and betrayals in the rearguard – indeed much of his pessimism stems from his experience of such machinations in the Civil War.[59] Pirandello, a character in *Campo del Moro*, no longer has any faith in human nature as a result: 'Ya no creo ni en la libertad ni en la fraternidad ni en la igualdad. He visto demasiadas cosas que me hacen desesperar de la naturaleza humana. Todo lo que nos mueve son intereses pequeños. El hombre es malévolo, hipócrita, incapaz' (pp. 126–27). Most of Aub's criticism, however, is narrowly focussed on certain individuals rather than the whole human race. Vicente Calvo, in *Campo de sangre*, falsely denounces Templado's father as a Falangist because he owes him 10,000 pesetas, and it is only pure chance that saves the latter from death. 'Robespierre', a police informer, willingly divulges to Anarchist militiamen that his brother is a Falangist, an admission which leads to the latter's death (p. 454). In *Campo abierto*, Alfredo Meliá is falsely denounced as a Falangist by his young wife and her lover, and shot as a result. The anonymous 'chiquillo de Melilla' takes his own life in prison, although he is innocent: 'Se suicidó con una cuchara, que se hundió en la garganta. Lo había denunciado su cuñado, un catolicón que no le podía ver . . . La verdad es que el muchacho nunca se había metido en nada' (p. 180).

The conflict between values on the one hand, and political theories (or simple expediency) on the other, is one of Aub's constant themes. For one critic, 'the frequency with which the Aubian hero engages in the theme of friendship is proof that Max Aub gives the human drama priority over the ideological controversy.'[60] For another, Aub is a 'conciencia desgarrada entre la elementalidad zoológica y la vigencia de unos valores éticos'.[61] In this conflict of loyalties, some characters sacrifice personal values. Jorge Mustieles, in *Campo abierto*, is part of a tribunal which tries his father; he votes with the others to condemn him to death (p. 127). The judge Rivadavia, Templado's close friend in *Campo de sangre*, subjects him to an interrogation over his dealings with Lola Cifuentes, who has defected to France. Templado is devastated by this lack of trust:

De pronto se sintió solo, completamente solo. ¿Tú también, bruto? [*sic*] pensó. Este que me conoce . . . El mundo le hizo daño. Le dieron ganas de gritar, de arañar el aire, de desesperarse con grandes alharacas . . . Siente el latigazo de la sospecha, el no poder contar con nadie, el no poder suponer siquiera que alguien le conoce. Una vez más se le derrumba su confianza en el hombre.   (pp. 452–453)

The complicated sub-plot of this novel, involving the SIM informer López Mardones, reveals the same atmosphere of fear and distrust that Barea describes in *La llama*. Secret Nationalist agents in Barcelona are getting papers to Burgos via contacts in Perpignan. Teresa Guerrero of the Teatro Barcelona is implicated, as is an under-secretary at the Generalitat. The informers brought in to keep watch on these activities (Mardones, Julio Jiménez, Peruzzi) are some of the most unpleasant characters Aub creates anywhere; they constitute a dim underworld in which loyalty and friendship have no place, but where brutality, corruption and immorality flourish.[62] If Aub's disillusionment is not total, it is because it is mitigated by the acts of human solidarity we have described elsewhere, and by relationships like that of Vicente and Asunción which survive the trauma of social disintegration. There is no doubt, however, that his faith in his fellow Spaniards, and indeed in human nature, was profoundly shaken by his experiences.

As we have seen, Sender's political disillusionment at the actions of the Left is expressed above all in *Ariadna*. In *El rey y la reina* he expresses more general disillusionment, at the impossibility of man's achieving his ideal. Since at one level Rómulo may be seen as a symbol of the Spanish people, and the duchess a symbol of their aspirations, the tragedy stems from the fact that in trying to attain their aspirations the people destroy them.[63] The duchess makes us aware of this truth when she reads the following in the *Esiemplos de las Monarquías*:

El universo es una inmensa monarquía. Los pobladores del universo estamos sometidos fatalmente a ella y somos a nuestra vez reyes de la realidad que nos rodea. Todo lo que el hombre ha soñado, ambicionado, creado, lo ha sido por esta monarquía del hombre – rey – y la ilusión, su propia ilusión – reina. El hombre y la ambición ideal que lleva consigo son el rey y la reina del universo . . .
    Pero cuando el rey – el hombre – quiere cumplirse en la posesión ideal de la reina hasta alcanzar los absolutos de Dios, la armonía se rompe y el orden del matrimonio se acaba. Que alcanzar la ilusión es matarla.   (p. 143)

A. Tovar writes that 'con razón algunos críticos que vivieron la guerra del lado republicano encuentran esta novela objetiva, impasible, imparcial. Tiene la impasibilidad del verdadero arte. Y nos hace sentir la crueldad de la vida.'[64] What is significant is that critics have related the novel to the war at all, since it pays scant regard to historical details, even avoiding acronyms like CNT or UGT when it would be much more natural to use them.[65] They are right to consider it a war novel, however, in that Sender's own personal experiences of the conflict are distilled and presented in symbolic form. His disillusionment with what he saw may well have played an important role in determining the form of the novel.[66] Certainly, there are signs in this novel as well as in *Ariadna* that the author needed to distance himself from the historical events by means of various literary devices. His disillusionment with the war years can be explained, not so much by the direct utterances of the characters, as by the general sense of frustration and failure that pervades the work. A further tragic dimension is added when one considers the likely fate of the protagonist Rómulo, of which we remain ignorant. His words on becoming the guardian of the palace (ending with: 'Acepté el brazalete republicano y la pistola' (p. 24)) have the flavour of a statement to a tribunal, and the duchess's warning to him may well have foreshadowed some form of retribution when the Nationalists entered Madrid: 'Terminó diciendo que tuviera cuidado con sus actos porque quizás un día tendría que explicarlos' (p. 26). According to such an interpretation, Rómulo not only fails to capture his fleeting illusion, but pays dearly for the pursuit of it.

Barea, as we have seen, does not disguise his abhorrence of violence by his own side. 'Su testimonio registra no sólo el heroísmo del pueblo español, sino también su ceguera, su locura monstruosa.'[67] Like the characters of many Civil War novels (Vicente Dalmases in *Campo de sangre*, Jorge Mustieles in *Campo abierto*, José Torres in 'La cabeza de cordero') Barea is described vomiting at moments of crisis, thus giving expression to the nausea he feels at the direction events have taken. Barea sees that his Socialist ideals are far from being realised. On a visit with Ilsa to Valencia, they are surprised to see how well people are living, while Madrid starves. In Murcia, the disparity is even more evident. He describes the scene in the hotel dining-room:

Estaban en pequeños grupos; los huertanos de la vieja casta de propietarios rurales, inquietos, malhumorados y silenciosos; los grupos más numerosos de los huertanos nuevos, hombres que habían sido explotados miserablemente toda su vida y habían llegado, a fuerza de sacrificios crueles, a convertirse a su vez en explotadores implacables y que ahora realizaban ganancias fabulosas en la escasez; y por último los grupos de los trabajadores, torpes, ruidosos, alardeando descaradamente de la libertad que habían ganado, exhibiéndose con sus pañuelos negros y rojos de anarquistas como para asustar con ellos a los amos odiados. Era una atmósfera de alegría forzada y falsa, con una subcorriente de desconfianza mutua, de tensión eléctrica, de disfrute desesperado. (pp. 738-739)

Compare this with the earlier descriptions of the *casinos* of Novés, one for the rich, one for the poor. What is described in Murcia is no real advance, simply a bringing together of the disparate elements under one roof. Their mutual distrust remains; some of the exploited have become, in their turn, exploiters. *Homo homini lupus.*

Because of his vocation, Arana's priest in *El cura de Almuniaced* is in a privileged position to moralise about the lessons of the Spanish revolution. Arana (like Ayala and Gironella) believes there must be a fundamental change in the hearts of men before social change can successfully follow. The class hatred and materialism unleashed by the Civil War was no basis on which to construct a just society. 'El hombre es libre de dentro a fuera y no de fuera a dentro ... Nadie libera a nadie. La libertad económica ... no es la libertad en sí, sino uno de los factores que la propician y que hacen posible su desarrollo' (p. 57). Mosén Jacinto achieves tragic stature because he pits himself against the awesome forces on each side in the belief that some form of reconciliation is possible. He is obsessed with having wasted his life in an attempt to change the hearts and minds of those around him. '¡Tratar de convencer aquí con la palabra y el ejemplo! ¡Tanto valía empeñarse en abrir ostras tañendo la guitarra! No le había entendido nadie ... (p. 26). The forces are already out of control: 'Es el tiempo de la manada contra el hombre; la hora de los infras, de los incompletos, aplastando todo lo que ha crecido más allá de su nada. La furia humana rompe y se deshace en ellos como una ola muy pequeña. El mismo Cid perecería ...' (p. 85). Arana's disillusionment, then, stems from a sense of hopelessness that nothing could be done to prevent the tragedy, for which he blames Republicans as well as Nationalists.

Paul Ilie writes that 'a commonplace of exile studies in all nations is that the exilic sensibility tends towards a universal limbo of immobile idealism'.[68] A study of the war novelists does not lead me to this conclusion. While their condemnation of Francoism is a constant, their critical awareness of their own side's defects develops steadily with time. Nowhere is this more clearly seen than in the evolution of Sender (from *Contraataque* to *Ariadna*) or Aub (from *Campo cerrado* to *Campo del Moro*). Marra-López simplifies Aranguren's categories of exiled writers to two: 'los beligerantes y los que han superado esa beligerancia'.[69] This seems a sensible classification, provided one realises that there is great diversity within the second category. S.G. Eskin rightly identifies a certain cynicism towards political solutions among these novelists. 'A writer may emphatically challenge the validity of the whole political dimension by asserting the moral claims of a private world of feelings and personal relationships, possibly in conjunction with spiritual and religious values.'[70] While he does not give examples, they are not difficult to find. In *Ariadna*, 'Javier solía repetir: yo no soy político, ni creo que lo seré nunca' (p. 52) – a view Sender repeats in the prologue to the novel (p. viii). Aub's magnificent creation Jacobo, the crow in 'Manuscrito cuervo' (*Cuentos ciertos*), gives a definition of politics: 'Definición: arte de dirigir. Medio: hacer virtud de la hipocresía' (p. 209). As for definitions of Fascism and anti-Fascism, 'Los fascistas no permiten huelgas. Los antifascistas acaban con las huelgas a tiros . . .' (*idem.*). The Republican minister who comes to address the troops in *Génaro* (p. 148) speaks in clichés; the author's contempt is clear from the description he gives. Saulo and don Eugenio, in *La vida por la opinión*, are typical of many Anarchist characters in that they believe in the people but not in their politicians. Significantly, the only optimistic note in *Caravana nazarena* is struck in the description of the human relationships between the three students and their girlfriends. When nothing else is left, and they are forced to flee to France, they are sustained in adversity, in an atmosphere of corruption and immorality, by friendship and love for each other. Love and sex, powerful elements in many of these war novels, often represent the only constant values in a chaotic universe. In *Ariadna*, such a bond exists between Ariadna and Javier. In Aub's *Campos*, erotic scenes are commonplace and loving relationships develop between Paulino Cuartero and Rosario, Vicente Dalmases and Asunción, Víctor Terrazas and Rosa María, and many others. Deep friendships between men and women are also frequently described. Arturo Barea's relationship with Ilsa, described in *La llama*, enables him to retain his sanity. M.T. León gives prominence, in *Juego limpio*, to the love story of Claudio and Angelines. In *El cura de Almuniaced* the priest's physical love is sublimated to a communion with nature. The memory of an adolescent love affair, 'amor ingenuo y dulce', for example, is inseparable from the landscape which nostalgically reminds him of it (p. 16). Prior to the outbreak of war, he sees the world through the innocent eyes of a child, and the pleasures of life – taking the morning sun, the daily walk to the hermitage – are keenly felt. This communion with a nature in which he sees God's work sustains the priest in his 'pasar constante hacia la muerte' (p. 115). By the end of the novel, however, his joy in nature is gone; what is ostensibly the same scene outside his window has lost its beauty:

El cielo es limpio ahora, recién mudado de invierno a primavera, pero él lo siente viejo, como rayado de miradas. En toda aquella inmensidad no queda ni un milímetro limpio de angustia o de blasfemia, ni un punto que no haya lamido la tristeza del hombre. (p. 90)

In the war novel, the phenomenon that Ilie has termed the 'exilic symptom' is often in evidence. It must be appreciated that writers are often seeing the war from the vantage point of exile, and this must inevitably colour their view of earlier events. Arturo, the protagonist of Sánchez Barbudo's *Sueños de grandeza*, encapsulates the thesis that Ilie examines in *Literature and Inner Exile* when he says: 'Todos notamos la falta de la otra mitad' (p. 189). Exilic symptoms in the war novel may be described as feeling cut off from others, failing to communicate with others, being subjected to strange behaviour by others, not knowing where to go or what to do. Arturo experiences many of these symptoms: he is first described at the front on his own, pondering on the war (ch. 1): when he visits his cousin Leopoldo's house in Madrid he enters an atmosphere reminiscent of Carmen Laforet's *Nada* (p. 44ff.); he fails to communicate with his cousin Asunción: 'Empezaba a sentir la desagradable sensación de que no se entendía, que no se entendería ya nunca con ella, como, quizás tampoco con otras personas' (p. 76), and he witnesses violent family disputes. He is described as 'indeciso en cuanto al rumbo a tomar' (p. 96), in a scene in which he hallucinates about past events in the streets of Madrid.

In Aub's *Campos* the constant separations that take place are an anguished reminder of exile; this is nowhere better expressed than in Vicente's relationship with Asunción:

Tal es su destino: haberse conocido, haberse reconocido para siempre uno de otro, y separarse, unirse, volver a separarse, buscarse en el infortunio, por fin encontrarse y tener que separarse de nuevo ... Un sí, un no; y una línea quebrada que desde la negación del vacío aspira a reconquistar la afirmación de la plenitud.[71]

The plight of Herrera in his tank in *Campo de sangre*, without radio communication or supply line, is another example of separation: 'En el tanque ... estás solo, cerrado, encerrado. Completamente solo, a la gracia de Dios ... y ciego. Sin saber nada de nada' (p. 433). Vicente complains in the dark days of November, 1936: '¿Para qué seguir? Nos han dejado solos. Solos, a cada uno de nosotros, sin remedio' (*Campo abierto*, p. 264). In *Campo del Moro* numerous characters try frantically to get friends out of prison during the Casado coup; their pleas nearly always fall on deaf ears.

It is not necessary to be an exile to display exilic symptoms. Barea would probably have been alienated even without living in England: 'Este héroe tan entretenido de *La forja* está como dividido – muy fiel a la condición humana de nuestra época – entre su soledad esencial, de la que quiere desprenderse a todo trance ... y su soledad "social".'[72] These symptoms, however, are exacerbated by the prospect of an extended exile.

Under the heading 'La soledad como circunstancia', J. Uceda discusses this aspect of *Réquiem por un campesino español*.[73] She points out that the caves Paco visits with the priest lack light, fire, air and water – all the elements essential to life, according to the ancients. The scene with the dying man symbolises a total lack of communication: 'En cada una de aquellas personas había una forma distinta de soledad y una total incomunica-ción.'[74] Paco's death too takes place in an atmosphere of total abandonment. He is enclosed, alone in his hideout until he agrees to emerge; then at the moment of his death he is abandoned by the priest.

It is clear from these examples of disillusionment that the phenomenon is more widespread and more profound in the Republican novel than in its Nationalist counterpart. This is explained by the relative freedom to express their thoughts enjoyed by Republican writers, the factionalism that inevitably sets in when an enterprise fails, and certain international developments such as the Hitler–Stalin pact, which suggested that they may have been little more than pawns in a game played out between the great powers. Aranguren maintains that Unamuno supplants Ortega as the guiding light of many of the exiled writers because his tragic sense of life is more in tune with their ideas. 'La contradicción anímica que, por decirlo así, constituía la sustancia misma de don Miguel y el trance de contradicción interior en que ha puesto a los emigrados el suceso del destierro, tenía que empujar a éstos hacia él.'[75] These writers do not, on the whole, indulge in the 'desperate and consuming nihilism' referred to earlier, which Benson identifies in many foreign writers on the war. They continue to adopt a critical stance towards the ideas of the Right, from Traditionalism to Fascism, but no longer see any easy political solutions. The duplicity of the Communists, under orders from Moscow, meets widespread condemnation, as does their over-emphasis on political theory (or expediency) at the cost of human values, their exaggerated sense of discipline and obedience to the Party, and their preparedness to use any means to attain their ends.

The Republican novel shares with the Nationalist novel a preoccupation with the horrors of war, but often puts the descriptions to different use: they are included not to glorify the exploits of the soldier, but to condemn the carnage. The fighting soldier on both sides often receives praise from his enemy. Not so the armchair warrior on the home front to which the soldier occasionally returns, unshaven, evil-smelling and lice-ridden, to find that such people know more about what is happening at the front than he does himself. Participants on both sides are also frequently disillusioned to see that one area of the country and one sector of the population is suffering deprivation, while another is reaping profits.

On the Nationalist side, disillusionment is most strongly felt by a group of Falangists, who see that their ideals of social renewal have been subverted. In addition, the lofty ideals of Nietzsche, discussed in an earlier chapter, have been sadly adulterated: 'La Voluntad se hizo Violencia, la Aristocracia desembocó en Autoritarismo, el Individualismo en Anarquía fracasada, la glorificación de la Vida en desesperación respecto al sentido humano y solidario de la vida.'[76]

All those who lived through the war realise that, as well as seeing man at his most courageous, they have also plumbed the depths of human degradation. The victors succeeded in stifling much of the soul-searching that would otherwise have taken place in Spain, and it was left to the exiles to express these thoughts, together with their continuing resentment, in most cases, at the Nationalist victory. Most writers of sensitivity saw their faith in their fellow Spaniards, and in man himself, severely shaken. While many displayed a 'pedagogy of optimism' in political solutions before the war, few could cling to such beliefs afterwards. As Rieuneau has pointed out in his study of the novel of the First World War, certain writers came to the conclusion that war does not degrade man, it simply reveals him as he is. He concludes: 'La philosophie de l'histoire est désespérante.'[77] Some of that despair, in varying degrees, is to be found in the novel of the Spanish Civil War.

Notes

1   D. Ridruejo, *Escrito en España* (Buenos Aires, 1962). I have used the second, corrected edition of 1964.
2   Of his resignation as editor of *Escorial* he writes: 'La dimisión fue aceptada de hecho sin que se le diese publicidad alguna. Tales eran los usos' (*Escrito en España*, p. 21). The regime was clearly attempting to portray itself as a seamless robe during these years, and provided it could guarantee censorship, was able to do so.
3   *Ibid.*, p. 15.
4   *Ibid.*, p. 17.
5   *Ibid.*, p. 18.
6   *Idem.*
7   *Ibid.*, p. 25.
8   *Ibid.*, pp. 34–35.
9   *Ibid.*, p. 81.
10 *Ibid.*, p. 103.
11 Ridruejo accepts responsibility, as a 'falangista notorio', for many of the atrocities during the Civil War. In an eloquent *mea culpa*, he confesses: 'Conviví, toleré, di mi aprobación al terror con mi silencio público y mi perseverancia militante' (*ibid.*, p. 93 footnote 1).
12 When unification is mentioned in the Nationalist novel it is never criticised; indeed it is more likely to be larded with praise. In Pablo Muñoz's *Aquellas banderas de Aragón*, for example, Falangists are described as being 'aumentados ahora con el magnífico Decreto de la Unificación

que el Caudillo tuvo el acierto de concebir'. None of the problems posed by unification is given serious consideration by the novelist.

13 *Tendencias en la novela española actual* (Paris, 1970), p. 73.

14 *Ibid.*, p. 75. As Georgel points out, this decree was applied to works as diverse as *Madame Bovary* and the *Discours de la méthode* (J. Georgel, *Le Franquisme* (Paris, 1970), p. 219).

15 *Spain and the Rule of Law* (Geneva, 1962), *passim.*

16 *Ibid.*, p. 49.

17 IPI Survey No. 5, *The Press in Authoritarian States* (Zurich, 1959), p. 146. Quoted in *Spain and the Rule of Law*, p. 48.

18 *Spain and the Rule of Law*, Appendix 9 (pp. 152–153).

19 The 1966 Law replaced prior censorship with the dubious principle of 'consulta voluntaria'. An author who risked publication without advice from the Ministry of Information could be fined up to a quarter of a million pesetas (Article 69).

20 Even when some were published in the slightly more liberal atmosphere between 1966 and the repeal of Francoist legislation (after the death of the dictator), references to sensitive issues were removed. In the following passage from Ayala's 'El tajo', the section in italics was excised in the 1972 Magisterio Español edition: 'Así se llegó discutiendo abuelo y nieto, hasta el final de la lucha: Entraron los moros en Toledo, salieron los sitiados del Alcázar, el viejo saltaba como una criatura, *y él, Pedro Santolalla, despechado y algo desentendido, sin tanto cuidado ya por atajar sus insensatas chiquilladas, pudo presenciar ahora, atónito, el pillaje, la sarracina* . . . Poco después se incorporaba al ejército . . . (Quoted in M. Joly, *Panorama du roman espagnol contemporain* (Montpellier, 1979), p. 349).

21 R. Gullón writes of the post-war Spanish novel: 'La violencia refleja la crueldad y el miserabilismo de la época; de una sociedad caracterizada por su conflicto permanente con el hombre, por el individuo pugnante por realizarse en libertad. El hombre ha pasado a ser víctima de una colectividad tiránica . . . El hombre moderno es el eventual acusado de cada instante, el sospechoso, y en cualquier momento puede convertirse en objeto, presa destinada a la destrucción en la máquina trituradora del todopoderoso Estado' ('La novela española moderna', *La Torre*, 42 (1963), 45–68 (pp. 61–62)).

22 I. Criado Miguel finds little formal innovation in the Republican novelists either: 'Con excepción de Francisco Ayala, la evolución de la novela española se debe al esfuerzo supremo de unos cuantos que se quedaron' ('Mito y desmitificación de la guerra en dos novelas' in A. Gallego Morell [ed.], *Estudios sobre literatura y arte* (Granada, 1979), 333–356 (p. 338)).

23 *Literature and Inner Exile. Authoritarian Spain 1939–1975* (Baltimore, 1980), pp. 3–4.

24 I. Soldevila-Durante maintains that around 1940 a directive was issued to the effect that writers should abandon the theme of the Civil War. ('La novela española actual (Tentativa de entendimiento)', *Revista Hispánica Moderna*, 33 (1967), 89–108 (p. 98)).

25 'En el libro de Reguera no hay tópicos políticos o sentimentales, ni blandas patrioterías, sino la vida del soldado . . . en toda su verdad' (Alborg, *Hora actual de la novela española*, 1 (Madrid, 1962), p. 218).

26 It seems extraordinary that García Serrano should have succeeded in getting into print sentiments such as those expressed here. It should be remembered, however, that Falange enjoyed freedoms denied to other groups. A memorandum of 1 May 1941, for example, exempted the Falangist press from censorship. The International Commission of Jurists commented: 'As the Falange is controlled by the State, this immunity obviously causes the regime to run no risk' (*Spain and the Rule of Law*, p. 50) but as we have seen, dissident Falangists occasionally did constitute a risk.

27 Contradictions of this kind abound in the war novel. Benítez de Castro writes in *Se ha ocupado el kilómetro 6*, 'La guerra es execrable' (p. 160); 'La Artillería es la más sublime de las armas' (p. 179).

28 *Writers in Arms* (London, 1968), p. xxviii.

29 *Ibid.*, p. xxix.
30 '¿Para quién escribimos nosotros? Yo, español en América, ¿para quién escribo? . . . Pues si nos preguntáramos: ¿Para quién escribimos nosotros? Para todos y para nadie sería la respuesta. Nuestras palabras van al viento: confiemos en que algunas de ellas no se pierdan' (*El escritor en la sociedad de masas* (Buenos Aires, 1958), pp. 7 and 21).
31 This surge of Republican novels matches a pattern detected by H. de Keyserling in the sales of First World War novels in 1929. He explains this phenomenon by saying that participants in the war would have made a positive effort to forget it immediately afterwards as an unpleasant experience; interest returned after a period of 10–11 years (*Meditaciones suramericanas* (Madrid 1933), p. 80). M. Rieuneau, too, identifies a second wave of First World War novels 'dix ou douze ans après' (*Guerre et révolution dans le roman français de 1919 à 1939* (Paris, 1974), p. 213). In Spain, the Nationalist novel is faithful to this trend – it reappears after a lengthy absence in 1950 – though, as we have seen, censorship may have accentuated the pattern in this case.
32 Aub was present at the Paris exhibition when Picasso's 'Guernica' was unveiled to the public for the first time. It is not inconceivable that the image of the disembowelled horse originates in that painting.
33 See J. Blanco Amor, 'A 20 años de *La forja de un rebelde*', *Cuadernos Americanos*, 185 (1972), 213–222 (p. 216). The final section of *La forja de un rebelde*, dealing with the siege of Madrid, is preceded by the following verse by William Blake:
   . . . When the senses
   Are shaken, and the soul is driven to madness,
   Who can stand? When the souls of the oppressed
   Fight in the troubled air that rages, who can stand?
34 B. Vance, 'The Civil War (1936–39) as a Theme in the Spanish Contemporary Novel' (PhD thesis, Wayne State University, 1968), overstates the case when she writes: '[The Spanish Civil War novelists'] protest is directed, in the case of the Nationalist authors, against the other side, and in the Republican authors mainly against elements in their own side' (p. 344). This is certainly not the case. However, it is true to say that examples of mordant self-criticism are more frequently found among Republican novelists.
35 *Ramón J. Sender en los años 1930–36* (Ghent, 1980), p. 69.
36 *The God that Failed* (London, 1950), p. 63.
37 *Ibid.*, p. 119.
38 *Ibid.*, pp. 187–188.
39 *Ibid.*, p. 247. Spender became a Communist because of the Civil War, which he described as 'in part an anarchist's war, a poet's war' (p. 245).
40 *Yo fui un ministro de Stalin* (Mexico, 1953), p. 173.
41 It will be recalled that in *Contraataque*, Russian arms *work*. E. Rodríguez Monegal writes: 'La amargura con que Javier denuncia en 1957 las actividades de los comunistas en España no habría sido posible si, entre 1936 y 1938, Sender no hubiese creído en ellos.' As he points out, praise for Communist leadership is lavish in *Contraataque* (pp. 66, 73, 114, 148, 149, 164, 167, 182, 226, 227, 284 and 286) (*Tres testigos españoles de la guerra civil* (Caracas, 1971), p. 31).
42 H. Thomas corroborates that such activities as these took place: 'The NKVD secured the passports of all dead (and some alive) members of the International Brigade, and they were despatched to Moscow: here a pile of nearly a hundred of them "mainly American" were observed by Krivitsky . . . Then new bearers were issued with these, and entered America as, apparently, reformed citizens (*The Spanish Civil War* (London, 1971), p. 426 footnote 2).
43 This view was shared by André Gide. 'In the Soviet Union it is accepted for once and for all that on every subject – whatever may be the issue – there can only be one opinion, the right one. And each morning *Pravda* tells the people what they need to know, and must believe and think' (*The God that Failed*, pp. 184–85).

44 Michael says mockingly: 'Parece que el realismo socialista es el que insulta a América y a Francia y a Inglaterra, y el burgués el que no se preocupa de insultar a nadie y dice las cosas más o menos como son' (p. 130).

45 'El anarquismo en las obras de Ramón J. Sender'. Unpublished PhD thesis (University of Illinois, 1970), p. 244. This work later appeared in published form in Ed. Playor (Madrid, 1979).

46 Gide reported after his visit to Russia that his interpreter there had refused to send a telegram to Stalin which included the personal pronoun 'you' without qualification. 'It was not decent, he declared, and something must be added. He suggested "You leader of the workers" or else "You Lord of the people"' (*The God that Failed*, p. 194). He also learned that words like 'destiny' should always be preceded by the word 'glorious' when it referred to the destiny of the Soviet Union (*idem.*). Sender uses such language freely in his satirical references to the Vodz.

47 The references are to La Pasionaria and Lister, both of whom went to live in Moscow at the end of the Civil War and continued to lead the Spanish Communist Party in exile.

48 *The Grand Camouflage* (London, 1961), He accuses the Communists of adopting 'a policy of duplicity and dissimulation of which there is no parallel in history' (p. 17).

49 Honest critics have admitted that they simply do not understand parts of *Ariadna*: 'El embrollo es tal que la obra alcanza la categoría de ininteligible' (Marra-López, *Narrativa española fuera de España* (Madrid, 1963), p. 378).

50 'Este... es comunista y tiene la manía de los letreros. Si no andamos con ojo, en menos de una semana la casa estará llena de carteles y rótulos' (*El rey y la reina* (Barcelona, 1979), p. 101).

51 'The Servicio de Investigación Militar... was to establish a set of torture chambers in Barcelona which were unearthed by the Nationalists after their victory' (H. Thomas, *The Spanish Civil War*, p. 557). Although Barea does not mention torture specifically, his reference to a prisoner looking like an 'animal perseguido' and the obvious relief he expresses in getting out of the building (pp. 766–767) point to the fact that this was such a *checa*.

52 I. Soldevila Durante, *La obra narrativa de Max Aub* (Madrid, 1973), p. 223.

53 *Ibid.*, p. 225.

54 *Ibid.*, p. 264.

55 *Ibid.*, p. 265.

56 S.G. Eskin, 'The Literature of the Spanish Civil War: Observations on the Political Genre', *Genre*, 4, no. 1 (1971), 76–99 (p. 85).

57 This is explained perhaps by the fact that the author is not Spanish but Argentinian. His notes for the novel were written in Madrid after Franco's victory in 1939.

58 'Aub fully appreciates the war effort sustained by the Communist Party and its Soviet Russian and Spanish representatives, but clearly rejects in all of his novels the application of the Communist doctrine as a solution, not only to Spain's but to man's problems in general' (P.P. Kohler, 'The Literary Image of the Spanish Civil War of 1936–39 in Max Aub's *El Laberinto Mágico*', unpublished PhD thesis (University of Toronto, 1970), p. 447).

59 Aub himself was falsely denounced in France after the war and imprisoned in Marseilles as a suspected Communist. His tribulations in the concentration camps stem from this, which explains why it is a haunting theme (I. Soldevila Durante, *La obra narrativa de Max Aub*, p. 77 footnote).

60 P.P. Kohler, 'The Literary Image', p. 126.

61 M. Tuñón de Lara, 'El laberinto mágico' in 'Homenaje a Max Aub', *Cuadernos Americanos*, 187, no. 2 (1973), 85–90 (p. 87).

62 Aub seems to take pleasure in punishing such characters. The secret policeman Ramiro Garizurieta is being cuckolded by López Mardones (*Campo de sangre*, p. 380). The wife of the informer Julio Jiménez is brutally raped by her stepson shortly after she has killed her husband and mutilated his body (pp. 464–466).

63 See M.C. Peñuelas, *Conversaciones con Ramón J. Sender* (Madrid, 1970), p. 165, where Sender admits: 'La duquesa es la España tradicional.'

64 'Dos capítulos para un retrato literario de Sender', *Cuadernos del Idioma*, 4 (1966), 17–35 (pp. 21–22).

65 The Hispano car which is requisitioned by the militiamen is daubed with 'tres iniciales blancas'. Rómulo admits to belonging to a trades union 'que tiene esas mismas iniciales' (p. 22). When he is asked by a Republican officer which union he is a member of, Rómulo is saved from having to reply by a militiaman, who interposes: 'De la misma central sindical que yo' (p. 102). By such devices Sender avoids ever naming the union.

66 While it is difficult to demonstrate that the novel of the war was a form of psychotherapy for some authors, it does not seem an unreasonable hypothesis.

67 This was the view of a *Times Literary Supplement* critic. Quoted in F. Yndurain, 'Resentimiento español: Arturo Barea', *Arbor*, 85 (1953), 73–79 (p. 75).

68 *Literature and Inner Exile* (Baltimore, 1980), p. 11.

69 *Narrativa española fuera de España*, p. 79.

70 'The Literature of the Spanish Civil War', p. 92.

71 G. Sobejano, 'Asunción en el laberinto', *Cuadernos Americanos*, 188, no. 3 (1973), 98–105 (pp. 101–102).

72 D. Pérez Minik, *Novelistas españoles de los siglos XIX y XX* (Madrid, 1957), p. 308.

73 In 'Realismo y esencias en Ramón Sender', *Revista de Occidente*, 82 (1970), 39–53.

74 *Ibid.*, p. 49.

75 'La evolución espiritual de los intelectuales españoles en la emigración', *Cuadernos Hispanoamericanos*, 38 (1953), 123–157 (p. 138).

76 G. Sobejano, *Nietzsche en España* (Madrid, 1967), p. 664.

77 *Guerre et révolution dans le roman français de 1919 à 1939* (Paris, 1974), p. 494.

7
—

The novel
as chronicle:
Gironella's trilogy

Los cipreses creen en Dios

NOT SATISFIED with describing his own experience of the war, as
Barea has done, Gironella wants to novelise the whole phenomenon,
including its antecedents and consequences. The novelist who wants to
present such a panoramic vision of history in the course of his narrative, and
sustain at the same time the relationship he has developed between his
readership and his literary creations, is faced with a major difficulty. The
picaresque tradition in Spain offered one solution to this problem: we could
follow a sympathetic Lazarillo from master to master, studying as we did so
a whole society in its evolution. A measure of unity was provided by the
strong personality of the central character. In more modern times the
cinematographic technique offers a similar solution. The main character,
like a camera, records the events around him as he moves from place to
place, interpreting the action through his own personality. This technique
is well suited to the war novel that describes a section of the front, or a
particular action (as in Benítez de Castro's *Se ha ocupado el kilómetro 6*), or the
experiences of the soldier throughout several actions (as in Fernández de la
Reguera's *Cuerpo a tierra*). In a more ambitious enterprise however, it has to
be abandoned. There is a limit to the number of actions in which a soldier
can participate, and also to the variety of people he can meet at the front.
Gironella's treatment of the middle-class Alvear family is dictated by the
ambitious nature of his project. Firmly anchored in the town of Gerona,
they are able to act as the microcosm for the rest of Spain. News of what is
happening elsewhere comes to us generally through them, or the people we
meet via them. Matías, the head of the family, is a telegraph operator who

has been transferred, due to the nature of his employment, from his native city of Madrid to Jaén and Málaga before finally settling in Catalonia. Carmen Elgazu, his wife, was born in Bilbao, the industrial heart of the Basque country. Both Matías and Carmen remain in contact with their respective families, so that events in other parts of Spain are lived within their home. (Bilbao, Burgos, Madrid and Málaga, all of which are closely connected with the Alvear family, lie on a line which runs from North to South and divides Spain symbolically in two.)

Every problem with which the Second Republic was confronted during its turbulent existence finds an echo in *Los cipreses*. Carmen, whose family is described as 'vasca, tradicional y católica hasta la médula' (p. 19), is representative of most Spanish women of her generation in that she is apolitical: 'Ella no entendía de política' (p. 31). But she is drawn into the conflict of ideologies in spite of herself. Azaña's statement of October 1931 that 'España ha dejado de ser católica',[1] and the subsequent anti-religious measures of the Republic, arouse her indignation. Matías, on the other hand, comes from a revolutionary and anti-clerical background. His brother in Madrid is a militant Anarchist; another brother in Burgos is a UGT Socialist. Matías himself, 'republicano de toda la vida, y también anticlerical' (p. 18), has mellowed with the years. He surreptitiously votes for the Left in the election of 1933, knowing that Carmen has voted Right; but he feels no sense of resentment towards her. He accepts that life is a perpetual compromise, and placing common sense above dogma, tries to be 'siempre ecuánime e intentando ver las cosas con equilibrio y perspectiva' (p. 386). The name of the café he frequents is in itself symbolic: 'el Neutral'. It is no surprise that the elder son draws closer to his father as the war approaches, for Matías's ability to understand the other side of every question is the quality Ignacio is trying to cultivate. Such compromise and self-control, however, is not to be seen in the society which revolves around the Alvear family; and it is here that Ignacio, the real protagonist of the novel, has to formulate his political and moral values.

When Ignacio leaves the seminary and takes a job at a bank, the range of his acquaintances widens; although all the employees are mostly from the same social class, their political ideas are extremely varied: Padrosa and 'La Torre de Babel' are UGT Socialists; two more are Left Republicans; Cosme Vila is a Communist; the under-manager is a supporter of the CEDA, while the manager is a Radical and Freemason. When confronted with these new sets of values, Ignacio's first reaction is to defend those he finds in his own home. When later, his own opinions are respected and he is no longer on the defensive, he begins to see some positive aspects in these new values, and to question his own. His brother César, on his summer vacation from the seminary where he has replaced Ignacio, follows his ascetic inclinations by seeking catacombs and the ancient ruins of churches around Gerona. His mother comments, without meaning to ask a question: '¿En qué mejor emplear las vacaciones?' Ignacio's reply is trenchant: 'En pensar en los pobres' (p. 78). Gironella carefully constructs a mosaic of the religious problems of his country. In no novel among those under study have they been explored so thoroughly. Worthy elements in the Church are to be found side by side with the unworthy. The isolation of the bishop in his palace is counterbalanced by the altruism of a humble priest who risks his life to give extreme unction to the first victims of the Revolution. In this way Gironella is taking the middle road between Republican writers like Barea, whose priests are invariably hypocrites and liars, and Nationalist writers like Ricardo León, who seem unaware of the Church's faults.

The individual conscience of a priest during the Civil War has been studied in other novels, notably in Sender's *Réquiem por un campesino español*, Arana's *El cura de Almuniaced* and Gomís Soler's *Cruces sin Cristo*. Leaving aside the artistic merits these novels may have, none of them reflects the situation as totally as Gironella's *Los cipreses*. This is due in part to his avowed purpose to correct what he considers a deformed version of history, in its non-political as well as its political aspects:

El aspecto político es el que menos me importa de la cuestión. Lo que duele positivamente no es que Koestler calumnie a la guardia civil, que Bernanos baraje cifras erróneas, que se afirme que la guerra fue un capricho sanguinario. Lo que duele es que se falsee la arquitectura espiritual del hombre español.[2]

It may well be, on the other hand, that Gironella makes religion one of his central themes because he believes, like Ricardo León, that 'en el fondo de todas las grandes cuestiones políticas hay siempre una cuestión teológica'.[3] Certainly the spiritual halo that surrounds even some of his Atheist characters would support this view.

The period Gironella is describing is one in which all the ideologies of Spain's recent history, from Carlism to Falangism, were the subject of active debate. Consequently it is difficult to single out any one of these as a central issue; but religion is a common factor, since it aroused strong feelings in every political faction, and the Government of the day was passing highly contentious anti-clerical laws.[4] Nora suggests that Gironella distorts history by focussing too narrowly on metaphysical questions.[5] It is true that the major characters are preoccupied in some way with religious questions, but other problems are not excluded. The major part of the novel is concerned with describing the growth of the political parties, and the resonance that they have in the life of Ignacio. This central character, by his eternal vacillation between the various factions, and his ability to see some good in them all, is meant to symbolise the deep schisms which divided Spaniards on every important issue.

Because of his method of introducing characters whose origins are conveniently diverse to allow him to cover events in the whole of Spain, and his insistence on presenting all the political groups of the Republic in all their complexity, Gironella has laid himself open to the charge of 'schematizing his human material'.[6]

Claudio Guillén, referring to *Los cipreses*, writes: 'Si Proust dans *Le Temps retrouvé* ramenait la politique à la psychologie, Gironella, par contre, soumet ses personnages aux exigences de l'histoire. C'est bien là, par l'intrusion du collectif dans l'individuel, que semble résider la faiblesse de ce livre en tant que roman psychologique.'[7] Making comparisons with *War and Peace* (which Gironella read just before writing *Los cipreses*),[8] another critic writes: 'The Alvears have their reality and charm but they never overwhelm their environment as the huge figure of Pierre, stumbling through Tolstoy's novel, blots Russia out.'[9] In the socio-political novel this delicate balance between environment and character is one of the novelist's most serious problems, and one which Gironella finds increasingly difficult to resolve as his trilogy progresses. But it is never the intention of the historical novelist to 'blot out' the background; if it were, he would no longer be a historical novelist.

Gironella has described himself as 'un hombre de mi tiempo'[10] and sees his work as a 'novela-documento' which has superseded the psychological novel or the *costumbrista* novel of the nineteenth century: 'La novela de puro pasatiempo ha muerto con el cine . . . La novela de hoy . . . tiene que ser documento, dato.'[11] This view of his work, however, as being something which introduces a new and vital element into the Spanish novel, is not shared by the majority of his critics, who accuse him of having 'una concepción pretérita, ochocentista',[12] of presenting us with 'héroes típicos y bien sabidos'[13] and of recreating 'las obras naturalistas del siglo pasado, la sociología novelesca'.[14]

The author's attempt at an impartial interpretation has aroused much disfavour. J.L. Cano sums up the majority view when he writes: 'Yo creo que frente a las guerras, y más frente a las guerras civiles, ser asépticamente imparcial es tanto como no ser nada. Un poco de pasión y de simpatía, aun involuntarias, es inevitable e incluso legítimo, independientemente de que tenga o no razón.'[15] While subjectivity is inevitable, no-one could approve of the bitter diatribes, often thinly disguised as novels, that each side had cast at the other. Gironella's impartiality can be seen as a reaction, as much against the fanatical Nationalist novels, particularly of 1937–42, as against those foreign works he mentions in his prologue; but being a reaction, it tends to swing too far towards the opposite pole, taking refuge in a neutrality which satisfies neither side.

All neutrality is relative, however, and the final 80 pages describing the bloodless right-wing coup, followed by the reversal of fortune and the left-wing seizure of power, undoubtedly tip the balance in favour of the Francoist interpretation of history. While the Nationalists are described as exercising restraint, the Anarchists and Communists engage in a brutal and systematic purge of their political opponents, priests and members of religious houses. This apparent partiality has led one critic to term Gironella a 'Falangist author',[16] and another to describe the novel as 'un plaidoyer en faveur de la participation nationaliste à la guerre'.[17] These are harsh judgements, perhaps. Scenes like those described at the end of *Los cipreses* did occur in Spain at the outbreak of war – indeed, they could have taken place in Gerona itself. For the benefit of the sceptical, it might be of interest to quote the figures Antonio Montero gives for losses in the diocese of Gerona: out of 935 priests, 194 lost their lives – almost all in the early days of the war.[18] It would not be just to criticise Gironella from a historical viewpoint, for his information is sound enough; but he has abandoned his pattern of presenting the two sides of every question and allowing the reader to come to his own conclusions. Here we have one side of the question only: a Goyaesque description of militiamen firing on a group of nuns, from behind, as they pray; the same men dressing up in priests' robes and going through the motions of a Holy Communion, disinterring the skeletons of nuns (an event which really occurred in Barcelona),[19] defiling the convent beds, burning altars, etc. In these scenes, whether he intends it or not, the author turns us against many characters who previously seemed to merit our sympathy: el Responsable is suddenly revealed as a sadist who likes feeling his victims' wounds as they die (p. 855); a prostitute enjoys leading prisoners to be shot (p. 857); Cosme Vila and Teo, whom previously we had almost respected, are enthusiastic organisers of the mass assassination. The final martyrdom of César, the total innocent, is just one more in a series of crimes by the militant Left which makes it impossible to regard them dispassionately any longer. Nor does the occasional good deed by a militiaman like Dimas, or the knowledge that in Barcelona, Madrid and Oviedo it is the workers who have suffered heavy losses (p. 869), do anything to diminish the impression that the Republicans are fundamentally evil.

Gironella would have been truly impartial had he been able to suggest more clearly in the final pages of the novel how the Civil War had been the logical consequence of deep-rooted economic and social problems. The mutual mistrust and intransigence of all groups was something which was well expressed in the earlier chapters, and the fair-mindedness with which he described these aspects was exemplary. Then, at the very moment when the point needs to be stressed, he is silent. The Army and the Falange are described as being noble in victory and in defeat. No lives were lost in their takeover, which makes the ensuing revenge of the Left all the more unjustified. Why did Gironella allow this imbalance to mar the last part of *Los cipreses*? It may be that he wanted to redress the balance by some description of Nationalist brutality (of which there is ample testimony), but knew that this would not be accepted by the censor.[20] Whatever the cause, the defect remains.

In the quotation with which his novel begins, he asks, in the words of St James: '¿De dónde nacen las riñas y pleitos entre vosotros? ¿No es de vuestras pasiones, las cuales hacen la guerra en vuestros miembros?' In relating the words of the disciple to the Civil War it is regrettable that Gironella could not sustain what began as a noble endeavour to be fair to both sides.

Un millón de muertos

Shortly after the publication of the first two volumes in the series *El ruedo ibérico*, Valle-Inclán was asked to comment on his work and on the historical novel in general. He replied:

Hay tres modos de ver el mundo artística y estéticamente: de rodillas, en pie o levantado en el aire. Cuando se mira de rodillas – y ésta es la posición más antigua en la literatura –, se da a los personajes, a los héroes una condición superior a la condición humana, cuando menos a la condición del narrador o del poeta ... Hay una segunda manera, que es mirar a los protagonistas novelescos como de nuestra propia naturaleza, como si fuesen nuestros hermanos, como si fuesen ellos nosotros mismos, como si fuera el personaje un desdoblamiento de nuestro yo, con nuestras mismas virtudes y nuestros mismos defectos ... Y hay otra tercera manera que es mirar al mundo desde un plano superior y considerar a los personajes de la trama como seres inferiores al autor, con un punto de ironía.[21]

In any historical, political or social novel, the author's attitude to his subject determines to a large extent the style of his narrative. Valle's own historical novels, reflecting an extremist temperament, fall into either the first category he describes (*La guerra carlista*, for example, has a distinctly epic tone), or the third (*El ruedo ibérico* is a satire on the court of Isabel II). The novelist's early admiration for the Carlists produced larger-than-life characters whose heroism was matched only by their ruthlessness, whose sacrifices to the cause took on the dimensions of legend. His healthy dislike of the orthodox monarchy and its acolytes, on the other hand, led him to employ the style of the *esperpento* to describe them.

Gironella builds his labyrinth of history and fiction in the middle ground that Valle avoids. Not for him the extremes, stylistic or political, of the earlier writer; no system of concave mirrors to deform reality; no effervescence of words and images to intoxicate the reader and make him accept a new version of history; no apotheosis, and above all no smile of contempt. In the prologue to *Un millón de muertos*, Gironella testifies to the efforts he has made to approach his characters sympathetically and without prejudice: 'Procuré amar sin distinción a cada uno de los personajes, salpicarles a todos de ternura, fuesen asesinos o ángeles, cantaran este himno, ese otro o el de más allá' (p. 11). He is able to do this because he has placed himself from the beginning on the same level ('en pie', to use Valle's expression) as the characters whose experiences he has shared. It is this personal involvement which distinguishes the novels of the Civil War from the traditional historical novel. The distinction can be made with reference to the *Episodios nacionales* of Galdós and to the historical works of Valle. Born in 1866, the latter wrote, when no longer a young man,[22] of events which took place in the first ten years of his life; his task was one of reconstruction rather than recollection. We know, for example, that he used ample documentation in the form of contemporary histories and collections of newspapers.[23] His historical deformations, whether epic or satirical, are the deliberate adornment of his art and at the same time the expression of a view of life, never the result of ignorance; but he is able to manipulate real events and characters freely, without the upsurge of emotion experienced by those describing an episode from their own lives. Gironella saw quite rightly that for the kind of novel he wanted to write, he too would have to immerse himself in a study of the war and not rely simply on his own recollections. According to his own admission in the prologue (p. 11), he consulted a great many newspapers of the period, talked to Spaniards and foreigners who had taken part, and read almost a thousand books and pamphlets on the subject. Such ample documentation, while contributing to a certain measure of success in *Los cipreses*, may explain the artistic failure of *Un millón de muertos*.

The prologue to the second novel gives us an idea of the struggle that is going on between the historian and the novelist in Gironella. While informing us that 'como siempre, lo que primordialmente me ha importado ha sido el rigor psicológico, la meteorología ambiental', Gironella goes on to add: 'También pretende ser mi obra una *crónica* para los propios españoles ... Urgía, creo, efectuar un *inventario* ...' (the emphasis is my own). The result is that some of the pages, especially the later ones, are mere chronicles of events in which the fictional names seem strangely out of place (see, for example, pp. 790–791), and are often included only so that we shall not lose sight of the characters completely. In situations such as these the fictional characters play a passive role and are totally submerged by the mass of historical information. 'Uno de los aciertos del autor', one critic wrote with reference to *Los cipreses*, 'es haber conseguido ese ajuste perfecto de ficción e historia'.[24] This assessment of *Los cipreses* could hardly be applied to *Un millón de muertos*. (Nor does the claim seem tenable that this second volume in the trilogy is superior to the first.)[25]

The action which occupies a central position in the two works taken together is undoubtedly the violence at the beginning of the hostilities: the 'Red terror' in Gerona, in which César and many others are killed. A study of the five parts that make up *Los cipreses* shows that while the first part covers a period of more than two and a half years, the second covers only ten months, the third (by far the longest section) sixteen months, the fourth six months and the last part only a fortnight. It can be seen from this that as the novel progresses, and the war approaches, so the attention to historical detail grows: what could previously be described in ten pages, now takes twenty. Contributing to this process is the author's concern to describe the psychological development of an ever-increasing number of characters in this crucial stage of their lives. This slowing down of the novel in purely chronological terms has quite the opposite effect on the pace and action. It is in the last 200 pages, which describe only two weeks in the life of Gerona, that we find the most rapid action and the greatest emotion. In *Un millón de muertos* this trend is reversed; the outbreak of the war forms the explosive beginning to the novel, after which each side wages a war of attrition and the struggle settles into a routine. The first novel had focussed more and more closely on a conflict that was about to flare up; the second departs from this point, and tends to devote less and less space to describing the psychology, development and interplay of characters, taking longer historical strides as the two and a half years go by. Together with this increasing interest in historical detail goes the gradual disintegration of the novel's balanced structure, for instead of describing imaginary events in Gerona, or situating there real events which occurred somewhere else, the author has chosen a much more literal approach to his subject. Much of the careful preparation made in the earlier novel is now squandered.

César's ghost haunts the early pages of *Un millón de muertos* as a constant reminder of left-wing violence; but as on previous occasions, when Gironella sees his objectivity in question, he takes corrective measures: 'En Castilla, en Navarra, en el Sur, los falangistas, los requetés, ¡para no hablar de los moros . . .!, estaban cometiendo los mismos horrores, a las mismas horas y con idéntica saña que sus adversarios en Gerona. Lo cual no era de extrañar, pues la raza era la misma . . .' (p. 30). The expression of such sentiments as these brought upon Gironella's head some of the most vitriolic criticism ever directed at a modern novelist; his claims to objectivity were dismissed by one Nationalist apologist as 'anémicas reservas y endebluchos considerandos'.[26]

The early scenes of the novel continue to be centred on Gerona, with occasional glimpses of revolutionary Barcelona nearby, which was the pattern established in *Los cipreses*. Soon, however, the scope of the novel widens to describe the Aragon front and the progress of the various militia units there. In his usual methodical manner the author creates a structure which will enable him to cover as much historical ground as possible and follow his characters naturally at the same time. In the Durruti column advancing on Zaragoza we recognise many familiar faces, among them José Alvear, Dr Rosselló, el Cojo, Porvenir, Ideal, etc.; in the Ortiz column further South towards Teruel we find Murillo, Canela and the *murcianos*; North towards Huesca, in the Ascaso columns are Teo and Gorki. In this way the whole of the Aragon front, which was successfully held by the Republic until the spring of 1938, is covered.

Immediately he disperses his characters, Gironella is faced with the very real problem of forging links between them all so that the novel is an organic and flexible whole. The technical problems here are greater than ever before. A structure like that of Cela's *La colmena* might have been better suited to the author's purpose than the strictly chronological scheme he has chosen, for it is clear that he has not resolved in *Un millón de muertos* the 'arduos problemas de construcción' he laments in the prologue (p. 10). The links between characters are often exceedingly tenuous;[27] if the function of these links is to give the novel a compact structure to compensate for the total disintegration of unity of place, they do not succeed. In many ways they serve to emphasise the superficial nature of much of the narrative. Alborg maintains that 'un novelista hubiera dirigido el proyector de su atención hacia una parte determinada para inundarla con su luz'.[28] Gironella has fallen victim to his own ambition to 'meterse toda la guerra en su alforja.'[29] The same conclusion is reached by E. de Nora: 'El error básico de Gironella está, a mi juicio, en no haber esquivado la tentación de que su obra reflejara, "íntegramente," los tres largos años de la contienda en ambas zonas.'[30] As Nora realised, the wish to cover both zones in all their important developments meant creating a vast repertoire of characters, thus reducing the importance of others whose role had hitherto been crucial.

Of the 185 fictional characters that appear in *Un millón de muertos*,[31] there are clearly some who embody and express the author's personal convictions. Such a character, surely, is Ignacio,[32] and it is significant that his role diminishes as the novel progresses. 'Un nuevo Hamlet a escala español',[33] Ignacio exemplifies the intellectual who is unable to come to terms with the realities that surround him. The internal conflict between reason and emotion reduces him to inertia. In his conversation with Mosén Francisco he is but the shadow of the young radical who had attacked the conservative priest Mosén Alberto. He now sees so many imponderables in any situation that he is unable even to suggest a solution. 'Puedo poco . . . No puedo nada' (p. 220), he murmurs, in despair at his own weakness. On the sentimental plane, too, he is still torn between the committed Falangist Marta and the bourgeois Ana María, whose preoccupation with her own happiness ('Yo tampoco nací para guerras, ¿sabes? Yo nací . . . para estar tranquila' (p. 229)) must make Ignacio suspect his own motives for standing aloof from the struggle. It is at this point, in a mood of utter moral confusion, that he finds solace in the traditional values of his family, united now in the desire for a Nationalist victory. Matías, who voted for the Left in the elections of 1933, dances for joy when he hears that Málaga has fallen to the Nationalists (p. 403). Ignacio resolves to join the Republican Army to work in the hospital service, only in order to desert to Nationalist Spain. Carmen dismisses the Republicans as 'esa gentuza' (p. 382). Pilar's essentially apolitical character is transformed by her love for the Falangist Mateo, and she is sorely tempted to join the Nationalist underground movement in Gerona. Nowhere is the unity of the Alvear family greater than in these pages.

While admirable as a study of the middle classes ('el retrato más acabado, más perfecto, más estudiado de nuestra clase media')[34] the unity of the Alvear family tends to make Ignacio a less significant character. In agreement now with many views he would have rejected six months earlier, he becomes secondary in importance to the action. His participation in the rearguard of the Brunete offensive saves him temporarily from insignifi-cance, and shows that flashes of the old Ignacio still exist. While training at Barcelona he had seriously contemplated sabotaging Republican medical supplies (p. 431); faced with the wounded of the International Brigades, he realises that such a step would have been to betray his own deepest beliefs. For this reason Brunete is the most important political event in Ignacio's life since the war began: 'Casi olvidó sus propósitos de fuga. La batalla de Brunete lo subyugó, constituyendo para él una lección comparable a la que recibió el 19 de julio en el cementerio de Gerona' (p. 516). Here for the first time Ignacio is seeing the results of Nationalist violence. Though not directly comparable with the civilian purges he has seen in Gerona, it is equally merciless. It shows him too that the Republicans are not merely rearguard terrorists. The resolution of those defending the Madrid front is described with great force by Gironella. Nationalist apologists have been quick to attack these pages for what they consider to be distortion. (It grieves them particularly that in no single engagement is Nationalist heroism described in such terms as the Republic's defence of Madrid on 6 November, 'la única página heróica, el solo pasaje épico de toda la novela'.)[35] Ignacio fraternises with the foreign volunteers he is tending at the hospital, but still has no real doubts about where his deeper sympathies lie. In some ways he has become a realist, tinged with the cynicism of Moncho, the character he so much admires. He suspects, for example, that his whole-hearted dedication to tending the wounded is based on the conviction that they are the inevitable losers, and therefore no longer a threat: 'En cierto modo, se arrogaba la generosidad de quien se sabe ineluctablement¿ vencedor' (p. 517). Later, visiting Burgos, he feels no compassion when he hears of the death of his Socialist uncle and the subsequent hardships suffered by the family (p. 591). 'Notó que, tratándose del enemigo, tenía seco el corazón' (p. 596). Such glimpses of Ignacio's psychology, sadly, have become all too rare by the time one reaches this stage in the novel; his role and stature are diminishing and 146 historical characters are vying for his place in the drama.

Once Ignacio has found himself an *enchufe* in the Nationalist Army far from the scene of the main battlefields, there is little to prevent Gironella embarking on a detailed historical description of the war without the commentary of this key character. It is not easy to determine whether the gradual withdrawal of the Alvears, and Ignacio in particular, is the cause or effect of the massive increase in historical detail which occurs in *Un millón de muertos*, but the latter seems the more likely. Gironella's claims in the prologue that he is not primarily concerned with history or sociology have not convinced his critics. 'El hecho de haber redactado una obra politizada ... desde la primera a la última página sitúa al escritor bajo el foco de la crítica política y no sólo literaria, sin que el reiterado anuncio de haber escrito una "novela," y no un "ensayo político o histórico," pueda servir de excepción dilatoria.'[36] That much of the novel is thinly disguised history is difficult to deny.

An exhaustive list of examples would be both tiresome and unnecessary to show the primacy of historical matter over imagined characters and situations. Let us examine instead one short paragraph whose structure is typical of many in the work; it illustrates well the problems inherent in such an ambitious historical novel. The first half of chapter 14 gathers together many of the historical loose ends of the novel up to that point (the autumn of 1936), in accordance with Gironella's aim to give a panoramic view. Mola's northern campaign is briefly described: the fall of Oviedo, Irún and San Sebastián. Then, before going on to discuss the strategic importance of the fall of Badajoz, the advance on Toledo and the abortive Republican attack on Mallorca, the novelist attempts to relate the events to his characters in the following short paragraph:

La victoria del General Mola en un sector tan estratégico como la provincia de Guipúzcoa desató en toda la zona 'nacional,' desde Galicia y Castilla hasta Extremadura y Andalucía, una explosión de entusiasmo. Queipo de Llano dijo por la radio: 'Les dimos una patada en un lugar que yo me sé.' Mateo, ya incorporado al frente, en el Alto del León, en unión de José Luis Martínez de Soria, tensó su brazo hasta casi tocar una estrella. El camarada Nuñez Maza, entregado de lleno a los servicios de Propaganda, se desgañitó con los altavoces y María Victoria masticó en Valladolid un chicle especial. Por el contrario, en la zona 'roja' la sorpresa fue triste. El Gobierno no dio con la palabra precisa para justificar aquello. Axelrod, el hombre nacido en Tiflis, y con él los militares rusos que trabajaban a su lado, se indignaron contra el Ministerio de la Guerra. En Barcelona, Ana María consiguió como siempre introducir el parte en el cesto de la comida destinado a su padre, que seguía en la Cárcel Modelo. Su padre comprendió. En Gerona, el coronel Muñoz se pasó toda una tarde mirando a través de los ventanales.   (p. 237)

The historical event itself was of the utmost importance. The Nationalist capture of the industrial North may be seen as the greatest loss the Republic suffered in the whole war. The vulgar remark by Queipo shows the scorn one side felt for the other. Then there follows a section of utter banality: the characters Gironella has created add nothing to the understanding of the events, but merely go through the motions of tired actors in a second performance. The character-symbols of *Los cipreses* were rounded figures whose convictions came from deep within them. Ignacio, who bore the seeds of civil conflict within himself, is a good example. In *Un millón de muertos*, however, Gironella fails to select his material with sufficient rigour. It should have been apparent to him that to continue the analysis of the various political factions, as well as giving full coverage to the military strategies of the war, was to inflict too great a strain on the structure of the novel. The novelist finds himself in an impasse, his progress blocked by an insurmountable mass of facts, figures and identities. Because history now occupies the stage, the evolution of the characters must take place outside our field of vision, sometimes to be abandoned altogether. The complicity that is mentioned between Ignacio and the girl telephonist in the health department in Barcelona (pp. 429, 454) is never explained or developed. 'Ignacio había cambiado', we are told at another point (p. 693); we have to take the author's word for it. The seduction scene between Ignacio and his landlady in Barcelona is summarily dismissed in a few sentences (p. 497), and on we rush to descriptions of Republican casualties in the hospital. As a substitute for the penetrating analysis of the political scene balanced by sound character portrayal to be found in *Los cipreses*, we are confronted with a failure to convince on both counts in *Un millón de muertos*. Nationalist critics have lamented the brevity of passages dealing with the Alcázar de Toledo, Simancas, Santa María de la Cabeza, Huesca and Oviedo.[37] Republicans might wonder whatever happened to Guernika, and why more attention was not given to Unamuno's momentous speech at Salamanca. Of course all these events are mentioned, but none is given the emphasis that it must have received at the time. Even the argument, therefore, that the failure of the characters is counterbalanced by the degree of historical accuracy and detail is not convincing.

With regard to historical accuracy, it is only fair to say that in many cases of apparent error, Gironella has merely used artistic licence to change the course of certain events. So it is, for example, that he describes the assassination of the bishop of Gerona by militiamen (p. 198), when in fact it was his political enemies who helped the bishop to escape to Italy, where he survived the holocaust.[38] Such distortions, however, are justifiable for they do not contradict the greater truths of the Civil War. Religious persecution was a regrettable fact, and a Spanish bishop did lose his life in Gerona.[39] Minor factual errors do, however, occur: the underground station of Velázquez is described as being a refuge during an air-raid (p. 463), when it did not even exist at that time; it is suggested (p. 777) that Prieto was formerly leader of the UGT, confusing him with Largo Caballero; the fictional Dr Rosselló is made to travel from Madrid to Gerona direct (this is to say, via Aragon) in the spring of 1937, when much of the territory in his path would have been in enemy hands (p. 461). In his description of the siege of Madrid, Gironella considerably underestimates the number of Nationalist troops ('cinco mil hombres cansados' (p. 332)) taking part.[40]

For P. Ilie, Gironella's trilogy rests on a fundamental structural weakness, in that he combines two irreconcilable elements – a national framework of real historical events and a fictional world centred on Gerona – which leads to a 'disjunction of history and fiction'.[41] (As we have seen in an earlier chapter, Ortega would have gone further than this to adduce the general principle that the horizons of history and fiction will always refuse to merge satisfactorily, so condemning the historical novel to ultimate failure.) The intrinsic difficulty confronting Gironella is that he is reporting national events dispassionately, while narrating the vicissitudes of the Alvear family and their circle in a much more personal tone. Confronted with the choice of whether to interpret historical events by means of his characters, or concentrate on the verisimilitude of his fictional creations within a framework of historical events, Gironella is accused by Ilie of opting for the latter, thus engaging in historiographical evasion in 'the formulation of issues that dissolve the rational basis of historical enquiry. The derationalizing method includes asking questions that are humanly poignant but historically irrelevant, interpreting events without regard to causality, and encouraging ideological confusion.'[42] A principal cause of this failure is Ignacio Alvear, whose 'total egoism, lack of ideals . . . incomprehension . . . (and) inability to transcend personal sorrow in order to comprehend history makes him an unconvincing agent for a historical novel'.[43] Ilie's thesis is that the true substance of Gironella's novels is non-historical, and that despite the massive accumulation of historical data in his work, the author is 'a sentimentalist in the guise of a historian, a novelist with a psychological perspective who in appearance is writing a historical narrative'.[44] This is a harsh judgement, but one the novelist brings upon himself through his incapacity to deal with the excessive amount of historical data he introduces into his narrative, other than in the most mechanical way.

A major criticism of *Un millón de muertos* (as of *Los cipreses*) relates to the author's quest for impartiality. Difficult as it was in the description of the pre-war situation, it is doubly so in the treatment of the Civil War itself. Writers such as Orwell, Koestler and others would in any case question the desirability of an aseptic impartiality, even if it could be achieved, since it may be seen as depriving the writer's work of its vigour. There is clearly a point at which personal commitment (not to be confused with political commitment) is both desirable and useful. The reader may accept or reject the author's view, but a least he is involved. Tolstoy's bias for the Russian victims of Napoleon in *War and Peace*, Zola's sympathy for the victims of the Prussian invasion in *La Débâcle*, Galdós's affection for the nineteenth-century liberals in his *Episodios*, all serve ultimately to enrich the novels, because 'más que a una política dada, ellos obedecen veraz y emocional-mente a los contenidos de su personal conciencia'.[45] Ignacio might have been the ideal character to fulfil this function. His outlook is that of the humanitarian rather than the politician; his own conscience, and not political expediency, is his guide. Vila Selma considers that 'Ignacio Alvear es la expresión de las convicciones de Gironella: el cansancio de España cesará con una transformación del material humano, de las actitudes humanas; cuando los hombres crean que lo importante no son las opiniones políticas – mesianismo fanático de cuna totalitaria – sino la fidelidad a la misión personal.'[46] Another critic writes: 'Todo sucedido político puede ser estudiado como cosa de hombres y nada más', implying that Gironella has used this approach.[47] 'Gironella's most important asset as a novelist', writes another, 'is his interest in humanity, his sympathy and understanding of people.'[48] All these judgements show that Gironella emphasises human values above all else. But given that this is the case, it seems self-defeating to have chosen a method of novelising which involved the introduction of a mass of historical data which inevitably led to a decline in the novels' poetic intensity.[49]

Some would argue that the mixed reception accorded to *Un millón de muertos* can be explained by the political prejudices existing in a large section of his audience. Thus, what to one reader is a comprehensive and just account,[50] to another is 'little more than a caricature in its biased historical documentation of the three years of the war, accompanied by a tendentious interpretation of the facts involved'.[51] Nor is this extremist reception confined to questions of veracity. Gironella's literary style receives similar treatment. One critic finds his prose 'simple, clear'[52] while another terms it 'opaca, incorrecta'.[53] Such are the hazards faced by any novelist of the Civil War. But in Gironella's case we see an author who has set himself a particularly difficult objective: to provide a comprehensive range of historical information without subjecting the data to rigorous historical analysis. This has led, inevitably, to the charge of historiographical irresponsibility. The paradox is that this excess of uninterpreted data also leads to deficiencies in characterisation, so that the 'novelist with a psychological perspective' ends up being neither effective novelist nor perceptive witness of his times.

Ha estallado la paz

The author's obsession with information, in *Ha estallado la paz* as in *Un millón de muertos*, becomes less easy to disguise as the narrative progresses, and finally engulfs the novel. Ignacio's role continues to be ambiguous. He is a member of Falange, and even admits to having been moved by the party anthem on more than one occasion (p. 64), but rarely shows any real enthusiasm for its aims. When he sees the Republican refugees interned in the French concentration camps of Argelès and St Cyprien his reaction is one not of compassion but of repugnance: 'Una oleada de repugnancia le atenazaba la garganta. Aquellas playas eran el resumen de todas las teorías antipatrióticas . . .' (p. 121). Yet he himself is soon to tire of the hollow patriotism of the new regime, and complains: '¡España, España! . . . Con perdón, pero estoy un poco harto. Quiero ser Ignacio . . . Hay personas que parecen haber olvidado ya su nombre y llamarse "acto de servicio" o "Alcázar de Toledo"' (p. 224). Basically a good man, Ignacio finds his ideals being tainted by memories of the trenches and the brothels; his intellectual schizophrenia deepens. Ana María, who considers that Ignacio has returned from the war a better person (p. 225), knows nothing of his immoral adventures.

Ignacio loses more in the war than he gains: ambition and cynicism replace a burning desire for justice. But the major change in his personality was brought about by the murder of his brother at the beginning of the war, and there is only limited development in his character now. Intellectually, Ignacio contributes little to *Ha estallado la paz* that has not been said before. On the sentimental plane, his problems remain to the end as they were half-way through *Los cipreses creen en Dios*, except that Marta has been replaced by Adela in the love triangle. Such a static situation in one who is meant to play a key role in the series only leads to an endless repetition of themes and a consequent loss of interest on the part of the reader. Ignacio's reaction to the explosive news that the United States has been drawn into world war is to seek solace in the arms of a woman (p. 758), thus avoiding serious consideration of the issue. In such situations as this, Gironella is evading his responsibility as a historical novelist. The events should be seen through the eyes of the characters if their inclusion is to have any justification at all. We can learn the cold facts of history by picking up any textbook on the subject. But history to the novelist, like a landscape, is a state of mind. The many elements of which it is composed may take different forms to different people, and seldom do two views coincide. Impassioned debate may arise; in a novel it is the balance and interplay of views in such a debate that should determine its objectivity, not the dispassionate way the debate is conducted. In inhibiting Ignacio, Gironella shows the confusion that exists in his own mind between the two issues. We see this clearly in the description of the Blue Division's participation in the war in Eastern Europe: 'El paso de los divisionarios por los pueblos de Polonia fue recibido con entusiasmo por los sacerdotes católicos y por la población en general; en cambio en Lituania cruzaron zonas de ambiente triste, miserable, un tanto hostil, debido a las represalias de que habían sido objeto, por parte de los soldados alemanes, las comunidades judías que allí había, muchos de cuyos miembros habían sido tatuados en la espalda con una marca amarilla' (p. 692). 'The prophet of the low tone of voice' cannot be forgiven for such understatement, in which he often indulges.[54] The moment he is describing is one at which over 136,000 Jews had been slain in Lithuania, and when the city of Warsaw alone was a massive concentration camp and torture chamber for 400,000 more.[55] To limit oneself to descriptions of gaiety and heroism among the Spanish division in the face of such a grotesque mathematical reality is to distort history. To balance the enthusiasm of the Catholic priests (whose role in Poland at the time, Hitler considered, was 'to keep the Poles quiet, stupid and dull-witted')[56] with the 'rather hostile' attitude of the persecuted Lithuanians, is to create an illusion of impartiality and nothing more.

Conclusion

Gironella's trilogy is a monumental undertaking. A venture of such magnitude could only be brought to a successful conclusion by an artist of genius, capable of sustaining the reader's interest in his myriad fictional characters as they make their way through the historical labyrinth. Of the novelists under study, he undoubtedly provides the greatest volume of historical information. (In preparing *Un millón de muertos*, in 1959, he went to live in Zurich so that he could use the extensive library of Ricardo Simó Prats, a former major in the Republican Army.)[57] But just as those who wrote fictional accounts of the war immediately after the event gave an excessively subjective and distorted view of it, so Gironella becomes obsessed with the opposite aim, that of a thoroughly documented impartiality. The trilogy can only be understood in the context of the poorly documented and intensely partisan literature which preceded it, to which it is a reaction. In shying away from the Falangist hero, Gironella creates an anti-hero who begins as a tortured conscience but ends as an indecisive and somewhat nondescript character lost in the crowd. Because of their concern with events, as R. Schwartz has shown, 'Gironella's war novels . . . show little psychological capacity',[58] while P. Ilie makes a strong case for saying that because of their concern with a psychological perspective they create 'fictive history':

[Ignacio's] very inability to transcend personal sorrow in order to comprehend history makes him an unconvincing agent for a historical novel . . . By concentrating on Ignacio the author declines to write a historical novel that articulates explanations and awareness.[59]

The enterprise on which Gironella embarked grew to such proportions that ultimately he was unequal to the task of integrating these two perspectives of psychology and historical causality.

Notes

1 *Diario de Sesiones de las Cortes Españolas*, 13 October 1931. Also quoted in Gironella, *Los cipreses*, p. 43.
2 Gironella, '¿Por qué no se conoce la novela española?' *Correo Literario*, 57 (1952), 1 and 10 (p. 10).
3 R. León, *Cristo en los infiernos* (Madrid, 1941), prologue, p. 10.
4 A partial but informative study of the Republic's anti-clerical measures is given in A. Montero Moreno's *Historia de la persecución religiosa en España (1936–1939)* (Madrid, 1961).
5 E. de Nora, *La novela española contemporánea*, 3 (Madrid, 1962), p. 100. M. de Gogorza Fletcher also takes issue with Gironella for confusing these questions: 'Gironella's interpretation of politics on the model of religion is quite unfortunate' (*The Spanish Historical Novel, 1870–1970* (London, 1974), p. 139).
6 M. Van Doren, 'The Thousand Faces of Spain', *The Reporter* (16 June 1955), 35–37 (p. 36).
7 C. Guillén, 'José María Gironella', *Critique*, 11 (1955), 571–573 (p. 573).
8 Gironella testifies to this in *SP*, 1, no. 27 (1957), 24–28 (p. 28).
9 M. Van Doren, 'The Thousand Faces of Spain'.
10 Gironella, *Ha estallado la paz* (Barcelona, 1966), p. 10.
11 Gironella, in an interview in *SP*, p. 28.
12 J.L. Alborg, *Hora actual de la novela española*, 1 (Madrid, 1962–63), p. 146.

13 D. Pérez Minik, *Novelistas españoles de los siglos XIX y XX* (Madrid, 1957), p. 296.

14 I. Elizalde, 'La novela social contemporánea en España', *Fomento Social*, 16, no. 63 (1961), 255–269 (p. 259).

15 J.L. Cano, 'J.M. Gironella', *Insula*, 89(1953), 6–7 (p. 7).

16 F.R. Benson, *Writers in Arms* (London, 1968), p. xxvi.

17 I. Soldevila, 'Les romanciers devant la Guerre Civile espagnole', *La Revue de l'Université de Laval*, 14, no. 5 (1960), 428–442 (p. 438).

18 A. Montero Moreno, *Historia*, p. 763.

19 H. Thomas, *The Spanish Civil War* (London, 1971), p. 230.

20 In a lecture given at the Ateneo two months after *Los cipreses* first appeared, Gironella openly attacked censorship for the pernicious influence it exercised on Spanish novelists: 'En tanto que novelista no puedo menos de manifestar que la influencia de la censura no hay que medirla por el número de obras que pasan o son rechazadas, ni por los párrafos mutilados [. . .] La censura realmente importante es la que el autor se ve obligado a ejercer *a priori* sobre su obra . . . Este punto es, a mi entender, decisivo y capaz por sí solo de frustrar la obra de toda mi generación' (*El novelista ante el mundo* (Madrid, 1954), pp. 34–35).

21 G. Martínez Sierra, 'Hablando con Valle-Inclán. De él y su obra', *ABC* (7 December 1928), 1.

22 Valle began publishing the novels on the Carlist Wars when he was 42, and did not begin *El ruedo ibérico* until some 20 years later.

23 For a detailed list of works consulted by Valle in the preparation of his historical novels, see the evidence of his son Carlos recorded in G. Gómez de la Serna's *España en sus Episodios Nacionales* (Madrid, 1954), pp. 61–62.

24 J.L. Cano, 'José María Gironella', 6.

25 Such is the view expressed by R. de la Cierva: 'Después de *Los cipreses creen en Dios*, novela grande con más orfebrería que aerodinámica, novela importante pero no definitiva, *Un millón de muertos* es la gran excepción al aforismo de las segundas partes, y es quizá el libro más hondo y más ancho que se ha escrito sobre la guerra española' (*Cien libros básicos sobre la Guerra de España* (Madrid, 1966), p. 298). This critic's adulation, in retrospect, seems somewhat exaggerated: 'Conservo mi ejemplar de la primera edición de este libro (*Un millón de muertos*) con el mismo amor anticipado con que algún intuitivo lector de Cervantes conservaría, sin duda, la primera edición del *Quijote* al terminar de leerla.'

26 L.E. Calvo-Sotelo, 'Crítica y glosa de *Un millón de muertos*', *Ya* (11 May 1961). This is one of a series of articles published in *Ya* which later appeared as a single volume, *Crítica y glosa de 'Un millón de muertos'* (Madrid, 1961).

27 See pp. 248–259, where the evolution of numerous characters is described in sequence, or pp. 373–382, where the only link between those mentioned is how happy they feel at the time.

28 *Hora actual de la novela española* (Madrid, 1962), 1, p. 158.

29 '*Un millón de muertos* de J.M.G.', *Estafeta Literaria* (15 May 1961), 20.

30 *La novela española contemporánea*, 3, p. 102.

31 This figure is an approximation; Gironella's own list at the end of the novel is larger, but there are repetitions (Antonio Casal, Julio García, Carlos Ayestarán, comandante Campos, coronel Muñoz, who are all Masons as well as belonging to a political party or the Army) and at least one omission (the bishop of Gerona).

32 L.E. Calvo-Sotelo, in an article entitled 'El pacifismo en Gironella', *Ya* (19 May 1961), points out that to attack Ignacio is to attack Gironella. (He goes on to attack Ignacio.)

33 *Ibid.*

34 J. Gich, '*Los cipreses creen en Dios*', *Correo Literario*, 70 (15 April 1953), 4.

35 L.E. Calvo-Sotelo, 'La épica en *Un millón de muertos*', *Ya* (22 April 1961).

36 L.E. Calvo-Sotelo, 'Los límites de la tragedia', *Ya* (16 April 1961).

37 L.E. Calvo-Sotelo, 'La épica en *Un millón de muertos*'; R.M. Hornedo, 'José María Gironella',

Razón y Fe, 164 (1961) 222–231; J.L. Vázquez Dodero, 'El arte y la historia en *Un millón de muertos*', *Nuestro Tiempo*, 14 (1961), 732–742 (p. 741).

38 H. Thomas, *The Spanish Civil War*, p. 232.

39 Monsignor Polanco, bishop of Teruel, was murdered in Gerona in 1939.

40 H. Thomas writes: 'The battle which began on the west of Madrid on 8 November was one of the most extraordinary in modern war. An army, well equipped but only *about 20,000 strong*, mainly Moroccans and legionaries . . .' (*The Spanish Civil War*, p. 409; the emphasis is mine).

41 P. Ilie, 'Fictive History in Gironella', *Journal of Spanish Studies*, 2, no. 2 (1974), 77–94 (p. 80).

42 *Ibid.*, p. 83.

43 *Ibid.*, p. 84.

44 *Ibid.*, p. 84.

45 D. Pérez Minik, *Novelistas españoles de los siglos XIX y XX*, p. 294.

46 J. Vila Selma, *Tres ensayos sobre la literatura y nuestra guerra* (Madrid, 1956), p. 55.

47 J.M. de Llanos, 'Reflexiones ante *Un millón de muertos*', *Ya* (29 April 1961), 5.

48 W.J. Grupp, 'José María Gironella, Spanish Novelist', *Kentucky Foreign Languages Quarterly*, 4, no. 3 (1957), 133.

49 In '*Así escribí Un millón de muertos*' in *Todos somos fugitivos* (Barcelona, 1961), Gironella explains how, incapable of writing his novel due to bouts of depression, he spent the time listing the events of the war in 2,000 pages of notes: 'Había ordenado cronológicamente los acontecimientos de nuestra guerra, mes por mes, semana por semana' (p. 329). This perhaps explains the surfeit of historical data, which he was incapable of integrating effectively into the second novel of the trilogy.

50 B. Marshall, '*Un millón de muertos*', *ABC* (18 February 1961), 46.

51 F.R. Benson, *Writers in Arms*, p. xxvi.

52 E.S. Urbanski, 'Revolutionary Novels of Gironella and Pasternak', *Hispania*, 43 (1960), 195.

53 D. Santos, 'Gironella, novelista útil' in *Generaciones juntas* (Madrid, 1962), p. 150.

54 This description of Gironella was coined by A. Kerrigan in 'J.M. Gironella and the Legend of Black Spain', *Books on Trial*, 14 (1956), 343.

55 W.L. Shirer, *The Rise and Fall of the Third Reich* (London, 1960), pp. 962 and 975 respectively.

56 *Ibid.*, p. 938.

57 '[Simó Prats] puso a su disposición sus dos mil volúmenes sobre el tema y . . . sus vivencias de protagonista en los sucesos.' J.M. Salso, *José María Gironella* (Madrid, 1981), p. 78.

58 *J.M. Gironella* (New York, 1972), p. 84.

59 P. Ilie, 'Fictive History in Gironella', 84.

8

–

The novel
as symbol:
La cabeza del cordero

IN AN ESSAY published in 1944, Ayala attacked the distorted view of Spain that emerges from reading *For Whom the Bell Tolls* (New York, 1940):

No es ya cuestión de las inexactitudes de detalle . . . ni tampoco siquiera de esa particular deformación de la realidad a que lo lleva su posición de testigo foráneo y que da el curioso resultado de que, según la fábula, en la guerra de España no cupiera a los españoles mismos otro papel que el de elemento perturbador, dificultosamente manejado por abnegados e inteligentes extranjeros; pues resulta disculpable que un literato en visita cuyo campo de movimiento está limitado por las circunstancias especiales y que ha de actuar dentro de los círculos de corresponsales de prensa y observadores militares, adquiriendo ahí sus datos, incurra en la ilusión óptica de agrandar las proporciones de este primer plano y olvide llevar a cabo la corrección que imponen las leyes de la perspectiva. Lo lamentable no es eso . . . Lo lamentable es que [*For Whom the Bell Tolls*] arroja una visión esencialmente falsa . . . de España.[1]

It is significant that Ayala's criticism is made more from an ethical than an aesthetic standpoint. The fact that Hemingway has distorted reality disturbs the Spanish novelist more than any failure in the technical aspects of the novel. His later classification of Hemingway, therefore, 'entre las [plumas] más ilustres',[2] implies no contradiction. It is a tribute to the intellectual honesty of writers like Ayala (and Barea, in such articles as 'Not Spain but Hemingway')[3] that they repudiated literature which, in political terms, was more favourable than hostile to their cause. Like many of his countrymen, Ayala would have watched the increasing flow of novels and short stories on the war with a proportionate sense of dissatisfaction. Critics were beginning to lament that *the* novel of the war, or *the* short story, was still to be written. Given this state of affairs as Ayala saw it, it is hardly surprising that he chose to come out of voluntary retirement as a novelist (his last volume of fiction had been published in 1930),[4] to make his own contribution to the literature of the war.

The first sign of this new interest was the appearance in December 1948 of a remarkable short story, 'El mensaje'.[5] Shortly afterwards, in August 1949, another story appeared, entitled 'El tajo'.[6] The same year, a volume of four stories (including these two) was published with the collective title *La cabeza del cordero*. This, together with one short story in *Los usurpadores* ('Diálogo de los muertos'), was to be Ayala's sole contribution to the literary discussion of this theme, but it is a contribution of outstanding merit and significance.

Before going on to evaluate *La cabeza del cordero* as war literature, let us first consider its position in relation to Ayala's earlier work. Such a study proves particularly illuminating in the case of this author, for in no other is the post-war trend towards realism more marked. Here we can see clearly the change in attitude which took place in the years leading up to the Civil War and during the turbulent decade that followed. That a change took place is reflected, firstly, in the fact that during the years of the Second Republic (1931–39) Ayala's literary production was nil. He devoted himself entirely to sociology, politics and law; one of his publications during these years was *El derecho social en la constitución de la República española* (1932). Secondly, even the most cursory glance at the author's last volume before he left for the wilderness testifies to the remarkable transformation that later took place. *Cazador en el alba* (Madrid, 1930) is a literary landmark of great importance; it shows Ayala at his most baroque, showering the reader with erudite and ornate metaphors and indulging in flights of fancy. To this strange mixture of ultramodern and gothic, Ayala adds his own personal stamp. The result is summed up thus by one critic: 'Sus páginas poseen un aire mezcla de guiñol y farsa surrealista, como un poema de Alberti y de feria andaluza entre Góngora y Lorca.'[7] A brief example will suffice to show how justified this description is. The scene is a dance hall at which the young girl, Aurora, has just accepted a rustic soldier's invitation to dance: 'Y cuando otra vez la pianola comenzó a peinarse su larga melena, cuando otra vez se ordenó la corriente humana, compleja y sideral, puso la mano en el hombro de Antonio, y adelantó la pierna, redonda en blanca seda. Su cintura era ingrave, cambiante, reiterada marea . . .'[8] Intoxicated with the heady wine of *arte puro* and the dehumanising ideas of Ortega's *Revista de Occidente*, Ayala was unconcerned with the social dimensions of literature, but only with 'el álgebra superior de las metáforas.'[9] In his comments on

Hemingway quoted above, however, Ayala upbraids the American for creating an 'ilusión óptica', and demands respect for 'las leyes de la perspectiva'. What is responsible for this aesthetic revolution? The best answer to that is given by the author himself in the prologue to *La cabeza del cordero*:

A la vez que mi juventud primera, pasó pronto la oportunidad y el ambiente de aquella sensual alegría que jugaba con imágenes, con metáforas, con palabras, y se complacía en su propio asombro del mundo, divirtiéndose en estilizarlo. Todo aquel poetizar florido, en que yo hube de participar también a mi manera, se agostó de repente; se ensombreció aquella que pensábamos aurora con la gravedad hosca de acontecimientos que comenzaban a barruntarse, y yo por mí, me reduje a silencio . . . Mi permanencia en Berlín por los años 29 y 30 (los años de despliegue del nazismo . . .) infundió en mi ánimo la intuición – y por cierto, la noción también – de las realidades tremendas que se incubaban, ante cuya perspectiva ¿qué sentido podía tener aquel jugueteo literario, estetizante y gratuito a que estábamos entregados? Poco después . . .   (pp. 28–29)

The golden age of dehumanised art in Spain was during the dictatorship of Primo de Rivera. Once the dictatorship collapsed and the pressures to change the structure of society grew, so the 'new literature' faded. Ayala was privileged to have a glimpse of Spain's future when he visited Berlin: he saw aligned there political forces which only existed in embryo in his own country. Hence his decision to part company with writers like Benjamín Jarnés and Antonio Espina, who continued along the dehumanised path.

After a silence of two decades, in which he has had time to gain a profound knowledge of man's inhumanity to man, Ayala's voice is heard again. 'Un Ayala grave, transcendente, enraizado, recogido en una dolorida serenidad, movido al más implacable enfrentamiento con el mundo real . . . un Ayala cuyas raíces podríamos buscar, todavía, en la más desolada y grave posición noventayochista . . . el escritor preocupado, el moralista que inquiere con angustia sobre el *ser* de España y del hombre español – calando lo bastante hondo para encontrar en su problema el enigma general humano, las condiciones y límites de la existencia misma – es lo que encontramos tras casi veinte años de concentrado silencio.'[10] Marra-López, referring especially to the author's style, expresses the metamorphosis in more plastic terms, comparing the early Ayala to Chagall, the post-war Ayala to Zurbarán.[11]

We draw attention to this contrast in the knowledge that Ayala himself and some of his critics have tended in recent years to play down the importance of the transformation. In his conversations with R. Hiriart, for example, Ayala says of his *vanguardista* period: 'Se (han) tomado con exageración ciertas frases de mi proemio a *La cabeza del cordero*, interpretándolas en el sentido de que yo condenara lo hecho en aquel entonces o renegara de ello. No hay tal.'[12] This appears to be a case of the writer being influenced in his analysis by the aesthetic climate of the later period at which he is speaking. As J. Butt has shown, for a considerable time after the war, there was a reluctance among writers to indulge in or condone what Ayala had dismissively termed 'jugueteo literario'.[13] From the mid-1960s onwards, however, the premises of social realism were increasingly being questioned, so that it became quite respectable in succeeding decades to express admiration for the *vanguardismo* of the pre-war era. Ayala now sees his work as a natural progression, during which he accommodated his style to his subject matter, at any given moment. G. Sobejano comes nearest to making an accurate assessment, perhaps, when he refers to the author's 'evolución . . . desde el antisentimentalismo de Vanguardia hacia la nueva conciencia humanista existencial'.[14] That a considerable change took place seems undeniable.

In *La cabeza del cordero* Ayala seeks to show the essentially destructive qualities that are predominant in man, in the hope that by bringing into the light of day these flowers of darkness he may cause them to wither and die. 'El tajo' is the only story in *La cabeza del cordero* which is set in the war, but even there the reference is a brief one. This oblique approach does not alter the fact that this collection is as much a novel of the Spanish Civil War as *Un millón de muertos*; it is simply the treatment of history that is different. While Gironella was concerned to write a chronicle of events as well as to create fictional characters of human dimensions, Ayala is intent upon excluding anecdotal material in order to concentrate on the essentials: 'El tema de la guerra civil es presentado en estas historias bajo el aspecto permanente de las pasiones que las nutren; pudiera decirse: la guerra civil en el corazón de los hombres' (p. 33). The historian will search in vain for information on the details of the war; almost any novel published in Spain in the post-war era would contain as many direct references to historical events as one finds here. We learn that the Aragon front did not see much action, that the Moors committed atrocities on entering Toledo, that the Nationalists carried out purges in Santiago, but little else. My intention here will be to consider how successful Ayala has been in his oblique approach to the war, examine the main themes in each of the stories of *La cabeza del cordero*, and finally, relate this work to the other main Civil War novels.

The first story, 'El mensaje', is a brilliantly constructed tale in which the

Civil War is seen to be already gnawing at the innermost being of the characters. Set in a period which is never once specified, but which we may assume to be the Second Republic, the story reveals the depths of scorn, envy and distrust which exist in the hearts of men. At no time is direct reference made to political differences, for Ayala considers the problem a moral rather than a political one. The anti-hero, Roque, 'mezquino, vanidoso y lleno de envidia' (p. 35), is an amalgam of the vices we see in other individuals in the same story. The use of the first person gives the author ample scope to lay bare the psychology of this petty and hateful commercial traveller. The failure to communicate, which is at the root of much human conflict, is stressed unknowingly by Roque with his very first words: 'La verdad sea dicha: Cada vez entiendo menos a la gente' (p. 37). The remainder of the story shows the truth of this apparent platitude. By their own blindness, the inhabitants of Roque's native village are bringing upon themselves the cataclysm of civil war; like Gironella's Gerona, the village is the microcosm of Spain.

The bare bones of the plot are concerned with the nocturnal conversation between the commercial traveller, who is briefly passing through his village after an absence of eight years, and his cousin Severiano, who tells the strange tale of a piece of paper, bearing an indecipherable message, which had been left at the local inn some years before by another transient visitor. When Roque tries to see the message next morning, it is found to have disappeared.

The arguments over the message prior to Roque's arrival in the village, and those in which he becomes embroiled during the night he spends at his cousin's house, signal the disintegration of a social structure. Like characters in a Calderonian drama,[15] all will contribute to the final act of destruction. For this reason Ayala has termed the characters of the first story 'inocentes-culpables o culpables-inocentes' (p. 34); to a greater or lesser degree, all Spaniards had to bear responsibility for the Spanish Civil War. At the same time, Ayala refrains from pointing an accusing finger at his creations. They are tragic in the classical tradition: their words are somehow prophetic of the disaster that will soon overtake them, and as they sense this disaster, 'caminan en su vida oprimidos por ese destino que deben soportar, que sienten merecido y que, sin embargo, les ha caído encima desde el cielo, sin responsabilidad específica de su parte' (p. 34). Roque comments at one point: '¿Por qué había de lamentarme? Cada cual su suerte' (p. 39), revealing the mood of resignation to which Ayala refers. The characters' communication among themselves grows steadily more difficult until they abandon their attempts altogether. Roque laments, after trying to explain to his country cousin how a code works, 'fue imposible llevar a cabo mi explicación. Quién sabe tampoco si él hubiera sido capaz de comprenderla. Renuncié...' (p. 53). When the dialogue ceased in other spheres of society, and in the Cortes, the only alternative was violence.

The gradual disintegration of the social structure is expressed in the tension that develops between the two main characters. Roque feels deep resentment for his cousin's affluence; the latter has acquired his wealth unjustly, Roque believes, merely by sitting back and waiting for things to happen, whereas he (Roque) has ruined his digestion living in cheap boarding houses and rushing from one end of Spain to the other in the pursuit of orders. To this primitive resentment is added the scorn that Roque, the city dweller, feels for the rustic Severiano. It is significant that the political differences between city and country, which were vividly illustrated in the elections of April 1931,[16] never enter into the Severiano/Roque relationship; they are at loggerheads even without the stimulus of political enmity. It pleases Roque to think that his cousin is trapped in his parochial environment (variously described as 'ratonera' (p. 37), 'agujero' (p. 39), 'pesebre' (p. 39)), until death delivers him. Showering his cousin with mental abuse, 'un palurdo empedernido' (p. 39), 'el muy simplón' (p. 40), 'aquel tontaina de Severiano' (p. 40), '¡Qué bruto! ¡Qué grandísimo terco!' (p. 52), 'el muy bruto' (p. 53), 'el pobre es bastante duro de mollera' (p. 53), 'el muy lerdo' (p. 54), Roque manages to gain some sense of his own superiority. Ironically, it is this wish to dominate his cousin that leads to all Roque's tribulations. His fabrications about travelling abroad and learning foreign languages prompt his cousin to seek his help in translating the message. Once the lie is told, he is trapped into agreeing to examine the piece of paper: 'Severiano lo tomaba en serio y me cerraba cualquier salida; de manera que no hubo sino seguirle la corriente' (p. 40). Here is fate at work.

It might appear from too hasty a study of the Severiano/Roque relationship that Roque is the guilty party, always goading and criticising his cousin, and that Severiano is innocent of all blame; but let us remember Ayala's terms of reference: the characters are both innocent and guilty at the same time. In his dealings with other people, Severiano displays many of the characteristics so evident in his cousin. He expresses annoyance that Antonio, a villager he describes as 'un perfecto borrico' (p. 47), does not show him the deference he thinks he deserves: 'Para él no hay respeto, no hay distancias. El hecho de haber sido compañeros de escuela...' (pp. 41–

42). He takes the same pleasure as Roque might have done in the inability of the local priest to decipher the message, taunting him: '¿De qué le valen todos los latines al padre cura si no es capaz de entender cuatro frases en idioma extranjero?' (p. 46). If he is unable to treat Roque in this way it is because he cannot find a weapon to do so. As for Antonio (a character who never appears but is described by Severiano), he employs even more outrageous tactics to arouse the anger of others. Apart from taking the same pleasure as Severiano in the failure of the village intellects to translate the message – he humiliates the tax-inspector (p. 43), and almost comes to blows with the village chemist over this (pp. 46–47) – he deliberately goads his wife into a white-hot rage by criticising her loudly to Severiano below the window where she is working. Roque, Severiano, Antonio – all are in the same mould.

Each relationship described in 'El mensaje' deteriorates as soon as contact is made between the two people involved. For this reason, it is an immensely bleak and depressing vision of humanity. One has the certainty that Roque and Severiano, although they part on superficially friendly terms, never want to see each other again. (Severiano's bluff farewell: '¡A ver si vuelves pronto, Roquete . . .!' (p. 64) is plainly ironical.) Roque is going off to meet a business acquaintance who is 'soberbio y grosero' (p. 58), and who will certainly not improve his digestion. Severiano will be left at the mercy of his sisters who, like Roque, continually harass him and force him out of bed if ever he has reason to want to stay there (p. 38). As well as the continual resentment felt by the various characters towards each other, violent quarrels are described between Antonio and his wife, Antonio and the chemist, Severiano and Juana. In short, what Ayala is describing is a little hell on earth. In 'El mensaje' he has reproduced the claustrophobic atmosphere of Sartre's *Huis clos*, published in 1944.[17] The basic theme – 'L'enfer, c'est les Autres'[18] – is expressed in both works as the deliberate infliction of psychological suffering, generally by humiliation, by one character on another: Antonio's criticism of his wife is meant to be overheard by her; in *Huis clos*, Garcin goes a stage further and brings his mulatto mistress to live with him, insisting that his wife bring them breakfast in bed every morning. In both works, part of the infernal atmosphere is due to the characters' realisation that they cannot escape consciousness by drifting into sleep, for sleep is denied them: 'Vous sentez vos yeux qui se ferment, mais pourquoi dormir? Vous vous allongez sur le canapé et pfft . . . le sommeil s'envole. Il faut se frotter les yeux, se relever et tout recommence',[19] moans Garcin. Compare this with Roque's dogged determination not to let his cousin have any sleep, despite the fact that he himself is exhausted too: 'Cansado sí que lo estaba; ¿no había de estarlo? Pero ya se me había pasado el sueño con tanta y tanta conversación . . . Y era justamente ahora cuando este bueno de mi señor primo sentía sueño y me mandaba, como se le manda a un niño, que me durmiera. – Pues no, señor: no estoy cansado' (pp. 49–50). At one point in Sartre's play, the lesbian Inès analyses herself and concludes: 'J'ai besoin de la souffrance des autres pour exister.'[20] It is precisely this need which seems to drive on the characters of 'El mensaje'. Though less *tremendista*, perhaps, than Sartre's deserter, infanticide and lesbian, the inhabitants of this village are motivated by the same misanthropic urges, and condemned ultimately to pay the same penalties for their lack of humanity.

In the passage already quoted from the *proemio* (p. 29), Ayala refers to his stay in Nazi Germany: 'Infundió en mi ánimo la *intuición* – y por cierto la noción también – de las realidades tremendas que se incubaban.' In an interview with A. Amorós, he claims that his writing comes from 'una íntima necesidad expresiva: la de dar forma a una *intuición* del mundo en que nos hallamos'.[21] In both cases, Ayala is concerned with reality, for the understanding of which he considers reason alone is insufficient. Marra-López terms Ayala 'una conciencia lúcida', adding: 'Si tuviéramos que resumir la figura de Francisco Ayala con una palabra, ninguna mejor que la de *intelectual*.'[22] While these latter judgements are true of Ayala the man, it should be realised that what makes Ayala a good novelist is not his intellect, but his perceptive intuition. For this reason, unlike Malraux, Aub or Sender,[23] he rarely creates intellectual heroes who analyse and probe in an attempt to understand themselves and their environment. Generally, his characters speak a simple language; but their words are often charged with a meaning – the author's intuition – that they themselves do not apprehend. It is this ineffable quality that is often expressed in great art, and it is doubtless the same quality which R. Gullón is trying to put into words when he writes: 'El gran don de Ayala es la capacidad de restituir a lo trivial su misterio, su capacidad para mostrarnos las cosas, no en su engañosa apariencia sin secreto, sino en su realidad arcana, empapadas en el gran misterio que llena la vida del hombre.'[24] Hence the poignant undertones in Roque's 'Cada vez entiendo menos a la gente', and other platitudes.

Santolalla, a first lieutenant in the Nationalist army and the protagonist of the second story, 'El tajo', is the only character in *La cabeza* to approximate to those intellectual heroes mentioned earlier. Described by the author as 'un carácter blando, solitario, soñador . . . el burgués cultivado capaz de análisis finos y de sentimientos generosos' (p. 35), he resembles the Ignacio of *Un millón de muertos*. Little wonder, then, that one discerning critic speaks of 'el hamletiano Santolalla'.[25] This nervous, anti-heroic Nationalist officer from Toledo is to give us not a panoramic description, however, but a brief glimpse of the war in an apparently trivial event which takes place in August 1938, somewhere on the Aragon front. He gives very few clues as to his exact position on this front. All that we know is that he has been there for 'un año largo' (p. 67), and that there has been absolutely no action during that time. (The only part of the Aragon front which coincides historically with the lieutenant's description is the far south of Teruel province, around Albarracín for example. Had he been on the eastern front, he would have moved at least 50 miles during those months to occupy positions to the east captured from the Republicans, and in the south-east, he would surely have been involved in the August counter-offensive across the Ebro.)

Santolalla's version of the war corresponds to that of realists like Orwell, who suffered 'boredom and discomfort' on other parts of the Aragon front, in 'a life as uneventful as a city clerk's'.[26] Uneventful, that is, until one day the peaceable lieutenant goes grape-picking in no-man's land and stumbles upon a Republican militiaman engaged in the same pastime. Before the latter has time to do anything except register surprise, Santolalla has instinctively drawn his revolver and shot him twice in the stomach, killing him outright. There follows the silent *crise de conscience*, which is all the more painful since this incident is Santolalla's only active contribution to the war, and because he finds he has killed someone from Toledo, his home town. The insensitivity and vulgarity of his fellow officers, coupled with his sense of shame, impel him to ask for transfer to an active front, but before this can be done, the Aragon front collapses and the war ends. Some time after returning home, Santolalla, now a schoolteacher, decides he must at least offer to help the family of his war victim. His pretence, however, that he has been the companion-in-arms, and not the killer, of the militiaman, is tacitly rejected by the man's mother, who has by now lost a second son and her husband in Nationalist reprisals. Santolalla's soft hands, middle-class vocabulary and comfortable economic position betray him immediately as a *señorito* (one of his haunting obsessions), and drive a wedge between him and this proletarian family he has helped to destroy. He is forced to leave, his conscience unappeased.

Such a summary of the plot cannot, of course, convey the sense of hopelessness that the author creates when confronting us with this rift between the two Spains, a rift that he portrays as being greater in 1941 than in the Second Republic, despite the intervening 'war of liberation'. Herein lies the profound pessimism of 'El tajo'. Deep-rooted human foibles, like those illustrated in 'El mensaje', underlie the tragedy, which is described as only one in a recurring cycle in Europe. The countries to which Spain has looked for inspiration during the last century – France and Germany – do not escape the fate of Spain herself, being ravaged by two great wars in succeeding generations. One of the many childhood memories recounted by Santolalla is the baiting of his father – a Francophile – by his grandfather – a Germanophile.[27]

El abuelo ... después de haber plegado su periódico dejándolo junto al plato y de haberse limpiado con la servilleta, bajo el bigote, los finos labios irónicos, decía: 'Pues tus queridos franchutes (corrían por entonces los años de la Gran Guerra) parece que no levantan cabeza.' Y hacía una pausa para echarle a su hijo, todo absorto en la meticulosa tarea de pelar una naranja, miraditas llenas de malicia; añadiendo luego: 'Ayer se han superado a sí mismos en el arte de la retirada estratégica' ... Desde su sitio, él, Pedrito [Santolalla], observaba cómo su padre, hostigado por el abuelo, perfeccionaba su obra, limpiaba de pellejos la fruta con alarde calmoso, y se disponía – con leve temblorcillo en el párpado, tras el cristal de los lentes – a separar entre las cuidadas uñas los gajos rezumantes. No respondía nada; o preguntaba, displicente: '¿Sí?' Y el abuelo, que lo había estado contemplando con pachorra, volvía a la carga: '¿Has leído hoy el periódico?' No cejaba, hasta hacerle que saltara, agresivo: y ahí venían las grandes parrafadas nerviosas, irritadas, sobre la brutalidad germánica, la civilización en peligro, la humanidad, la cultura, etcétera, con acompañamiento, en ocasiones, de puñetazos sobre la mesa.
                                                                    (p. 71)

While this family enmity is outwardly on a political level, there are clearly less rational forces at work. This view is supported by the incidence of similar antagonistic situations: the beatings dealt out to the family laundress by her drunken husband (p. 73); the enjoyment experienced by a classmate of Santolalla's when he has to tell him he has found his pet dog beaten to death (pp. 76–77); the violence and humiliation inflicted on the young Santolalla by Rodríguez, the son of a working-class family who envies the relative good fortune of the señorito (p. 80). But Santolalla too, outwardly balanced and educated, is just as much a victim of his passions as his neighbours. His compassion for the laundress is mingled with a desire to see the husband punished, and soon turns to contempt for the woman when he sees what a passive creature she is; his feelings for his grandfather turn to resentment when the latter obstinately refuses to join the family in Madrid;

his childhood longing for vengeance on Rodríguez grows into a murderous fantasy: '"Deseo," "anhelo," no son las palabras; más bien habría que decir: una necesidad física tan imperiosa como el hambre o la sed, de traerlo a casa, atarlo a una columna del patio y, ahí, dispararle un tiro con el pesado revólver del abuelo. Esto es lo que quería con vehemencia imperiosa, lo que dolorosamente necesitaba' (pp. 80–81). Ayala might have interpreted this as the beginning of a social upheaval having as its basis inequality (compare, for example, Barea's description of his tribulations as the son of a laundress in Madrid during the preceding decade).[28] But he does not pur' sue this line of thought, continuing to describe the problem as being moral rather than economic. This is consistent with his view of the Civil War, which he has described elsewhere as 'un acontecimiento no sólo peninsular sino universal por su alcance y consecuencias morales'.[29] Even the political differences which still separate Santolalla's father and grandfather are left without comment. We learn by the father's fright at seeing his son appear in Nationalist uniform that his liberal sympathies are still present, and the addition to the family of a Falangist son-in-law will have increased internal tension, but all this is left as a matter for conjecture. The only indication that Ayala has any political emotion left is the recurring image (pp. 75, 79, 81) of the column of savage Moors occupying Toledo and massacring Republican soldiers as they lie in their beds in the hospital.[30] It might be argued that as a Nationalist soldier, Santolalla would have chosen one of the examples of brutality on the Republican side; his intimate connections with Toledo, however, make it quite credible that the horror of violence in familiar surroundings would provide a more lasting impression.

On the question of impartiality, Ayala is among the most scrupulous of the writers who have dealt with the Civil War. His very concept of the characters as being a mixture of innocence and guilt makes him from the outset an impartial observer.[31] In 'El tajo', his particular care in choosing his words bears witness to this preoccupation. Madrid, whose defence is a hotly debated item of propaganda both during and after the war, is given a fleeting reference in the epithet 'hervidero de heroísmo y de infamia' (p. 69). In the description of the war in Toledo, the same careful balance is to be found in the expression 'la furia y el valor . . . el entusiasmo y la cólera popular' (p. 69), which neither wholly condemns nor wholly condones. In the *proemio*, Ayala writes: 'En "El tajo," el relato se hace más impersonal, en busca de una objetividad de la forma que compensara de la mayor interiorización del tema' (p. 34). The choice of the third person here, while all the other stories are narrated in the first person, is indicative of Ayala's wish to make a cool appraisal of the war itself. So too is his deliberate avoidance of anecdote, which invariably exposes the author to accusations of unfair selection. Even now, Ayala has laid himself open to the same charge as Gironella by creating a negative character, an anti-hero who does not uphold any of the ideals of the Right he is defending. Santolalla, like all the other characters, is a victim of circumstances rather than a manipulator of events. The war drives him hither and thither like flotsam on the tide. His presence on a quiet sector of the front with *emboscados* like himself is due to the good offices of his grandfather, who is a general in the reserve. The shooting of the militiaman is a reflex, the cumulative effect of anger and frustration at being away from his family and being reminded of the troubled moments of his childhood. Santolalla's guilt grows out of the realisation that this killing was not in self-defence; it was the unleashing on a hapless individual of all the pent-up emotions hitherto contained behind a civilised façade, the desire to wound, hurt and eventually destroy, which he has already seen, to a greater or lesser degree, in those around him.

The tragedy of 'El tajo' is that of collective guilt ('diffused responsibility', to use Parker's definition of a similar technique in Golden Age drama). This is the only satisfactory explanation for the inclusion of so many flashbacks to Santolalla's formative years, where he describes the friction that exists in so many relationships around him. Responsibility for what has happened lies with all those who have contributed to this state of affairs: Rodríguez, Rita and her husband, Santolalla's father and grandfather and the whole background of discord from which Santolalla has emerged. 'Each single error trickles down and combines with all the others to form the river that floods the tragic stage of life.'[32] Although the guilt may be shared, however, the conscience is not. Pedro Santolalla is regarded as an oddity for his sensitive reaction, and cannot reveal his tortured conscience to his comrades, who would simply laugh: 'Este – hubieran dicho – se complica la existencia con tonterías' (p. 81). But the eye of conscience pursues him as relentlessly as it pursued Hugo's Cain. Santolalla, though far from being the epic figure of *La Légende des siècles*, is condemned to a similar fate. The man he has killed in cold blood is, in symbolic terms, his brother; his dream of making amends to the bereaved family and receiving forgiveness on bended knee never becomes a reality. This is an example of the punishment by frustration which befalls the biblical Cain: 'When thou tillest the ground, it shall not henceforth yield unto thee her strength.'[33] The symbolic direction of his departure, 'calle abajo' (p. 91), leaves no doubt in our minds that this fratricide of the twentieth century is doomed to live with his remorse.[34]

R. Skyrme has shown that 'El tajo' is a brilliant illustration of the divided self, the estranged individual trying to reintegrate his personality.[35] The state of scission develops 'in precisely those forms of association in which one expects to find close cohesion: in Santolalla's family, in his relationship with childhood companions and acquaintances, and with his comrades in arms'.[36] The first part of the story is a demonstration of the estrangement the protagonist feels in these three relationships – based on blood, age and politico-military affiliation – while the language of the final part shows an unmistakable attempt to reintegrate the divided whole; the tragedy of the story lies, as we have seen, in the frustration of this attempt. When Santolalla remembers his childhood he seems to see himself in a photograph: 'Se veía a sí mismo . . . extrañamente, desde fuera, como la imagen recogida en una fotografía' (p. 70). It is no coincidence that he carries around with him the photograph of the militiaman he has killed, whose rotting corpse brings back other childhood memories. For the dead man is symbolically part of himself: 'His act in the vineyard is one of self-alienation, which leaves Santolalla not only changed but incomplete, needing to reintegrate the severed halves of his divided self',[37] like the grotesque figure of a Dalí painting.

Critics have hailed 'El tajo' as 'una obra maestra . . . lo mejor del libro',[38] 'el (relato) más completo, profundo e impresionante del libro'.[39] It is, without doubt, the most complete and convincing statement among the novels under study on the moral tragedy of the Civil War. Surprisingly enough, despite the differences in the end-products, Ayala's starting point is identical to Gironella's. *Ha estallado la paz*, as has been noted earlier, opens with Papini's words: 'No basta con cambiar los sistemas; hay que cambiar los ánimos y los corazones de los hombres.' Few statements could be more appropriate to Ayala's own view. Like Gironella, he would define the systems and political parties as transient and secondary, while the underlying passions which divide men are permanent and of primary importance. His oblique approach to the war involves the exclusion of almost all the transient elements in favour of the permanent elements, at the same time leaving enough markers to indicate clearly that his subject is indeed the Spanish Civil War.

In his *proemio* (p. 35), Ayala describes the protagonist of 'El regreso' as 'sano de alma, astuto, y un tanto brutal'. Returning to Spain in 1948 after nine years in exile in Buenos Aires, the anonymous ex-captain in the Republican army spends a month in Santiago de Compostela laying the ghosts of the past. As in the case of Barea's Antolín in *La raíz rota*, the reasons put forward for the exile's return – commitment to the family – are unconvincing. Both novelists are simply enacting in fictional terms the event they themselves yearn for in real life. The hope expressed in the exile's refrain, 'cuando vuelva a España . . .', remained unfulfilled in the case of Barea, and Ayala's story of the return of the exile was written prior to his own return.

Unlike Barea, who seeks to recreate the social environment of the late 1940s, Ayala continues to portray the Civil War in its effect on the human spirit: 'Ayala ha tomado la guerra por el lado que más quema: por el lado de las conciencias.'[40] Barea is specific when he describes the atrocious conditions of the lowest classes in Madrid in 1949,[41] but his detailed descriptions have a hollow ring: this is patently *la España inventada*. Ayala mentions certain of the post-war phenomena such as *estraperlo* (p. 102), but does not elaborate on them. He deliberately obscures this reference to *estraperlo*, for example, by inserting it in a garbled conversation between the old aunt and her nephew. He never loses sight of the fact that his main theme is one of morality: the betrayal of the protagonist by his childhood friend Abeledo: 'La vieja, estúpida, me explicaba cosas del negocio, ¿cómo iba a prestarle atención hoy?: vender y comprar, amistades, influencias, conchavos, estraperlo, ayer mismo sin ir más lejos, mañana a más tardar . . . De pronto, la interrumpí: "¿Y Abeledo?" One can imagine what Barea would have made of a scene such as the conversation between the returned exile and his barber. The barber would have been a member of the illegal UGT, would have roundly condemned the social policies of the Franco régime and taken the returned exile to see the low quarters of the city. Ayala simply reveals how far apart these men are after their experiences, with nothing meaningful to say to each other.

'¡Cuánto hace ¿eh? que no nos veíamos!' 'Hace sí – corroboró –: así es: el tiempo pasa; la gente se va, y luego, vuelve; es así . . . ¿Qué se proponía sugerir con eso? Mejor no cavilar en ello.
– Y por acá ¿qué novedades hay? – me adelanté a preguntar entonces.
– Ninguna. ¿Novedades? ¡Ninguna!
– Pues el caso es que – insistí – yo, apenas he llegado, digo: Voy a acercarme hasta la peluquería, a ver qué cuenta el amigo Castro.
– Llegó ayer, ¿no? – fue su incongruente réplica. Y, a raíz de ella, manifestó deseo de información acerca de si yo preferiría muy corto el pelo, para absorberse sin demora en su trabajo profesional.
– Y ¿qué gente viene por aquí? – reincidí en preguntarle tras de una pausa –. ¿Sigue viniendo siempre la misma gente?
– La misma, poco más o menos. Ya se sabe: unos se van, otros vienen . . . Poco más o menos, la misma gente.   (pp. 107–108)

Ayala makes his point well. The situation we have encountered in 'El mensaje' and 'El tajo', namely that of a deeply divided society which could not resolve its internal differences peaceably, is replaced in 'El regreso' by a society which is broken and disillusioned. There are no supporters of the régime to make jubilant references to the 'New State'. Instead, the 'deber que cumplía [Abeledo] por la causa' on the Nationalist side is shown to stem from selfish motives (p. 131); similarly, the exterminating fervour that swept over the Left in the first weeks of the war seems insane when the protagonist considers it in retrospect: 'Ni la comunidad de la sangre era excusa frente a aquella otra comunión insensata' (p. 117). The war does not seem to have solved any of the problems expressed in 'El mensaje'; indeed, the returned exile of 'El regreso' displays a degree of cynicism and selfishness which is reminiscent of Roque, the protagonist of the first story. The exile's treatment of his mistress, (pp. 96–97) and of María Jesús (p. 131), the terms in which he speaks of his aunt (pp. 102, 106), and his final abandonment of her (p. 134), all take us back to the themes of the earlier story.

Ayala has not changed either his approach or his message, then, in this third story of *La cabeza del cordero*. He is still concerned with the problems 'within the hearts of men' and remains scrupulously even-handed. His approach to the war – in the numerous flashbacks which punctuate 'El regreso' – is best summed up in his own words: 'Los escritores han de buscar la radical autenticidad del ser humano a través de una interpretación directa y sin compromiso – la sinceridad constituye el único compromiso del verdadero artista – de la concreta coyuntura en que se encuentran.'[42] He is contemptuous of political commitment in literature because it undermines this sincerity; in particular, he attacks the European left-wing movement espoused by so many post-war novelists: 'En esa Europa próspera y socialmente avanzada – mucho más avanzada socialmente que la Unión Soviética – el "engagement" de numerosos escritores no pasa de ser un lujo más que se conceden, el último toque de la *sophistication*, mediante el cual asumen verbalmente posiciones hostiles frente al sistema de cuyas ventajas disfrutan sin aprensión.'[43]

R. Gullón and J.R. Marra-López have written (in almost identical terms) that one of the achievements of Ayala is the avoidance of what they term 'la voluntad de probar'.[44] Mention has already been made of the fleeting reference to *estraperlo*. He is equally sparing in his treatment of other aspects of the war and its consequences. The shortage of Republican arms is briefly mentioned (p. 103); a *registro* by a Nationalist patrol is sketched (p. 100); everything is left to our imagination in such expressions as 'sangrientas noticias' (p. 92), 'montón de horrores' (p. 93), which refer to

Franco's Spain. Very occasionally the author allows himself a little irony: 'los héroes de retaguardia' (p. 95), the café Cosmopolita, whose dangerously internationalist name is quickly changed to 'Nacional' after the Civil War (p. 109).[45]

In the description of Abeledo's work in the dawn patrol (pp. 130–131), Ayala comes closest, it might appear, to abandoning his objectivity. Here we have a sadist who insists on recounting to his sister the horror of the Nationalist purge in which he is taking part: 'Hacía burlas, morisquetas; imitaba los sudores, balbuceos y pamplinas que los tipos hacían a la hora de la verdad' (p. 131). But Ayala does not exaggerate the brutality itself. (Galicia, in spite of its support to the Republic through the CNT, UGT and Galician Nationalist movement, fell to the Nationalists in its entirety within the first days of the war and the subsequent purge carried out by the Nationalists was swift and brutal.[46] There would have been little opportunity for a purge by the Left in this clerical city of Santiago.)

In portraying the sadism of Abeledo, Ayala shows how a weak character is distorted by violence and tension; having set out along the road of suppressing his enemies to ensure his own safety, he is then carried along by the events themselves. No mention here of 'imperio', 'Dios', 'patria' or 'rey'. For Abeledo, as for Santolalla in 'El tajo', the war is a squalid event. Both men, in different ways, are the antithesis of the clean-limbed Falangist hero we find in the work of Francisco de Cossío or Domingo Manfredi, and the crusading Carlist we find in the novel of Jorge Claramunt; the author is resolute in his intention not to glorify the violence. By 1949, when 'El regreso' was written, the less partisan novelists were already reacting against the extremism of the committed war writers. We have seen that for Ayala sincerity was above commitment; he is not ashamed, therefore, of depicting the Republican exile as embittered, cynical and no longer preoccupied with the political dimensions of the conflict. The 'transient' elements are once more secondary and the 'permanent' elements – the underlying passions which divide men – come to the fore. Like Severiano and Roque in 'El mensaje', Abeledo and the returned exile would be at loggerheads even without the stimulus of political enmity.

The air of unreality which permeates 'El regreso' may be explained by the frequent use of flashback during which the main action is frozen, and by the fact that the drama of the story is based on a fear which proves to be unfounded. We discover when the story reaches its dénouement that Abeledo was killed during the war and no longer poses a threat to the protagonist, as feared. At the symbolic level, however, the protagonist's failure to find Abeledo is a failure to find part of himself. As G. Plaza has shown, 'en su deseo de retorno no busca, se busca'.[47] 'Lo que mueve la persistencia de la búsqueda de Abeledo no es sino la búsqueda integradora.'[48] In their days in the seminary the two boys had been 'compañeros inseparables', and Abeledo had shown towards him 'un sentimiento fraterno que está por encima de cualesquiera diferencias' (p. 104). So much so that the unnamed narrator had found it impossible to feel physically attracted to Abeledo's sister because of her 'excesivo parecido con el hermano . . . ¿Cómo hubiera podido yo tocarla sin pensar de inmediato en Abeledo González?' The barely disguised symbolism of the name Abeledo, in the context of the other stories in this collection, makes it clear that Ayala is exploring the theme of the Cain–Abel relationship, and the estranged self. When the narrator meets Abeledo's sister in the post-war era it is by chance, in a brothel. But in satisfying his sexual urge, 'cuya satisfacción tenía pagada de antemano' (p. 131), he does not find any part of himself or any spiritual satisfaction: this is purely a commercial transaction on his part. He returns to Buenos Aires having achieved nothing: 'No había hecho nada, y ese nada había sido por nada, puro disparate' (p. 133). Ayala's restless protagonists, wherever they happen to be, soon feel an urge to be somewhere else. Roque, Santolalla, José Torres and this unnamed character are all described in this way at the end of their story. In 'El regreso' there is an interesting variation, in that the pursued becomes the pursuer in the course of the narrative. 'Es extraño cómo en esta dualidad de búsqueda tanto Abeledo como [el protagonista] buscan algo que de alguna forma no llega a concretarse en un hecho físico, en el encuentro que libere.'[49] All these stories end, therefore, with a sense of failure.

The story which gives its title to the collection, 'La cabeza del cordero', is narrated in the first person by 37-year-old José Torres, a native of Almuñécar, who visits the Moroccan city of Fez on a business trip after the war. A family there which bears the same surname as he does learns of his arrival and, certain he must be a relative, invites him to join them for dinner. This consists of a whole lamb which has been cut up in portions (including the severed head) and served on a large platter. After the meal, José returns to his hotel, where he is haunted by feelings of guilt for the ignoble part he played in the Civil War in Málaga. In an act of self-deception, he blames the meal for his discomfort: 'La cabeza del cordero me pesaba ya insoportablemente; me arañaba con sus dientes en las paredes del estómago, y me producía náuseas. Me tiré de la cama, y me fui de prisa para el cuarto de baño, haciendo bascas' (p. 175). The reader is not so easily deceived: José has in any case eaten no part of the lamb's head; that cannot be the explanation for his vomiting.

'La cabeza del cordero' offers one of the most powerful symbols of guilt in the narrative fiction of the Civil War, and complements thematically 'El tajo', in the same volume. While Santolalla is conscious of his remorse, and tries unsuccessfully to purge it in the visit to his victim's family in Toledo, José Torres is seemingly uncaring until a fortuitous sequence of events in Fez brings his subconscious feelings to the surface. Ayala's protagonists in all four stories of the first edition ('La vida por la opinión' was added later) are individuals who are deeply divided in themselves, and alienated from those around them. As Irizarry indicates, 'vemos en todos los relatos a personajes que parecen alejarse de su cuerpo y figura para contemplarse desde fuera'.[50] Just as Santolalla sees his *alter ego* in the photograph of the militiaman he has killed (a fellow Toledan), José Torres sees himself in Yusuf Torres and in the medallion portrait of Yusuf's great-great-grandfather, Mohamed ben Yusuf. The expression of self-disgust when José is confronted with this portrait is unequivocal: 'Tuvo por lo pronto el poder de suscitar en mí una curiosa y repentina sensación de náusea, un movimiento de las entrañas por escapar de mí mismo, huir de mi figura y encarnación' (p. 151). The reason for such a violent reaction is not immediately explained, but is revealed later to be José's failure to save his uncle, Jesús, from being assassinated by the Left; as a member of the CNT and leader of workers' committee, José was plainly in a position to have exerted influence to help him. Later, when the Right took power, he had quickly switched allegiance to the victorious side, abandoning many of his fellow workers to death by firing squad. 'Los pobres diablos no sabían qué hacerse ni qué pensar viendo al *camarada responsable*, con quien hasta el día antes habían bebido mano a mano el jerez y el coñac de la empresa, ahora otra vez a partir un piñón con la gerencia' (p. 172). For José, described by Ayala in the *proemio* as 'inteligente, cínico, burlón, canalla' (p. 35), thoughts of self-preservation and self-aggrandisement overcome moral principles or political ideology. One senses in Ayala profound disillusion-ment at the depths to which individuals sank during these years, and although he concedes that some people's conduct was 'generoso y abnegado,'[51] he provides few examples. From the comments he makes in *Confrontaciones* it is clear that he considers there is a chasm between the high ideals expressed by both sides, and their actions, which is why he feels unable to confront the war directly in its historical dimension: 'A los móviles elevados y generosos de la contienda sólo con reticencia, con leve ironía, se alude, porque destacarlos – dicho queda – hubiera resultado sarcástico.'[52] Ayala creates instead Nationalist and Republican anti-heroes, of whom Santolalla and José Torres are respective examples. Such characters are confronted with their own estrangement from themselves and others around them and attempt, to a greater or lesser degree, to harmonise their personalities, their system of values and their beliefs; in other words, to rediscover some internal coherence in their lives. But in the present in which they live there prevails a sense of 'being-in-history'; the shadow of the past appears and reappears in scenes remembered, sometimes voluntarily, sometimes not. The lamb's head in Ayala's story serves a similar function to Proust's device of the *madeleine*, albeit with more violent consequences. As Rodríguez Padrón observes:

Estas historias se sustentan sobre una bipolaridad (pasado–presente) que es constante y que permite una recuperación reveladora del pasado: que permite una investigación sobre una intriga mantenida por el personaje al situarse ante aquel hecho inesperado, ante aquel acontecimiento rompedor de la monotonía que le obliga a saberse parte de una historia, de la que no podrá prescindir.[53]

In his Moroccan relatives (if relatives they are), José Torres finds an image of himself as he might have been, 'el perfil moral de su mejor "yo"'.[54] His *alter ego*, Yusuf, unlike himself, accepts his responsibilities as head of the family, respects the memory of his ancestors and shows deference to religious tradition; his extreme courtesy in greeting José Torres disconcerts the latter, and his attachment to Almuñécar, the native town of his ancestors, seems incomprehensible to the cynical narrator. Mohamed ben Yusuf, the ancestor José resembles, is described as 'el mejor hombre de toda la familia, aquel que logró restituir aquí, en Africa, la importancia que antes había tenido en Andalucía' (p. 150). Significantly, when José is taken to the cemetery, he expresses interest in seeing this man's grave. Yusuf's reply, for once, is unhelpful ('"Ese no está enterrado aquí," fue su única respuesta'), and José's wish is frustrated. Destiny has brought him face to face with an idealised image of himself, which vanishes when he reaches out to possess it. Like the protagonists of the other three stories, his frustration may be seen as a punishment, symbolising the fate that befell Ayala's generation following the social disintegration of Spain. The punishment meted out to José's uncle Jesús and his cousin Gabriel by opposing sides in the war took the form of execution – a form of retribution whose result is immediately apparent, palpable. Not so the punishment suffered by the survivors. José's frequent assertions that he was one of the lucky ones ('Salvé el cuero', 'Tuve ... suerte', 'La cosa me salió ... muy bien') have a hollow ring when he is described vomiting into a lavatory pan after the meal in Fez. For E. Irizarry, Ayala's message in 'La cabeza del cordero' is essentially pessimistic because José Torres does not learn anything from his experience; 'he reverts to his former complacency after the symbolic expulsion of the lamb's head'.[55] This is perhaps to take at face value José's expressions of total relief and well-being the morning after, and to believe, with him, that 'total, no se había perdido gran cosa'. In fact, the mere sight of Yusuf's messenger again through the window of the bus in which he is leaving throws him into a fit of alarm: 'Tuve un sobresalto y (¡qué tontería!) miré para otro lado.' One senses that José's flight to Marrakech will not rid him of his guilt, and that like Santolalla he is destined for the rest of his life to be pursued by the eye of conscience. This interpretation does not make Ayala's message seem any less pessimistic, needless to say: what was done in the Civil War cannot be undone, however remorseful the participants may feel after the event.

Ayala's oblique approach consists of his recreating the insecurity and tension, anguish and fear of the Civil War, rather than a recreation of the events themselves. It is not easy to identify precisely which elements contribute to the vibrant tension which is the most characteristic feature of the novel. The reader is left with the same feeling of *malaise* he would experience after reading a mysterious tale of Edgar Allan Poe or a legend of Bécquer. In 'El mensaje' the tension undoubtedly develops out of the mysterious message; it grows by feeding on the multiple conflicts that spring up, the enormous reserves of suppressed violence that the characters feel towards each other. In 'El tajo', as we have seen, Santolalla is naturally alienated within the family, within his age group and among his comrades-in-arms; he is often described at the front seeking solitude. In 'El regreso' the tension stems from the anticipated violence between Abeledo and the protagonist, which never materialises; it is heightened by the dreamlike atmosphere in which the events take place. In 'La cabeza del cordero', the temporal planes of present, recent past and distant past form a complex labyrinth through which the protagonist moves uneasily. In all these cases, personal resentment or guilt is more powerfully expressed than political antagonism.

Ayala's skill in depicting these personal conflicts, 'su capacidad poética de identificarse con el vivir ficticio de sus criaturas',[56] and above all his avoidance of the anecdotal, are the key to his success in his approach to the war. He has adopted this technique, according to M. Joly, because he considers the traditional 'episodic' approach has outlived its usefulness. 'Ese descubrimiento de una nueva línea se debe a una especie de movimiento pendular que, agotadas las posibilidades de la perspectiva histórica, lleva a Ayala a interesarse por el partido que podría sacar de una versión reelaborada del esperpento.'[57] G. Sobejano praises Ayala for eschewing the technique that perhaps came most easily to him, namely satire; instead, he has chosen 'la vía lúcida de la alusión'.[58]

It seems clear from Ayala's explanation in *Confrontaciones* that his motives for choosing this oblique approach stemmed from the painful nature of the recollection:

Si yo he tratado literariamente de manera oblicua el tema de la Guerra Civil es para establecer de este modo la distancia necesaria a la objetivación artística, ya que los acontecimientos me quedaban demasiado próximos, emocional y temporalmente, para haber podido asumirlos y transfigurarlos en su enorme y dura inmediatez.[59]

Indeed, the painful nature of the recollection is evident more than 40 years after the event in his conversations with R. Hiriart, in which he shows a marked reluctance to discuss the issue at length.[60]

Because Ayala sets out to 'transfigure' the events he is describing, he is one of the few authors of the Civil War essentially to capture that tragic style whose absence is so lamented by G. Steiner in *The Death of Tragedy*. Avoiding the rhetoric and the authorial intrusions so typical of the writers of his generation on this subject,[61] Ayala succeeds more than any other in recreating the atmosphere of tension and conflict of his country during these years. In Ayala's prose, words once again give their full yield of meaning; instead of rhetoric there is true style, and bathos gives way to a genuinely tragic dimension.

Significantly, commenting on the French war novel of the twentieth century, two French critics come to the independent conclusion that the oblique approach has yielded most positive results. With reference to Aragon's *Le Monde réel*, M. Rieuneau writes:

Sans être des romans de guerre, puisqu'ils ne la décrivent pas, les trois premiers romans du *Monde Réel* sont fortement unis par le thème de la guerre de 1914, envisagée dans sa genèse. On voit maintenant pourquoi cette approche était plus féconde, aux yeux d'Aragon, qu'une mise en scène directe de l'événement: elle lui permettait de remonter aux causes et de mettre au jour les rouages de la société qui, selon lui, engendre la guerre. Au lieu d'un effet de pure émotion, pathétique, tragique, héroïque ou pittoresque, elle donnait aux romans la portée d'une analyse historique infiniment riche d'enseignements pour le présent et pour l'avenir.[62]

R. Pomeau, referring to more recent wartime experiences, writes: 'Il se confirme encore combien peu maniable est la guerre en sa phase intense pour le romancier qui veut aller au-delà du témoignage. Quand Camus dessine un symbôle du Mal, c'est la peste qu'il choisit . . .'[63] In avoiding recounting directly his painful personal experience Ayala has, whether consciously or not, made it possible to concentrate on the quintessential elements of the conflict in a way few other novelists have succeeded in doing.

Notes

1 'La excentricidad hispana', *Histrionismo y representación* (Buenos Aires, 1944), p. 183.

2 *La cabeza del cordero*, 2nd edn (Buenos Aires, 1962), p. 32. Although this second edition is the one to which detailed reference is made, we have not included the fifth story, 'La vida por la opinión', in our analysis; it was absent from the first edition and is not directly concerned with the Civil War, but its aftermath.

3 *Horizon* (May 1941), 350–361.

4 Occasional short stories appeared in *Sur*, such as 'Diálogo de los muertos' (December 1939) and 'La campana de Huesca' (August 1943); 'El hechizado' was published in 1944. These did not appear in a volume, however, until 1949 (*Los usurpadores*).

5 *Sur*, 170 (December 1948), 19–53.

6 *Realidad*, 6, no. 16 (July–August 1949), 59–87.

7 J.R. Marra-López, *Narrativa española fuera de España (1939–1961)* (Madrid, 1963), p. 230.

8 *Cazador en el alba* (Madrid, 1930), pp. 50–51. Quoted in H. Rodríguez-Alcalá, 'Metáforismo, "criaturalismo" y sátira en la obra novelística de Francisco Ayala', *Revista Hispánica Moderna*, 25, no. 4 (1959), 291–303 (p. 293).

9 Ortega's definition of modern poetry in 'La deshumanización del arte', *Obras completas* (Madrid, 1946), 3, p. 372.

10 Nora, *La novela española contemporánea*, 2, pp. 247–248.

11 Marra-López, *Narrativa española*, pp. 227 and 242.

12 R. Hiriart, *Conversaciones con Francisco Ayala* (Madrid, 1982), p. 72. This same disclaimer is repeated on p. 79.

13 'Ortega politicised modernism: he identified it as the literature of a "natural" ruling class which hates democracy. The aura of political suspicion surrounding any Spanish literature of imagistic or syntactic complexity has never since been dispelled' (J. Butt, *Writers and Politics in Modern Spain* (London, 1978)).

14 'Observaciones sobre la lengua de dos novelistas de la emigración: Max Aub y F. Ayala', *Diálogos*, 65 (1975), 27–30 (p. 27).

15 R. Molina, in *Estudios* (Madrid, 1961), draws attention to Ayala's use of Calderonian themes and techniques (in *Muertes de perro*).

16 The cities were massively Republican, the country districts Monarchist. See H. Thomas, *The Spanish Civil War* (London, 1971), p. 39.

17 *Huis clos* (Paris, 1947). In an interview with Ayala in 1987, the author assured me that this resemblance is coincidental.

18 *Théâtre* (Paris, 1966), p. 182.

19 *Ibid.*, pp. 129–130.
20 *Ibid.*, p. 157.
21 *Revista de Occidente*, 68 (1968), 145–171 (p. 149).
22 Marra-López, *Narrativa española*, p. 219.
23 In *L'Espoir*, the *Campos* and *Los cinco libros de Ariadna*, respectively.
24 R. Gullón, '*La cabeza del cordero*', *Insula*, 51 (15 March 1950).
25 Nora, *La novela española contemporánea*, 3, p. 251.
26 *Homage to Catalonia* (London, 1964), p. 25.
27 In a later interview, Ayala reveals that this schism between Francophiles and Germanophiles was 'una división que separó a los miembros de mi propia familia' (E. Brandenberger, 'Francisco Ayala y Alemania', *Cuadernos Hispanoamericanos*, 329–330 (1977), 308–310 (p. 308)).
28 *La forja*, Part 1, *passim*.
29 F. Ayala, *El escritor en la sociedad de masas* (Buenos Aires, 1958), p. 8.
30 H. Thomas, *The Spanish Civil War*, p. 263, describes the bloodbath in the hospital of San Juan, adding in a footnote that this incident may have been caused by 'the fact that certain unwounded militiamen took refuge in the hospital and so drew the fire of the Moors in that direction'. Whatever the ultimate truth of the matter, the censors of the Franco regime showed themselves to be particularly sensitive to Ayala's constant references to the incident: 'El tajo' was conspicuously absent from the early Gredos anthology of Ayala's work, *Mis páginas mejores* (Madrid, 1965), and the Aguilar edition of his complete works (Madrid, 1968).
31 For an interesting attempt to interpret 'El tajo' as a pro-Republican *novela de tesis*, see J. Díaz and R. Landeira, '"El tajo" de Francisco Ayala: un caso de conciencia', *The American Hispanist*, 4 (1978), 7–12. These critics spoil their case when they claim, for example, that 'lo único que falta para que Pedro (Santolalla) sea *prototipo* del falangista es una mayor conciencia ideológica' (p. 10). Santolalla bears no resemblance to the Falangist prototypes described in this study. Nor does it seem very rational for the critics in question to take the author's repeated denials that his novel displays a Republican bias as a basis for proving that the opposite is true.
32 A.A. Parker, 'Towards a Definition of Calderonian Tragedy', *Bulletin of Hispanic Studies*, 39 (1962), 222–237 (p. 233).
33 Genesis 4: 12. J. Díaz, in Díaz and Landeira, '"El tajo" de Francisco Ayala', has drawn attention to the biblical resonance of the vineyard in which the killing takes place; it evokes the killing by Cain of his brother Abel, and the theme of paradise lost to which Ayala returns in other stories such as 'Nuestro jardín' and 'A las puertas del Edén'.
34 The scene at the home of the dead militiaman has been variously interpreted. N.R. Orringer considers that in describing the mother's rejection of Santolalla's expression of condolence for her son's death, 'Ayala . . . está subrayando el fracaso de impulsos genéricamente humanos frente al particularismo intransigente' ('Responsabilidad y evasión en "La cabeza del cordero"', *Hispanófila*, 52 (1974), 51–60 (p. 54)). R. Skyrme comes to a quite different conclusion: 'Santolalla's motive is, by his own admission, a truly selfish one: "*para mí* sería una satisfacción muy grande poderles ayudar en algo"' ('The Divided Self: The Language of Scission in "El tajo" of Francisco Ayala', *Revista Canadiense de Estudios Hispánicos*, 6, no. 1 (1981), 91–109 (p. 103)). The second of these interpretations seems to me to be the correct one, given Ayala's depiction of Santolalla as an ambivalent and anti-heroic character.
35 R. Skyrme, 'The Divided Self'.
36 *Ibid.*, 92.
37 *Ibid.*, 101. The phenomenon of *desdoblamiento* in Ayala is further discussed in E. Irizarry, *Teoría y creación literaria en Francisco Ayala* (Madrid, 1971).
38 H. Rodríguez-Alcalá, 'Metaforismo', 298.
39 R. Dieste, '*Los usurpadores* y *La cabeza del cordero*', *Boletín del Instituto Español*, 10 (February 1950), 26–27 (p. 27).

40 *Ibid.*, p. 27.

41 A. Barea, *La raíz rota* (Buenos Aires, 1955), ch. 4 *et passim*.

42 F. Ayala, 'Función social de la literatura', *Revista de Occidente*, 2, no. 10 (1964), 97–107 (p. 105).

43 *Ibid.*, 105.

44 '[Los cuentos] responden a un tipo de narración muy actual, habitado por las preocupaciones de nuestro tiempo, y libres de la quizá más grave tacha de la llamada "literatura comprometida": la voluntad de probar' (R. Gullón, *Insula*, 51 (15 March 1950), 4).

   'Una de sus características principales es la de que siendo un escritor comprometido plenamente con su tiempo – como lo demuestra toda su obra de posguerra – ha sabido librarse de uno de los más difíciles escollos de la actual literatura: la voluntad de probar' (J.L. Marra-López, *Narrativa española*, p. 253).

45 Cf. Gironella, *Ha estallado la paz*, p. 25, where similar symbolism is employed: 'Frente al Café Neutral – que ahora se llamaba Café Nacional . . .' The change in the names of streets, cafés, cinemas, etc. took place in every Spanish town when the Nationalists entered.

46 For examples, see H. Thomas, *The Spanish Civil War*, pp. 149, 160–161 and 161 n.1.

47 'Un relato de Francisco Ayala: realidad imaginada o soledad intransferible', *Cuadernos Hispanoamericanos*, 329–330 (1977), 429–440 (p. 431).

48 *Ibid.*, 438.

49 *Ibid.*, 436.

50 E. Irizarry, *Teoría y creación literaria en Francisco Ayala*, pp. 74–75.

51 F. Ayala, *Confrontaciones* (Barcelona, 1972), p. 90.

52 *Ibid.*, p. 121. Later in this same volume, Ayala condemns partisan attitudes to the war: 'Durante la Guerra Civil, los españoles, exasperados, llegamos a sentir el Bien supremo como vinculado a la causa respectiva' (p. 233).

53 'La oblicuidad de Francisco Ayala', *Camp de l'Arpa*, 13 (1974), 24–25 (p. 25).

54 N.R. Orringer, 'Responsabilidad y evasión en "La cabeza del cordero"', 56.

55 *Francisco Ayala* (Boston, 1977), p. 63.

56 H. Rodriguez Alcalá, 'Metaforismo', 300.

57 'Francisco Ayala: Ensayo de interpretación de su obra narrativa posterior a la guerra', *Cuadernos Hispanoamericanos*, 329–330 (1977), 366–383 (p. 368).

58 G. Sobejano, 'Observaciones sobre la lengua de dos novelistas de la emigración', 27. Aub, on the other hand, he describes as having chosen 'el camino cálido del recuerdo'. The contrast between two approaches to the problem of novelising the Civil War could hardly be more marked.

59 *Confrontaciones*, p. 40.

60 *Conversaciones con Francisco Ayala* (Madrid, 1982), p. 26. Ayala devotes a mere paragraph to the war, adding dismissively: 'En último análisis, ese acontecimiento trascendental no opera sobre las existencias individuales de manera distinta a tantos otros de importancia quizá menos y aun mínima.' This change of perspective may have been brought about by a surfeit of questions by interviewers on the same theme. Ayala was by this time in his mid-seventies.

61 Ayala warns of the dangers of authorial intrusion in the following comment: 'Si los personajes viven con una autonomía y responden a sus propias leyes, y no hacen como títeres lo que el autor quiere que hagan, sino que hacen lo que corresponde a ellos, entonces habrá acierto' (N.R. Orringer, 'Entrevista con F. Ayala', *Cuadernos Americanos*, 34, no. 4 (1975), 223–229 (p. 227)). As we have seen, this was one of the major faults of Civil War novelists before Ayala.

62 *Guerre et révolution dans le roman français de 1919 à 1939* (Paris, 1974), pp. 414–415.

63 'Guerre et roman dans l'entre-deux-guerres', *Revue des Sciences Humaines* (January–March 1963), 77–95 (p. 94).

9

Irrationalism
and anti-historicism
in the later novels of
the Civil War (1967–1975)

THE PUBLICATION of Lera's *Las últimas banderas* in 1967 marks a new phase in the production of Civil War novels. For the first time in Franco's Spain, a Republican ex-combatant was allowed to publish his account of events. Up to the time of Franco's death, only a handful of former Republicans would succeed in doing the same: L. Perpiñá Castellá (*El miliciano Borrás*, 1971); M. Andújar (*Historias de una historia*, 1973); A. de la Granda (*Hospital militar 28*, 1975). A more numerous band of Republicans (M. Aub, R. de Belausteguigoitia, M. Carreño, F. Parés Guillén, J.A. Rial, R. Ruiz, J. Sanz Saínz) continued to publish abroad, mainly in Mexico, during this same period (1967–75). Meanwhile, in Spain itself, a stream of Civil War novels continued to be produced by former Nationalists, or by the new generation of writers who had been too young to experience the war.

It is important to realise that the last decade of Franco's rule in Spain was characterised by considerable social and political unrest. The events of May 1968 in Paris had repercussions on university campuses throughout Europe; Basque terrorists were bent on frustrating the continuation of Francoism after Franco; the Catalan protest movement grew more insistent in its demands. Though supported by the United States for geo-strategic reasons the Franco regime sat uncomfortably among the European democracies. The Civil War still cast a heavy shadow over Spain.

In the war novel, the tradition of social realism, by now almost exhausted, still received the patronage of the Right: A. Duque's *El mono azul* was awarded the Premio José Antonio Primo de Rivera in 1974. The régime's abandonment of prior censorship in 1966 may have led writers to begin preparing material they had hesitated to offer to publishers before that date. Whatever the reason, more Civil War novels were published in Spain in 1969 than in any other year since 1939.

For many writers, their personal experience of the Civil War still formed the basis of their novels. A. Albalá's *Los días del odio* (1969) describes the war in Coria (Cáceres), where the author was born in 1924; the war is seen through the eyes of Fernando, the adolescent son of a middle-class family – clearly the author himself. The protagonist of Cela's *San Camilo 1936* (1969) was 20 when the war broke out (p. 251), suffered tuberculosis (pp. 183, 304) after a sickly childhood (p. 354), and at Madrid University had preferred, like Cela, to attend Pedro Salinas's classes (p. 16) to those that would prepare him for his chosen career. A. de la Granda's *Hospital militar 28* is a story based on the author's experiences as director of the military hospital in Madrid's Puerta del Sol during the War.

Lera's *Las últimas banderas* is closely modelled on his own experiences, as his biographer makes clear.[1] Founder of the Partido Sindicalista in La Línea de la Concepción, Lera was active in left-wing politics, especially after October 1934. The graphic description in the novel of his visit by taxi on 18 July 1936 to the crossroad at El Toril and his encounter with a contingent of Civil Guards is entirely factual. Lera was fortunate to escape with his life. Later, when La Línea was taken, he slipped through the back door of the Bar Belmonte and escaped his Falangist persecutors. As friend and confidant of Angel Pestaña, he was involved in negotiations at the highest level during the war: on 17 October 1936 he attended a meeting with Largo Caballero, Alvarez del Vayo and Rosenberg (p. 204). Immediately afterwards he was sent as a war commissar to the Madrid front (Torrejón de Velasco), where he was clearly impressed by the General in command ('alto, delgado . . .' (p. 225)), whose identity in the novel is not revealed (but we know to be Asensio). On 7 November 1936, Lera was given the task of rallying the population of Madrid to the defence of the city. He was later to serve as a commissar with Cipriano Mera in the 4th Army Corps in Guadalajara, and El Campesino in the Alcarria, before ending the war in Madrid during the Casado coup. The nights in the flat in the Carrera San Jerónimo, the escape to Castelló, 99, to a flat belonging to his uncle, his subsequent arrest and the tram journey to a makeshift jail in San Bernardo are all real events. Not surprisingly, perhaps, the novel stops short of describing the torture he witnessed in the Nationalist jails during this period.[2]

Benet's *Volverás a Región* is punctuated with his own memories of the war. At the age of nine he was separated from his parents, an event which by his own admission caused him great distress.[3] Worse was to come: in 1936, his father was shot. In the novel, mystery surrounds the young boy who awaits with anguish his mother's return, while a woman is haunted by 'la imagen . . . del marido, envuelta en el aura de la mañana con un rictus siniestro y una sonrisa macabra al . . . rascar su camisa para mostrar las terribles heridas y el agujero negro in el centro del pulmón' (p. 21). Nothing demonstrates more vividly the power of Civil War images to survive the passing of time.

By the last decade of the Franco regime, despite these painful memories, revanchist novels of the Civil War are a thing of the past. The disillusionment that characterised some earlier writers on both sides now takes the form of profound pessimism, and scepticism that anything good could have come out of the conflict, whichever side won. Some opponents of the regime, realising that their attempts to influence Spanish public opinion through social realism had produced few changes, sought new forms of expression. 'De un naturalismo, basado en las motivaciones y acciones del hombre externo, se pasa a la existencia psíquica, al hombre interno.'[4] The profusion of historical analyses of the conflict that had appeared by this time may also have deterred some from following in the footsteps of Gironella, whose work stood as the ultimate achievement of the historical school of writing. Aub brought his cycle of *Campos* to a conclusion in 1968 with *Campo de los almendros*. Agustí's *Guerra civil*, in 1972, marked the end of the series *La ceniza fue árbol*, a vast fresco of Spanish social history which includes the Civil War. As these traditional novel forms become exhausted, authors become preoccupied with discovering new modes of expression for an essentially bleak view of the society in which they live, as well as the immediate past they describe in their novels.

A good example of the new aesthetic is to be found in J. Benet's *Volverás a Región*. Benet is an engineer by profession, who began writing a surrealist novel in 1951 after reading Frazer's *The Golden Bough*. The name of the anonymous location, Región, was coined at that time, and the figure of Numa – a symbol of prohibition and retribution – borrowed from Frazer. Benet moved in opposition circles: he was a friend of Martín Santos and Dionisio Ridruejo; his brother helped Republican prisoners to escape from Franco's jails.[5] The knowledge of post-war Spanish society he gained in his travels around the country working on hydraulic projects led him to profoundly pessimistic conclusions, but these go beyond social criticism:

Durante ocho años había estado recurriendo una buena parte del noroeste de la península y en cada comarca, en cada tierra, en los arrinconados y podridos burgos y en los quejumbrosos monasterios, había seguido espiando la presencia de aquel guarda maldito, el fundador de la maldita dinastía que mantenía a raya tantas extraviadas comunidades sujetas a su propia tierra por su propio terror. Semejante experiencia viajera me llevó a aclarar algunas ideas y . . . a entenebrecer otras que, por demasiado contundentes, se me antojaban inexactas. Entonces llegué a la conclusión de que rara vez la verdad alumbra, o en otras palabras, que de semejarse a algo es a *las tinieblas que se cierran tras el relámpago del error.*[6]

This is a text of fundamental importance in that it questions the validity of historical analysis: the only certainty the author appears to cling to is that nothing is certain. Any judgement he may make on the Civil War and its legacy will carry within it the germ of its own contradiction. The novel of ambiguity is born. As Julia Wescott has written, Benet does not set out to write a readerly novel. This work, and the other two novels in the trilogy (*Una meditación, Un viaje de invierno*), are written in the structuralist mode, making it impossible to formulate a traditional pattern of character attributes from actions or statements. There is fragmentation of events, chronology is destroyed and there is ambiguity in the narrative stance, deliberately creating confusion. The characters thus lose their intrinsically human qualities of intelligibility and coherence, so that their analytical attempts to order the significance of the past are unsuccessful.[7] One critic has compared Benet's technique to the 'suspended meaning' which Roland Barthes defines as the essence of literature: 'He opens up a meaning about the world, and in the very act of offering it, he arrests it and prevents its completion . . .'[8] Given that the novel was redrafted four times before publication, it seems clear that its incoherence is intentional, 'un implacable y sistemático proceso de autodestrucción individual y colectiva que constituye el tema'.[9] The accounts of the military campaigns in Región are factual and straightforward, for the most part, as are the minutely detailed descriptions of the geographical and geological features of the area. These contrast starkly with the confused identities and motivations of the characters. The Republican leader, variously named as Rombal, Rumbal, Rembal, Robal, Rubal and Rumbás, deals in those 'verdades palmarias e incontestables' (p. 31) we know the author to distrust. Rombal is made to appear a ridiculous figure, likened to a reluctant performing elephant in a circus act (p. 33) and unfit to lead others (p. 184). The constant references to the gambling incident in the casino which leads to the wounding of the army officer Gamallo reminds us that it is passion ('enojo') and destiny ('un montón de fichas de nácar') which send the horsemen in pursuit of the fleeing gambler (p. 183). 'It is basically vengeance that impels the horsemen against the gambler, the same force that moved Spain (Región) into the nightmare of the Civil War.'[10] In the discussion of people's motives for taking part in the war, Dr Sebastián predicts that historians will oversimplify the reasons: 'La historia dará en su día su fallo que es muy distinto al de los contemporáneos porque no somos capaces de conformarnos con una simplificación.' But just when we expect a discussion of the issues, the doctor resorts to anti-historicism and obfuscation: 'Lo que sí creo es que cuando una sociedad ha alcanzado ese grado de desorientación que llega incluso a anular su instinto de supervivencia, espontáneamente crea por sí misma un equilibrio de fuerzas antagónicas que al entrar en colisión destruyen toda su reserva de energías para buscar un estado de paz – en la extinción – más permanente' (p. 184). Having abandoned any scientific analysis, Dr Sebastián takes refuge in the vague historiography of the Generation of '98. Another recurring metaphor for Spanish society is that of a collection of separate particles suspended in a liquid (an image worthy of Ortega y Gasset), particles which precipitate 'al solo anuncio de la guerra civil'. Precisely what role the principle of historical causality can play in such an analysis is not clear, particularly when the image of Numa, guardian of the forest, is immediately juxtaposed to confuse the analogy (p. 181). Political militants welcome the arrival of war as an opportunity to display their courage, indulge their resentment or commit acts of vengeance (p. 183). It is significant that these are all psychic needs rather than political aspirations. The mass of the people fear anything that disturbs their passivity: when a manifesto appears calling them to political action, 'nadie quería leerlo, era demasiado terrible, lo más terrible era encontrar una finalidad de los actos y un motivo de lucha' (p. 32). The proof that Dr Sebastián advances to show that there was little rational basis for the Civil War is that, even in the case of committed Republicans, 'si hubieran cambiado un par de circunstancias, es posible que hubieran combatido del otro lado' (p. 187). While there are occasional references to the agrarian question ('La ley no ha servido – a la vuelta de los años – sino para convertir al pequeño propietario rural en el enfiteuta de los grandes señores' (p. 48)), little sympathy is expressed for the victims of greedy landowners. Nor are solutions to the problem proposed. While there is historical reality in the novel there is an absence of historicism. Irrational and even magic elements abound: Numa, the god of the forest; a boat-woman who has all the attributes of a witch; a gold coin which motivates much of the novel's action; red flowers which spring up wherever mortal remains lie buried. It would be wrong to seek a coherent symbolism in the novel, as some critics have done.[11] While some images may lend themselves to such an interpretation, most do not. Rather, Benet attempts to destroy coherence and causality, reproducing in the reader the experience of psychic disintegration. 'La dimensión sociológica de la novela no se funda en símbolos, sino en la experiencia creada: la transformación de una realidad concreta en sensación fantasmal.'[12] When Benet wishes to treat the Civil War socio-politically, he does so in an essay: ¿Qué fue la guerra? (Barcelona, 1976). He refuses, however, to assign a social function to the novel, maintaining that this is to undermine the potential of a work of art. Spanish social realism, he claims, has always been a vulgar type of literature, written for a public that had no choice but to 'tolerate and even applaud under the coercion of collective guilt'.[13] It is a frustrating exercise to look for rational explanations for historical phenomena in this novel. The explanations a historian would give for the prolongation of the war might include the aid that both sides received from abroad, the hope on the Republican side that a European war would soon erupt, the incompetence of military commanders, or a number of other factors. A recurrent theme of the novel, however, is that the war was prolonged by the Republicans so that their own defeat, when it came, would be totally deserved: 'La mejor razón para prolongar aquella guerra había que buscarla entre las compensaciones de la derrota. Que la guerra había que perderla, costase lo que costase . . . para perder definitivamente toda confianza en la historia y en su porvenir' (p. 176). Benet spurns rationalism and historicism, depicting the war as a product of collective psychic disintegration and self-destruction. He raises the novel of the Civil War to new heights of literary expression, while declining to interpret the underlying cultural, political and socio-economic motives for the conflict.

Cela's San Camilo 1936 shares with Volverás a Región a number of the features described above, notably an anti-historical approach to the events of 1936 (despite a wealth of factually accurate information) and an interpretation of the war as a psychic epidemic. 'El individuo que no encuentra sentido personal en la vida se une a los demás con la excusa de participar en la acción común, parapetándose en ésta para dar rienda suelta a sus deseos ancestrales de destrucción.'[14] Cela too renounces interpretation; instead, he creates confusion and uncertainty by the free expression of subconscious thoughts which defy rational analysis. Not surprisingly, he has laid himself open to irresponsibility. Like Volverás a Región the novel was published in 1969, towards the end of Franco's dictatorship, when dispassionate and informed political debate was needed to steer Spain through a difficult transition towards a more democratic form of government. The text is liberally punctuated with references to real people and real events in 19–21 July 1936. 'We must consider the author as being obliged, in the light of his non-fictional references, to allude further to the socio-economic circumstances in which his historical facts occurred. He might be expected, short of that, to suggest the motivating ideologies behind the figures and events cited in his narrative. What Cela offers instead is a version of cultural psychology which explains political history by theorising on sexual repression, hormonal functions and defective sexual release.'[15] Republican Madrid is a vast whorehouse in which the author projects 'a maze of trivialities which all but bury the outbreak of the Civil War in a grotesque accumulation of low, mean or petty words and deeds'.[16] 'Politicians of both left and right . . . seem to spend a disproportionate amount of time in bawdy houses, brothels or more elegant houses of prostitution. Indeed, the reader can hardly escape the conclusion that Cela means to imply that most of the decisions concerning the war – on both sides – were made in whorehouses.'[17] Cela substitutes for historical analysis the absurd claim that Spaniards could avoid political violence if they fornicated more – a thesis some critics appear to take seriously.[18] Underlying this cynical advice (presumably to the youth of 1969 as well as that of 1936) is a profound distrust of ideology: 'Cela busca la salvación no en la historia sino unamunianamente en la intravida, en la interioridad del individuo, y por eso su mensaje se aparta en lo fundamental de las más conocidas ideologías sociales . . . Se percibe en la novela . . . aborrecimiento por los conceptos abstractos y las ideas fijas, por la *ideocracia* . . .'[19] Hence Cela's emphasis on psychoanalysis, represented by the young man studying himself in a mirror throughout the novel. It seems very probable that Cela is exploring his own feelings of guilt in these descriptions since this is a past he prefers to forget.[20] Like Benet, Cela minimises the political differences between Spaniards, suggesting that if he had been born a few years earlier he might well have become a Republican.[21] Political violence is not distinguished from any other form of violence; the death of Calvo Sotelo is no different from that of a prostitute, or a drunk who is knocked down while vomiting in the street (p. 101). The church burning of the 1930s is attributed by Tío Jerónimo to the pyromania that afflicts all Spaniards: 'Detrás de tanta llama no hay una motivación política y menos aun económica, sino religiosa y mágica' (p. 298). As Ilie points out, such semi-mystical ideology harks back to the Generation of '98 and does nothing to enlighten the reader on the realities of the political situation. The consequence of irrationalist explanations is a deformation of history. In insisting on sexual release as a panacea, for example, Cela wilfully diverts the reader's attention from objective causes of unrest: 'Not the economics of class but libidinal economy, as Reich puts it, holds the key to social equilibrium. No better method for evading the history of a society could be devised.'[22] Tuñón de Lara has gently chided his old friend Cela for such distortion, pointing out that the real issues in 1936 were (a) agrarian reform, (b) the regional issue, (c) the alliance of the Church and the owning classes, (d) an Army with too many officers, (e) cultural backwardness. He also calls attention to the high degree of politicisation of the Madrid working classes, as evidenced by the number of workers (134,000) affiliated to the unions of the Casa del Pueblo.[23] For these objective causes, Cela substitutes masturbatory fantasies. The author's defence that this is a novel '"en la guerra" no "de la guerra"' is unconvincing. There is so much accurate historical detail that when fiction is juxtaposed we give it credence. Though the narrator admits he lies to himself and to us (p. 355), 'the real events of history are mentioned frequently enough (to) give the reader . . . confidence in the narrator's veracity'.[24] But the contradictory images in the mirror and in the narrator's mind convince us only that any search for meaning in the Civil War is an exercise in futility. The event is a psychic epidemic, a contagion ('Zabalegui solo no es fascista pero se contagia' (p. 242)) for which the numerous quack remedies mentioned will have no effect. As the narrator tells himself in the mirror: 'Te enfrentas con el problema, pero es inútil, no sabes resolverlo' (p. 17). Cela's response to history is effectively to deny objective causes for class conflict and take refuge in irrationalism and semi-mysticism. It is significant that in the epilogue, Tío Jerónimo quotes not Marx but Unamuno and Ganivet to elucidate his country's past.

The examination of conscience we find in Cela's novel is matched only by the searching self-analysis made by the Republican president in Carlos Rojas's *Azaña*. Drawing heavily on the president's published memoirs, Rojas describes the events of 1936–39, as recalled by Azaña in defeat and exile. This latter detail has profound implication for the tone of the novel and the interpretation given to previous events. Republican resistance which, at the time, seemed to many the most rational policy to adopt, came to be condemned later as an act of gross irresponsibility. Azaña's disillusionment with politics is such that he denies human rationality and inveighs against historical interpretation: '¿Qué sentido tiene . . . haber ideado la razón cuando siempre ocurre lo arbitrario, lo inesperado y lo incomprensible? ¿Qué sentido inventar la historia cuando la conducta humana es inconsecuente?' (p. 34). If the war, for the narrator of *San Camilo*

1936, was a 'carnaval de sangre', a recurrent theme of *Azaña* is that 'el mundo no es sino el sueño de un carnaval' (p. 40). The ailing president remembers attending a fancy dress ball in Madrid in 1928 dressed as Cardinal Mendoza; this serves to symbolise the unreality of the events he is living now, to which he reacts with total indifference. When news comes to him of the seizure of the Barcelona Telephone Exchange by Assault Guards in 1937, leading to internecine warfare on the Republican side, he quickly puts it out of his mind and returns to writing *La velada en Benicarló* (p. 74). Azaña's response to the tragedy of the Civil War is to retreat into spiritual exile, where he can no longer be accused or reviled. He takes the advice of the Devil in Byron's *Cain*: 'Think and endure and form an inner World / In your own bosom where the outward fails. / So shall you be nearer the spiritual / Nature, and war triumphant with your own' (p. 74). The war, Azaña considers, has been reduced to a meaningless bloodbath and it no longer matters who wins. Indeed, victory would be even more painful to endure than defeat: 'De todas las desdichas de la contienda civil la peor es, con mucho, la victoria' (p. 213). As in *Volverás a Región* there is no future to look forward to; there is only a future-in-the-past: 'El futuro en este país suele parecerse al pasado' (pp. 213–214). In identifying the reasons for the war, Azaña adopts the same anti-historical stance as that of Cela's characters, remaining at the level of generalisation: '¿Cómo llegamos a esta matanza? La respuesta está en el odio, en el hambre y quizá en el miedo' (p. 163). The workers burn the churches out of 'afán purificador' (p. 192), not to destroy religion but to return it to its pristine state. More important than the political future of the country is the art collection from the Prado, temporarily stored in the castle of Perelada: 'El Museo del Prado ... es más importante que la República y la Monarquía juntas' (p. 11). But the ultimate indictment of history is that a Civil War which was avoidable, once begun, could have been won by the Republicans: 'Cobardes ... salimos los dirigentes, incapaces de prevenir una guerra evitable y capitulando luego cuando aún podía ganarse' (pp. 252–253). This anti-historical claim, originally made by Negrín, is sustained by Azaña on his deathbed (p. 269). Rojas's intention in *Azaña* is to synthesise the historical events of the war and express them artistically.[25] Whether the view of the war, in defeat, from Azaña's deathbed could give due consideration to the principle of historical causality is doubtful. When Azaña says '¿Qué importa la guerra, y ... qué importamos nosotros?' (pp. 21–22), he renounces historical analysis.

The problem of a distorted historical perspective (which P. Ilie terms 'perspective réversible') also arises in Lera's *Las últimas banderas*. The exhortations to violent resistance by Largo Caballero and Alvarez del Vayo in 1936 are recalled in the midst of the futile struggles of 1939. When seen in this perspective, they make the Republican leaders look irresponsible: 'Insérés dans ce genre de structure narrative, ces discours prennent automatiquement l'aspect d'un monstrueux aveuglement historique.'[26] Lera, like Rojas, suggests that war was avoidable; the Republican leaders should have looked for political solutions rather than lurch into war: 'Nuestro fuerte debería haber sido la política, porque ¿qué sabíamos nosotros ni las masas de la guerra? Sin embargo, nuestra dirección política estuvo siempre dando bandazos . . .' (p. 32). That the military plotters are not held accountable in this analysis is an extraordinary piece of historical distortion.

It· is apparent from the above examples that interpretations by some writers of the historical events of 1936–39 had, by the last decade of the Franco era, become radically depoliticised. The magnitude of the tragedy remained, but the focus of attention had moved from socioeconomic and political interpretations to an exploration of more mysterious and irrational forces within the human psyche. *Las últimas banderas* is a delayed form of the traditional war novel but its ambiguity and ideological confusion still remind us of Benet's 'relámpago del error'. Despite his early radicalism, Lera appears to have lost faith, even during the war itself, in political ideology.[27] Thirty years later, when a new generation of Spaniards is rapidly tiring of the Franco dictatorship, Lera gives them little encouragement to seek radical reform. The only character in the novel who retains any vestige of revolutionary principles is Molina ('Nos quedan muchas batallas delante . . . Las ideas no mueren' (p. 356)), but he ends up in a Nationalist jail. Other revolutionaries, like Casanova and Cubas, die violent deaths for their radical principles but their sacrifice is futile. The Nationalists' pragmatism, and the political skill of Franco, on the other hand, receive the plaudits of this former Republican commissar (p. 87). Lera deliberately avoids the role of political mentor to the new generation so willingly adopted by certain writers prior to the Second Republic: '¿Qué me dices de aquellos célebres escritores e intelectuales que trajeron la República y que fueron nuestros maestros? Ellos nos lanzaron (me refiero a los estudiantes de mi generación) a la lucha por una España nueva, y luego, a la hora de la verdad, se pusieron al margen y nos dejaron en la estacada' (p. 368). This judgement by the revolutionary Molina does much to explain the ambiguity of this novel, and indeed of the others studied in this chapter. These authors, far from taking sides, cast the reader into doubt and confusion about the issues of the war. Rojas presents us with an Azaña who is deeply divided; 'el hombre de la carne' and 'el hombre del espíritu' contradict each other throughout the novel, the one responding with humanitarian feeling, the other with indifference to terrestrial affairs. To confuse matters further, Azaña claims to have a double – a pharmacist who works in a hospital in Gerona – with the same name as himself, with identical handwriting and tone of voice (pp. 186–187). The reality of this person is, of course, more than doubtful. But, then, Azaña frequently doubts his own reality, and even that of Rojas, who will eventually tell his story (p. 197). Dreams unfold within dreams (p. 201), and reality and illusion are often inseparable. At the level of politics, too, contradictions abound; Azaña, the politician who mesmerised a crowd of half a million at the Comillas stadium in October 1935, has Ortega's *La rebelión de las masas* on his bedside table (p. 141). Cervantes and Shakespeare are admired because 'don Quijote y Hamlet resultan paradójicos e irónicos, porque constantemente se desdicen e impugnan' (p. 264). This ambiguity and contradiction have already been identified in Benet's novel, where a character may have half a dozen different names, and where Numa, the guardian of the forest, may in fact be a Republican refugee, Luis I. Timoner '(I. de incógnito)' (p. 36). Cela's anti-hero, fantasising in a mirror, knows who he is *not* (Napoleon, St Paul, Buffalo Bill, Roland, Viriatus, Caesar, el Cid, William Tell, King Cyril(!)) but implies that he is less certain about who he *is*. Characters in this novel, too, have names which may change from time to time (Tránsito/Toisha, Sr. Asterio/Sr. Ricardo) or which they share with someone else (don Roque Barcia). Given a choice between one action and another, the protagonist is blind to any moral distinction: 'Defender con uñas y dientes la legalidad republicana y democrática acostarse con esta mujer que huele a sudor y a comida o . . . no acostarse con esta mujer . . .' (p. 258). The ambiguity which results from 'the *sí/no* dialectic, name-switching and negative presentation' is a fundamental element in the novel;[28] it leads to doubt, uncertainty and indefinite conclusions about the source or significance of the conflict, recording only the psychic disintegration of an individual conscience. 'La sociedad descrita en *San Camilo* es una sociedad enajenada vista desde la enajenación del individuo, el cual, pese a su examen de conciencia no penetra en la conciencia de nadie, sólo en la suya para encontrarla escindida, informe, absolutamente vacía de cualquier proyecto que pueda trascender hacia los otros con sentido afirmativo y creador.'[29] Such pessimism, descending frequently into nihilism, makes it impossible to draw any lessons from the history of the Civil War. Rojas too, because of his choice of subject and historical moment, ends in nihilism, making Azaña say at one point, 'Nadie hizo nunca nada por nadie' (p. 261). The president, once famed for his 'clarity and technical competence',[30] now cuts a sorry figure. Caught in the crossfire at one point between warring Republican factions in Barcelona, and abandoned by the Generalitat, he is isolated and alienated. His contempt for Negrín is totally reciprocated by the Republic's last prime minister (p. 14). Other politicians he meets (Hidalgo de Cisneros, operational chief of the Air Force; Marcelina Pascua, Spanish ambassador in Paris; Abad de Santillán, an intellectual of the FAI, and others) generally encounter the same disdain. Other characters, too, are alienated from each other: Casares and Prieto; Negrín and Besteiro, Casado, Jiménez de Asúa. These divisions simply illustrate the *cabilismo* Azaña identifies as a basic defect in the Spanish character (pp. 105–106). (Franco would later come to categorise these national vices as 'demonios familiares'.) In Benet's novel the divisions are symbolically described with characteristic incisiveness: rustic properties are separated by 'enormes tapias de fábrica, coronadas de alambre de espino y cristales de botella de bordes afilados . . . Tal es el burgo, tal es su pacífica convivencia' (p. 49). Though each villager goes in fear of 'la voracidad de su vecino', all are united in their hatred for the shepherds, considering them to be the 'brazo secular del terrateniente extremeño o castellano' (p. 49), sent each summer by their masters to spy on the inhabitants of Región. When a shepherd's hut accidentally catches fire the ancestral pyromaniac urge of the villagers is aroused: 'la hoguera . . . es recibida en los pueblos con júbilo y alivio, con disparo de bombas y toque de campanas' (p. 51). This apparently irrational juxtaposition by Benet of popular enthusiasm, fire, explosions and bells conjures up the church burnings of the 1930s and, by extension, espouses the same fundamental Spanish characterology expressed by Cela ('El español es más amigo del fuego que del agua' (p. 316)) and Rojas (in Azaña's references to *afán purificador*). From which the reader of any of these three novels would deduce that Spaniards, irrespective of moment or context, are essentially bent on destruction.[31]

The tradition of social realism persisted in many novels written in the last years of the Franco regime, as Lera's work testifies. A small group of gifted writers sought new vehicles of expression for their confused feelings about the war. In pursuing innovation, however, they failed to capture the tragic essence of the conflict. A more serious charge might be that in a period of political transition, they also failed in their moral responsibility to confront a new generation of Spaniards with the realities of their past.

Notes

1 R. Hernández, *Angel María de Lera* (Madrid, 1981). This contains bibliographical information (pp. 149–156) as well as a biography and anthology of Lera's writing.

2 *Ibid.*, pp. 44ff. Lera was sentenced to death, but the sentence was commuted to 30 years; he was released in 1947.

3 '[La guerra civil] fue lo que más influyó en él: verse separado de los padres, vivir las dos Españas y, por una de esas paradojas de la vida, desfilar en Madrid con los pioneros de Lenin y ver en San Sebastián el desfile de los falangistas' A. Núñez, 'Encuentro con Juan Benet', *Insula*, 269 (April 1969), 4.

4 J. Ortega, 'La dimensión temporal en *Volverás a Región*' in *Ensayos de la novela española moderna* (Madrid, 1974), pp. 137–152 (p. 138).

5 See V. Cabrera, *Juan Benet* (Boston, 1983), p. 2. Juan Benet was mistakenly arrested in 1949 after his brother, with the help of Norman Mailer's sister and another American girl, had helped two Republican prisoners (Nicolás Sánchez Albornoz and Manuel Lamana) to escape from Cuelgamuros.

6 J. Benet, 'Breve historia de *Volverás a Región*', *Revista de Occidente*, 134 (May 1974), 160–165 (p. 160). The emphasis is my own. This also appears as a prologue to the second edition of the novel.

7 J.L. Wescott, 'Subversion of Character Conventions in Benet's Trilogy' in R.C. Manteiga et al., *Critical Approaches to the Writings of Juan Benet* (Hanover N.H., 1984), pp. 72ff.

8 S.J. Summerhill, 'Prohibition and Transgression in *Volverás a Región* and *Una meditación*' in R.C. Manteiga et al. *Critical Approaches*, p. 63.

9 P. Gimferrer, 'En torno a *Volverás a Región* de Juan Benet', *Insula*, 266 (January 1969), 14.

10 V. Cabrera, *Juan Benet*, p. 14.

11 'Yo creo que el doctor Daniel Sabastián simboliza la vieja generación, apolítica y liberal, que no supo actuar con energía durante la guerra civil, contribuyó a perderla y ha quedado desde entonces marginada y paralizada; la mujer misteriosa representa la juventud española, perseguida por las fuerzas autoritarias y totalitarias de derechas y de izquierdas . . . El viejo guarda que ronda por los montes simboliza a Franco y sus seguidores. El muchacho enfermo . . . es, quizá, la imagen de las futuras generaciones, que habrá, algún día, de repudiar la pasividad y la abulia con que tantos españoles han aceptado la situación social y política de su país' M. Durán, 'Juan Benet y la nueva novela española', *Cuadernos Americanos*, 183 (July–August 1974), 193–205 (pp. 201–202).

12 R.C. Spires, '*Volverás a Región* y la desintegración total' in *La novela española de la posguerra* (Madrid, 1978), p. 245.

13 See 'Respuesta al señor Montero', *Cuadernos para el Diálogo*, 23 (December 1970), 13–15. Quoted in V. Cabrera, *Juan Benet*, p. 10.

14 A. Echave, 'Historia e intrahistoria in *San Camilo 1936*', unpublished PhD thesis, University of Emory (Atlanta, Georgia, 1980), p. 69. This analysis owes much to the work of Erich Newmann, a disciple of Jung.

15 P. Ilie, 'The Politics of Obscenity in *San Camilo 1936*', *Anales de la Novela de Posguerra*, 1 (1976), 25–63 (p. 28).

16 J. Díaz, 'Techniques of Alienation in Recent Spanish Novels', *Journal of Spanish Studies*, 3 (Spring 1975), 5–16 (p. 11).

17 J. Pérez, 'Historical Circumstances and Thematic Motifs in *San Camilo 1936*', *Review of Contemporary Fiction* 4, no. 3 (1984), 67–80 (p. 70).

18 See J.S. Bernstein, 'Confession and Inaction in *San Camilo*', *Hispanófila*, 17, no. 3 (1974), 47–63. This critic takes Cela literally, seeing sex as an attempt to return to a lost national communion: 'If anything can preserve or restore the communion of Spain's people, it is sex' (pp. 60–61). One is prompted to ask why, with so much sexual gratification taking place, the characters of the novel are not contented.

19 G. Roberts, 'La culpa y la búsqueda de la autenticidad in *San Camilo 1936*, *Journal of Spanish Studies*, 3, no. 1 (Spring 1975), 73–84 (p. 82).

20 *Fuerza Nueva*, 558 (17 September 1977) contains a photocopy (reproduced here as Plate 19) of an application to the Nationalist authorities by Cela in March 1938 to work for the Cuerpo de Investigación y Vigilancia. In this application he wrote of himself: 'Habiendo vivido en Madrid y sin interrupción durante los últimos 13 años, cree poder prestar datos sobre personas y conductas que pudieran ser de utilidad.' Speaking to F. López in *Mazurca para Camilo José Cela* (Madrid, 1986), Cela plays down the Civil War, calling it a 'guerra a palos,' 'un partido de rugby', adding: 'Lo que hay que hacer es correr un tupido velo y tratar de olvidar' (p. 96). He had been equally reluctant to discuss it in the Twayne World Authors series with D.W. McPheeters, *Camilo José Cela* (New York, 1970), in which less than ten lines were devoted to his wartime activities.

21 Cela once commented in an interview: '[Miguel Hernández] tenía seis años más que yo. Esos seis años fueron clave, porque si la guerra me coge con seis años más, lo probable es que hubiera acabado en México, como todos' F. López, *Mazurca*, p. 96.

22 P. Ilie, 'The Politics of Obscenity', p. 49.

23 'La circunstancia histórica de la novela *San Camilo 1936*, *Papeles de Son Armadans*, 69, no. 207 (1970), 229–252. He concludes: 'En ambos bandos hubo muchos más héroes que criminales.'

24 J.S. Bernstein, 'Confession and Inaction', p. 51.

25 'Creo firmemente que tanto la historia como la novela tienden a abarcar la experiencia humana total, si bien aquélla lo hace de forma analítica y ésta de modo sintético' (p. 275).

26 P. Ilie, 'Le roman de l'ambigüité historique' in M. Hanrez (ed.), *Les Ecrivains de la guerre d'Espagne* (Paris, n.d.), pp. 157–163 (p. 161).

27 See R. Hernández, *Angel María de Lera*, passim. During the Casado coup, 'Lera, hastiado, permanece al margen de estos hechos' (p. 42). By 1962, he was working for the Monarchist newspaper *ABC*.

28 J. Pérez, 'Historical Circumstances', p. 72.

29 G. Sobejano, *La novela española de nuestro tiempo* (Madrid, 1975), p. 129.

30 G. Jackson, *The Spanish Republic and the Civil War* (Princeton, 1965), p. 52.

31 See P. Ilie, 'The Politics of Obscenity', for a discussion of Cela's generalisations on the Spanish character. For Ilie 'such massive disorientation belongs to a larger anti-historicism in Spanish literature in this period' (p. 56).

Conclusion

STENDHAL MAINTAINED that politics in a work of literature is like a pistol shot in the middle of a concert: something loud and vulgar, and yet a thing which it is not possible to ignore. To extend this metaphor, the novels of the Civil War are punctuated by regular bursts of gunfire which threaten to drown out the sound of the orchestra altogether. It is difficult not to conclude, with Ortega y Gasset, that the fictional world and the world of historical events are ultimately irreconcilable; this seems particularly true in cases where the reader is familiar with the history being described, to which he will provide his own, idiosyncratic emotional and intellectual response which may well be disproportionate to his reaction to the imaginary world of the novel, with its different resonance and significance. The organisatio-nal skills, too, demanded of the novelist attempting such a feat, are of quite a different order from those normally required, and more than one writer, as we have seen, has renounced the attempt to integrate the two worlds in the face of the technical difficulties. P. Lubbock makes the point that even the great Tolstoy alternates his treatment of the imaginary and the real worlds: it is not surprising that lesser novelists than he are forced to do likewise. Those novelists who have chosen to weave a large-scale tapestry of the Civil War (notably Gironella and Aub) have met with limited technical success. Many of Gironella's characters appear occasionally as though to remind us they are still there, but play a less and less effective role as the trilogy progresses. Aub's characters engage in extensive monologues and dialogues during which his novels' action comes to a halt. This is not to say that *El laberinto mágico* is not a masterpiece; but it is a masterpiece in *spite* of these technical failures. The success of the second-wave novels by comparison with those of the first wave is not unconnected with a reduction, in many of them, in the amount of anecdotal, political and historical material included.

221

This reduction goes hand-in-hand with a gradual decline in propagandist intention, the 'voluntad de probar' mentioned by several critics. (Writers such as Gironella and Manfredi Cano are exceptional in that they *increase* the documentary component of their work, taking advantage of the extensive bibliography of historical analyses that existed by that time.) There are unmistakable signs in some writers of a growing awareness that historical material, by its nature, exposes the author to accusations of partisanship. The very process of selection situates a writer in one camp or the other, and once selected, the material must be interpreted and commented on by the characters, or at least play some role in the novel which will justify its selection. It is possible to see the process by which two of the greatest novelists of the Civil War, F. Ayala and R. Sender, have finally opted for an indirect approach (in *La cabeza del cordero* and *El rey y la reina*, respectively) which involves the exclusion of virtually all anecdotal material. Their novels remain, nevertheless, as statements on the Civil War: Ayala recreates the climate of tension and political antagonism brilliantly, and Sender expresses eloquently the social divisions of the time. But these works also have a timeless quality which makes them accessible to the reader who knows nothing of the history of the Civil War. They may be read as statements on the human condition as well as on the turbulent, political events they describe. The universal is contained within the particular; rather than 'transcending' the social reality, by giving it symbolic significance they enhance its role in the novel. If some Republican novelists have been more successful in achieving this than their Nationalist counterparts, it is because their public was not always acquainted with the political complexities of the period being described; their novels therefore had to exist on (at least) two levels.

I have attempted to demonstrate the deadening effect of propaganda on language, in support of statements made by G. Steiner and others in the context of English letters. There seems little doubt that mass communica-tion in the twentieth century has created a sense of numbness in the reader, listener or (more recently) viewer, which anaesthetises the individual's sensitivity to language and images. The output of propaganda from both sides in the Spanish Civil War was prodigious; much of it came to be adopted as slogans which would make thoughtful analysis redundant. (I have read no study of the incidence of war slogans in the literature of the period, but it may well be the case that the numerous novelists who described the defence of Madrid in such epic terms were inspired, at least in part, by slogans such as 'No pasarán', or 'Madrid será la tumba del fascismo'. The emotive resonance of 'No pasarán' is evidenced by the fact that it has since become familiar to millions of people all over the world.) The language of propaganda slogans and official statements describing the daily progress of the war has left its mark, and in order to dispel the resulting mental numbness, the successful novelist must find ways of defamiliarising language and images. None succeeds in this better than F. Ayala, whose characters' apparently trivial speech is often unconsciously ironic. The first-wave Nationalist novelist may be forgiven as an individual, it could be argued, for not perceiving the numbing effect of propaganda because such writers are contributing to this effect collectively as they write. As part of the process, they cannot be expected to foresee its result. They would be unlikely to be over-concerned, even if they did. They are mostly writing 'short-range' works for immediate effect, as part of the propaganda of agitation and integration that all revolution and counter-revolution requires. Other writers may be concerned to write straight, honest prose or create the mystery of words that lies at the source of tragic poetry; not they. The novel is thus pressed into service as a propaganda weapon in a way that is unique in Spanish literature. The appendix (p. 229) shows that the Nationalists produced far more of these early, propagandist works than the Republicans, which is perhaps surprising, given that most publishing before the war took place in Madrid and Barcelona – centres which remained in Republican hands between 1936 and 1939. The explanation for this discrepancy in the quantities of novels produced may lie in the fact that large numbers of the educated middle class fought on the Nationalist side; the Republicans, while boasting more *eminent* artists and writers of all kinds, had proportionately many fewer potential novelists in their ranks. A second factor may be morale among the Republicans, whose military victories were few and far between. There is also evidence to show that those who did write novels were dismayed, too, by the factionalism on their own side; this may have discouraged some from writing at all. Finally, when paper was in short supply, better use may have been found for it (for example, in printing posters) on the Republican side.

I have suggested that while the novel of the Spanish Civil War has similarities with the nineteenth-century *episodio*, its highly politicised nature makes it dangerous to carry these comparisons too far. It shares certain characteristics, too, with the earlier novels of the First World War, but as we have seen, the revolutionary nature of the struggle in Spain, involving the existence of an extensive home front bustling with revolutionary and counter-revolutionary activity, makes this novel substantially different in a number of respects. In particular, there is hardly any evidence, at least in the novels of the first and second waves, of pacifist ideas.

The political novelist is the conscience of his generation, describing the ideological and emotional dimensions of the debate which took place around the central issues of the time. But he is expected to do more than deal in commonplaces, transmitting the conventional wisdom of received ideas. He must penetrate the surface of these ideas and express the conflict they generated in individuals and social groups. For most of the early novelists of the war, these issues are expressed in quite dogmatic terms, so that there is no inner tension possible in the central characters. With time, experience suggests that the extravagant claims of the propagandists do not bear analysis: right is not conveniently located on one side. It is at this moment, when self-doubt begins, that there is potential for art. At that point, the characters become representations of the author's divided self and serve as a vehicle for the exploration of truth. No-one exemplifies this process better than Aub, whose characters are involved in endless debate with themselves and with others. The development of the collective protagonist, so common in these novels, may respond in part – especially in the second wave – to such a need for self-examination: the author's *alter ego* is multiplied and a constructive debate takes place on the validity of his ideas. In some writers, this is achieved by the creation of a solitary figure, whose divided self, tortured with uncertainty, allows the exploration of contradictory ideas. Arana, Ayala and Barea come to mind as examples of writers who develop their thoughts in this way. For Nationalist writers, censorship was a major impediment to the expression of anti-heroic sentiments, and it is to Gironella's credit that he signals a new departure in this regard, with the publication of *Los cipreses creen en Dios*. But the long-awaited 'great' novel of the Civil War could not have been written in Spain under these circumstances except in the most oblique and symbolic terms. Instead, many writers abandoned the war theme and expressed their *angst* in the description of post-war society. This effectively deprived the novel of the Civil War of much potential artistic talent, leaving it impoverished as a result. The contrast between the energy which Nationalist writers, in particular, devoted to describing the Civil War up to 1941, and their abandonment of it thereafter until the early 1950s, is quite striking. Noticeable also is the dearth of radical, anti-Catholic novels of the Right, like those of Céline in France.

This study has been restricted to the novel. The length of the works studied varies enormously, however, from under a hundred to several thousand pages. The intensity with which an author can sustain the dramatic events of war and the description of human behaviour in a limit situation has implications for the success or otherwise of this genre. There seems little doubt that some of the most effective writing, from the point of view of the emotional response elicited in the reader, is not to be found in the novel, but in the short story. Aub's 'La llamada', occupying one page, is a masterpiece in miniature. 'El Cojo', another story by Aub, is also a magnificent (and more typical) example. In the novels that are the object of this study, some of the shorter works by Arana, Ayala and Sender (*El cura de Almuniaced, La cabeza del cordero* and *Réquiem por un campesino español*, respectively) are the most memorable. This is not unconnected with the intensity of description that is possible in the shorter novel. By contrast, those novels that provide extensive historical background, while more informative, make less of an emotional impact on the reader. Sometimes the memorable sections of the longer, labyrinthine works are in effect short stories of a kind. (Take the episode describing the death of the American, Earl, in Sender's *Ariadna*, for example.) It has already been pointed out that poetry is wellsuited to the immediacy of war. The problem posed for the novelist is how to sustain the tragic intensity achieved by war poetry over an extended period. If the 'great' novel of the Civil War is expected, in the public aesthetic, to have this quality, it may be asking too much that it should serve also as a vehicle for analysing the historical and political complexities of the war. Certainly, the novelistprotagonists have proved incapable of producing such a work, and later writers like Benet resort to a magic realism that recreates the psychic tensions of the war without penetrating its objective cause.

A major part of this study has been concerned with the ways in which both sides elaborated an ideal which would sustain them through the Civil War. On the Right, this ideal attained the proportions of a myth, fuelled by the creative rhetoric of Falange and Catholic propagandists. I had not realised before embarking on this study to what an extent the resources of the novel had been harnessed to promote the 'mito creador'. It is only by examining the novel in its subliterary as well as in its literary forms that this has become clear. The 'bad novel' is also an interesting indicator of ideology and class consciousness, since a great deal can be surmised about the aesthetic and political ideas of the public for which the novelist is writing. The geopolitical division of Spain into two halves between 1936 and 1939 meant that the novelist on each side was in an unaccustomed position, writing for a 'captive' readership which was barred access to political writing which might subvert the values of the respective régimes. The writer was expected to reinforce the ideas already being expressed in official propaganda; this was a degree of *dirigismo* which far exceeded earlier authoritarian practices. In Nationalist Spain, a large number of writers accepted their new, propagandist role, resurrecting as the bearer of their values a figure long forgotten in Spanish literature: the epic hero. A small group of Falangist writers draw inspiration from Nietzsche in their depiction of this hero (a character in one of the Republican novels (C. Cimorra's *El bloqueo del hombre*, p. 105) comments on 'el nietzscheísmo utilizado en escoria por algunos intelectuales de la zona facciosa de España'). Many more adopt the facile *aristocraticismo* which appears to have been prevalent in right-wing circles in Spain, following the publication of Ortega's *La rebelión de las masas*. Militant Catholicism, too, plays a part in the creative myth once the Civil War achieves the status of a Crusade.

Meanwhile, on the Left, the growing realisation during the war of the inevitability of defeat, and the eventual exile of all the novelist-protagonists included in this study, create a far more diffident attitude. Although the enemy is caricatured, and class consciousness and anti-clericalism are a pronounced feature of these novelists, they do not match the Right in propagandist output. Because their characters often display inner tensions, there is more potential here for a genuinely tragic dimension. Aub exploits the contradictions between the dictates of friendship and the personal conscience, on the one hand, and the ethics imposed by ideology on the other. Their protagonists have far more in common with the existentialist heroes of the post-war European novel than with their Nationalist counterparts. While all Spaniards, in one way or another, bore the scars of the Civil War for years after the event, the defeat and exile of the Republicans were additional wounds which went deep, and in their case never properly healed at all.

Because the exiles were not subject to the same restrictive censorship, it is possible to see much more clearly in their work the abandonment of narrow political commitment and the return to humanistic values. In the 1930s these writers still have faith in specific political solutions to the problems of Spain, and elaborate theories of commitment which place the novel, together with other art forms, at the service of politics. An unfortunate consequence of this otherwise laudable determination to make art socially responsible was that anything modernist and experimental became branded as 'bourgeois formalism'. It would take writers like Sender, one of the luminaries of the Left in the 1930s, many years to escape the influence of these ideas, but the obscure surrealism of *Los cinco libros de Ariadna* is surely a direct literary reaction to it. While it lasted, the literary 'Popular Front' which developed in Spain was an object lesson to European intellectuals in how art might serve politics. It is sometimes forgotten that the theories of *engagement* elaborated by Sartre in the 1940s, for the description of which literary historians continue to use the French term, were current in Spain a decade earlier. Writers like Sender deserve more credit, perhaps, for the contribution they made to the formulation of these ideas, which were being freely discussed at the Second International Congress of Writers, held in Valencia in 1937. There can be no doubt that the world's attention was focussed during these years on events in Spain, and that the artist was expected to play a key role in interpreting them. Looking back on these events, Republican writers are sadder and wiser: while they retain a strong sense of personal commitment to the Republican cause, they have become politically sceptical about specific remedies. Above all, they no longer display any 'pedagogy of optimism'.

In one section of this study a number of technical aspects of the Civil War novels were discussed, particularly those of the first wave which have received little critical treatment to date. What soon became apparent here was that the *novela popular*, a previously apolitical genre, had rapidly become politicised during the war and its immediate aftermath. The political question, however, is approached in a superficial way; the absence of a 'problematic' in these works is determined by the fact that the captive readership prefers to have its ideas confirmed rather than challenged, and even if this were not the case, the Department of Press and Propaganda would insist that publications conformed to the regime's directives, official or otherwise. This imposes a certain homogeneity on the early novels in terms of ideology. There is no reason, however, why there should not have been greater technical innovation in these works, other than the fact that they were probably written in great haste to serve the immediate cause. Many of the writers were also actively contributing to the war effort in other ways. The French novelist, Céline, is reported to have said: 'On n'écrit pas un roman d'amour pendant qu'on fait l'amour.' By the same token, it is difficult to write a war novel while one is waging war. These apprentice novelists adapted forms that were familiar to them: crime novels, detective novels and adventure stories. It is an interesting fact that the Nationalists (and *only* the Nationalists) also adapted the *novela rosa* to their needs, creating an interesting hybrid in the *novela rosa de guerra*. The Republicans shun this, presumably considering it to be a bourgeois and decadent art form.

An examination of the novels of the Spanish Civil War can teach us much about the relationship between art and literature. In particular, they demonstrate the need for the artist to retain not only personal integrity but also respect for a diversity of values other than his own; today's orthodoxy may appear indefensible to future generations. Many of these works had a utilitarian purpose: once that purpose was served, they became expendable. They are interesting today, not as artistic creations, but for what they tell us of the emotional and intellectual climate in which they were written. A small number will continue to be republished: these are works of permanent value which point to the universal implications of the issues confronting Spaniards between 1936 and 1939. While all the works are of outstanding documentary interest, it is this latter group of novels that will remind future generations that they should 'never send to know for whom the bell tolls'.

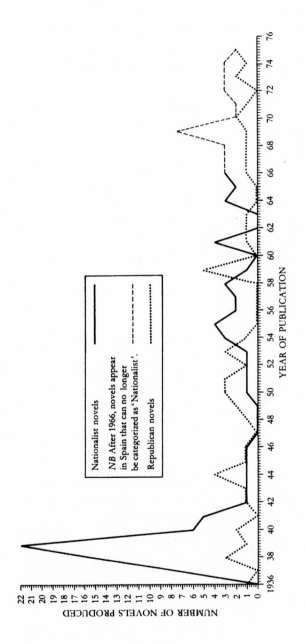

NUMBER OF NOVELS PRODUCED

YEAR OF PUBLICATION

Nationalist novels

NB After 1966, novels appear
in Spain that can no longer
be categorized as 'Nationalist'.

Republican novels

APPENDIX: *Novels of the Spanish Civil War 1936–1975*

GLOSSARY OF CIVIL WAR TERMS

A description of the main political organisations, together with their abbreviations, is to be found in many of the standard works on the Civil War and will not be repeated here. The following list contains terms, often colloquial, which appear to have been in common use during the Civil War. All examples have been taken from the novels which are the subject of this study. The list is by no means intended to be exhaustive, but provides a definition of over 200 items, many of which might perplex the reader of today.

abisinios	Originally, any enemy of Italy, after the Abyssinian campaign. Later applied to Republicans by Nationalists. Sometimes abbreviated to 'bisinios'.
Abuelo	(a) A large Republican cannon situated in the Retiro, in Madrid.
	(b) A nickname given to Pablo Iglesias by his supporters.
acero	(a) Company founded by the Communist Party; part of the Fifth Regiment.
	(b) Member of such a battalion.
aguilucho	A young member of the FAI; Anarcho-syndicalist.
alférez provisional, cadáver efectivo	An axiom which refers to the high mortality rate among the Nationalist soldiers of this rank. See also 'provisional'.
ametralladoras	Pejorative term applied by Nationalists to women in the Republican militia, because of the number of men they put out of action through venereal disease.

ángeles exterminadores	Absolute Monarchists. Also known as 'nietos del Angel Exterminador'.
antediluviano	Tank.
Año Triunfal	The period 18 July 1936–17 July 1937 was termed by the Nationalists 'primer Año Triunfal'. There followed a second and third, then the 'Año de la Victoria'.
apepinar	To fire on.
arco iris	Pejorative term for the Republican Air Force.
argos de la madrugada	Police patrols in Madrid.
Atilano	A Republican cannon on the Teruel front.
Ausente	Term applied to José Antonio Primo de Rivera after his death. The Nationalist dead are often referred to as 'ausentes'.
ausente (f.)	Pejorative term for the Republican Air Force.
auto fantasma	Car used by fifth columnists in their surprise attacks on their enemy.
aval	Document showing that the bearer was politically trustworthy. Its use extended into the immediate postwar era in Franco's Spain.
Avenida del Quince y Medio	The Gran Vía in Madrid, so called because of the heavy shelling it received from Nationalist cannon of this calibre.
azul	Nationalist.
Bandera	Battalion of the Legion or Falangist militia.
Barba Eléctrica	Nickname of the Italian general, Bergonzoli, commander of the Littorio Division.
Batallón de Hierro	Anarchist battalion famous for its part in the siege of Teruel. Also known as the 'Columna de Hierro', it contained 2,000–3,000 men, including a large group of exconvicts.
bermejo	Republican.
besugo	Corpse. The term is usually confined to victims of street fighting and 'paseos'.
bien pagá	The title of a popular song in the thirties, this term was also applied to the Republican Air Force because of the relatively high salaries paid to its members.
bisinios	See 'abisinios'.
blanco	Nationalist.
boina roja (m.)	Carlist 'requeté'.
bombones	Bombs.

borrego	New recruit.
Botas	Nickname of Alcalá Zamora, who often wore 'botas de elástico'.
Braguetón	General Sanjurjo.
brigada de las siete cuaren⁄ta	Police patrols in Madrid.
brigada del amanecer	Police patrols in Madrid.
Brigadas	(a) In Nationalist territory, 'las Brigadas de Navarra' were six huge brigades, more like divisions, that Navarre contributed to the war. (b) In Republican territory, the International Brigades.
buey	Savoia S 81 Nationalist bomber.
buzón del miliciano	Section which Republican newspapers devoted to requests and letters from soldiers at the front.
Cabra	Republican machine⁄gun in the Alto del León.
Café	Falangist slogan, provided by the initial letters of '¡Camaradas, arriba Falange Española!'
camisa azul	Falangist.
camisa negra	Italian Fascist.
camisa nueva	Falangist who joined the movement after 16 February 1936, the date of the electoral victory of the Popular Front.
camisa vieja	Falangist who joined the movement before 16 February 1936.
Campesino	Nickname of Valentín González, the famous Republican military leader.
caña	Rifle, in soldiers' slang.
Cara al sol	Hymn of the Falange. 'Estar cara al sol' could mean 'to be actively serving in the Falangist cause' or, when used cynically, 'to be dead'.
caramelo	Hand grenade, in soldiers' slang.
carca	Pejorative term for a Carlist, and by extension, for any member of the Right.
carnicero de Albacete	André Marty, the French Communist leader.
carro de la leche	Early morning Nationalist bomber over Madrid.
Casa	Communists' term for Moscow.
cenetista	Member of the CNT; Anarcho⁄syndicalist.
Chacales del Progreso	A column of Republican militiamen.
chapelgorri	Carlist 'requeté'.

chaquetear	(a) To turn one's back on the enemy; to run away.
	(b) To engage the enemy; to fight.
	(c) To change sides.
chato	Republican single-seater bi-plane.
checa, cheka	Republican political prison.
chíbiri, chíviri	Nationalist term for a young Socialist.
chino	Communist.
chivato	A 'planted' prisoner. It was common practice to try to obtain information in this way.
churrero	Early morning Nationalist bomber or reconnaissance plane. See also 'lechero'.
cinturón de hierro	The defences around Bilbao which supposedly made the city impregnable.
coleta (m.)	Communist; so called because of the pig-tail traditionally associated with the Chinese.
colorado	Republican.
Columna de Hierro	See 'Batallón de Hierro.'
columna menguada	Pejorative term for the 'columna Mangada', whose military capability was impaired by an infection of venereal disease.
corrida de toros	Execution.
currito	Nationalist gunman.
DCA	Anti-aircraft guns ('defensa contra aero-naves').
desabrochar	To kill.
Desdentada	Death.
deserción	A euphemism for execution.
detente, detente bala	Motto, generally embroidered by mother or girlfriend, worn over the heart by Catholic soldiers.
diez con cinco	Artillery piece of this calibre.
dolor de garganta	A euphemism for fear, often used by General Millán Astray.
echarse al plato	To assassinate, execute.
emboscado	Someone who avoided taking part in the fighting.
enchiquerar	(a) To imprison.
	(b) To assassinate, execute.
enchufado	Coined long before the war, but used from late 1936 as a synonym for 'emboscado' (q.v.).
enfriar	To assassinate, execute.

escachifollar	To blow up.
escamots	Green-shirted Catalan militia at the service of the Generalitat before the war, later to become part of the Catalan Army.
escuadrilla del amanecer	Republican police patrols.
faccioso	Republican term for a Nationalist.
facha	Fascist, and by extension a Nationalist. 'Fachista' and 'facista' are also found.
Faenas	Nickname for Azaña.
faicista	Pejorative term applied to members of the FAI by their Communist rivals, thus identifying them with the enemy.
faiero, faísta	Member of the FAI; Anarcho-syndicalist.
failangista	Pejorative term coined by the reactionary Right to describe militant Falangists, thus identifying them with the enemy.
falange (m.), falangio	Slang terms for a Falangist.
fascio	Fascism; the Fascist powers.
Felipa	A machine-gun in the Guadarrama.
Felipe	(a) Republican 30.5 cannon in the Retiro; also known as 'El Abuelo' (q.v.).
	(b) Republican battery near Peñarroya.
flecha (m.)	Youngest member of a Falangist unit.
Flechas Azules	Mixed division of Spaniards and Italians formed in early 1937.
Flechas Negras	Spanish division which fought with the Italian forces of the CTV.
Flechas Verdes	Mixed division of Spaniards and Italians.
fortificar es vencer	Communist slogan coined early in the war to try to persuade the militias to adopt military tactics.
frac	Soldier's battle dress.
fulana	Soldier's slang for knife. Hence 'meter la fulana'.
Gloriosa	Republicans' term for their own Air Force.
GNR	'Guardia Nacional Republicana'; title given in Republican territory to the former 'Guardia Civil' in August 1936.
guá	Name given to the Glorieta de Bilbao (and also by some to the Telefónica) because of the frequency with which it was shelled.
guardia de los luceros	In Falangist mythology, those who died for the

	cause became guardians of the heavens. 'Hacer guardia sobre los luceros' and similar expressions are used to describe this.
gudari	Basque Nationalist soldier.
Gutiérrez	Name given by the Left to Alfonso XIII.
harca, harka	Group of Moroccan soldiers under a Spanish officer.
Hienas Antifascistas	A Republican column of militiamen.
hijos de la Pasionaria	Communists.
hijos de Negrín	The forces raised by Negrín, which together with the former Cuerpo de Carabineros constituted the shock troops of the Republican Ejército Popular, were known as the 'cien mil hijos de Negrín'.
Himno de Riego	The Republican national anthem.
huevo frito	(a) Republican insignia indicating that the bearer was attached to the General Staff. (b) Eight-pointed star worn by a major.
incontrolado	Someone who killed and plundered on the home front. Often applied to Anarcho-syndicalists.
Inda	Indalecio Prieto was given the nickname 'don Inda' by the Right wing.
jabalí	Anarchist.
katiuska	(a) Republican S-B 2 bomber. (b) A high boot worn by women during the war.
lechero	(a) Nationalist cannon outside Madrid which began firing in the early morning. (b) Early morning Nationalist bomber or reconnaissance plane.
leer el periódico	To de-louse oneself (in soldiers' slang).
Legionaria	Name given by Nationalists to the Italian Air Force in Spain.
Lenin español.	Largo Caballero.
león del Rif	General Sanjurjo.
leona	12.40 cannon.
Leones Rojos	A column of Republican militiamen.
ley de las cunetas	One of the many euphemisms for 'to execute' was 'aplicar la ley de las cunetas'.
ley de reforma agraria	Another euphemism for 'to execute' was 'aplicar la ley de reforma agraria'.

libertad	A coded order to execute a prisoner. 'Libertar', 'dar libertad absoluta', or the single letter 'L' were often used to order an execution.
Linces de la Victoria	A column of Republican militiamen.
loro	Republican bi-plane.
luises	Monarchists.
macarrones	Pejorative term for Italian troops.
madrina	Female correspondent that every soldier acquired, if he could, to send him letters and bring him luck.
mandarina	A shell, in soldiers' slang.
mantecados	Eight-pointed stars of the colonel and lieutenant colonel's uniform.
miliciano	Republican militiaman.
mohamed	Moorish soldier.
mono azul	Republican militiaman's uniform.
mosca (m.)	Russian conversion of the Boeing A32 fighter plane.
moscón	Republican bomber.
motorizada	Militant group of Prieto Socialists, mostly young, who served as a bodyguard.
nacional	Supporter of the Nationalist cause; nationalist soldier.
Napoleonchu	The Nationalists' term for Aguirre, the Basque leader.
naranjero	Light sub-machine gun.
naranjitas	Small Italian hand grenades.
Narizotas	Pejorative term for Alfonso XIII.
natacha (m.)	Republican bi-plane.
Negrilla	Name given by the Nationalists to the Condor Legion.
negus	Name given to certain Republican planes which regularly flew over the Somosierra front.
nicanora	Mortar; short cannon.
Nicéforo	Alcalá Zamora was known to his enemies by a variety of names ('Niceto I', 'El Bobo de Coria'), including 'don Nicéforo'.
nietos de la Nelken	Republicans (Margarita Nelken was a Socialist deputy).
nietos del Angel Exterminador	Absolute Monarchists.
Niña Bonita	The Republicans' term for the Second Republic.

¡no pasarán!	The slogan of the besieged population of Madrid.
novia	Death.
novio de la muerte	Soldier in the Foreign Legion. (The battle hymn of the Legion bears the same name.)
nueve (largo)	A pistol of this calibre.
Optimista	Name given to the statue of Neptune in wartime Madrid, due to the fact that he appeared to be holding a fork in anticipation of a meal. (Hence 'Plaza del Optimista'.)
Oriamendi	Hymn of the Carlist requetés.
paco	Sniper; a familiar hazard from the rooftops of the large cities as well as at the front.
pagano	Name given to the Falangists by militant Catholics.
paisa	Originally a Moorish term for a Spanish soldier, it came to be used to denote a Nationalist soldier.
pájaro	A term originally applied by Moors to describe an aeroplane, it came to be used by Spaniards also.
Pancho Villa	Name adopted by revolutionary leaders in Valencia and a number of other Republican-held cities.
papagayo	Nationalist term applied to Republican bombers.
paquete	Coded word for venereal disease. Hence 'coger un paquete'.
pasaportar	To assassinate. Also 'dar el pasaporte'.
paseo	A prisoner's journey to his death. (Hence, 'dar el paseo', 'pasear'.)
Pasionaria	Dolores Ibarruri, the Communist leader.
pasionario	Communist.
pava	Nationalist Heinkel 46 or Junker 52 bomber.
pavo	Nationalist Heinkel 45.
pelayo	A young Carlist requeté.
picadero	Place where executions took place.
picar	To execute, assassinate.
Pichi	Name given to improvised 7.5 anti-aircraft gun in the Alto del León in the early days of the war.
píldoras del doctor Negrín	Lentils, which in the later stages of the war became the staple diet of the Republic. (A well-

	known brand of pills at the time were called 'pastillas del Dr. Andreu'.)
pipa	Revolver, in soldiers' slang.
pluma	Truncheon favoured by Falangists in street battles.
Potez	Republican bomber.
¡presente!	The cry of Falangists commemorating the death of a comrade. 'Estar presente' had the same meaning, paradoxically, as 'estar ausente'.
protomártir	Calvo Sotelo, who was assassinated by the Left in July 1936.
,provisional	Though there were 'provisionales' at the rank of sergeant, lieutenant and captain, the term usually signifies 'alférez provisional'; these second lieutenants in the Nationalist army were usually former University students.
queso de Gruyere	The Telefónica, which frequent shelling had left in the state described.
quince y medio	Artillery piece of this calibre.
quinta columna	Fifth columnists. The phrase is traditionally ascribed to Mola, who led one of the four columns converging on Madrid, confident that the fifth would contribute from within to the downfall of the city.
quinta del biberón	The Republican draft of July 1938 for the Ebro campaign included all men between 16 and 42. The younger elements were given this nickname.
quinta del SEU	First draft of University students into the Nationalist army.
rabassaire	Catalan vine grower.
rasante	Republican bi-plane.
rata	Small Republican fighter aircraft.
rebelde	Generally a term applied by Republicans to a member of the Nationalist side; sometimes vice versa.
recado	Death. Hence 'dar un recadito'.
refrigerar	To execute.
Regulares	Moorish units in the Spanish army.
remigio	Pejorative term applied by the Nationalists to a Republican soldier.
requeté	(a) Carlist militiaman.

	(b) Carlist militia unit made up of six 'escuadras'.
¡resistir!	Battle cry launched by Juan Negrín.
responsable	Leader of a group, often Anarchist. Such groups would not accept the concept of leadership or hierarchy, hence this neutral term.
ricinazo	A form of punishment favoured by some Falangists; it consisted of making their victim drink castor oil.
rogelio	Republican.
roja y gualda	The Monarchist (later Nationalist) flag.
rojo	Nationalist term for Republican (irrespective of political affiliation of the latter). The diminutive 'rojillo' is often used contemptuously.
saca	The taking of prisoners from a jail to be shot.
San Bartolomé (f.)	Mass killing (after the killing of French Huguenots on this day in 1572).
Semana del Niño	Republican version of Epiphany.
señor	One of the terms used by Monarchists to describe Alfonso XIII was 'el señor'.
siete y medio	Mortar of this calibre.
simio	Nationalist term for a Republican SIM (military intelligence) agent.
submarino	Informer. See also 'chivato'.
Tabor	Unit of Moroccan troops in the Spanish army.
Tercio	(a) Unit of Carlist army, made up of 3 'Requeté' units.
	(b) Foreign Legion.
Tigres de la República	A column of militiamen (the 26th Division of the Republican army).
viaje	'Hacer el viaje' is one of the many euphemisms used to describe someone going to his death.

BIBLIOGRAPHY

The bibliography is divided into five sections: Bibliographical sources; Background reading; Novels of the Spanish Civil War (with two subsections, one arranged by date of publication, the other by title); Books and articles (general criticism); and Books and articles on individual authors.

1 Bibliographical sources

Amador Carrandi, Florencio. *Ensayo bibliográfico de las obras y folletos publicados con motivo del Movimiento Nacional* (Bermeo, 1940).

Amo, Julian and Shelbey, Charmion. *La obra impresa de los intelectuales españoles en América, 1936–1945* (Stanford, 1950).

Bertrand de Muñoz, Maryse. 'Bibliografía de la novela de la guerra civil española', *La Torre*, 61 (1968), 215–242.

'Suplemento a la bibliografía de la novela de la guerra civil española', *La Torre*, 66 (1969), 119–131.

La guerra civil española en la novela. Bibliografía comentada, 2 vols. (Madrid, 1982).

Cierva, Ricardo de la. *Bibliografía general sobre la guerra de España (1936–39) y sus antecedentes históricos* (Madrid, 1968).

Comín Colomer, Eduardo. 'Bibliografía de la Guerra de Liberación', *Revista de Estudios Políticos*, 43 (1952), 341–378.

Fresco, Mauricio. *La emigración republicana española. Una victoria de México* (Mexico, 1950).

García Durán, Juan. *Bibliografía de la Guerra Civil española* (Montevideo, 1964).

Montes, M./J. 'La guerra española en la creación literaria' in *Cuadernos Bibliográficos de la Guerra de España* (Anejo no. 2) (Madrid, 1970).

2 Background reading

The following list represents only a small proportion of the available literature on the subject. It consists of those works which have been referred to in footnotes or which have otherwise proved useful in the preparation of this study.

Aguilera-Malta, Demetrio. *¡Madrid!* (Santiago de Chile, 1937).

Alvarez Puga, Eduardo. *Diccionario de la Falange* (Barcelona, 1977).

Aparicio, Juan (ed.) *La Conquista del Estado* (Barcelona, 1939).

Arrarás, Joaquín. *Historia de la Segunda República Española*, 3 vols. (Madrid, 1956–68).

    (ed.) *Historia de la Cruzada española* 8 vols. (Madrid, 1940–44)

Aub, Max. *Cuentos ciertos* (Mexico, 1955).

    Morir por cerrar los ojos (Barcelona, 1967).

    No son cuentos (Mexico, 1944).

Aznar, Manuel. *Historia militar de la guerra de España* (Madrid, 1940).

Barea, Arturo. *La raíz rota* (Buenos Aires, 1955).

Benavides, Manuel D. *La escuadra la mandan los cabos* (Mexico, 1944).

Benda, Julien. *La Trahison des clercs* (Paris, 1927).

Bernanos, Georges. *Les Grands Cimetières sous la lune* (Paris, 1938).

Bolín, Luis. *Spain: The Vital Years* (London, 1966).

Bolloten, Burnett. *The Grand Camouflage* (London, 1961).

Borkenau, Franz. *The Spanish Cockpit* (Michigan, 1983).

Brenan, Gerald. *The Spanish Labyrinth* (Cambridge, 1943).

Broué, Pierre, and Témime, Emile. *La Révolution et la guerre d'Espagne* (Paris, 1961).

Carr, Raymond. *Spain, 1808–1939* (London, 1966).

    The Spanish Tragedy: The Civil War in Perspective (London, 1977).

Carro, Conchita. *Paco y las duquesas* (Madrid, 1939).

Colodny, Robert G. *The Struggle for Madrid* (New York, 1958).

Coverdale, J. *Italian Intervention in the Spanish Civil War* (Princeton, 1975).

Crossman, Richard (ed.) *The God that Failed* (London, 1950).

Díaz del Moral, J. *Historia de las agitaciones campesinas andaluzas* (Madrid, 1967).

Ellul, J. *Propaganda: The Formation of Men's Attitudes* (New York, 1973).

García Serrano, Rafael. *Diccionario para un macuto* (Madrid, 1964).

García Venero, Maximiano. *Falange en la guerra de España: la Unificación y Hedilla* (Paris, 1967).

Garosci, Aldo. *Gli intellettuali e la Guerra di Spagna* (Rome, 1959).

Georgel, Jacques. *Le Franquisme* (Paris, 1970).

Gil Robles, J.M. *No fue posible la paz* (Barcelona, 1968).

Giménez Caballero, Ernesto. *Genio de España* (Madrid, 1936).

    La nueva catolicidad (Madrid, 1933).

Hemingway, Ernest. *For Whom the Bell Tolls* (New York, 1940).

Hernández Tomás, Jesús. *Yo fui un ministro de Stalin* (Mexico, 1953).

Inquisidor, El Gran. 'Antifascistas en España: J. Ortega y Gasset', *Fe*, 1, no. 1 (1933), 12.

International Commission of Jurists. *Spain and the Rule of Law* (Geneva, 1962).

Jackson, Gabriel. *The Spanish Republic and the Civil War, 1936–39* (Princeton, 1965).

Kemp, Peter. *Mine Were of Trouble* (London, 1957).

Kitchen, Martin. *Fascism* (London, 1976).

Koestler, Arthur. *Spanish Testament* (London, 1937).

Ledesma Ramos, Ramiro. *Discurso a las juventudes de España* (Madrid, 1935).
  El sello de la muerte (Madrid, 1924).
Luca de Tena, Juan Ignacio. *A Madrid 682* (Santander, n.d.).
Madariaga, Salvador de. *Spain: A Modern History* (New York, 1958).
Maeztu, Ramiro de. *Defensa de la hispanidad* (Madrid, 1934).
Malraux, André. *L'Espoir* (Paris, 1937).
Marrero, Vicente. *La guerra española y el trust de los cerebros* (Madrid, 1961).
Matthews, Herbert. *The Yoke and the Arrows* (New York, 1957).
Maura, Miguel. *Así cayó Alfonso XIII* (Mexico, 1962).
Ministerio de Justicia. *Causa general: la dominación roja en España* (Madrid, 1943).
Mintz, Jerome R. *The Anarchists of Casas Viejas* (Chicago, 1982).
Montero, Antonio. *Historia de la persecución religiosa en España (1936–1939)* (Madrid, 1961).
Ortega y Gasset, José. *Notas* (Madrid, 1928).
Orwell, George. *Homage to Catalonia* (London, 1938).
Pablo Muñoz, José de. *Aquellas banderas de Aragón* (Valencia, 1942).
Payne, Robert. *The Civil War in Spain, 1936–39* (London, 1963).
Payne, Stanley. *Falange: A History of Spanish Fascism* (London, 1962).
  Falange (Stanford, 1970).
Peers, Allison. *The Spanish Tragedy, 1930–36* (London, 1937).
Preston, Paul. *The Coming of the Spanish Civil War* (London, 1978).
  (ed.) *Revolution and War in Spain, 1931–1939* (London, 1984).
Primo de Rivera, José Antonio. 'La política y el intelectual: Homenaje y reproche a don
  José Ortega y Gasset', *Haz*, 12 (15 December 1935).
  Obras completas (Madrid, 1942).
Puente, José Vicente. *Viudas blancas* (Burgos, 1937).
Rama, Carlos M. *La crisis española del siglo XX* (Mexico, 1960).
Regler, Gustav. *The Great Crusade* (London, 1940).
Remarque, E.M. *All Quiet on the Western Front* (London, 1928).
Ridruejo, Dionisio. *Escrito en España* (Buenos Aires, 1962).
Salas, Jaime de. *El frente de los suspiros* (Madrid, 1939).
Salas Larrazábal, Ramón. *Pérdidas de la guerra* (Barcelona, 1977).
Salaverría, José María. *Cartas de un alférez a su madre* (Madrid, 1939).
Sartre, Jean-Paul. *Théâtre* (Paris, 1966).
Seco Serrano, Carlos. *Historia de España: Tomo VI* (Barcelona, 1962).
Segura, (Cardinal). Letter to *El Sol*, 7 May 1931.
Shirer, William. *The Rise and Fall of the Third Reich* (London, 1960).
Southworth, Herbert R. *El mito de la cruzada de Franco* (Paris, 1963).
  Antifalange (Paris, 1967).
Suñer, Enrique. *Los intelectuales y la tragedia española* (San Sebastian, 1937).
Thomas, Hugh. *The Spanish Civil War* (London, 1971).
Tuñón de Lara, Manuel. *El movimiento obrero en la historia de España* (Madrid, 1972).
  La España del siglo XX, 3 vols. (Barcelona, 1974).

Welles, Benjamin. *Spain: The Gentle Anarchy* (London, 1966).

Woodcock, George. *Anarchism* (London, 1963).

3   Novels of the Spanish Civil War

Those works which are asterisked have been the subject of detailed study in the preparation of this work; the remainder are known to be 'Civil War novels' in the full sense in which the term has been used in this study, and are included for bibliographical reference. Republican novels are distinguished by bold letters.

3.1   Novels of the Spanish Civil War, arranged by date of first publication. Where the edition used was not the first, details of both editions have been provided.

1936

Palma, Elías. *Gavroche en el parapeto* (Madrid, Nueva Imprenta Radio).

1937

*Carriedo de Ruiz, Carmen. *En plena epopeya* (Cordoba, Imprenta Provincial).

*Claramunt, Jorge. *El teniente Arizcun* (Burgos, Editorial Española).

Cossío, Francisco de. *Manolo* (Valladolid, Editorial Santarén).

*Espina, Concha. *Retaguardia* (Cordoba, Editorial Nueva España). (Edn cit.: San Sebastian, Librería Internacional, 1937).

Muñoz San Román, José. *Las fieras rojas* (Cordoba, Instituto Social de Bellas Letras).

*Sepúlveda, María. *En la gloria de aquel amanecer* (Cordoba, Editorial Española).

Viza, Juan Bautista, *La mochila del soldado* (Seville, Editora Nacional).

1938

Aguilar de la Sierra, Joaquín. *Cinco flechas y un corazón* (Vigo, Talleres Gráficos Cartel).

Belausteguigoitia, Ramón de. *Euzcadi en llamas* (Mexico, Ediciones Botas).

Cirre Jiménez, José. *Memorias de un combatiente de la Brigada Internacional* (Granada, Editorial Prieto).

Collantes, Juan A. *Las vestales* (Cadiz, Establecimientos Cerón).

*Espina, Concha. *Esclavitud y libertad* (Valladolid, Ediciones Reconquista).

Las alas invencibles (Burgos, Imprenta Aldecoa).

*Foxá, Agustín de. *Madrid de Corte a checa* (San Sebastian, Librería Internacional). (Edn cit.: Madrid, Prensa Española, 1964.)

*García Serrano, Rafael. *Eugenio o proclamación de la Primavera* (Burgos, Editora Nacional). (Edn cit.: *La guerra*, Fermín Uriarte Editor, Madrid, 1964.)

Herrera Petere, José. *Cumbres de Extremadura* (Madrid, Editorial Nuestro Pueblo).

*Martel, Carmen. *La guerra a través de las tocas* (Cadiz, Editorial Cerón).

*Miquelarena, Jacinto. *El otro mundo* (Burgos, Imprenta Aldecoa).

*Muñoz San Román, José. *Del ruedo a la trinchera* (Granada, Editorial Prieto).
  Señorita en la retaguardia (Cadiz, Editorial Cerón).
*Salazar, Miguel de. *De anarquista a mártir* (Santander, Librería Moderna).
*Salinas Quijada, Francisco. *Retoños de la gesta triunfal. Un alférez de cursillos* (Zaragoza, Talleres Gráficos El Noticiero).
*Sender, Ramón. *Contraataque* (Madrid, Editorial Nuestro Pueblo).
Ubreva, Eduardo Luis. *Un caballero legionario* (Seville, Imprenta San Antonio).
*Vázquez, José Andrés. *Armas de Caín y Abel* (Cadiz, Editorial Cerón).

1939

*Arauz de Robles, Carlos. *Mar y tierra* (Valladolid, Editorial Santarén).
*Benítez de Castro, Cecilio. *El espantable caso de los 'tomadores' de ciudades* (Barcelona, Gráficas Marcos).
  Se ha ocupado el kilómetro 6 (Barcelona, Editorial Juventud). (Edn cit.: 2nd edn, Editorial Juventud, Barcelona, n.d.)
Bonmatí de Codecido, Francisco. *Pilar* (Valladolid, Editorial Santarén).
Borrás y Bermejo, Tomás. *Oscuro heroísmo* (Seville, Ediciones Españolas).
*Caballero Alvarez, Agapito. *Romance en la guerra* (Barcelona, Ediciones BYP).
*Camba, Francisco. *Madridgrado* (Madrid, Ediciones Españolas).
*Carrere, Emilio. *La ciudad de los siete puñales* (Madrid, Ediciones Españolas).
Castro, Cristóbal de. *Mariquilla, barre, barre* (Madrid, Ediciones Españolas).
Cruzado, El. *Escenas vividas en la Guerra Española* (Bilbao, Editorial Palomeque).
*Espina, Concha. *Luna roja* (Valladolid, Librería Santarén).
*Fernández Flórez, Wenceslao. *Una isla en el mar rojo* (Madrid, Ediciones Españolas). (Edn cit.: 9th edn, 1940.)
López de Haro, Rafael. *Fuego en el bosque* (Madrid, Ediciones Españolas).
Martín de Lucenay, A. *El teniente Zacatecas* (Mexico, Ediciones Cicerón).
*Morales López, José. *Méndez, cronista de guerra* (Badajoz, Gráficas Corporativa).
Morgado, Pedro. *Los horizontes en los ojos* (Madrid, Ediciones Españolas).
Pérez de Olaguer, Antonio. *Amor y sangre* (Seville, Editorial Sevillana).
  Elvira, Tomas Rúfalo y yo (San Sebastian, Editorial Española).
Reyes Huertas, A. *La grandeza del hombre* (Madrid, Ediciones Españolas).
Ros, Samuel. *Meses de esperanza y lentejas* (Madrid, Ediciones Españolas).
*Soler Moreu, José. *Navidades sin pan* (Barcelona, Editorial Ibérica).
Vázquez, José Andrés. *Héroes de otoño* (Madrid, Ediciones Españolas).
*Ximénez de Sandoval, Felipe. *Camisa azul* (Valladolid, Editorial Santarén).

1940

*Borrás y Bermejo, Tomás. *Checas de Madrid* (Madrid, Editorial Escelicer). (Edn cit.: Editorial Luis de Caralt, Barcelona, 1956.)
*Cimorra, Clemente. *El bloqueo del hombre* (Buenos Aires, Claridad).

*Espina, Concha. *Princesas del martirio* (Barcelona, Ediciones Armiño).

Jauregui, G. *¡Sangre en los riscos!* (Palencia, Jauregui).

Landy, Lino. *Coloquios del frente* **(Mexico, A. del Bosque, Impresor).**

Ortoll de Galingo, María Mercedes. *Nuevos horizontes* (Madrid, Ediciones Españolas).

*Pérez y Pérez, Rafael. *De una España a otra* (Barcelona, Editorial Juventud).

Romano, Julio. *La luz en las tinieblas* (Madrid, Espasa-Calpe).

1941

Fernández Flórez, Wenceslao. *La novela número 13* (Zaragoza, Librería General).

*Giménez Arnau, José Antonio. *El puente* (Madrid, Ediciones Españolas). (Edn cit.: 2nd edn, 1941).

*León, Ricardo. *Cristo en los infiernos* (Madrid, Librería Victoriano Suárez).

*Noguera, Enrique. *La mascarada trágica* (Zaragoza, Gráficas Uriarte).

Romano, Julio. *La casa del padre* (Madrid, Espasa-Calpe).

1942

*Pedro, Valentín de. *La vida por la opinión* (Buenos Aires, Editorial A. López).

*Salazar Allende, Ricardo. *Tú no eres de los nuestros* (Madrid, Editora Nacional).

1943

*Aub, Max. *Campo cerrado* (Mexico, Editorial Tezontle). (Edn cit.: Ediciones Alfaguara, Madrid, 1982.)

*García Serrano, Rafael. *La fiel Infantería* (Madrid, Editora Nacional). (Edn cit.: *La guerra*, Madrid, Fermín Uriarte Editor, 1964.)

1944

*Barea, Arturo. *La forja* (in English: *The Clash*) (London, Faber and Faber). (Edn cit.: *La forja de un rebelde*, Buenos Aires, Editorial Losada, 1966.)

Cabello Lapiedra, Xavier. *¡Hombre!* (Madrid, Gráfica Informaciones).

*Masip, Paulino. *Diario de Hamlet García* (Mexico, M.L. Sánchez).

*Samblancat, Angel. *Caravana nazarena* (Mexico, Ediciones Orbe).

*Sancho Granados, Romualdo. *98 horas* (Mexico, Gráfica Panamericana).

1945

*Aub, Max. *Campo de sangre* (Mexico, Ediciones Tezontle).

García Suárez, Pedro. *Legión 1936* (Madrid, Ediciones Estudiantes Españoles).

1946

*Sánchez Barbudo, Antonio. *Sueños de grandeza* (Buenos Aires, Editorial Nova).

Siria, Barón de. *Isabel, la mujer legionaria* (Madrid, Ediciones Patria).

1947

1948

*Martínez Pagán, Antonio. *Génaro* (in French) (Paris, Editions du Pavois).

1949

*Ayala, Francisco. *La cabeza del cordero* (Buenos Aires, Editorial Losada). (Edn cit.: Buenos Aires, Compañía General Fabril Editora, 1962.)

*Sender, Ramón. *El rey y la reina* (Buenos Aires, Editorial Jackson). (Edn cit.: Barcelona, Destino, 1979.)

1950

*Alba, Víctor. *La vida provisional* (Mexico, Compañía Importadora y Distribuidora de Ediciones).

*Arana, José Ramón. *El cura de Almuniaced* (Mexico, Colección Aquelarre). (Edn cit.: Madrid, Ediciones Turner, 1979.)

*Fórmica, Mercedes. *Monte de Sancha* (Barcelona, Editorial Luis de Caralt).

Hermanos, Juan. *El fin de la esperanza* (in French: *La Fin de l'espoir*) (Paris, Ed. René Julliard).

1951

*Aub, Max. *Campo abierto* (Mexico, Editorial Tezontle).

*Barea, Arturo. *La llama* (Buenos Aires, Editorial Losada). (Edn cit.: *La forja de un rebelde*, Buenos Aires, Editorial Losada, 1966.)

   La ruta (Buenos Aires). (Edn cit.: as above.)

*García Serrano, Rafael. *Plaza del Castillo* (Madrid, Editorial Saso). (Edn cit.: *La guerra*, Madrid, Fermín Uriarte Editor, 1964.)

1952

Gomis Soler, José. *Cruces sin Cristo* (Mexico, Compañía General de Ediciones).

*Oliver, Angel. *Los canes andan sueltos* (Madrid, Editora Nacional).

1953

*Andreu, José María Tomás. *La alegría del vivir* (Mexico, Ediciones Orbe).

Botella Pastor, Virgilio. *Por qué callaron las campanas* (Mexico, Ediciones Libertad).

*Gironella, José María. *Los cipreses creen en Dios* (Barcelona, Planeta). (Edn cit.: 15th edn, 1958.)

*Sender, Ramón. *Mosén Millán* (Mexico, Colección Aquelarre). (Edn cit.: *Réquiem por un campesino español*, Buenos Aires, Editorial Proyección, 1966.)

1954

Arima, Jacobo. *Abismos de papel* (Barcelona, Ediciones Eler).
*Fernández de la Reguera, Ricardo. *Cuerpo a tierra* (Barcelona, Editorial Garbo). (Edn cit.: 3rd edn, 1955.)
Nácher, Enrique. *Volvió la paz* (Valencia, Diputación Provincial).
*Sender, Ramón. *Los cinco libros de Ariadna* (Mexico, Colección Aquelarre). (Edn cit.: New York, Ediciones Ibérica, 1957.)

1955

*Manfredi, Domingo. *Las lomas tienen espinos* (Barcelona, Luis de Caralt).
Marrero, Angel. *Todo avante* (Madrid, Editorial Prensa Española).
*Martín Artajo, Javier. *No me cuente Vd. su caso* (Madrid, Editorial Biosca).
Mateos, Francisco. *Dos amores* (Barcelona, Ed. Rumbos).

1956

Escalante, Pedro de. *La vida por la muerte* (Madrid, Editorial Afrodisio Aguado).
*Ruiz-Ayúcar, Angel. *Las dos barajas* (Barcelona, Luis de Caralt).

1957

Castañón, José Manuel. *Bezana roja* (Madrid, Editorial Aramo).
*Romero, Emilio. *La paz empieza nunca* (Barcelona, Planeta).

1958

*Diego, Luis de. *La presa del diablo* (Valladolid, Ediciones Gerper).
García Serrano, Rafael. *Los ojos perdidos* (Madrid, Ed. Eskua).
Matute, Ana María. *Los hijos muertos* (Barcelona, Planeta).

1959

*Cepas, Juan. *Provisional* (Barcelona, Luis de Caralt).
Fernández Granell, Eugenio. *La novela del Indio Tupinamba* (Mexico, Ed. Costa-Amic).
Lamana, Manuel. *Los inocentes* (Buenos Aires, Editorial Losada).
*León, María Teresa. *Juego limpio* (Buenos Aires, Editorial Goyanarte).
Palencia, Isabel de. *En mi hambre mando yo* (Mexico, Libro Mex).
Valdosín, Simón de. *Retó a la muerte* (Mexico, Imprenta Laura).

1960

1961

*García de Pruneda, Salvador. *La soledad de Alcuneza* (Madrid, Ediciones Cid).
*Gironella, José María. *Un millón de muertos* (Barcelona, Planeta).

Masoliver, Liberata. *Barcelona en llamas* (Barcelona, Editorial Barna).

Ortas, Francisco M. *Soldado y medio* **(Mexico, Editorial Nuevas Generaciones).**

*Soler, Bartolomé. *Los muertos no se cuentan* (Barcelona, Editorial Juventud).

1962

Castañón, José Manuel. *Andrés cuenta su historia* **(Caracas, Editorial Arte).**

1963

*Aub, Max. *Campo del Moro* **(Mexico, Editorial Joaquín Mortiz).**

1964

Castillo Puche, José Luis. *El perro loco* (Madrid, Ediciones Alfaguara).

Matute, Ana María. *Los soldados lloran de noche* (Barcelona, Ediciones Destino).

Riudavets de Montes, Luis. *Al final del camino* (Madrid, Editorial Agesa).

1965

Agustí, Ignacio. *19 de julio* (Barcelona, Planeta).

Vázquez Azpiri, Héctor. *La navaja* (Madrid, Ediciones Alfaguara).

1966

Alós, Concha. *El Caballo Rojo* (Barcelona, Planeta).

Contreras Pazo, Francisco. *Sinaí* **(Montevideo, Ediciones CISA).**

*Gironella, José María. *Ha estallado la paz* (Barcelona, Planeta).

López-Sanz, Francisco. *Llevaban su sangre* (Pamplona, Editorial Gómez).

1967

*Benet, Juan. *Volverás a Región* (Barcelona, Ediciones Destino).

*Lera, Angel María de. *Las últimas banderas* **(Barcelona, Planeta).**

Lueiro Rey, Manuel. *Manso* (Buenos Aires, Oberón).

Masoliver, Liberata. *La retirada* (Barcelona, Editorial Peñíscola).

1968

Aub, Max. *Campo de los almendros* **(Mexico, Joaquín Ortiz).**

Martín-Vigil, José Luis. *Muerte a los curas* (Oviedo, Richard Grandio Ed.)

Martínez Orejón, Félix. *Cuando las cruces no se alzan al cielo* (Barcelona, Planeta).

Muñíz Martín, Oscar. *El coronel* (Oviedo, Gráf. Summa).

1969

Ahumada Zabal, Fernando. *Los responsables* (Madrid, Prensa Española).

Albalá, Alfonso. *Los días del odio* (Madrid, Guadarrama).

Barco Teruel, Enrique. *Valle del Jarama. Brigada Internacional* (Barcelona, Ed. Marte).

Barrios, Manuel. *El miedo* (Barcelona, Planeta).
*Cela, Camilo José. *San Camilo 1936* (Madrid, Alfaguara).
Padilla, Pedro Pablo. *Casa Paco* (Madrid, Literoy).
Piñeiro, Jaime. *La traición de los héroes* (Barcelona, Edisven).
Rial, J.A. *La prisión de Fyffes* (Caracas, Monte Avila).

1970

Belausteguigoitia, Ramón de. *La novela de un refugiado* (Mexico, Costa-Amic Ed.).
Heredia, Manuel de. *El Chepa* (Madrid, Afrodisio Aguado).
Rojas, Carlos. *Aquelarre* (Barcelona, Ed. Nauta).
Ruíz, Roberto. *Los jueces implacables* (Mexico, Joaquín Mortiz).

1971

Fernández Serrano, Juan Antonio. *El convertidor* (Barcelona, Planeta).
Granero, Sancho, Emilio. *Barras y estrellas* (Valencia, Prometeo).
Perpiñá Castellá, Luis. *El miliciano Borrás* (Barcelona, A.T.E.).

1972

*Agustí, Ignacio. *Guerra civil* (Barcelona, Planeta).
Díaz Garrido, Carmen. *Los años únicos* (Madrid, Ed. Prensa Española).
Salom, Jaime. *La casa de las Chivas* (Barcelona, Planeta).

1973

Andújar, Manuel. *Historias de una historia* (Madrid, Al-Borak).
Badell, Gabriel. *Las cartas cayeron boca abajo* (Barcelona, Ediciones Destino).
Castañón, Luciano. *Los huidos* (Bilbao, Ed. La Gran Enciclopedia Vasca).
*Rojas, Carlos. *Azaña* (Barcelona, Planeta).
Sanz Saínz, Julio. *Los muertos no hacen ruido* (Mexico, Ed. Asociados).

1974

*Duque, Aquilino. *El mono azul* (Barcelona, Destino).
Manfredi Cano, Domingo. *Juan, el negro* (Barcelona, Luis de Caralt).
Parés Guillén, Francisco. *Entre la verdad y la mentira* (Mexico, Costa-Amic).
Royo, Rodrigo. *Todavía* (Barcelona, Planeta).

1975

Carreño, Mada. *Los diablos sueltos* (Mexico, Novaro).
Granda, Antonio de la. *Hospital militar 28* (Madrid, Sedmay).
Jurado Morales, José. *Un hombre de la CNT* (Barcelona, Rondas).
Valdeón, José Aurelio. *Murieron los de siempre* (Barcelona, Sedmay).

3.2 Novels of the Spanish Civil War, arranged by title. The date given is that of the first edition in each case. Republican novels are distinguished by bold letters.

Abismos de papel, Arima, Jacobo (Barcelona, 1954).

Al final del camino, Riudavets de Montes, Luis (Madrid, 1964).

Amor y sangre, Pérez de Olaguer, Antonio (Seville, 1939).

Andrés cuenta su historia, Castañón, José Manuel (Caracas, 1962).

Aquelarre, Rojas, Carlos (Barcelona, 1970).

***Armas de Caín y Abel, Vázquez, José Andrés (Cadiz, 1938).**

***Azaña, Rojas, Carlos (Barcelona, 1973).**

Barcelona en llamas, Masoliver, Liberata (Barcelona, 1961).

Barras y estrellas, Granero Sancho, Emilio (Valencia, 1971).

Bezana roja, Castañón, José Manuel (Madrid, 1957).

*Camisa azul, Ximénez de Sandoval, Felipe (Valladolid, 1939).

***Campo abierto, Aub, Max (Mexico, 1951).**

***Campo cerrado, Aub, Max (Mexico, 1943).**

Campo de los almendros, Aub, Max (Mexico, 1968).

***Campo de sangre, Aub, Max (Mexico, 1945).**

***Campo del Moro, Aub, Max (Mexico, 1963).**

***Caravana nazarena, Samblancat, Angel (Mexico, 1944).**

Casa Paco, Padilla, Pedro Pablo (Madrid, 1969).

*Checas de Madrid, Borrás y Bermejo, Tomás (Madrid, 1940).

Cinco flechas y un corazón, Aguilar de la Sierra, Joaquín (Vigo, 1938).

Coloquios del frente, Landy, Lino (Mexico, 1940).

***Contraataque, Sender, Ramón (Madrid, 1938).**

**Cristo en los infiernos*, León, Ricardo (Madrid, 1941).

Cruces sin Cristo, Gomis Soler, José (Mexico, 1952).

Cuando las cruces no se alzan al cielo, Martínez Orejón, Félix (Barcelona, 1968).

*Cuerpo a tierra, Fernández de la Reguera, Ricardo (Barcelona, 1954).

Cumbres de Extremadura, Herrera Petere, José (Madrid, 1938).

**De anarquista a mártir*, Salazar, Miguel de (Santander, 1938).

**De una España a otra*, Pérez y Pérez, Rafael (Barcelona, 1940).

**Del ruedo a la trinchera*, Muñoz San Román, José (Granada, 1938).

***Diario de Hamlet García, Masip, Paulino (Mexico, 1944).**

19 de julio, Agustí, Ignacio (Barcelona, 1965).

Dos amores, Mateos, Francisco (Barcelona, 1955).

***El bloqueo del hombre, Cimorra, Clemente (Buenos Aires, 1940).**

El Caballo Rojo, Alós, Concha (Barcelona, 1966).

El Chepa, Heredia, Manuel de (Madrid, 1970).

El convertidor, Fernández Serrano, Juan Antonio (Barcelona, 1971).

El coronel, Muñiz Martín, Oscar (Oviedo, 1968).

***El cura de Almuniaced, Arana, José Ramón (Mexico, 1950).**

**El espantable caso de los 'tomadores' de ciudades*, Benítez de Castro, Cecilio (Barcelona, 1939).

El fin de la esperanza (in French: *La Fin de l'espoir*), Hermanos, Juan (Paris, 1950).

El miedo, Barrios, Manuel (Barcelona, 1969).

El miliciano Borrás, **Perpiñá Castellá, Luis (Barcelona, 1971)**.

*El mono azul, Duque, Aquilino (Barcelona, 1974).

*El otro mundo, Miquelarena, Jacinto (Burgos, 1938).

El perro loco, Castillo Puche, José Luis (Madrid, 1964).

*El puente, Giménez Arnau, José Antonio (Madrid, 1941).

El rey y la reina*, **Sender, Ramón (Buenos Aires, 1949).

**El teniente Arizcun*, Claramunt, Jorge (Burgos, 1937).

El teniente Zacatecas, **Martín de Lucenay, A. (Mexico, 1939)**.

Elvira, Tomás Rúfalo y yo, Pérez de Olaguer, Antonio (San Sebastian, 1939).

**En la gloria de aquel amanecer*, Sepúlveda, María (Cordoba, 1937).

En mi hambre mando yo, **Palencia, Isabel de (Mexico, 1959)**.

*En plena epopeya, Carriedo de Ruiz, Carmen (Cordoba, 1937).

Entre la verdad y la mentira, **Parés Guillén, Francisco (Mexico, 1974)**.

Escenas vividas en la Guerra Española, Cruzado, El (Bilbao, 1939).

**Esclavitud y libertad*, Espina, Concha (Valladolid, 1938).

**Eugenio o proclamación de la Primavera*, García Serrano, Rafael (Burgos, 1938).

Euzcadi en llamas, **Belausteguigoitia, Ramón de (Mexico, 1938)**.

Fuego en el bosque, López de Haro, Rafael (Madrid, 1939).

Gavroche en el parapeto, **Palma, Elías (Madrid, 1936)**.

*Génaro (in French), **Martínez Pagán, Antonio (Paris, 1948)**.

*Guerra civil, Agustí, Ignacio (Barcelona, 1972).

**Ha estallado la paz*, Gironella, José María (Barcelona, 1966).

Héroes de otoño, Vázquez, José Andrés (Madrid, 1939).

Historias de una historia, **Andújar, Manuel (Madrid, 1973)**.

¡Hombre!, Cabello Lapiedra, Xavier (Madrid, 1944).

Hospital militar 28, **Granda, Antonio de la (Madrid, 1975)**.

Isabel, la mujer legionaria, Siria, Barón de (Madrid, 1946).

Juan, el Negro, Manfredi Cano, Domingo (Barcelona, 1974).

*Juego limpio, **León, María Teresa (Buenos Aires, 1959)**.

La alegría del vivir*, **Andreu, José María Tomás (Mexico, 1953).

La cabeza del cordero*, **Ayala, Francisco (Buenos Aires, 1949).

La casa de las Chivas, Salom, Jaime (Barcelona, 1972).

La casa del padre, Romano, Julio (Madrid, 1941).

**La ciudad de los siete puñales*, Carrere, Emilio (Madrid, 1939).

**La fiel Infantería*, García Serrano, Rafael (Madrid, 1943).

*La forja (in English: *The Clash*), **Barea, Arturo (London, 1944)**.

La grandeza del hombre, Reyes Huertas, A. (Madrid, 1939).

**La guerra a través de las tocas*, Martel, Carmen (Cadiz, 1938).

*La llama, **Barea, Arturo (Buenos Aires, 1951)**.

La luz en las tinieblas, Romano, Julio (Madrid, 1940).

**La mascarada trágica*, Noguera, Enrique (Zaragoza, 1941).

La mochila del soldado, Viza, Juan Bautista (Seville, 1937).

La navaja, Vázquez Azpiri, Héctor (Madrid, 1965).

La novela de un refugiado, Belausteguigoitia, Ramón de (Mexico, 1970).

La novela del Indio Tupinamba, Fernández Granell, Eugenio (Mexico, 1959).

La novela número 13, Fernández Flórez, Wenceslao (Zaragoza, 1941).

*La paz empieza nunca, Romero, Emilio (Barcelona, 1957).

*La presa del diablo, Diego, Luis de (Valladolid, 1958).

La prisión de Fyffes, Rial, J.A. (Caracas, 1969).

La retirada, Masoliver, Liberata (Barcelona, 1967).

*La ruta, Barea, Arturo (Buenos Aires, 1951).

*La soledad de Alcuneza, García de Pruneda, Salvador (Madrid, 1961).

La traición de los héroes, Piñeiro, Jaime (Barcelona, 1969).

La vida por la muerte, Escalante, Pedro de (Madrid, 1956).

*La vida por la opinión, Pedro, Valentín de (Buenos Aires, 1942).

*La vida provisional, Alba, Víctor (Mexico, 1950).

*Las alas invencibles, Espina, Concha (Burgos, 1938).

Las cartas cayeron boca abajo, Badell, Gabriel (Barcelona, 1973).

*Las dos barajas, Ruiz-Ayúcar, Angel (Barcelona, 1956).

Las fieras rojas, Muñoz San Román, José (Cordoba, 1937).

*Las lomas tienen espinos, Manfredi, Domingo (Barcelona, 1955).

*Las últimas banderas, Lera, Angel María de (Barcelona, 1967).

Las vestales, Collantes, Juan A. (Cadiz, 1938).

Legión 1936, García Suárez, Pedro (Madrid, 1945).

Llevaban su sangre, López-Sanz, Francisco (Pamplona, 1966).

Los años únicos, Díaz Garrido, Carmen (Madrid, 1972).

*Los canes andan sueltos, Oliver, Angel (Madrid, 1952).

*Los cinco libros de Ariadna, Sender, Ramón (Mexico, 1954).

*Los cipreses creen en Dios, Gironella, José María (Barcelona, 1953).

Los diablos sueltos, Carreño, Mada (Mexico, 1975).

Los días del odio, Albalá, Alfonso (Madrid, 1969).

Los hijos muertos, Matute, Ana María (Barcelona, 1958).

Los horizontes en los ojos, Morgado, Pedro (Madrid, 1939).

Los huidos, Castañón, Luciano (Bilbao, 1973).

Los inocentes, Lamana, Manuel (Buenos Aires, 1959).

Los jueces implacables, Ruíz, Roberto (Mexico, 1970).

Los muertos no hacen ruido, Sanz Saínz, Julio (Mexico, 1973).

*Los muertos no se cuentan, Soler, Bartolomé (Barcelona, 1961).

Los ojos perdidos, García Serrano, Rafael (Madrid, 1958).

Los responsables, Ahumada Zabal, Fernando (Madrid, 1969).

Los soldados lloran de noche, Matute, Ana María (Barcelona, 1964).

*Luna roja, Espina, Concha (Valladolid, 1939).

*Madrid de Corte a checa, Foxá, Agustín de (San Sebastian, 1938).

*Madridgrado, Camba, Francisco (Madrid, 1939).

Manolo, Cossío, Francisco de (Valladolid, 1937).

Manso, Lueiro Rey, Manuel (Buenos Aires, 1967).

*Mar y tierra, Arauz de Robles, Carlos (Valladolid, 1939).

Mariquilla, barre, barre, Castro, Cristóbal de (Madrid, 1939).

Memorias de un combatiente de la Brigada Internacional, Cirre Jiménez, José (Granada, 1938).

*Méndez, cronista de guerra, Morales López, José (Badajoz, 1939).

Meses de esperanza y lentejas, Ros, Samuel (Madrid, 1939).

*Monte de Sancha, Fórmica, Mercedes (Barcelona, 1950).

*Mosén Millán, Sender, Ramón (Mexico, 1953). Later retitled Réquiem por un campesino español.

Muerte a los curas, Martín⁄Vigil, José Luis (Oviedo, 1968).

Murieron los de siempre, Valdeón, José Aurelio (Barcelona, 1975).

*Navidades sin pan, Soler Moreu, José (Barcelona, 1939).

*No me cuente Vd. su caso, Martín Artajo, Javier (Madrid, 1955).

*98 horas, Sancho Granados, Romualdo (Mexico, 1944).

Nuevos horizontes, Ortoll de Galingo, María Mercedes (Madrid, 1940).

Oscuro heroísmo, Borrás y Bermejo, Tomás (Seville, 1939).

Pilar, Bonmatí de Codecido, Francisco (Valladolid, 1939).

*Plaza del Castillo, García Serrano, Rafael (Madrid, 1951).

Por qué callaron las campanas, Botella Pastor, Virgilio (Mexico, 1953).

*Princesas del martirio, Espina, Concha (Barcelona, 1940).

*Provisional, Cepas, Juan (Barcelona, 1959).

*Réquiem por un campesino español. See Mosén Millán above.

*Retaguardia, Espina, Concha (Cordoba, 1937).

Retó a la muerte, Valdosín, Simón de (Mexico, 1959).

*Retoños de la gesta triunfal. Un alférez de cursillos, Salinas Quijada, Francisco (Zaragoza, 1938).

*Romance en la guerra, Caballero Alvarez, Agapito (Barcelona, 1939).

*San Camilo 1936, Cela, Camilo José (Madrid, 1969).

¡Sangre en los riscos!, Jauregui, G. (Palencia, 1940).

*Se ha ocupado el kilómetro 6, Benítez de Castro, Cecilio (Barcelona, 1939).

*Señorita en la retaguardia, Muñoz San Román, José (Cadiz, 1938).

Sinaí, Contreras Pazo, Francisco (Montevideo, 1966).

Soldado y medio, Ortas, Francisco M. (Mexico, 1961).

*Sueños de grandeza, Sánchez Barbudo, Antonio (Buenos Aires, 1946).

Todavía, Royo, Rodrigo (Barcelona, 1974).

Todo avante, Marrero, Angel (Madrid, 1955).

*Tú no eres de los nuestros, Salazar Allende, Ricardo (Madrid, 1942).

*Un alférez de cursillos. See Retoños de la gesta triunfal above.

Un caballero legionario, Ubreva, Eduardo Luis (Seville, 1938).

Un hombre de la CNT, Jurado Morales, José (Barcelona, 1975).

*Un millón de muertos, Gironella, José María (Barcelona, 1961).
*Una isla en el mar rojo, Fernández Flórez, Wenceslao (Madrid, 1939).
Valle del Jarama. Brigada International, Barco Teruel, Enrique (Barcelona, 1969).
*Volverás a Región, Benet, Juan (Barcelona, 1967).
Volvió la paz, Nácher, Enrique (Valencia, 1954).

4 Books and articles (general criticism)

AEAR (Association des Ecrivains et des Artistes Révolutionnaires), letter from Spanish branch, Commune (September–October 1934), 289–294.
Alborg, Juan Luis. Hora actual de la novela española, 2 vols. (Madrid, 1962–63).
Alonso, Amado. Ensayo sobre la novela histórica (Buenos Aires, 1942).
Amorós, Andrés. Introducción a la novela contemporánea (Madrid, 1971).
Sociología de una novela rosa (Madrid, 1968).
Subliteraturas (Barcelona, 1974).
Armstrong, Douglas Holcombe. 'The Novel of the Spanish Civil War: A Thematic Appraisal, 1936–1960'. Unpublished PhD dissertation (University of Michigan, 1967).
Aub, Max. Discurso de la novela española contemporánea (Mexico DF, 1945).
Ayala, Francisco. El escritor en la sociedad de masas (Buenos Aires, 1958).
'Función social de la literatura', Revista de Occidente, 2, no.10 (1964), 97–107.
Histrionismo y representación (Buenos Aires, 1944).
'¿Para quién escribimos nosotros?', Cuadernos Americanos, 1 (1949), 36–58.
Azorín, 'Nietzsche en España', El Pueblo Gallego (Vigo), 18 February 1941.
Baker, C. (ed.) Ernest Hemingway. The Writer as Artist (Princeton, 1963).
Baquero Goyanes, Mariano. Problemas de la novela contemporánea (Madrid, 1951).
Proceso de la novela actual (Madrid, 1963).
Barea, Arturo. 'Not Spain but Hemingway', Horizon (May 1941), 350–361.
Beccari, G. Scrittori di guerra spagnoli, 1936–1939 (Milan, 1941).
Benson, Frederick R. Writers in Arms. The Literary Impact of the Spanish Civil War (London, 1968).
Bertrand de Muñoz, Maryse. 'La Guerre Civile espagnole dans le roman européen et américain.' Unpublished doctoral thesis (Université de la Sorbonne, Paris, 1962).
'Reflejo de los cambios políticos, sociales, históricos y lingüísticos en las novelas recientes de la guerra civil', Camp de l'Arpa, 19 (1975), 16–20.
Bousoño, Carlos. 'La novela española en la posguerra', Revista Nacional de Cultura, 19, no. 124 (1957), 157–167.
Brenan, Gerald. The Literature of the Spanish People (Cambridge, 1951).
Brown, Reginald F. La novela española, 1700–1850 (Madrid, 1953).
Buckley, Ramón. Problemas formales en la novela española contemporánea (Barcelona, 1968).
Buendía, Felicidad. Antología de la novela histórica española, 1830–1844 (Madrid, 1963) (Estudio preliminar, pp. 9–36).

Butt, John. *Writers and Politics in Modern Spain* (London, 1978).

Calvo Serer, Rafael. *La literatura universal sobre la guerra de España* (Madrid, 1962).

Cano, José Luis. 'La novela española', *Revista Nacional de Cultura*, 19, no. 125 (1957), 18–22.

Carrillo, V. et al. *L'infralittérature en Espagne aux XIXe et XXe siècles* (Grenoble, 1977).

Castro, Américo. 'Emigrados', *Cuadernos del Congreso por la Libertad de la Cultura*, 17 (1956), 5–14.

Chabás, Juan. *Literatura española contemporánea* (Havana, 1952).

Cierva, Ricardo de la. *Cien libros básicos sobre la Guerra de España* (Madrid, 1966).

Corrales Egea, José et al. *Los escritores y la Guerra de España* (Barcelona, 1977).

Davison, P. et al. *Literary Taste, Culture and Mass Communication, Vol. 11: The Writer and Politics* (Cambridge, 1978).

Díaz, Janet W. 'Spanish Civil War and Exile in the Novels of Aub, Ayala and Sender' in Moeller, Hans Bernard (ed.), *Latin America and the Literature of Exile* (Heidelberg, 1983).

Dietrich, Anton. 'Spanien: Leiden am Burgerkrieg. Zwei Neuerscheinungen und ein Kollektivneurose', *Wort und Wahrheit*, 17, no. 3 (1962).

Doménech, R. 'Una generación en marcha' in *Insula*, nos. 162–165 (1960).

Donnelly, J.P. 'Spanish Views on the Civil War', *The Month*, 28, no. 6 (1962), 335–341.

Elizalde, I. 'La novela social contemporánea en España', *Fomento Social*, 16, no. 63 (1961), 255–269.

Eoff, Sherman H. *The Modern Spanish Novel* (New York, 1961).

Eskin, Stanley G. 'The Literature of the Spanish Civil War: Observations on the Political Genre', *Genre*, 4, no. 1 (1971), 76–99.

Fernández-Cañedo, Jesús A. 'La guerra en la novela española, 1936–1947', *Arbor*, 12, no. 37 (1949), 60–68.

 'La joven novela española (1936–1947)', *Revista de la Universidad de Oviedo*, 9, nos. 49–50 (1948), 45–79.

Ferreras, Juan Ignacio. *La novela por entregas, 1840–1900* (Madrid, 1972).

 Tendencias de la novela española actual (Paris, 1970).

 Teoría y praxis de la novela (Paris, 1970).

Ford, Hugh D. *A Poet's War: British Poets and the Spanish Civil War* (Oxford, 1965).

Foulkes, A.P. *Literature and Propaganda* (London, 1983).

García Viñó, M. *La novela española actual* (Madrid, 1967).

Gil Casado, Pablo. *La novela social española, 1942–1968* (Barcelona, 1968).

Gilhodes, Lucienne. 'Le Roman espagnol sur le thème de la guerre civile de 1936–39.' Unpublished dissertation, Diplôme d'Etudes Supérieures (Université de la Sorbonne, Paris, 1958).

Giménez Caballero, Ernesto. 'Pío Baroja, precursor del fascismo.' Prologue to Baroja, Pío, *Comunistas, judíos y demás ralea* (Valladolid, 1938), pp. 3–13.

Gironella, José María. *El novelista ante el mundo* (Madrid, 1954).

 '¿Por qué no se conoce la novela española?', *Correo Literario*, 3, no. 57 (1952), 1 and 10.

Gogorza Fletcher, Madeleine de. *The Spanish Historical Novel (1870–1970)* (London, 1974).

Gómez de la Serna, Gaspar. *España en sus episodios nacionales* (Madrid, 1954).

Goytisolo, Juan. 'Para una literatura nacional popular', *Insula*, 146 (1959), 6 and 11.

Gullón, Ricardo. 'La generación de 1936', *Asomante*, 1 (1959), 64–69.

'La novela española moderna,' *La Torre*, 42 (1963), 45–68.

Hanrez, Marc (ed.) *Les Ecrivains et la guerre d'Espagne* (Paris, n.d.)

Howe, Irving. *Politics and the Novel* (New York, 1957).

Hoyos, A. de. *Ocho escritores actuales* (Murcia, 1954).

Iglesias Laguna, Antonio. *Treinta años de novela española, 1938–1968* (Madrid, 1969).

Ilie, Paul. *Literature and Inner Exile: Authoritarian Spain, 1939–1975* (Baltimore, 1980).

'Nietzsche in Spain, 1890–1910', *Publications of the Modern Language Association of America*, 79 (1964), 80–96.

Joly, Monique et al. *Panorama du roman espagnol contemporain, 1939–1975* (Montpellier, 1979).

Keyserling, Hermann de. *Meditaciones sudamericanas* (Madrid, 1933).

Klein, Holger (ed.) *The First World War in Fiction* (London, 1976).

Lamana, Manuel. *Literatura de postguerra* (Buenos Aires, 1961).

Lloréns, Vicente. 'Entre España y América. En torno a la emigración republicana de 1939' in *Literatura, historia, política* (Madrid, 1967) by the same author.

Longhurst, Carlos. *Las novelas históricas de Pío Baroja* (Madrid, 1974).

Lo Ré, Anthony George. 'The Novel of the Spanish Civil War, 1936–1960.' Unpublished PhD thesis (University of North Carolina, 1965).

López Aranguren, José Luis. 'La evolución espiritual de los intelectuales españoles de la emigración', *Cuadernos Hispanoamericanos*, 14, no. 38 (1953) 123–157.

Lubbock, Percy. *The Craft of Fiction* (New York, 1960).

Macmahon, D. 'Changing Trends in the Spanish Novel', *Books Abroad*, 34 (1960), 227–230.

MacNeice, L. 'The Poet in England Today', *New Republic*, 102 (1940), 412–413.

Magny, C.E. *Histoire du roman français* (Paris, 1950).

Mainer, José Carlos. *Falange y literatura* (Barcelona, 1971).

'Recuerdo de una vocación generacional, II. Creación literaria en *Vértice* (1937–1940)', *Insula*, 254 (1968), 7 and 10.

Mander, John. *The Writer and Commitment* (London, 1961).

Marañón, Gregorio. *Españoles fuera de España* (Madrid, 1964).

Marra-López, José R. *Narrativa española fuera de España (1939–1961)* (Madrid, 1963).

'Precisiones a una crítica de Guillermo de Torre', *Insula*, 202 (1963), 4.

Marrast, Robert. 'Le théâtre à Madrid pendant la guerre civile. Une expérience de théâtre politique' in Jacquot, J., *Le Théâtre Moderne* (Paris, 1957), pp. 257–274.

Martínez, Carlos. *Crónica de una emigración* (Mexico, 1959).

Martínez Cachero, J.M. *Historia de la novela española entre 1936 y 1975* (Madrid, 1979).

'Cuatro novelistas "de" y "en" la Guerra Civil (1936–39)', *Bulletin Hispanique*, 85, nos. 3–4 (1983), 281–298.

Martínez Sierra, G. 'Hablando con Valle-Inclán. De él y su obra', *ABC* (7 December, 1928), 1.

Medina, J.T. *Spanish Realism* (Potomac, 1979).

Molina, R. *Estudios* (Madrid, 1961).

Montesinos, José F. *Costumbrismo y novela: Ensayo sobre el redescubrimiento de la realidad española* (Madrid, 1960).

Moufflet, André. 'Le style du roman-feuilleton', *Mercure de France*, 15 Jan 1931.

Muste, John M. *Say That We Saw Spain Die: Literary Consequences of the Spanish Civil War* (London, 1966).

Nicholson, Helen S. 'The Novel of Protest and the Spanish Republic', *University of Arizona Bulletin*, 10, no. 3 (1939), 3–42.

Nora, Eugenio de. *La novela española contemporánea*, 3 vols. (Madrid, 1958–62).

Norrish, P.J. *Drama of the Group. A Study of Unanimism in the Plays of Jules Romains* (Cambridge, 1958).

Ortega y Gasset, José. *Obras completas*, 5 vols. (Madrid, 1946).

Orwell, George. *Collected Essays* (London, 1961).

Pageard, R. 'Romanciers et conteurs espagnols actuels', *Mercure de France*, 1, no. 123 (1957), 530–537.

Parker, A.A. 'Towards a Definition of Calderonian Tragedy', *Bulletin of Hispanic Studies*, 39 (1962), 222–237.

Pérez Bowie, José Antonio. *El léxico de la muerte durante la Guerra Civil española* (Salamanca, 1983).

Pérez Minik, Domingo. *Novelistas españoles de los siglos XIX y XX* (Madrid, 1957).

Pomeau, René. 'Guerre et roman dans l'entre-deux-guerres', *Revue des Sciences Humaines* (January–March 1963), 77–95.

Ponce de León, José Luis S. *La novela española de la guerra civil, 1936–1939* (Madrid, 1971).

Rieuneau, Maurice. *Guerre et révolution dans le roman français de 1919 à 1939* (Paris, 1974).

Rodríguez Alcalde, L. *Hora actual de la novela en el mundo* (Madrid, 1959).

Rodríguez Monegal, Emir. *Tres testigos de la guerra civil: Max Aub, Ramón Sender, Arturo Barea* (Caracas, 1971).

Romeiser, John Beals (ed.) *Red Flags, Black Flags: Critical Essays on the Literature of the Spanish Civil War* (Madrid, 1982).

Romero Tovar, Leonardo. *La novela popular española del siglo XIX* (Barcelona, 1976).

Ruhle, Jurgen. *Literatura y revolución* (Barcelona, 1963).

Sáinz de Robles, F.C. *Ensayo de un diccionario de la literatura* (Madrid, 1949).

Santonja, Gonzalo (ed.) *La novela proletaria* (Madrid, 1979).

Santos, Dámaso, *Generaciones juntas* (Madrid, 1962).

'Guerra y política en la novela contemporánea', *Estafeta Literaria*, 251 (1962), 4.

Sartre, Jean-Paul. *Situations, I* (Paris, 1947).

Situations, II (Paris, 1948).

Schwartz, Kessel. 'A Fascist View of Nineteenth Century Literature, 1936–1939', *Romance Notes*, 7 (1966), 117–122.

Sender, Ramón. 'El novelista y las masas', *Leviatán*, 24 (1936), 31–41.

Sérant, Paul. *Le Romantisme fasciste* (Paris, 1959).

Serge, Victor. *Littérature et révolution* (Paris, 1976).

Serrano Poncela, Segundo. 'La novela española contemporánea', *La Torre*, 2 (1953), 105–128.

Sobejano, Gonzalo. *Nietzsche en España* (Madrid, 1967).

La novela española de nuestro tiempo (Madrid, 1970).

Soldevila Durante, Ignacio. 'La novela española actual', *Revista Hispánica Moderna*, 33 (1967), 89–108.

'Les romanciers devant la Guerre Civile espagnole', *La Revue de l'Université de Laval*, 14, no. 4 (1959), 326–339 and no. 5 (1960), 428–442.

Spender, Stephen. 'Spain Invites the World's Writers', *New Writing*, 4 (1937), 250.

World within World (London, 1953).

Steiner, George. *Language and Silence. Essays on Language, Literature and the Inhuman* (New York, 1976).

The Death of Tragedy (London, 1961).

Torre, Guillermo de. 'Hacia más allá del realismo novelesco', *Revista de Occidente*, 4 (1963), 106–114.

'Respuesta a José R. Marra López', *Insula*, 204 (1963), 3.

Torrente Ballester, Gonzalo. 'Los problemas de la novela española contemporánea', *Arbor*, 9, no. 27 (1948), 395–400.

Unamuno, Miguel de. *Ensayos*, 2 vols. (Madrid, 1966).

Valbuena Prat, Angel. *Historia de la literatura española*, 3 vols. (Barcelona, 1960).

Vance, Birgitta Johanna. 'The Civil War (1936–39) as a Theme in the Spanish Contemporary Novel.' PhD thesis (Wayne State University 1968). Later published as *A Harvest Sown by Death: The Novel of the Spanish Civil War* (New York, 1975).

Vila Selma, J. *Tres ensayos sobre la literatura y nuestra guerra* (Madrid, 1956).

Wattelet, P. 'Grandeur et misère des romanciers', *Confluences: Problèmes du roman*, 21–24 (1943), 414–415.

Weintraub, Stanley. *The Last Great Cause: The Intellectuals and the Spanish Civil War* (London, 1968).

Werrie, Paul. 'Le Roman espagnol d'aujourd'hui', *La Table Ronde*, 193 (1964), 91–101.

Whitmore, S.G. 'History Versus the Novel: A Sartrean Concern and its French Antecedents.' Unpublished PhD thesis (University of Washington, 1974).

Wilson, Edmund. 'Marxism and Literature' in Lodge, David (ed.), *Twentieth Century Literary Criticism* (London, 1972), pp. 241–252.

Yerro Villanueva, Tomás. *Aspectos técnicos y estructurales de la novela española actual* (Pamplona, 1977).

Yndurain, Francisco. 'Novelas y novelistas españoles', *Rivista di Letterature Moderne*, 3, no. 4 (1952), 277–284.

5 Books and articles on individual authors

Agustí, Ignacio

Miranda, Wenceslao. *Ignacio Agustí: el autor y la obra. Interpretación y realismo de la guerra civil* (Washington, 1982).

Aub, Max

Andújar, Manuel. 'Cita con Max Aub en *El laberinto mágico*', *Cuadernos Americanos*, 188 (1973), 58–61.

Carenas, Francisco. 'Análisis de los grupos sociales en *Campo cerrado*', *Cuadernos Americanos*, 174 (1971), 197–213.

Corro. See López Corro.

Doménech, Ricardo. See his introduction to Aub's *Morir por cerrar los ojos* (Barcelona, 1967), pp. 9–64.

Domingo, José. 'Con Max Aub en el laberinto', *Insula*, 264 (1968), 7.

Durán, Manuel. 'Max Aub, *El laberinto mágico* y la novela de la guerra civil española' in Horanyi, Matyas (ed.), *Actas del simposio internacional de estudios hispánicos* (Budapest, 1978).
'Max Aub o la vocación del escritor', *Papeles de Son Armadans*, 31, no. 92 (1963), 125–138.

Embeita, María. 'Max Aub y su generación', *Insula*, 22, no. 253 (1967), 1 and 12.

Fernández Figueroa, J. 'Campo abierto', *Indice de Artes y Letras*, 32, no. 53 (1952).

García Lora, José. 'Algunos laberintos de Max Aub', *Cuadernos Americanos*, 188, no. 3 (1973), 70–75.

Gil Mariscal, Félix. '*Campo de sangre*, de Max Aub', *Universidad de México* (Organo de la Universidad Autónoma de México), 1, no. 7 (1947).

González López, E. '*Campo cerrado*', *Revista Hispánica Moderna*, 11 (1945), 251–252.

Kohler, Paul Peter. 'The Literary Image of the Spanish Civil War of 1936–39 in Max Aub's *El laberinto mágico*.' Unpublished PhD thesis (University of Toronto, 1970).

Llacer, Juan L. 'Aproximación a Max Aub', *Cuadernos Hispanoamericanos*, 289–290 (1974), 473–476.

Longoría, Francisco A. *El arte narrativo de Max Aub* (Madrid, 1977).

López Corro, Raymond. 'El tema de España en las novelas de Max Aub.' Unpublished PhD thesis (University of Utah, 1971).

Mainer, José Carlos. 'Max Aub: Entre la antiespaña y la literatura universal', *Insula*, 28 (1973), 6–12.

Marra-López, José R. 'La obra literaria de Max Aub', *Primer Acto*, 52 (1964), 8–13.

Prats Rivelles, Rafael. *Max Aub* (Madrid, 1978).

Rodríguez Monegal, Emir. 'Max Aub en su laberinto', *Cuadernos Americanos*, 188, no. 3 (1973), 91–99.

Siebenmann, G. 'Max Aub' (Introduction to German trans. of 'El Cojo'), *Neue Züricher Zeitung*, 23 October 1963.

Sobejano, Gonzalo. 'Asunción en el laberinto', *Cuadernos Americanos*, 188, no. 3 (1973), 98–105. See also this critic's entry under F. Ayala.

Soldevila Durante, Ignacio. 'El español Max Aub', *Insula* 160 (1960), 11 and 15. *La obra narrativa de Max Aub (1929–1969)* (Madrid, 1973).

Tuñón de Lara, Manuel. 'El laberinto mágico', *Cuadernos Americanos*, 187, no. 2 (1973), 85–90.

Ugarte, Michael. 'Max Aub's Magic Labyrinth of Exile', *Hispania*, 68, no. 4 (December 1985), 733–739.

Ayala, Francisco

Amorós, Andrés. See his introduction to Ayala's *Obras narrativas completas* (Madrid, 1969), pp. 9–92.

Bibliografía de Francisco Ayala (New York, 1973).

'Conversaciones con Francisco Ayala', *Revista de Occidente*, 68 (1968), 145–171.

Ayala, Francisco, *Confrontaciones* (Barcelona, 1972).

'La disputa de las escuelas críticas', in Beck, M.A. et al. (eds.), *The Analysis of Hispanic Texts* (New York, 1976).

Brandenberger, Erna. 'Francisco Ayala y Alemania', *Cuadernos Hispanoamericanos*, 329–330 (1977), 308–310.

Díaz, Janet and Landeira, Ricardo. '"El tajo" de Francisco Ayala: Un caso de conciencia', *The American Hispanist*, 4, nos. 30–31 (1978), 7–12.

'La "historia dentro de la historia" en tres cuentos de Francisco Ayala', *Cuadernos Hispanomericanos*, 329–330 (1977), 481–494.

Dieste, Rafael. '*Los usurpadores y La cabeza del cordero*', *Boletín del Instituto Español*, 10 (1950), 26–27.

Ellis, Keith. *El arte narrativo de Francisco Ayala* (Paris, 1964).

'El enfoque literario de la guerra civil española: Malraux y Ayala' in F. Ayala's *La cabeza del cordero* (Buenos Aires, 1962), pp. 9–23.

Embeita, María. 'Francisco Ayala y la novela', *Insula*, 244 (1967), 4 and 6.

Fernández Suárez, Alvaro. '*La cabeza del cordero*', *Sur*, 186 (1950), 64–67.

Guerrero, Obdulia. 'Francisco Ayala: El escritor y su obra', *La Torre*, 75–76 (1972), 11–35.

Gullón, Ricardo. '*La cabeza del cordero*', *Insula*, 51 (1950), 4.

Hiriart, Rosario. *Conversaciones con Francisco Ayala* (Madrid, 1982).

'Francisco Ayala: Vida y obra', *Cuadernos Hispanoamericanos*, 329–30 (1977), 262–275.

Los recursos técnicos en la novelística de Francisco Ayala (Madrid, 1972).

Irizarry, Estelle. *Francisco Ayala* (Boston, 1977).

Teoría y creación literaria en F. Ayala (Madrid, 1971).

Joly, Monique. 'Francisco Ayala: Ensayo de interpretación de su obra narrativa posterior a la guerra', *Cuadernos Hispanoamericanos*, 329–330 (1977), 366–383.

Luzuriaga, J. 'F. Ayala: *La cabeza del cordero*', *Realidad*, 6, nos. 17–18 (1949), 313–319.

Mallea, Eduardo. *Notas de un novelista* (Buenos Aires, 1954).

Marra-López, José R. 'Entrevista con F. Ayala', *Insula*, 203 (1963), 6.

Martínez Palacio, Javier. 'Tres aspectos de la novelística de F. Ayala', *Cuadernos Hispanoamericanos*, 43, no. 189 (1965), 291–302.

Orringer, Nelson R. 'Entrevista con Francisco Ayala', *Cuadernos Hispanoamericanos*, 34, no. 4 (1975), 223–229.

'Responsabilidad y evasión en *La cabeza del cordero* de Francisco Ayala', *Hispanófila*, 52 (1974), 51–60.

Plaza, Galvarino. 'Un relato de Francisco Ayala: Realidad imaginada o soledad intransferible', *Cuadernos Hispanoamericanos*, 329–330 (1977), 429–440.

Rodríguez-Alcalá, Hugo. 'Metaforismo, "criaturalismo" y sátira en la obra novelística de Francisco Ayala', *Revista Hispánica Moderna*, 25, no. 4 (1959), 291–303.

Rodríguez Padrón, Jorge. 'La oblicuidad de Francisco Ayala', *Camp de l'Arpa*, 13 (1974), 24–25.

Skyrme, Raymond. 'The Divided Self: The Language of Scission in "El Tajo" of Francisco Ayala', *Revista Canadiense de Estudios Hispánicos*, 6, no. 1 (1981), 91–109.

Sobejano, Gonzalo. 'Observaciones sobre la lengua de dos novelistas de la emigración: Max Aub y Francisco Ayala', *Diálogos*, 65 (1975), 27–30.

Soldevila Durante, Ignacio. 'Vida en obra de F. Ayala', *La Torre*, 42 (1963), 69–106.

Wiseman, C.C.F. '*The Lamb's Head*: A Translation and Critical Study'. Unpublished PhD thesis (University of Texas, 1971).

Barea, Arturo

Barea, Arturo. 'Not Spain but Hemingway', *Horizon*, May 1941, 350–361.

Benedetti, Mario. 'El testimonio de Arturo Barea', *Número*, 3, nos. 15–17 (1951), 374–381.

Blanco Amor, José. 'A 20 años de *La forja de un rebelde*', *Cuadernos Americanos*, 185 (1972), 213–222.

Castellet, José María. 'En la muerte de Arturo Barea, novelista español', *Papeles de Son Armadans*, 8, no. 22 (1958), 101–106.

Devlin, J.J. 'A. Barea and J.M. Gironella. Two Interpreters of the Spanish Labyrinth', *Hispania*, 41, no. 2 (1958), 143–148.

González López, E. 'A. Barea: *La forja de un rebelde*', *Revista Hispánica Moderna*, 19 (1953), 103–104.

Ortega, José. 'Arturo Barea, novelista español en busca de su identidad', *Symposium*, 25 (1971), 377–391.

Ruiz-Ayúcar, Angel. 'Arturo Barea o la forja de un hombre', *Arriba*, 18 August 1957.

'Después de Barea, Gorkín', *Arriba*, 9 January 1958.

Salazar Chapela, E. 'Arturo Barea', *Asomante*, 14, no. 1 (1958), 80–84.

Torre, Guillermo de. 'A. Barea: *La forja de un rebelde*', *Sur*, 205 (1951), 60–65.

'Grandeza nacional de un novelista: Arturo Barea', *Nacional*, 20 March 1958.

Yndurain, Francisco. 'Resentimiento español: Arturo Barea', *Arbol*, 24, no. 85 (1953), 73–79.

Benet, Juan

Benet, Juan. 'Breve historia de *Volverás a Región*', *Revista de Occidente*, 134 (May 1974), 160–165. Also appears as prologue to the second edn of the novel (Alianza Editorial).

'La entrada en la taberna' in *La inspiración y el estilo* (Madrid, 1965).

¿Qué fue la guerra civil? (Barcelona, 1976).

Cabrera, Vicente. *Juan Benet* (Boston, 1983).

Compitello, Malcolm Alan. *Ordering the Evidence: Volverás a Región and Civil War Fiction* (Barcelona, 1983).

Durán, Manuel. 'Juan Benet y la nueva novela española', *Cuadernos Americanos*, 183 (July–August 1974), 193–205.

Gimferrer, Pedro. 'En torno a *Volverás a Región*', *Insula*, 266 (January 1969), 14.

Guillermo, Edenia. See *La novelística española de los 60* (New York, 1970), pp. 129–150.

Gullón, Ricardo. 'Una región laberíntica que bien pudiera llamarse España', *Insula*, 319 (June 1973), 3 and 10.

Herzenberger, David K. 'The Emergence of Juan Benet: A New Alternative for the Spanish Novel', *The American Hispanist*, 1 (November 1975), 6–12.

The Novelistic World of Juan Benet (Clear Creek, 1976).

Manteiga, Roberto C. et al. *Critical Approaches to the Writings of Juan Benet* (Hanover, 1984).

Núñez, A. 'Encuentro con Juan Benet', *Insula*, 269 (April 1969), 4.

Ortega, José. 'La dimensión temporal en *Volverás a Región* de Juan Benet', in *Ensayos de la novela española moderna* (Madrid, 1974), pp. 137–152.

Roa Bastos, Augusto. *Juan Benet* (Amsterdam, 1976).

Schwartz, Ronald. See *Spain's New Wave Novelists 1959–74* (Metuchen, 1976), pp. 233–244.

Spires, Robert C. '*Volverás a Región* y la desintegración total' in *La novela española de posguerra* (Madrid, 1978), pp. 224–246.

Wescott, Julia Lupinacci. 'Creation and the Structure of Enigma. Literary Conventions and Juan Benet's Trilogy.' PhD thesis (University of Massachusetts, 1985).

Cela, Camilo José

Amorós, Andrés. '*San Camilo 1936*', *Revista de Occidente*, 87 (June 1970), 379–381.

Bernstein, Jerome S. 'Confession and Inaction in *San Camilo*', *Hispanófila*, 17, no. 3 (May 1974), 47–63.

Cela, Camilo José. See the letter claimed to be Cela's (dated 30 March 1938), in *Fuerza Nueva*, 558 (17 September 1977), 9.

Díaz, Janet W. 'Techniques of Alienation in Recent Spanish Novels', *Journal of Spanish Studies*, 3 (Spring 1975), 5–16.

Echave, Angelines. 'Historia e intrahistoria en *San Camilo 1936*.' PhD thesis (University of Emory, Atlanta, Georgia, 1980).

Giménez Frontín, José Luis. *Camilo José Cela: texto y contexto* (Barcelona, 1985).

Ilie, Paul. 'The Politics of Obscenity in *San Camilo 1936*', *Anales de la Novela de Posguerra*, 1 (1976), 25–63.

López, Francis. *Mazurca para Camilo José Cela* (Madrid, 1986).

McPheeters, D.W. *Camilo José Cela* (New York, 1970).

Pérez, Janet. 'Historical Circumstances and Thematic Motifs in *San Camilo 1936*', *The Review of Contemporary Fiction*, 4, no. 3 (Fall 1984), 67–80.

Roberts, Gemma. 'La culpa y la búsqueda de la autenticidad en *San Camilo 1936*', *Journal of Spanish Studies: Twentieth Century*, 3, no. 1 (Spring 1975), 73–84.

Tuñón de Lara, Manuel. 'La circunstancia histórica de la novela *San Camilo 1936*', *Papeles de Son Armadans*, 69, no. 207 (1973), 229–252.

Uriarte, Fernando. 'Apuntes sobre *San Camilo*', *Papeles de Son Armadans*, 59, no. 177 (1970), 323–335.

Espina, Concha

Maza, Josefina de la. *Vida de mi madre, Concha Espina* (Alcoy, 1957).

Fernández Flórez, Wenceslao

Mainer, José Carlos. *Análisis de una insatisfacción: Las novelas de W. Fernández Flórez* (Madrid, 1975).

Foxá, Agustín de

Gómez Santos, Marino. 'Pequeña historia de grandes personalidades: Agustín de Foxá cuenta su vida', *Pueblo*, 22–27 September, 1958.

Luca de Tena, J.I. 'Agustín de Foxá, Conde de Foxá', *Boletín de la Real Academia Española*, 39 (1959), 365–377.

García Serrano, Rafael

Fernández Figueroa, J. '*Plaza del Castillo* de R. García Serrano', *Indice de Artes y Letras*, 47 (1952).

Morales, R. 'La última novela de García Serrano', *Cuadernos Hispanoamericanos*, 11, no. 32 (1952), 304–305.

Gironella, José María

Alborg, Juan Luis. 'Los novelistas: J.M. Gironella', *Indice de Artes y Letras*, 34 (1956), 9.
'*Un millón de muertos* de J.M.G.', *Estafeta Literaria*, 217 (1961), 20.

Anon. 'Gironella: *Un millón de muertos* para *Los cipreses*', *SP*, 1, no. 27 (1957), 24–28.

Anon. 'Una enciclopedia de la guerra', *SP*, 5, no. 160 (1961), 64–66.

Botana, José. 'José María Gironella: Nuevos episodios nacionales', *Duquesne Hispanic Revue*, 6, no. 3 (1967), 13–33.

Calvo Sotelo, Luis Emilio. *Crítica y glosa de 'Un millón de muertos'* (Madrid, 1961). (Originally published as articles in *Ya*, 16, 22, 25, 28 April and 11 May 1961.)

Cano, José Luis. 'José María Gironella: *Los cipreses creen en Dios*', *Insula*, 89 (1953), 6–7.

Castro, F.✓G. de. 'Situación actual de la novela española', *Indice de Artes y Letras*, 62 (1953), 7.

Colomer, Eusebio. '*Un millón de muertos*', *Razón y Fe*, 163 (1961), 483–494.

Devlin, J.J. See this critic's entry under A. Barea.

Dial, John E. 'Gironella's Chronicles Revisited: A Panorama on Fratricide', *Papers on Language and Literature*, 10, no. 1 (1974), 98–110.

García✓Luengo, Eusebio. 'Gironella tardíamente. *Los cipreses creen en Dios*', *Indice de Artes y Letras*, 64 (1953).

Gich, J. 'Los libros de la quincena: *Los cipreses creen en Dios*', *Correo Literario*, 70 (1953), 4.

Gironella, José María. 'Así escribí *Un millón de muertos*' in *Todos somos fugitivos* (Barcelona, 1968) by the same author, pp. 301–341.

Gómez de la Serna, Gaspar. '*Los cipreses creen en Dios*', *Clavileño*, 22 (1953), 70–71.

Gómez Galán, Antonio. '*Ha estallado la paz*, de Gironella', *Arbor*, 45, no. 251 (1966), 93–95.

Grupp, W.J. 'J.M. Gironella, Spanish Novelist', *Kentucky Foreign Languages Quarterly*, 4 (1957), 129–135.

Guillén, Claudio. 'José María Gironella: Les cyprès croient en Dieu', *Critique*, 11 (1955), 571–573.

Hernández, Casimiro. 'Sobre cuatro gazapos de *Un millón de muertos*', *Estafeta Literaria*, 242 (1962).

Hornedo, R.M. 'J.M. Gironella', *Razón y Fe*, 164 (1961), 222–231.

Ilie, Paul. 'Fictive History in Gironella', *Journal of Spanish Studies: Twentieth Century*, 2, no. 2 (1974), 77–94.

Kerrigan, Anthony. 'J.M. Gironella and the Black Legend of Spain', *Books on Trial*, 14 (1956), 343–344 and 387–388.

Llanos, José María de. 'Reflexiones ante *Un millón de muertos*', *Ya*, 29 April and 17, 30 May 1961, 5–6 (in each case).

López✓Sanz, Francisco. *Un millón de muertos, pero con ¡héroes y mártires!* (Pamplona, 1963).

Magaña Schevill, I. 'A Day in Gerona with Gironella', *Hispania*, 42 (1959), 170–174.

Marshall, Bruce. '*Un millón de muertos*', *ABC*, 18 February 1961, 46.

Ponce de León, José Luis S. '*Ha estallado la paz*', *Estafeta Literaria*, 358 (1966), 17–18.

Salso, José Antonio. *José María Gironella* (Madrid, 1981).

Schwartz, Ronald, *J.M. Gironella* (New York, 1972).

Suárez-Torres, J. David. *Perspectivas humorísticas en la trilogía de Gironella* (New York, 1972).

Ulises. 'Ha estallado la paz', *La Codorniz*, 8 January 1967, 3.

Urbanski, E.S. 'Revolutionary Novels of Gironella and Pasternak', *Hispania*, 43, no. 2 (1960), 191–197.

Van Doren, Mark. 'The Thousand Faces of Spain', *The Reporter*, 16 June 1955, 35–37.

Vázquez Dodero, José Luis. 'El arte y la historia en *Un millón de muertos*', *Nuestro Tiempo*, 14 (1961), 732–742.

Velarde Fuertes, J. 'Gironella, la Segunda República y la economía española', *Correo Literario*, 5, no. 92 (1954), 8–9.

Vila Selma, J. 'El mundo de Gironella', *Punta Europa*, 1 (1956), 126–135.

León, Ricardo

Olivar Bertrand, Rafael. 'Política y literatura: Ricardo León', *Arbor*, 36 (1957), 459–466.

Vigón, Jorge. 'Roja y gualda, novela por Ricardo León', *Acción Española*, 11, nos. 62–63 (1934), 178–181.

Lera, Angel María de

Hernández, Ramón. *Angel María de Lera* (Madrid, 1981).

Ilie, Paul. 'Le roman de l'ambigüité historique' in Hanrez, M., *Les Ecrivains et la guerre d'Espagne* (Paris, n.d.).

Listerman, Mary Sue. *Angel María de Lera* (Boston, 1982).

Samblancat, Angel

Carrasquer, Francisco. 'Samblancat, Alaiz y Sender: Tres compromisos en uno', *Papeles de Son Armadans*, 76 (1975), 211–246.

Sender, Ramón J.

Bates, Ralph. 'R.J. Sender', *Saturday Review Literature*, 15 April 1944.

Bejar, Manuel. 'Existencia infinal o las latitudes del absurdo: Comentario a *Los cinco libros de Ariadna*', *Reflexión*, 2, nos. 2–4 (1973), 75–81.

Bernadete, José Mair. 'Ramón Sender, cronista y soñador de una España nueva.' Introduction to Sender's *Réquiem por un campesino español* (New York, 1960), pp. 83–115.

Bertrand de Muñoz, Maryse. 'Los símbolos en *El rey y la reina* de R.J. Sender', *Papeles de Son Armadans*, July 1974, 37–56.

Bly, Peter A. 'A Confused Reality and its Presentation', *International Fiction Review*, 5 (1978), 96–102.

Busette, Cedric. 'Religious Symbolism in Sender's *Mosén Millán*', *Romance Notes*, 11 (1970), 482–486.

Carrasquer, Francisco. *La verdad de Ramón J. Sender* (Leiden, 1982). See also this critic's entry under A. Samblancat.

Collard, Patrick. *Ramón J. Sender en los años 1930–1936: Sus ideas sobre la relación entre literatura y sociedad* (Ghent, 1980).

Criado Miguel, Isabel. 'Mito y desmitificación de la guerra en dos novelas de la posguerra' in Gallego Morell, A. (ed.) et al., *Estudios sobre literatura y arte dedicados al profesor Emilio Orozco Díaz*, 1 (Granada, 1979), pp. 333–356.

Ferrándiz Alborz, F. '*Los cinco libros de Ariadna*', *Ibérica*, 6, no. 1 (1958), 6–8.

Garnett, David. 'Current Literature', *The New Statesman and Nation*, 31 July 1937.

Godoy Gallardo, Eduardo. 'Problemática y sentido de *Réquiem por un campesino español* de Ramón Sender', *Letras de Deusto*, 1 (1971), 63–74.

Guillén, C. '*Los cinco libros de Ariadna*', *Books Abroad*, 32, no. 2 (1958), 137–138.

Henn, David. 'The Priest in Sender's *Réquiem por un campesino español*', *International Fiction Review*, 1 (1974), 106–111.

Iglesias, Ignacio. 'Sender: *Los cinco libros de Ariadna*', *Cuadernos del Congreso por la Libertad de la Cultura*, 28 (1958), 102–103.

'Acercamiento a Ramón Sender', *Nuevo Mundo* (September–October 1969), 97–116.

Iglesias Ovejero, Angel. 'Estructuras mítico-narrativas de *Réquiem por un campesino español*', *Anales de la Literatura Española Contemporánea*, 7, no. 2 (1982), 215–236.

Kazin, Alfred. 'R.J. Sender', *New Republic*, 5 April 1943.

King, Charles L. 'A Partial Addendum to Ramón J. Sender: An Annotated Bibliography, 1928–1974,' *Hispania*, 66, no. 2 (1983), 209–216.

Ramón J. Sender (New York, 1974).

'Sender: Aragonese in New Mexico', *Modern Language Journal*, 36 (1952), 242–244.

'Sender's Spherical Philosophy', *Publications of the Modern Language Association of America*, 69 (1954), 993–999.

'Surrealism in Two Novels by Sender', *Hispania*, 51, no. 2 (1969), 244–251.

'Una bibliografía senderiana española, 1928–1967', *Hispania*, 50 (1967).

López Alvarez, L. '*El rey y la reina* de R. Sender', *Cuadernos del Congreso por la Libertad de la Cultura*, 17 (1957), 122–123.

Lord, David. 'This Man Sender', *Books Abroad*, 14 (1940), 352–354.

Mainer, José Carlos. 'Actualidad de Sender', *Insula*, 231 (1966), 1 and 12.

Marra-López, José R. 'Ramón Sender, novelista español', *Insula*, 209 (1964), 5.

Mead, R.J. 'Sender: *Los cinco libros de Ariadna*', *Hispania*, 41 (1958), 234–235.

Nerja, Andrés. '*El rey y la reina*', *Las Españas*, 5, no. 13 (1949).

Nonoyama, Michiko. *El anarquismo en las obras de Ramón Sender* (Madrid, 1979).

Olstad, Charles Fredrick. 'The Novels of Ramón Sender: Moral Concepts in Development.' Unpublished PhD thesis (University of Wisconsin, 1961).

Ornstein, J. 'The Literary Evolution of R. Sender', *Modern Language Forum*, 36, no. 2 (1951), 33–40.

Penn, Dorothy. 'R.J. Sender', *Hispania*, 34 (1951), 79–84.

Peñuelas, Marcelino C. *Conversaciones con Ramón J. Sender* (Madrid, 1970).

La obra narrativa de Ramón J. Sender (Madrid, 1971).

Percival, A. 'Sociedad, individuo y verdad en *Réquiem por un campesino español*', *Ottawa Hispánica*, 4 (1982), 71–84.

Rivas, Josefa. *El escritor y su senda* (Mexico, 1967).

Rodríguez Méndez, J.M. 'Ramón Sender: *El rey y la reina*', *Cuadernos Hispanoamericanos*, 341 (1957), 388–389.

Schneider, Marshall J. 'Man, Society and Transcendence: A Study of the Thematic Structure of Selected Novels of Ramón J. Sender.' Unpublished PhD thesis (University of Connecticut, 1970).

'Politics, Aesthetics and Thematic Structure in Two Novels by Ramón J. Sender', *Hispanic Journal*, 4, no. 2 (1983), 29–41.

Schwartz, Kessel. 'Animal Symbolism in the Fiction of R.J. Sender', *Hispania*, 46 (1963), 496–505.

Skyrme, Raymond. 'On the Chronology of Sender's *Réquiem por un campesino español*', *Romance Notes*, 24, no. 2 (1983), 116–122.

Tovar, Antonio. 'Dos capítulos para un retrato literario de Sender', *Cuadernos del Idioma*, 4 (1966), 17–35.

Uceda, Julia. 'Realismo y esencias en Ramón Sender', *Revista de Occidente*, 82 (1970), 39–53.

Vilas, Santiago. '*Mosén Millán*', *Hispania*, 47 (1964), 678–679.

Soler, Bartolomé

Hornedo, Rafael M. de. 'Bartolomé Soler', *Razón y Fe*, 164 (1961), 231–236.

Index